English Duplicates

of

Lost Virginia Records

English Duplicates of Lost Virginia Records

compiled by

Louis des Cognets, Jr.

Baltimore
GENEALOGICAL PUBLISHING CO., INC.

First printing, 1958
Second printing, 1960
Reprinted, by arrangement,
Genealogical Publishing Co., Inc.
Baltimore. 1981, 1990
Library of Congress Catalogue Card Number 80-85117
International Standard Book Number 0-8063-0929-6
Made in the United States of America

❧

This book is dedicated to my grandmother

ANNA RUSSELL des COGNETS

in memory of the many years she spent

writing two genealogies about her

Virginia ancestors

❧

:£.

FOREWORD

This book was compiled from material found in the Public Record Office during the summer of 1957. Original reports sent to the Colonial Office from Virginia were first microfilmed, and then transcribed for publication. Some of the penmanship of the early part of the 18th Century was like copper plate, but some was very hard to decipher, and where the same name was often spelled in two different ways on the same page, the task was all the more difficult.

May the various lists of pioneer Virginians contained herein aid both genealogists, students of colonial history, and those who make a study of the evolution of names. In this event a part of my debt to other abstracters and compilers will have been paid.

Thanks are due the Staff at the Public Record Office for many heavy volumes carried to my desk, and for friendly assistance. Mrs. William Dabney Duke furnished valuable advice based upon her considerable experience in Virginia research. Mrs.Olive Sheridan being acquainted with old English names was especially suited to the secretarial duties she faithfully performed.

:£.

CONTENTS

CONTENTS

English Duplicates
of
Lost Virginia Records

List of Sheriffs Appointed 16th June 1680

New Kent County	Capt. Jno. Lewis
Accomack County	Capt. Edmund Scarburgh
Westmorland County	Col. Will'm Pierce
James City County	Mr. Edm'd Jenning

List of Sheriffs Appointed 22nd July 1680

Middlesex County	Co. Christ'r Wormeley
Gloster County	Maj'r John Armistead
Yorke County	Capt. Fran: Page
Isle of Wight	Mr. Thomas Pitt
Lancaster	Capt. Daniel Fox
Rappahanock	Mr. Henry Smith

List of Sheriffs Appointed 1699

Henrico	Thomas Cook	King & Queen	John Waller
Charles Citty	Robert Bolling	Glocester	Mordecai Cook
Surrey	Thomas Holt	Middlesex	Sr. Wm. Skipwith, Baronett
Isle of Wight	Anthony Holladay		
Nansemond	Francis Milner	Essex	John Talliaferro
Princess Anne	John Thorowgood	Richmond	-----------
Norfolke	Richard Church	Lancaster	Alexander Swann
Elizabeth City	Coleman Brough	Northumberland	Rhodham Kennor
Warwick	William Cary	Westmorland	Alexander Spence
James Citty	Henry Duke	Stafford	George Mason
Yorke	Thomas Ballard	Accomack	Thomas Welburne
New Kent	William Bassett	Northampton	Nathaniel Littleton

List of Surveyors Appointed 1699

Henrico	Rich'd Ligon	James City	John Soan
Charles City	Theodorick Bland	New Kent	James Minge
Surry & Isle of Wight	Thomas Swan	King & Queen	Richard Whitehead
		Middlesex	Edwin Thacker
Elizabeth City & Warwick	William Lowry	Accomack & Northampton	Edm'd Scarburgh
York & Gloucester	Miles Cary	Essex & Richmond	Wm. Moseley
		Stafford	Tho. Grigg
		Westmorland	Alexander Spence
Nansemond, Norfolk & Princess Ann	Thomas Milner	Northumberland	George Cooper

List of Sheriffs Appointed 1700

Henrico	Francis Epps	King & Queen	John Walker
Charles City	Littlebury Epps	Gloucester	James Ransone
Surry	Wm. Brown Jr.	Middlesex	Robert Dudley
Isle of Wight	Arthur Smith	Essex	James Bougham
Nansemond	George Norsworthy	Richmond	Sam'l Peachey
Norfolk	Richard Church	Lancaster	William Ball
Princess Anne	Wm. Cornex	Northumberland	Charles Lee
Elizabeth City	Walter Bayley	Westmorland	Willoughby Allerton
Warwick	Thomas Merry	Stafford	Rich'd Fossaker
York	Henry Tyler	Accomack	Geo. Nich'o Hack
James City	Thomas Cowles	Northampton	John Robbins
New Kent	Nich'o Meriwether		

List of Sheriffs Appointed 1701

Henrico	John Worsham	King & Queen	John Waller
Charles City	Micajah Lowe	Gloucester	John Gwin
Surry	Thomas Holt	Middlesex	Matt: Kemp
Isle of Wight	John Pitt	Essex	John Taliafero
Nansemond	Rich: Awburn	Richmond	John Tapley
Princess Ann	Adam Thorowgood	Lancaster	Alex: Swann
Norfolk	Tho: Willoughby	Northumberland	----------
Eliza: City	Coleman Brough	Westmorland	Charles Ashton
Warwick	Miles Wills	Stafford	John Waugh Jr.
York	Dan'll Taylor	Accomack	John Watts
James City	Tho: Mountfort	Northampton	Littleton Robins
New Kent	John King		

List of Sheriffs Appointed April 25th 1702

Norfolk	Samuell Boush	Glocester	Petter Kemp
Nansimond	Charles Drewry	King & Queen	Jno. Walker
Isle of Wight	Wm. Bridger	King William	Jno. Waller
Surry	----------	Middlesex	Sr. Wm. Skipwith
Charles Citty	Charles Goodrich	Essex	Tho. Merriwheather
Henerico	Giles Webb	Richmond	Jno. Downman
New Kent	Nich'o Merriweather	Lancaster	Henery Fleett
James Citty	Thomas Cowles	Northumberland	Jno. Harriss
York	Henery Tylor	Westmoreland	Lewis Markham
Warwick	Thomas Merry	Stafford	Charles Ellis
Elizabeth City	Nicholas Curle	Accomack	---------
		Southampton	---------

List of Sheriffs Appointed for 1706

Henrico	Jno. Bolling	King & Queen	John Walker
Charles City	R'd Bradford	Middlesex	Matt: Kemp
Prince George	Fra: Mallory	Gloucester	Conq't Wyatt
Surry	Tho: Holt	Essex	Tho: Merriwether
Isle of Wight	Nath: Ridly	Richmond	Wm. Tayloe
Nansemond	Luke Haveild	Lancaster	Jno. Turberville
Norfolk	Matt: Spivy	Northumberland	Rich'd Hanie
Princess Ann	Hen: Chapman	Westmorland	Will'o Allerton
Elizabeth City	Fra: Ballard	Stafford	Geo. Mason
Warwick	Tho: Haines	New Kent	Roger Thomson
York	Wm. Barber	King William	Mart'n Palmer
James City	David Bray		

LIST OF SHERIFFS APPOINTED April 25th 1707

Henrico	Jno. Bolling	New Kent	Roger Thomson
Charles City	Jno. Epps	King William	Marten Palmer
Prince George	Fr: Mallory	Gloucester	Conq: Wyat
Surry	Thos. Holt	Middlesex	Matt: Kemp
Isle of Wight	Nath: Ridley	Essex	Wm. Tomlin
Nansemond	Luke Harvild	Richmond	Wm. Tayloe
Norfolk	Sam'll Boush	Stafford	Wm. Fitzhugh
Princess Anne	Edw: Mosely	Westmoreland	Willoughby Allerton
Eliza: City	Fr: Ballard	Northumberland	Rich'd Hainie
Warwick	Thomas Haynes	Lancaster	Jno. Turbarville
York	Wm. Barbar	Accomack	Tully Robinson
James City	Jno. Geddes	Northampton	Jno. Luke

LIST OF SURVEYORS APPOINTED April 25th 1707

Miles Cary, Surveyor Generall

Thomas Grigg for Stafford
Wm. Thornton for Richmond
George Cooper for Northumberland
Thos: Thomson for Westmoreland
Thomas Cook for Middlesex

LIST OF J.P.s APPOINTED April 26th 1707

King William County: Sam'll Normant, Jno. Cesar, George Purchase, Wm. Chadwick

King & Queen County: Thos: Pettitt, John Maddison

List of Sheriffs Appointed April 28th 1708

Accomack	John Brodhurst	James City	John Frayser
Charles City	Wm. Epes	King William	Thomas Carr
Henrico	Wm. Randolph	King & Queen	Rich'd Anderson
Prince George	John Hamlin	Gloucester	Anthony Gregory
Surry	Joseph John Jackman	Essex	John Lomax
Isle of Wight	------	Richmond	Wm. Robinson
Nansemond	Thomas Jordan	Lancaster	Thomas Carter
Norfolk	Samuel Boush	Northumberland	George Cooper
Princess Anne	Edward Moseley	Westmorland	John Sturman
Elizabeth City	Thomas Tabb	Stafford	--------
Warwick	Matthew Jones	Northampton	Henry Stringer
York	Lawrence Smith	Middlesex	George Wortham
New Kent	George Keeling		

List of Sheriffs Appointed April 26th 1709

Accomack	Jno. Brodhurst	New Kent	Geo. Keeling
Charles City	Wm. Hunt	James City	Jno. Frayser
Henrico	Wm. Randolph	King William	Thomas Carr
Prince George	Jno. Hamlin	King & Queen	Rich'd Anderson
Surry	Jos: Jno. Jackman	Gloucester	Rob't Porteus
Isle of Wight	Henry Applewhite	Essex	Jno. Lomax
Nansemond	Thom's Jordan	Middlesex	Geo. Wortham
Norfolk	Matt'w Godfrey	Richmond	Wm. Thornton
Princess Anne	Jno. Rich'dson	Lancaster	Thos. Carter
Eliza: City	Thos. Tabb	Northumberland	Thos. Cooper
Warwick	Matt'w Jones	Westmorland	Jno. Sturmer
York	Lawrence Smith	Stafford	George Anderson
		Northampton	Hillary Stringer

List of Sheriffs Appointed April 19th 1710

Henrico	Francis Epes	York	William Timson
Prince George	Wm. Epes	Isle of Wight	Humphry Marshall
King & Queen	Samuel Matthews	New Kent	Joseph Foster
King William	Philip Whitehead	Eliza City	Anthony Armistead
Richmond	Edward Barrow	Charles City	Richard Bradford
James City	Edward Jaquilin	Nansemond	John Speir
Middlesex	Richard Kemp	Westmorland	Daniel McCarty
Essex	Robert Coleman	Stafford	George Anderson
Lancaster	Thomas Pinkard	Northumberland	Maurice Jones
Surry	Ethelred Taylor	Northampton	John Powell
Gloucester	Richard Bailey	Accomack	Tully Robinson
Warwick	Humphry Harwood	Norfolk	Matthew Godfrey
		Princess Anne	Thomas Richardson

List of J.P.s Appointed 27th April 1710

Essex	Stephen Loyd, Joseph Smith, Henry Robinson, Wm. Woodford, Paul Micon Gent.
Norfolk	William Langly, George Mason Gent.
King William	William Anderson, James Dabney Gent.
Charles City	James Joyeux Gent.

List of Coroners Appointed 29th April 1710

Richmond	Alexander Donaphan, Nicholas Smith, William Woodbridge, George Heale.

List of Sheriffs Appointed 27th April 1711

Norfolk	James Wilson	Gloucester	Thomas Buckner
Princess Anne	George Hancock	King & Queen	Samuel Matthews
Prince George	Joshua Wynne	King William	William Anderson
Henrico	Francis Epes	Middlesex	Oliver Segar
Charles City	James Joyeux	Essex	Richard Covington
New Kent	Joseph Foster	Richmond	Edward Barrow
James City	Edward Jacquelin	Westmorland	Daniel McCarty
York	William Timson	Stafford	Joseph Sumner
Warwick	Humphry Harwood	Northumberland	Maurice Jones
Eliza: City	John Moore	Lancaster	Thomas Pinkard
Accomack	Tully Robinson	Nansemond	Joseph Merredith
Northampton	John Powell	Isle of Wight	Humphry Marshall
		Surry	Ethelred Taylor

List of Sheriffs Appointed 22nd April 1712

Henrico	William Farrow	King William	William Anderson
Charles City	John Stith	King & Queen	Thomas Petit
Prince George	Randale Platt	Essex	Richard Covington
Surry	Henry Harrison	Middlesex	Oliver Segar
Isle of Wight	Andrew Woodlie	Gloucester	Thomas Buckner
Nansemond	Henry Baker	Lancaster	Hugh Brant
Norfolk	James Wilson Jr.	Northumberland	Peter Presly
Princess Anne	George Hancock	Westmorland	Francis Wright
Elizabeth City	John Moore	Stafford	Joseph Sumner
Warwick	Thomas Cary	Richmond	Nicholas Smith
York	Wm. Pinkethman	Accomack	Thomas Custis
James City	Mongo Ingles	Northampton	William Kendall
New Kent	Thomas Butts		

Justices Appointed to Court of Prince George County 22nd April 1712

Henry Duke, Stith Bottomey,
Sampson Meredith, James Thovay Gent.

LIST of Sheriffs Appointed 25th April 1713

Henrico	William Farrar	New Kent	Thomas Butts
Charles City	John Stith	King William	George Dabney
Prince George	Randle Platt	King & Queen	Thomas Petitt
Surry	William Edwards	Essex	Joseph Smith
Isle of Wight	Nathaniel Ridley	Middlesex	John Vivian
Nansemond	Henry Baker	Lancaster	Hugh Baine
Norfolk	Jonas Holliday	Gloucester	Ambrose Dudley
Princess Anne	John Cornick	Northumberland	Peter Presley
Eliza: City	Francis Ballard	Westmoreland	John Sturman
York	Thomas Roberts	Richmond	John Tayloe
Warwick	Thomas Cary	Stafford	George Mason Jr.
James City	Mongo Ingles	Northampton	William Kendall
		Accomack	Thomas Custis

List of Sheriffs Appointed 28th April 1714

Henrico	John Wortham	Charles City	Richard Dennis
Prince George	Sampson Meredith	King William	William Smith
Surry	Robert Ruffin	King & Queen	John Maddison
Isle of Wight	Nathaniel Ridley	Essex	Leonard Tarent
Nansemond	William Butler	Middlesex	John Vivian
Norfolk	Jonas Holliday	Gloucester	Philip Smith
Princess Anne	John Cornick	Stafford	George Mason Jr.
Eliza: City	Francis Ballard	Westmoreland	John Sturman
Warwick	Francis Jones	Richmond	Charles Barber
James City	William Manson	Northumberland	William Jones
York	Thomas Nutting	Lancaster	Thomas Lee
New Kent	Thomas Barber Jr.	Accomack	John Brodhurst
Northampton	John Powell		

Scales and Weights distributed to Agents Oct. 26th 1714

Henrico	Mr. William Randolph
Charles City	Mr. Littlebury Epes
Prince George	Mr. Robert Mountfort
Surry	Mr. William Gray, Mr. John Simmons
Isle of Wight	Mr. Joseph Godwin
Nansemond	Mr. Thomas Godwin
Norfolk	Mr. Samuel Boush
Princess Anne	Mr. Lemuel Newton
Eliza: City	---------
Warwick	Mr. Miles Wills
York	Mr. Wm. Buckner
James City	Mr. Henry Soane, Mr. Edw'd Jaqueline
New Kent	Mr. Thomas Carr
King William	Augustine Moore
Essex	Mr. Robert Beverley, Mr. Richard Buckner
King & Queen.	Mr. John Baylor
Gloucester	Mr. Joseph Smith Esq'r, Henry Whiting
Middlesex	Mr. Christ'r Robinson
Richmond	Mr. William Robinson
Stafford	Mr. John Waugh
Westmorland	Mr. Henry Fitzhugh
Northumberland	Mr. George Eskridge, Mr. Richard Neal
Accomack	----------

List of Sheriffs Appointed 25th April 1715

Henrico	John Worsham	Charles City	Rich'd Dennis
Prince George	Sampson Meredith	King William	Wm. Smith
Surry	Robert Ruffin	King & Queen	Tho: Maddison
Isle of Wight	Thomas Walton	Glouster	David Alexander
Nansemond	Wm. Butler	Middlesex	George Worsham
Norfolk	John Halstead	Essex	Leon'd Trent
Princess Anne	-----------	Stafford	James Jameson
Elizabeth City	Simon Hollier	Richmond	Charles Barber
Warwick	Fran: Jones	Westmoreland	Benja' Berryman
York	Tho: Nutting	Northumberland	William Jones
James City	Wm. Marston	Lancaster	Thomas Lee
New Kent	Tho: Barbar Jr.	Accomack	Edward Robins
		Northampton	John Powell

LIST OF COUNTY OFFICERS 1699

NORTHUMBERLAND COUNTY 8 June 1699

Rodham Konnor, Sheriff
Thomas Hobson, Clerk

WESTMORELAND 8 June 1699

William Peirce
William Horton
William Bridges
Francis Wright
Nicholas Spencer
Henry Ross
Alexander Spencer, Sherriff
Willoughby Allerton

QUORUM

Samuel Thompson
Lewis Markham
James Taylor
Charles Ashton
Caleb Butler
John Sturman
Gerrard Hutt
John Scott
George Weedon
John Elliott

James Westcomb, Clk. Court

LANCASTER

David Fox
Robert Carter
Joseph Ball
Henry Fleet
William Lester

QUORUM

William Ball
Alexander Swan, Sheriff
William Fox
John Turbervill
John Pinkard
Thomas Martin

Joseph Tayloe, Clk. Court

ESSEX

John Catlet
William Moseley
Thomas Edmondson
Edward Thomas
Francis Talliaferro
Bernard Gaines

QUORUM

Robert Brooks
John Battaile
John Talliaferro, Sheriff

James Boughan
Francis Goldman
Richard Covington
Daniell Dobbins
Robert Paine

Francis Meriwether, Clk. Court

NORTHAMPTON

John Robbins
John Custis
Philip Fisher
Obedience Johnson
Nathaniell Littleton, Sheriff
William Waters

QUORUM

Ralph Pigot
Wm. Harmanson
John Powell
Jacob Johnson
Thomas Savage
George Harmanson

Daniell Urrch (?) Clk. Court

LIST OF COUNTY OFFICERS 8th June 1699

RICHMOND

George Taylor
Samuell Peachey
William Underwood
Alexander Doniphin
Thomas Lloyd
John Deane

QUORUM

David Gwyn
John Baker
William Dolman
John Trapley- Sheriff
Rawleigh Traverse
Francis Sloughter (? Slaughter)

William Colston, Clk. Court

STAFFORD

George Mason - Sheriff
Matthew Thompson
John Harvey
Robert Alexander
Philip Buckner
Rice Hooe

QUORUM

Richard Fosaker
William Williams
John Washington
Robert Colston
Joseph Sumner
John Waugh Jr.
Edward Hart
Thomas Greg

Thomas Owsley, Clk. Court

NORFOLK

Lemuel Mason
John Hatton
Thomas Hodges
James Wilson
Richard Church - Sheriff
Thomas Butt

QUORUM

Samuel Boush
Tho. Willoughby
John Hodges
Matthew Godfrey
Thomas Mason
William Laungley

Malachy Thruston, Clk. Ct.

ACCOMACK

Edmond Scarburgh
George Nicholas Hack
Richard Bayley
Tho. Wolbourne - Sheriff
Edmond Custis

QUORUM

George Parker
Robert Hutchinson
Edward Moore
Robert Pitt
John Watts

John Washburne, Clk. Ct.

NANSEMOND

John Brassour
George Norsworthy
Thomas Swann
Luke Haveild
Francis Milner - Sheriff
Thomas Tilly

QUORUM

Thomas Milner
Charles Drury
John Spier
William Hunter
William Wright

Joseph Bridges, Clk. Court

WARWICK

Humphrey Harwood
Miles Cary
Samuell Rausha
Robert Hubbard
William Cary - Sheriff
Thomas Merry

QUORUM

Wm. Rascow
Thomas Charles
Matthew Jones
Miles Wills
Thomas Haynes
John Tignall

Miles Cary, Clk. Ct.

LIST OF COUNTY OFFICERS 9th June 1699

PRINCESS ANNE

Anthony Lawson
Wm. Cornex
Benoni Burroughs
John Thorowgood - Sheriff
Francis Morse

QUORUM

Edward Moseley
Elvan Jones
Henry Woodhouse
William Clowes
Robert Thorrowgood
Solomon White

Patrick Angus, Clk. Ct.

ELIZABETH CITY

William Wilson
Anthony Armistead
Pasco Curle
Wm. Lowry
Thomas Harwood
Augustus Moore

QUORUM

Coleman Brough - Sheriff
Thomas Curle
Matthew Watts
John Minson
Walter Bayley

Charles Jenings, Clk. Ct.

CHARLES CITY (17 June 1699

Richard Bland
Daniell Lewellain
Charles Goodrich
Robert Bolling - Sheriff
Littlebury Eppes
George Blighton

QUORUM

John Hardiman
William Hunt
Micajah Low
Richard Bradford
Joshua Wynn
John Torry

John Taylor, Clk. Ct.

JAMES CITY

Philip Lightfoot
Henry Soan
Henry Duke - Sheriff
Philip Ludwell Jr.
Michael Sherman

QUORUM

James Bray
David Bray
Thomas Cowles
Hugh Norvill
William Edwards
William Drummond

Chicheley Corbin Thacker, Clk. Court

YORK

Thomas Barber
Joseph Ring
Robert Read
Thomas Ballard
Thomas Roberts
Charles Hansford

QUORUM

William Buckner
Henry Tyler
Baldwin Matthews
John Page
James Whaley
John Goodwin
Daniell Taylor
Thomas Nutting

William Sedgwick, Clk. Ct.

KING & QUEEN (25 Feb. 1699)

William Leigh
Joshua Story
William Gough
Richard Gregory
Henry Fox
Thomas Paullin

QUORUM

John Walker
Wm. Claybourne
Willis Wilson
James Howell
John Waller - Sheriff
Richard Anderson

Robert Beverly, Clk. Ct.

LIST OF COUNTY OFFICERS 1699

HENRICO 17 June 1699

Richard Cock
William Randolph
Peter Feild
Francis Eppes
Wm. Farrer

QUORUM

John Worsham
Thomas Cock - Sheriff
Giles Webb
Joseph Royall
John Bolling

James Cock, Clk. Ct.

NEW KENT 17 June 1699

Joseph Foster
Lancelot Bathurst
William Bassett - Sheriff
Thomas Bray
Francis Burnell
John Lyddall

QUORUM

James Moss
John Stanop
Thomas Smith
John Lewis
Nicholas Meriwether
George Keeleing

Job Howse, Clk. Ct.

ISLE OF WIGHT 26 April 1698

Henry Applewaite
Samuel Bridger
Geo. Moore
Jer. Exum
Henry Baker

QUORUM

James Day
Thomas Giles
Anthony Holliday - Sheriff
Arthur Smith
Robert Key
Humphrey Marshall

Charles Chapman, Clk. Ct.

GLOUCESTER 6 Oct. 1699

James Ransome
Mordecai Cook, Sheriff
Conquest Wyatt
John Gwynn
Sands Knowles

QUORUM

Richard Booker
Ambrose Dudley
Thomas Todd
Thomas Buckner
Anthony Gregory

Peter Beverley, Clk. Ct.

MIDDLESEX 26 April 1698

Wm. Skipwith, Bart. - Sheriff
Matthew Kemp
Wm. Churchill
Wm. Wormeley
Gawin Corbin
Thomas Landon

QUORUM

Francis Weekes
Robert Dudley
Henry Thacker
John Smith
Richard Willis
John Grymes

Edwin Thacker, Clk. Ct.

SURREY 12 December 1698

Henry Tooker
William Brown
Thomas Holt - Sheriff
James Mason
Nathaniel Harrison

QUORUM

William Newsom
Wm. Cock
Thomas Drew
John Edwards

Francis Clements, Clk. Ct.

A LIST of the quantity of LAND, Number of Tithables, and Civill Officers in the Dominion of Virginia this 8th Day of July 1702

ACCOMACK COUNTY. 200,861 acres of land. 1,041 Tithables

BURGESSES - Tho: Welburn, Tully Robinson

SHERIFF - ________

JUSTICES - Edw'd Scarbrough; Geo. Nich. Hack, Rich. Bayly, Tho: Welburn, Benitt Scarbrough, Geo: Parker, Rob't Hutchinson, Edw. Moore, Rob't Pitt, Jno. Watts, Southy Littleton

ESCHEATOR - Edw. Scarbrough

CORONORS - Edw'd Scarbrough, Tho: Welburne, Geo: Parker

COUNTY CLERK - Jno. Washburne

SURVEYOR - Edw'd Scarbrough

CHARLES CITY. 169,901 Acres of land. 1,327 Tithables

BURGESSES - Rich: Bland, Jno. Wynn

SHERIFF - Char: Goodrich

JUSTICES - Rich: Bland, Dan: Luellin, Char: Goodrich, Robert Bolling, Little'y Epes, Geo: Blighton, Jno. Hardiman, Micajah Low, Jno. Wynn, Rich: Bradford, Jno. Terry

ESCHEATOR - Wm. Randolph

CORONORS - ________

COUNTY CLERK - Ben: Harrison

SURVEYOR - Rob't Bolling

ELIZABETH CITY. 29,560 acres of land. 478 Tithables

BURGESSES - Wm. Wilson, Wm. Armistead

SHERIFF - Nich'o Curle

JUSTICES - Wm. Wilson, Ant'o Armistead, Robert Beverley, Pascho (?) Curle, Wm. Lowry, August'n Moore, Coleman Borough, Walt'r Bayly, Nich'o Curle.

ESCHEATOR - John Lightfoot

CORONORS - ________

COUNTY CLERK - Charles Jenings

SURVEYOR - Wm. Lowry

ESSEX. 125,350 acres of land. 1,034 Tithables

BURGESSES - Jno. Catlett, Tho: Edmondson

SHERIFF - Tho: Merriwether

JUSTICES - Jno. Catlett, Tho: Edmondson, Francis Talliaferro, Bernard Gaines, Rob't Brookes, Jno. Battaile, Jno. Talliaferro, Jam's Boughan, Fra: Gouldman, Rich: Covinton, Dan'l Dobins, Rob't Paine, Tho: Meriwether, Wm. Tomlin, Benj: Mosely, Sam'l Thacker, Rob't Coleman

ESCHEATOR - Matt: Page

CORONORS - Jno. Catlett, Rob't Brookes, Jam's Boughan, Rich'd Covinton

COUNTY CLERK - Francis Meriwether

SURVEYOR - Charles Smith

GLOUCESTER. 142,479 acres of land. 2,626 Tithables

SPEAKER - Pet'r Beverley

BURGESS - Mord: Cook

SHERIFF - Pet'r Kemp

JUSTICES - Jam's Ransom, Mordecai Cook, Conquest Wyat, Jno. Gwin, Sands Knowles, Pet'r Kemp, Rich: Booker, Amb: Dudley, Tho: Tod, Thomas Buckner, Ant'o Gregory, Jno. Smith, Gabriel Throgmorton

ESCHEATOR - Matt: Page

CORONORS - _______

COUNTY CLERK - Pet'r Beverley

SURVEYOR - Miles Carey

HENRICO. 146,650 acres of land. 863 Tithables

BURGESSES - Tho: Cook, Wm. Farrar

SHERIFF - Giles Webb

JUSTICES - Rich'd Cock, Wm. Randolph, Peter Field, Francis Epes, Wm. Farrar, Jno. Worsham, Tho: Cock, Giles Webb, Jos: Royall, Jno. Bolling

ESCHEATOR - Wm. Randolph

CORONORS - Wm. Randolph, Wm. Cock, Peter Field, Seth Ward

COUNTY CLERK - James Cock

SURVEYOR - Richard Ligon

JAMES CITY. 108,366 acres of land. 1,193 Tithables

BURGESSES - Sam'l Bray, Geo: Marable, Rob't Beverley

SHERIFF - Tho: Cowles

JUSTICES - Phill: Lightfoot, Henry Duke, Benj: Harrison, Phill: Ludwell, Mich: Sherman, Jam's Bray, Thos. Cowles, Hugh Norwell, Wm. Edwards, Wm. Drumond, Tho: Mountfort, Jno. Frasier, Dionisius Wright, Jno. Geddis, Henry Soane

ESCHEATOR - Jno. Lightfoot

COUNTY CLERK - Chic. Corb: Thacker

SURVEYOR - Jam's Minge Jr.

ISLE OF WIGHT. 130,496 acres of land. 876 Tithables

BURGESSES - Hen: Applethwaite, Tho: Giles

SHERIFF - Wm. Bridger

JUSTICES - Hen: Applethwaite, Sam'l Bridger, Geo: Moor, Jerom: Exam, Hen: Baker, Tho: Giles, Ant'o Holliday, Arth: Smith, Rob't Key, Hump: Marshall, Pitt Bridger, Hen: Applethwaite Jr.

ESCHEATOR - Wm. Randolph

CORONORS - Hen: Applethwaite, Geo: Moore

COUNTY CLERK - Char: Chapman

SURVEYOR - Thomas Swain

KING & QUEEN. 209,102 acres of land. 1,848 Tithables

BURGESSES - Wm. Leigh, Jam's Taylor

SHERIFF - Jno. Walker

JUSTICES - Wm. Leigh, Rich: Gregory, Tho: Paulin, John Waller, Rich'd Anderson, Wm. Byrd, Jam's Taylor, Jno. Storey, Geo: Braxton, Hen: Fielding, Jno. Wyatt, John Major, Tho: Pettit

ESCHEATOR - Matt Page

CORONORS - ______

COUNTY CLERK - Rob't Beverley

SURVEYOR - Harry Beverley

KING WILLIAM. _____ acres of land. 803 Tithables

BURGESSES - Jno. West, Nath: West

SHERIFF - Jno. Waller

JUSTICES - Hen: Fox, Jno. Waller, Jno. West, Hen: Madison, Wm. Clayborne, Rich'd Gissedge, Martin Palmer, Dan'l Miles, Rog'r Mallory, Tho. Carr, Wm. Noy, Geo: Dabney, Tho: Terry

ESCHEATOR - Matt: Page

COUNTY CLERK - Wm. Aylett

SURVEYOR - Harry Beverley

LANCASTER. _______ acres of land. 926 Tithables

BURGESSES - Jos: Ball, Wm. Fox

SHERIFF - Hen: Fleet

JUSTICES - Dav: Fox, Jos: Ball, Hen: Fleet, Wm. Lester, Wm. Ball
Alex: Swan, Wm. Fox, Jno. Turbervill, Jno. Pinckard,
Tho: Martin, Rich'd Ball, Tho: Pinckard

ESCHEATOR - _________

CORONORS - Dav'd Fox, Jno. Turbervill

COUNTY CLERK - Jos. Tayloe

SURVEYOR - _________

MIDDLESEX. 48,200 acres of land. 814 Tithables

BURGESSES - Gawin Corbin, Edw'n Thacker

SHERIFF - Sr. Wm. Skipworth

JUSTICES - Sr. Wm. Skipworth Bar., Matt Kemp, Wm. Churchill,
Rob't Dudley, Gaw'n Corbin, Fra: Weekes, Henry Thacker,
Jno. Smith, Jno. Grimes, Corbin Griffin, Christ: Robinson,
Tobias Micklebrough, Harry Beverley

ESCHEATOR - Matt Page

CORONORS - Matt Kemp

COUNTY CLERK - Edw'n Thacker

SURVEYOR - Edwin Thacker

NANSEMOND. 130,500 acres of land. 1,030 Tithables.

BURGESSES - Tho: Milner, Dan'l Sullivan

SHERIFF - Char: Drury

JUSTICES - Geo: Nosworthy, Tho: Swan, Luke Havild, Fra: Milner,
Tho: Milner, Cha: Drury, Jno. Speir, Wm. Hunter,
Wm. Wright, Rich'd Awborn, Hen: Jenkins, James Lockhart

ESCHEATOR - Wm. Randolph

CORONERS - _________

COUNTY CLERK - Dan'l Sullivan

SURVEYOR - Tho: Milner

NORFOLK. 110,534 acres of land. 693 Tithables

BURGESSES - Rich'd Church, Matt: Godfrey

SHERIFF - Sam'l Boush

JUSTICES - Tho: Hodges, Jam: Wilson, Rich'd Church, Sam'l Boush, Tho: Willoughby, Jno. Hodges, Matt: Godfrey, Wm. Langley, Lem'l Mason, Geo: Mason, James Wilson Jr., Mathew Spivy

ESCHEATOR - Wm. Randolph

CORONORS - Tho: Willoughby, Sam'l Boush, James Wilson

COUNTY CLERK - Lem'l Wilson

SURVEYOR - Tho: Milner

NEW KENT. 175,334 acres of land. 1,245 Tithables

BURGESSES - Wm. Basset, Jos: Foster

SHERIFF - Nich'o Meriwether

JUSTICES - Jos: Foster, Lancel. Bathurst, Wm. Basset, Jno. Lyddall, Jam's Moss, Jno. Stanup, Tho: Smith, Jno. Lewis, Nich'o Merriwether, Geo. Keeling, Jno. King, Henry Chiles

ESCHEATOR - Jno. Lightfoot

CORONORS - Lanc: Bathurst, Jno. Stanup, Nich'o Merriwether, Jno. Lewis

COUNTY CLERK - Geo: Clough

SURVEYOR - James Minge Sr.

NORTHUMBERLAND. ______ acres of land. 1,189 Tithables

BURGESSES - Rodh'm Konnor, Tho: Hobson

SHERIFF - Geo: Cooper

JUSTICES - Sam'l Griffin, Hancock Lee, Char: Lee, Geo: Cooper, Rodh'm Konnor, Pet: Hack, Jno. Harris, Chris'r Neale, Jno. Crawly, Pet'r Coutanceau, Tho: Winder, Leon'd Howson, Jno. Eustace, Jam's Waddy, Jno. Howson

ESCHEATOR - ______

CORONORS - Jno. Harris, Rich: Flint, Pet: Coutanceau, Edw: Sanders

COUNTY CLERK - Tho: Hobson

SURVEYOR - George Cooper

NORTHAMPTON. 102,099 acres of land. 693 Tithables

BURGESSES - Wm. Waters, Jno. Powell

SHERIFF - ________

JUSTICES - Jno. Robins, Phill: Fisher, Obed: Johnson, Nath: Littleton, Wm. Waters, Jno. Custis Jr., Ralph Pigott, Wm. Harmason, Jno. Powell, Jacob Johnson, Tho: Savage, Geo: Harmason, Littleton Robinson

ESCHEATOR - Jno. Custis

CORONORS - Wm. Waters, Jac: Johnson, Geo: Harmason

COUNTY CLERK - Dan'l Neech

SURVEYOR - Edm'd Scarbrough

PRINCESS ANNE. 97,891 acres of land. 727 Tithables

BURGESSES - Adam Thorogood, Edw'd Moseley

SHERIFF - ________

JUSTICES - Benoni Burrough, Fra: Morse, Edw'd Moseley, Adam Thorogood, Tho: Lawson, Solom: White, Hen: Spratt, Joel Cornick, Jno. Richardson, Jno. Moseley, Horatio Woodhouse

ESCHEATOR - Wm. Randolph

CORONORS - Edw'd Moseley, Rob't Thorogood, Hen: Woodhouse, Patr. White

COUNTY CLERK - Chris: Cock

SURVEYOR - Thomas Milner

RICHMOND. ______ acres of land. 1,358 Tithables

BURGESSES - Wm. Tayloe, Geo: Taylor

SHERIFF - Wm. Downman

JUSTICES - Wm. Tayloe, Geo: Taylor, Sam'l P****, Wm. Underwood, Alex: Doniphan, Jno. Deane, Dav'd Gwin, Jno. Baker, Wm. Holman, Jno. Tarpley, Rawleigh Traverse, Francis Slaughter

ESCHEATOR - ________

CORONORS - Jno. Baker, David Gwin, Wm. Underwood, Alex: Doniphan

COUNTY CLERK - James Porlock

SURVEYOR - ______

SURRY. 102,425 acres of land. 739 Tithables

BURGESSES - Natt: Harrison, Sam'l Thompson

SHERIFF - ________

JUSTICES - Hen: Tooker, Wm. Brown Jr., Tho: Holt, Jam's Mason, Nat'l Harrison, Sam'l Thompson, Wm. Newsom, Wm. Cock, Tho: Drew, Jno. Edwards, Edw'd Jackman

ESCHEATOR - Wm. Randolph

CORONORS - Tho: Holt, Nat'l Harrison

COUNTY CLERK - Fra: Clements

SURVEYOR - Thomas Swan

STAFFORD. ______ acres of land. 828 Tithables

BURGESSES - Geo: Mason, Wm. Fitzhugh

SHERIFF - Char: Ellis

JUSTICES - Geo: Mason, Matt: Thompson, Rob't Alexander, Rice Hoe, Rich'd Fossaker, Jno. Washington, Jos. Sumner, Jno. Waugh, Jr. Edw'd Hart, Tho: Gregg, Rich'd Foole, Tho: Gilson, Phill: Alexander, Wm. Bunbury, Jno. West, Charles Ellis

ESCHEATOR - ________

CORONORS - ________

COUNTY CLERK - Wm. Fitzhugh

SURVEYOR - Tho: Gregg

WARWICK. 38,606 acres of land. 505 Tithables

BURGESSES - Miles Cary, Wm. Cary

SHERIFF - Tho: Merry

JUSTICES - Hump: Harwood, Miles Cary, Sam'l Ranshaw, Rob't Hubbard, Wm. Cary, Tho: Merry, Wm. Roscow, Thomas Charles, Matt: Jones, Miles Wills, Tho: Haynes, Jno. Tignall

ESCHEATOR - Jno. Lightfoot

CORONORS - Wm. Cary, Wm. Roscoe

COUNTY CLERK - Miles Cary Jr.

SURVEYOR - Wm. Lowry

WESTMORELAND. _______ acres of land. 1,083 Tithables

BURGESSES - Alex: Spence, Sam'l Westcomb

SHERIFF - Lem'l Markham

JUSTICES - Wm. Pierce, Francis Wright, Nich'o Spencer, Alex Spence, Willoughby Allerton, Lem'l Markham, Sam. Taylor, Char: Ashton, Caleb Butler, Jno. Sturman, Gerrard Hutt, Geo: Weedon, Jno. Elliott, Andr: Monroe, Hen: Ashton Jno. Bushrod

ESCHEATOR - ________

CORONORS - ________

COUNTY CLERK - Jam's Westcomb

SURVEYOR - Alex. Spence

YORKE. 61,196 acres of land. 1,180 Tithables

BURGESSES - Tho: Barbar, Tho: Ballard

SHERIFF - Hen: Tyler

JUSTICES - Tho: Barbar, Jos. Ring, Rob't Read, Tho: Ballard, Tho: Roberts, Char: Hansford, Wm. Buckner, Hen: Tyler, Baldwyn Mathews, Jno. Page, Jam: Whaley, Jno. Goodwin, Dan'l Taylor, Tho: Nutting

ESCHEATOR - Jno. Lightfoot

CORONORS - _______

COUNTY CLERK - Wm. Sedgwick

SURVEYOR - Miles Cary

Her Maj'y. Learned Councill in the law - Benj: Harrison

Clerke of her Maj'y Councill
Clerke of the Gen'l Assembly - Wm. Robinson

Clerke of the House of Burgesses - Wm. Randolph

Clerke of Secret Office
Clerke of the Gen'l Court - Chicheley Corbin Thacker

Mace Bearer and Messenger to the House of Burgesses - John Chiles.

By: E. Jenings.

THE PRESENT STATE OF VIRGINIA FOR THE YEAR 1714 WITH RESPECT TO THE COLONY IN GENERAL.

THE RIGHT HONORABLE GEORGE, , EARL OF ORKNEY,
HIS MAJESTY'S LT. GOVERNOR GENERAL

THE HONORABLE ALEXANDER SPOTSWOOD,
LT. GOVERNOR & COMMANDER IN CHIEF

COUNCIL

Robert Carter	William Cocke
James Blair	Nathaniel Harrison
Philip Ludwell	Mann Page
John Smith	Robert Porteus, Esq.
John Lewis	Wm. Robinson, Clerk
William Byrd	Wm. Cragg, Door Keeper

PRINCIPAL OFFICERS

COMMISSARY for ye Bishop of London	Rev'd Mr. James Blair
SECRETARY of ye Colony	William Cocke, Esq.
AUDITOR of His Maj'ty's Revenues	William Blathwait Esq.
RECEIVER GEN'LL of His Maj'ty's Revenues	Wm. Byrd Esq.
DEPUTY AUDITOR	Philip Ludwell Esq.
ATTORNEY GEN'LL	John Clayton Esq.

OFFICERS GEN'LL CT. & VICE-ADM'TY

JUDGES OF YE GENERALL COURT	Robert Carter	Wm. Byrd
	James Blair	Wm. Cocke
	Philip Ludwell	Nathaniel Harrison
	John Smith	Mann Page
	John Lewis	Robert Porteus Esq.
CLERK	Chicheley Corbin Thacker	
JUDGE OF YE SD. COURT OF VICE-ADM'TY	John Holloway	
ADVOCATE	John Clayton	
REGISTER	Cha. Jackson	
MARSHALL	Francis Tyler	

DISTRICT OFFICERS OF CUSTOMS

DISTRICT	COLLECTORS	NAVAL OFFICERS
Upper part James River	Edward Hill	Francis Lightfoot
Lower part James River	Francis Kanaday	John Holloway
ditto	George Walker, Searcher	
York River	Wm. Buckner	Nathan'l Burwell
do.	Robert James, Searcher	
Rappahanock	Rich'd Chichester	Chr. Robinson
Potomack	Dan'l McCarty	Thomas Lee
Eastern Shore	Henry Scarbrugh	Wm. Waters
do.	Robert Howsen, Surveyor	
Lynhaven Bay and Elsabeth (Elizabeth)	Sampson Trevelhan, Surveyor	

ESCHEATORS

For South Side James River	Wm. Byrd Esq.
Between James & York Rivers	Philip Ludwell Esq.
Between York & Rappahanock Rivers	John Lewis Esq.
For the Eastern Shore	Hancock Custis, Gent.

OFFICERS OF THE ASSEMBLY

SPEAKER	Peter Beverly
CHAPLAIN	Benj'a Goodwin
CLERK OF GEN'L ASSEMBLY	Wm. Robertson
CLERK OF HOUSE OF BURGESSES	Rich'd Buckner
CLERK OF COMMITTEE OF PROPOSITIONS & GRIEVANCES	John Clayton
CLERK OF COMMITTEE OF CLAIMS	Miles Cary
MESSENGER	Francis Tyler
4 Door Keepers	

THE PRESENT STATE OF VIRGINIA FOR THE YEAR 1714
with respect to the County in particular.

ACCOMACK COUNTY

ACRES	239,462
TITHABLES	1,055
STOREHOUSES	2
SHERIFF	Edward Robins
CORONER	Tully Robinson
JUSTICES OF THE PEACE	Wm. Custis, Edm'd Scarbrugh, Tully Robinson, Geo. Parker, Jno. Bradhurst, Hancock Custis, Jno. Watts, Chas. Bailey, Quorum. Edw'd Robins, Rich'd Kitson, Hen. Scarbrugh, Hen. Custis, Tho. Custis, Skinner Wallop, Wm. Burton
BURGESSES	Tully Robinson, Rich'd Drumond
TOBACCO AGENTS	Hen. Scarburgh, James Kemp
COUNTY CLERKS	Rob't Snead
SURVEYORS	Chas. Bailey
PARISHES	Accomack
MINISTERS	Mr. Black

CHARLES CITY

ACRES	57,939
TITHABLES	553
STOREHOUSES	1
SHERIFF	Rich'd Dennis
CORONERS	Littlebury Epes, Jno. Stith
JUSTICES OF THE PEACE	Jno. Stith, Rich'd Bradford, Drury Stith, Jno. Epes, Sam'l Harwood, Rich'd Dennis, Quorum Jos. Harwood, James Joyeux, Lewellin Epes, Geo. Hunt, James Maundes
BURGESSES	Littlebury Epes, Sam'l Harwood
TOBACCO AGENTS	Littlebury Epes
COUNTY CLERKS	Littlebury Epes
SURVEYORS	Rob't Bolling
PARISHES	Westover Port, Weyanoke
MINISTERS	Chas. Anderson

ELIZABETH CITY

ACRES	33,851
TITHABLES	610
WAREHOUSES	1
SHERIFF	Fra. Ballard
CORONER	Wm. Armistead
JUSTICES OF THE PEACE	Jno. Holloway, Wm. Loury, Wm. Armistead, Fra. Ballard, Tho. Tabb, Anth'o Armistead, Simon Hollier, Quorum. Wm. Boswell, John Bailey, John Moore, Tho. Wyth, Jno. King, Mark Johnson
BURGESSES	Wm. Armistead
TOBACCO AGENTS	Rob't Armistead
COUNTY CLERKS	Chas. Jennings
SURVEYORS	Wm. Loury
PARISHES	Eliz'a City
MINISTERS	Andr'w Thomson

ESSEX

ACRES	190,352
TITHABLES	1,653
WAREHOUSES	4
SHERIFFS	Leo. Farrent
CORONERS	Jno. Catlett, Law. Taliaferro
JUSTICES OF THE PEACE	Rich'd Covington, Jno. Lomax, Jos. Smith, Hen. Robinson, Quorum. Wm. Woodford, Paul Micou, Wm. Daingerfield, Wm. Young, Leo. Farent
BURGESSES	Fra. Gouldman, Jno. Hawkins
TOBACCO AGENTS	Rich'd Buckner, Rob't Beverly, Joseph Smith
COUNTY CLERKS	Rich'd Buckner
SURVEYORS	Aug't Smith
PARISHES	South Farnham, St. Ann's, St. Mary's
MINISTERS	Lewis Latane, Tho. Edwards, Owen Jones

GLOUCESTER

ACRES	133,544
TITHABLES	2,804
SHERIFFS	Phil Smith
CORONERS	Thos. Buckner, Amb. Dudley
JUSTICES OF THE PEACE	Mordeccy Cooke, Peter Kemp, Nath'l Burwell, Gab. Throckmorton, David Alexander, Quorum. Wm. Smith, Tho. Read, Phil. Smith, Hen. Armistead, Henry Whitings, Aug't Smith, Cha. Tomkies, Wm Kemp
BURGESSES	Peter Beverly, Mordeccy Cooke
TOBACCO AGENTS	Jno. Smith Esq., Henry Whitings, Giles Cooke
COUNTY CLERKS	Peter Beverly
SURVEYORS	Tho. Cooke
PARISHES	Abbington, Petso, Ware, Kingston
MINISTERS	Guy Smith, Em. Jones, James Clack, Fra. Mylne

HENRICO

ACRES	***
TITHABLES	1,355 (?)
SHERIFFS	Jno. Washburn (?)
CORONERS	Fra. Epes
JUSTICES OF THE PEACE	Fra. Epes, Wm. Farrar, Jno. Worsham (?), Jos. Royall, Jno. Bolling, Rich'd **cke (? Cocke) Tho. J**son, Quorum. Abra. Salle, Isham Epes, Wm. Kennon, Tho. Rudolph, Hen. R***ph Jr., Jno. A***, Jno. ***ford
BURGESSES	Jno. Bolling, Fra. Epes Jr.
TOBACCO AGENTS	Wm. Randolph, Fra. Epes, Jr., Wm. Kennon
COUNTY CLERKS	***
SURVEYORS	***
PARISHES	***
MINISTERS	***

JAMES CITY

ACRES	117,337
TITHABLES	1,535
WAREHOUSES	3
SHERIFF	Wm. Marston
CORONERS	Tho. Cowles, Jno. Geddis, David Bray
JUSTICES OF THE PEACE	James Bray, Jno. Frayser, Hen. Soane Jr., Wm. Brodnax, Edw'd Jaquelin, Fred. Jones, Quorum. Mongo Ingles, Arch. Blair, James Duke, David Morce, Fra. Lightfoot, Wm. Marston
BURGESSES	Geo. Marable, Henry Soane Jr., Edw'd Jaquelin, for ye City
TOBACCO AGENT	Henry Soane Jr.
COUNTY CLERK	Wm. Robertson
SURVEYOR	Simon Jeffrys
PARISHES	Wallingford, Willmington, James City, Bruton Port
MINISTERS	James Blair

ISLE OF WIGHT

ACRES	168,026
TITHABLES	1,223
WAREHOUSES	2
SHERIFF	Nath'l Ridley
CORONER	-------
JUSTICES OF THE PEACE	Anth'o Holladay, Arthur Smith, Tho. Pitt, Wm. Bridges, Hen. Applewait, Jos. Godwin, Tho. Hill, Andrew Woodley, Quorum. Nath'l Ridley, Tho. Walton, Geo. Norsworthy, James Day, Barnaby Mackkeny, Tho. Brewer,
BURGESSES	Wm. Bridger, Joseph Godwin
TOBACCO AGENTS	Joseph Godwin, Wm. Bridger
COUNTY CLERK	Henry Lightfoot
SURVEYOR	John Allen
PARISHES	Warwick Creek, Newport
MINISTERS	Alex. Forbes, And'w Monro

KING & QUEEN

ACRES	218,304
TITHABLES	1,814
WAREHOUSES	4
SHERIFF	Jno. Madison
CORONERS	Geo. Braxton, Tho. Pettit
JUSTICES OF THE PEACE	Jno. Holloway, Rich'd Anderson, Wm. Bird, James Taylor, Geo. Braxton, Tho. Pettit, Jno. Madison, Law'r Orill, Rob't Pollard, Quorum. Sam'l Mathews, Jer. Clowdes, Rich'd Johnson, Isaac Hill, Wm. Southerland, Gawin Corbin, John Baylor, Tho. Walker, Wm. Todd
BURGESSES	Jno. Holloway, Wm. Bird
TOBACCO AGENTS	Rob't Beverly, Jno. Baylor
COUNTY CLERK	C. C. Thacker
SURVEYOR	Harry Beverly
PARISHES	St. Stephen's, Stratton Major
MINISTERS	Ralph Bowker, Jno. Skaife

KING WILLIAM

ACRES	146,000
TITHABLES	1,226
WAREHOUSES	7
SHERIFF	Wm. Smith
CORONERS	Jno. Waller, Wm. Anderson
JUSTICES OF THE PEACE	Jno. Waller, Tho. West, Geo. Dabnoy, Nath'l West, Phil. Whitehead, Wm. Anderson, Jno. Butts, Aug't Moore, Quorum. Tho. Johnson, G** Purchase, Jno. Chiles, Tho. Carr Jr., Wm. Smith, Jno. Quarles, Ralph Crawford
BURGESSES	Jno. Waller, Orlando Jones
TOBACCO AGENTS	Jno. Waller, Wm. Aylett, Nath'l West, Tho. Carr, Tho. Butts
COUNTY CLERK	Wm. Aylett
SURVEYOR	Harry Beverly
PARISHES	St. Johns
MINISTER	Jno. Monro

LANCASTER

ACRES	Proprietors
TITHABLES	1,019
WAREHOUSES	2
SHERIFF	Tho. Lee
CORONERS	Wm. Ball, Jno. Tubervile
JUSTICES OF THE PEACE	Henry Fleet, Wm. Ball, Jno. Tubervile, Rich'd Ball, Tho. Pinkard, Quorum. Tho. Carter, Rich'd Chichester, Row'ld Lawson, Hugh Brent, Geo. Heale, Rawleigh Chin, Jos. Ball, Tho. Lee
BURGESSES	Wm. Ball, Edwin Conway
TOBACCO AGENT	Tho. Carter
COUNTY CLERK	Jos. Tayloe
SURVEYOR	-------
PARISHES	Christ Church, White Chappelle
MINISTERS	Jno. Ball

MIDDLESEX

ACRES	71,264
TITHABLES	926
WAREHOUSES	1
SHERIFF	Jno. Vivion
CORONER	Matt'w Kemp
JUSTICES OF THE PEACE	Sir Wm. Skipwith, Baronett, Matthew Kemp, Jno. Smith, Chr. Robinson, Geo. Wortham, Rob't Daniell, Jno. *****, Quorum. Roger Jones, Oliver Segar, Garrett Miner, James Walker, Jno. Grymes, Jno. Price, Jno. Vivion, Jno. Wormley
BURGESSES	Jno, Robinson, Chr. Robinson
TOBACCO AGENT	Jno. Robinson
COUNTY CLERK	Wm. Steward (?)
SURVEYOR	Tho. Cooke
PARISHES	Christ Church
MINISTERS	Bart'oly Yates

NANSEMOND

ACRES	142,834
TITHABLES	1,250
WAREHOUSES	5
SHERIFF	Wm. Butler
CORONERS	Tho. Jordan, Tho. Godwin, James Reddick
JUSTICES OF THE PEACE	Tho. Godwin, Tho. Milner, Cha. Drury, Wm. Wright, Jno. Lear, Rob't Peale, Henry Baker, Jos. Meredith, Quorum. Jno. Norsworthy, Tho. Jordan, Jno. Yeate, Wm. Butler, Jno. Wright, Edm'd Streator, Tho. Hausland, Gresham Coffield, Tho. Norfleet
BURGESSES	Tho. Godwin, Wm. Wright
TOBACCO AGENTS	Wm. Wright, Tho. Godwin
COUNTY CLERK	Mich'l Archer
SURVEYOR	Tho. Milner
PARISHES	Lower Parish, Upper Parish, Chuckatuck
MINISTERS	Wm. Ransford, Wm. Wallice

NORFOLK

ACRES	122,061
TITHABLES	891
WAREHOUSES	2
SHERIFF	Jonas Holladay
CORONERS	Tho. Willoughby, Sam'l Boush
JUSTICES OF THE PEACE	Sam'l Boush, Matth'w Godfrey, Wm. Langley, James Wilson, Matth'w Spivy, Quorum. Geo. Newton, Jonas Holladay, Jno. Holsted, Wm. Crawford
BURGESSES	Geo. Newton, Wm. Crawford
TOBACCO AGENTS	Sam'l Boush
COUNTY CLERK	Lem'l Wilson
SURVEYOR	Lem'l Newton

NEW KENT

ACRES	200,649
TITHABLES	1,852
WAREHOUSES	2
SHERIFF	Tho. Barbar
CORONERS	Jos. Foster, Jno. Dibdale, Nich'o Meriwether
JUSTICES OF THE PEACE	Joseph Foster, James Moss, John Stanup, Nich'o Merriwether, Geo. Keeling, Henry Chiles, Rich'd Littlepage, Roger Thompson, Quorum. Jno. Dibdale, Rob't Anderson, Jno. Scott, Tho. Butts, Jno. Foster, Tho. Barbar Jr., Alex. Walker, Jno. Sclater
BURGESSES	Nich'o Meriwether, Jno. Stanup
TOBACCO AGENTS	Tho. Carr, Tho. Butts, Rich'd Littlepage
COUNTY CLERK	Jno. Thornton
SURVEYOR	Val. Minge
PARISHES	Blisland, St. Peters, St. Pauls
MINISTERS	Dan'l Taylor, Wm. Brodie, Tho. Sharp

NORTHUMBERLAND

ACRES	Proprietors
TITHABLES	1,272
WAREHOUSES	3
SHERIFF	------
CORONERS	Jno. Sanders, Edw'd Sanders
JUSTICES OF THE PEACE	Peter Hack, Chr. Neale, Jno. Howson, Peter Presley Jno. Stepto, Jno. Claughton, Jno. Taylor, Jno. Ingram, Wm. Jones, Quorum. Rich'd Lee, Griffin Fauntleroy, Rich'd Neale, Rich'd Sp**n (Spann ?) Geo. Ball, Rich'd Hull, Jno. Coppage, Tho. Hughlet.
BURGESSES	Chr. Neale, Rich'd Neale
TOBACCO AGENTS	Rich'd Neale, Geo. Eskridge
COUNTY CLERK	Tho. Hobson
SURVEYOR	Jno. Coppage
PARISHES	Fairfeild, Wicocomico
MINISTERS	Mr. Spann

NORTHAMPTON

ACRES	103,840
TITHABLES	831
SHERIFF	Jno. Powell
CORONERS	Geo. Harmanson
JUSTICES OF THE PEACE	Benj'a Nottingham, Hillary Stringer, Jno. Harmanson, Jno. Powell, Wm. Kendall, Obedi. Johnson, Quorum. Jno. West, Wm. Kendall Jr., Jno. Marshall, Jno. Savage, Henry Blair, Jno. Hunt.
BURGESSES	Wm. Waters, Cha. Floyd
TOBACCO AGENT	------
COUNTY CLERKS	Rob't Howsen
SURVEYOR	Cha. Bailey
PARISHES	Hungars
MINISTERS	Pat. Faulkner

PRINCESS ANNE

ACRES	106,639
TITHABLES	921
WAREHOUSES	1
SHERIFF	Jno. Cornick
CORONERS	Edw'd Moseley, Jno. Moseley
JUSTICES OF THE PEACE	Edw'd Moseley, Solomon White, Hen. Spratt, Jno. Moseley, Horatia Woodhouse, Jno. Cornick, Hen. Chapman, Quorum. Wm. Smith, Geo. Hancock, Cha. Sayer, Tho. Keeling, Samp. Trevethan Jr., Edw'd Moseley, Tho. Corprew, Edw'd Lamont, Jno. Bollitho
BURGESSES	Alex. Boush, Tho. Walker
TOBACCO AGENT	**** Walker
COUNTY CLERK	Chr. Cooke
SURVEYOR	Lem'l Newton
PARISHES	Lynhaven
MINISTERS	Mr. Tenant

PRINCE GEORGE

ACRES	118,764
TITHABLES	1,040
SHERIFF	Sam'l Merlin
CORONERS	Wm. Harrison, Henry Ball
JUSTICES OF THE PEACE	Cha. Goodrich, John Hamlyn, Jno. Poythress, Peter Jones, Rand'h Platt, Rob't Mumford, Rob't **ll (? Ball), Henry Duke, Quorum. Stith Bolling, Sampson Meredith, James Thweat, Jno. ***tch, Rob't Bolling, Jno. Hardiman, Lewis Green Jr., Edw'd Wyatt, Jno. Patterson, Rich'd Hamlyn
BURGESSES	Edw'd Goodrich, Jno. Hamlyn
TOBACCO AGENTS	Rob't Mumford, Jno. Hamlyn, Rich'd Blair (?) Jno. Simmons
COUNTY CLERK	-------
SURVEYOR	Rob't Bolling
PARISHES	Bristoll Port, Martin Brandon
MINISTERS	Geo. Bolling, (?), Jno. Worden

RICHMOND

ACRES	Proprietors
TITHABLES	1,799
SHERIFF	Cha. Barbar
CORONERS	Edw'd Barrow, Nich'o Smith, Alex. Donaphon
JUSTICES OF THE PEACE	Alex. Donaphon, Jno. Tarpley, Cha. Barbar, Edw'd Barrow, Nich'o Smith, Joseph Deeke, Wm. Woodbridge, Wm. Thornton, Quorum. Tho. Griffin, Jno. Taylor, Moore Fantleroy, Jon'a Gibson, Rich'd Talliaferra, Aug't Brockenburgh
BURGESSES	Wm. Robinson, Wm. Thornton
TOBACCO AGENTS	Wm. Robinson, Wm. Thornton, Wm. Tayloe, Jno. Tarpley
COUNTY CLERK	Marm. Beckwith
SURVEYOR	Wm. Thornton
PARISHES	St. Mary's, Sittenborne, North Farnham
MINISTERS	Mr. Stagg, Peter Kippax

SURRY

ACRES	146,302
TITHABLES	1,320
SHERIFFS	------
CORONERS	Wm. Edwards
JUSTICES OF THE PEACE	Wm. Brown, Tho. Holt, Sam'l Thomson, Wm. Edwards, Wm. Cocke, Walter Cocke, Etheld'r Taylor, Rob't Ruffin, Hen. Harrison, Quorum. Jno. Simons, Wm. Gray, Jno. Nickells, Walter Flood Howell Edmonds, Jno. Holt, Wm. Snookins (?), Tho. Collyer, Wm. Drew
BURGESSES	Wm. Gray, Jno. Simons
TOBACCO AGENTS	Wm. Gray, Jno. Simons
COUNTY CLERK	JNO. Allen
SURVEYOR	Jno. Allen
PARISHES	Southwark, Lyons Creek
MINISTERS	Mr. Cargill

STAFFORD

ACRES	Proprietors
TITHABLES	1,069
SHERIFF	Geo. Mason Jr.
CORONERS	Jno. Waugh, Jno. West
JUSTICES OF THE PEACE	Geo. Mason, Rice Hooe, Jno. Washington, Jos. Sumner, Dade Massie, Jno. West, Quorum. Geo. Anderson, Jno. Waugh, Geo. Mason Jr., James Jameson, Hen. Fitzhugh, Tho. Lunn, Rawl. Travis, Jno. Mosely
BURGESSES	Henry Fitzhugh, Jno. Waugh
TOBACCO AGENTS	Jno. Waugh, Hen. Fitzhugh
COUNTY CLERK	Tho. Fitzhugh
SURVEYOR	Tho. Gregg
PARISHES	St. Pauls, Overworton
MINISTERS	Mr. Scott

WARWICK

ACRES	39,213
TITHABLES	604
WAREHOUSES	2
SHERIFF	------
CORONER	Tho, Merry
JUSTICES OF THE PEACE	Miles Wills, Tho. Charles, Matthew Jones, Tho. Haynes, Tho. Cary, Hump. Harwood, Quorum. Fra. Jones, Wm. Harwood, Nath'l Hoggard, Wm. Cole, Tho. Haynes Jr., Henry Cary Jr.
BURGESSES	Miles Wills, Wm. Harwood
TOBACCO AGENTS	Miles Wills
COUNTY CLERKS	Miles Cary
SURVEYOR	Wm. Loury
PARISHES	Mulberry Island, Denby
MINISTER	Mr. Sclater

THE PRESENT STATE OF VIRGINIA 1726
With respect to the Colony in General

The Right Honorable GEORGE, Earl of Orkney,
His Majesty's Lieut. & Governor General

The Honorable HUGH DRYSDALE,
Lt. Governor & Commander in Chief

COUNCIL

Edmund Jenings	Cole Digges
Robert Carter	Peter Beverly
James Blair	John Robinson
Phillip Ludwell	John Carter
William Byrd	Rich'd Fitzwilliam
Nath'l Harrison	John Grymes
Mann Page	Wm. Robertson, Clerk
	Jno. Basleroyle, Doorkeeper

PRINCIPAL OFFICERS BY PATENT & OTHERWISE

COMISARY for the Bp. of London	Rev'd James Blair
SECRETARY of ye Colony	John Carter, Esq.
AUDITOR of His Majesty's Revenues	Horatia Walpole Esq.
RECEIVER GEN'L of His Majesty's Revenues	John Grymes Es.
DEPUTY AUDITOR	Nath'l Harrison Esq.
ATTORNEY GENERAL	John Clayton Esq.

OFFICERS OF THE GEN'L COURT & VICE-ADMIRALTY

JUDGES OF THE GEN'L COURT	Edmund Jenings	Cole Digges
	Robert Carter	Peter Beverly
	James Blair	John Robinson
	Phillip Ludwell	John Carter
	William Byrd	Rich'd Fitzwilliam
	Nath'l Harrison	John Grymes
	Mann Page	Rich'd Hickman, Clerk.
JUDGE OF THE COURT OF VICE-ADMIRALTY	John Clayton Esq.	
ADVOCATE	Wm. Hopkins	
REGISTER	Thomas Crew	
MARSHALL	Wm. Gordon	

OFFICERS OF THE CUSTOMS

Rich'd Fitzwilliam Esq.
Surveyor General

DISTRICTS	COLLECTORS	NAVAL OFFICERS
Upper part James River	John Banister	Francis Lightfoot
Lower part James River	Thomas Michall	Wilson Cary
York	Richard Ambler	Wm. Robertson
Rappahanock	Adam Cockburn	Chr. Robinson
Potomack	Henry Moryson	Thomas Lee
Eastern Shore	Henry Scarburgh	Edm'd Scarburgh

Griffith Bowan, Survey'r of Cape Charles

PRESENT STATE OF VIRGINIA 1726

Keeper of the MAGAZINE at Wmburgh - Hen: Cary

GUNNERS OF THE BATTERIES

At James River, Oldpoint Comfort	George Walker
York River, York Town	Wm. Gordon
At Gloucester Town	John Lester
Rapp'a River, Corratomen	********
At Toppahanock	Rich'd Parker

ESCHEATORS

Between York & Rappahanock Rivers	John Robinson Esq.
Between James & York Rivers	Edmund Jenings Esq.
For the Eastern Shore	Hancock Custis Jr.
For the South Side of James River	Henry Harrison Jr.

OFFICERS OF THE ASSEMBLY

Speaker	John Holloway Esq.
Chaplain	William La Neve
Clk. of ye Gen'l Assembly	Wm. Robertson
Clk. of ye House of Burgesses	John Randolph
Clk. of ye Committee of propositions & Grievances	Godfrey Pole
Clk. of ye Committee of Claims	Miles Cary
Sergeant at arms & mace bearer	Phillip Finch
4 Door Keepers	

INDIAN INTERPRETERS

Pamunkey & Chickahomony Indians	James Adams
Nottaway, Maherin & Nansemond	Henry Briggs
Sapone, Occoneockes, Stuckanocks & Totewes	Charles Kymball

PRESENT STATE OF VIRGINIA 1726

ACCOMACK COUNTY

ACRES	230,720
TITHABLES	1,300
SHERIFF	John Kendall
CORONORS	Hen. Scarburgh, Hancock Custis
JUSTICES OF THE PEACE	Hen. Scarburgh, Hen. Custis, Edm'd Scarburgh, Rich'd Drummond, Wm. Burton, Dan'l Walburn, Jno. Kendall Quorum. Morris Shepherd, Hen. Bagwell, Hill Drummond, Wm. Bivans, Edw'd Revell, Geo. Parker
BURGESSES	Edm'd Scarburgh, Hen. Scarburgh
CLERK OF COUNTY COURT	Charles Snead
SURVEYOR	Mitchell Scarburgh
PARISHES	Accomack
MINISTER	Mr. Black
COUNTY LIEUTENANT	Hen. Scarburgh
SORT OF TOBACCO	Arromico

BRUNSWICK COUNTY

TITHABLES	160
SURVEYORS	Drury Stith, Tho. Cocke
PARISH	St. Andrew
SORT OF TOBACCO	Arromeco

CHARLES CITY COUNTY

ACRES	91,599
TITHABLES	1,082
SHERIFF	Fra. Hardyman
CORONERS	Littlebury Epes, Drury Stith
JUSTICES OF THE PEACE	Drury Stith, Hen. Soanes, James Duke, Fra. Lightfoot, Sam'l Harwood, Lewellin Epes, James Mander, Sam'l Harwood Jr. - Quorum. Fra. Hardyman, John Stith, Benj'a Harrison, John Edloe, Jno. Banister
BURGESSES	Sam'l Harwood, Jr., John Stith
CLERK OF COUNTY COURT	Littleberry Epes
SURVEYOR	Rob't Bolling
PARISHES	Westover
MINISTERS	Peter Fountain
LIEUTENANT	Wm. Byrd
SORT OF TOBACCO	Arromeco

ELIZABETH CITY

ACRES	33,748
TITHABLES	813
SHERIFFS	Joseph Selden
CORONERS	Anth. Armistead, James Servant
JUSTICES OF THE PEACE	Anth. Armistead, Simon Hollier, Tho. Wythe, John King, Joshua Curle, Rob't Armistead, John Lowry, Jacob Walker - Quorum. James Wallace, Sam'l Sweney, Joseph Banister, Joseph Selden, John Selden, Wilson Cary, Tho. Mitchell
BURGESSES	Tho. Wythe, Rob't Armistead
CLERK OF COUNTY COURT	Tho. Mingham
SURVEYOR	John Lowry
PARISHES	Eliz'a City
MINISTER	Mr. Thompson
LIEUTENANT	Cole Digges
SORT OF TOBACCO	Sweetscented

ESSEX COUNTY

ACRES	181,101
TITHABLES	2,472
SHERIFF	Tho. Waring
CORONERS	Jno. Lommax, Wm. Daingerfield
JUSTICES OF THE PEACE	Jno. Lommax, Wm. Daingerfield, Rand. Welch, Tho. Catlett, Tho. Waring, Salvador Muscoe, Quorum Rob't Brooke, Benj'a Robinson, Leon'd Hill, Fra. Thornton, Jno. Battail
BURGESSES	Wm. Beverly
CLERKS OF COUNTY COURT	Rob't Jones, Wm. Daingerfield
SURVEYOR	Rob't Brooke
PARISHES	South Farnham, Saint Anna, Saint Mary
MINISTERS	Louis Latane, Mi' Cawthorn, Owen Jones
LIEUTENANT	Peter Beverly
SORT OF TOBACCO	Sweetscented

GLOUCESTER COUNTY

ACRES	164,013
TITHABLES	3,421
SHERIFF	Fra. Willis
CORONERS	Giles Cook, Henry Willis
JUSTICES OF THE PEACE	Gab. Throckmorton, Hen. Armistead, Cha. Tomkins, Fra. Willis, Hen. Willis, Tho. Booth, Giles Cook, Quorum. Thomas Hayes, Tho. Read Jr., Geo. Nicholas, John Alexander.
BURGESSES	Giles Cook, Henry Willis
CLERK OF COUNTY COURT	John Clayton
SURVEYOR	Thos. Cook
PARISHES	Abingdon, Petso, Ware, Kingston
MINISTERS	Tho. Hughes, Emanuel Jones, John Richards, Mr. Wye
LIEUTENANT	Mann Page
SORT OF TOBACCO	Sweetscented

HANOVER COUNTY

ACRES	205,936
TITHABLES	1,941
SHERIFF	David Meriwether
CORONERS	David Meriwether, Isaac Winston, Cha. Clark, David Crawford
JUSTICES OF THE PEACE	Nich'o Meriwether, Roger Thompson, Cha. Chiswell, David Meriwether, Wm. Fleming, Isaac Winston, Cha. Hudson, Chr. Clark, David Crawford, Quorum. Peter Garland, John Anderson, James Overton Rich'd Harris, Tho. Anderson, Cha. Snelson, Rich'd Clough
BURGESSES	Nich'o Meriwether, Rich'd Harris
CLERKS	Arthur Clayton
SURVEYORS	John Syme
PARISHES	Saint Pauls, Saint Martins
MINISTERS	Mr. Brookes
LIEUTENANT	Wm. Byrd
SORT OF TOBACCO	Sweetscented

HENRICO COUNTY

ACRES	326,251
TITHABLES	2,453
SHERIFF	Jno. Radford
CORONERS	Jno. Worshan, Tho. Randolph
JUSTICES OF THE PEACE	Wm. Randolph, Tho. Jefferson, Wm. Kennon, Tho. Randolph, Hen. Randolph Jr., John Radford, Fra. Epes, Joseph Royal, Jr., Rich'd Randolph Henry Anderson, Quorum. Rich'd Kennon, John Soane, John Woodson, Bowles Cocke, John Bolling, Jr., Wm. Mayo, Edw'd Booker, Joseph Mayo, Dan'l Stoner
BURGESSES	Wm. Randolph, John Bolling
CLERKS CO. COURT	Henry Wood
SURVEYOR	Fra. Epes
PARISHES	Varina at Henrico, Bristol Port, King William, Saint James
MINISTERS	Wm. Finney, Geo. Robertson, Mr. Murdock
LIEUTENANT	Wm. Randolph
SORT OF TOBACCO	Arromicb

JAMES CITY

ACRES	87,217
TITHABLES	1,347
SHERIFF	Rob't Goodrich
CORONER	Edw'd Jacquelin
JUSTICES OF THE PEACE	John Clayton, Wm. Broadnax, Edw'd Jacquelin, Wm. Brown, Wm. Marston, Jno. Netherland, Benj'a Waldon, David Bray, Lewis Burwell, Quorum Henry Cary, Henry Powers, Rich'd Hickman, John Tyler, Rob't Goodrich, Joseph Eggleston
BURGESSES	Arth. Blair, Jno. Clayton
CLERKS CO. CT.	Mich. Archer
SURVEYOR	Wm. Comrie
PARISHES	James City, Bruton Port
MINISTERS	Wm. Letteve, James Blair
LIEUTENANT	Phillip Ludwall
SORT OF TOBACCO	Sweetscented

ISLE OF WIGHT

ACRES	214,966
TITHABLES	1,844
SHERIFF	Tho. Brewer
CORONERS	Arthur Smith, Wm. Wilkinson
JUSTICES OF THE PEACE	Arthur Smith, Wm. Bridger, Hen. Applewaite, Joseph Godwin, Tho. Walton, Geo. Norsworthy, Tho. Brewer, Matth. Jones, James Bonn, Quorum. Tho. Applewhite, Wm. Kinchin, Hardy Council, Wm. Wilkinson, John Edwards
BURGESSES	Hen. Applewaite, Joseph Godwin
CLERK CO. COURT	James Ingles
SURVEYOR	John Allen
PARISHES	Warwick Creek, Newport
MINISTERS	Mr. Barlow
LIEUTENANT	Arthur Smith
SORT OF TOBACCO	Arromico

KING GEORGE

ACRES	-----
TITHABLES	1,300
SHERIFF	Wm. Strother
CORONER	Wm. Thornton
JUSTICES OF THE PEACE	Wm. Robinson, Nich'o Smith, Wm. Thornton, Jon'a Gibson, Joseph Strother, John Spicer, Quorum Tho. Vivian, Meredith Price, Sam'll Skinker, Tho. Turner, Rowl'd Thornton, Benj'a Strother, Wm. Strother Jr.
BURGESSES	Nich'o Smith, Wm. Thornton
CLERK CO. CT.	Tho. Turner
SURVEYOR	John Savage
PARISHES	Hanover, Sittenburn Port
MINISTERS	John Prime, Mr. Blacknall
LIEUTENANT	Robert Carter
SORT OF TOBACCO	Arromeco

KING & QUEEN

ACRES	239,141
TITHABLES	2,685
SHERIFF	John Leigh
CORONERS	Gawin Corbin, Geo. Braxton, C.C. Thacker
JUSTICES OF THE PEACE	Gawin Corbin, James Taylor, Geo. Braxton, John Leigh, Rich'd Johnson, Wm. Southerland, Wm. Todd, Rob't Baylor, Quorum. Rob't Dudley, Hen. Hickman, Tho. Foster, Chr. Beverley, Phillip Todd, George Moore, Sam'll Smith, Ambr. Madison
BURGESSES	Rich'd Johnson, Geo. Braxton
CLERK	C. C. Thacker
SURVEYOR	Harry Beverley
PARISHES	Stratton Major, St. Stephens, Drysdale
MINISTERS	John Skaife, Mr. Dunbar, Jno. Harlow
LIEUTENANT	---------
SORT OF TOBACCO	Sweetscented

KING WILLIAM

ACRES	212,582
TITHABLES	2,389
SHERIFF	John Butts
CORONER	Aug's Moore
JUSTICES OF THE PEACE	Geo. Dabney, Phil. Whitehead, John Butts, Aug't Moore, Tho. Carr Jr., Wm. Smith, John Quarles Wm. Dandridge, Wm. Claiborn, Quorum. Henry Fox, Leon'd Claiborn, James Fountain, Henry Webber, Walter Chiles, John Sutton, Nath'l West, John Camm
BURGESSES	Wm. Aylett, Phil. Whitehead
CLERK CO. CT.	Wm. Aylett
SURVEYOR	Harry Beverly
PARISHES	St. Johns, St. Margarets
MINISTERS	Mr. Clark, Mr. Bromskill
LIEUTENANT	John Carter
SORT OF TOBACCO	Sweetscented

LANCASTER

ACRES	------
TITHABLES	1,249
SHERIFF	James Ball
CORONER	Jno. Turberville
JUSTICES OF THE PEACE	Henry Fleet, Wm. Ball, Jno. Turberville, Rich'd Ball, Tho. Carter, Rich'd Chichester, Geo. Heale, Joseph Ball, Quorum. Thomas Lee, Edwin Conway, James Ball, Cha. Burges, Hen. Fleet Jr.
BURGESSES	Edwin Conway, Wm. Ball
CLERK CO. CT.	Tho. Edwards
SURVEYOR	Jno. Coppedge
PARISHES	Christ Church, St. Marys, White Chappell
MINISTERS	Mr. Bell
LIEUTENANT	Rob't Carter
SORT OF TOBACCO	Arromico

MIDDLESEX

ACRES	73,696
TITHABLES	1,150
SHERIFF	Ch'r Robinson
CORONERS	John Price, Matt'w Kemp
JUSTICES OF THE PEACE	Chr. Robinson, Jno. Wormsley, Roger Jones, Oliver Segar, John Price, Edwin Thacker, Quorum. Matth. Kemp, Armistead Churchill, Edm'd Berkeley, Hump. Jones, Adam Cockburn
BURGESSES	Matth. Kemp, Edwin Thacker
CLERK CO. CT.	Wm. Standard
SURVEYOR	Tho. Cook
PARISHES	Christ Church
MINISTERS	Barth'o Yates
LIEUTENANT	John Robinson
SORT OF TOBACCO	Sweetscented

NANSEMOND

ACRES	150,960
TITHABLES	1,692
SHERIFF	Barnaby Kerny
CORONER	John Lear
JUSTICES OF THE PEACE	Tho. Jordan, Cha. Drury, Wm. Wright, Tho. Godwin, James Redick, John Lear, Henry Baker, Joseph Meredith, John Norsworthy, Tho. Jordan, Jr. Quorum. John Yates, Wm. Butler, John Wright, Edw'd Streater, Barnaby Kerney, Rob't Batty, Andrew Meade, Dan'l Pugh, David Osbene, John Milner
BURGESSES	Tho. Godwin, Henry Baker
CLERK CO. CT.	Chr. Jackson
SURVEYOR	Henry Baker
PARISHES	Upper parrish, Lower parrish, Chuckatunk
MINISTERS	Mr. Jones
LIEUTENANT	Tho. Godwin
SORT OF TOBACCO	Arromico

NEW KENT

ACRES	94,271
TITHABLES	1,348
SHERIFF	Jno. Sclater
CORONERS	John Scott, Jno. Armistead, Rich'd Richardson
JUSTICES OF THE PEACE	Hen. Holdcraft, John Scott, Tho. Butts, Jno. Sclater, Cha. Lewis, Wm. Mason, Nich'o Aldersey, Wm. Kenny, Rich'd Richardson, Quorum. Rob't Burbridge, John Armistead, Tho. Bray, Wm. Meriwether, Ebenezer Adams, Tho. Massie, Wm. Morris, Joseph Foster
BURGESSES	Jno. Thornton, Tho. Massie
CLERK	Jno. Thornton
SURVEYOR	John Syme
PARISHES	Blisland, St. Peters
MINISTERS	Mr. Taylor, Mr. Land
LIEUTENANT	Wm. Byrd
SORT OF TOBACCO	Sweetscented

NORFOLK

ACRES	123,632
TITHABLES	1,188
SHERIFF	John Hare
CORONER	Sam'l Boush
JUSTICES OF THE PEACE	Sam'l Boush Sr., James Wilson, George Newton, Wm. Crawford, Sam'l Smith, Sam'l Boush Jr., Rich'd Chastaine, Quorum. Edw'd Thurston, Willis Wilson, Nath. Newton, Tho. Willoughby, Thomas Scott, John Hane
BURGESSES	Wm. Craford, Geo. Newton
CLERKS CO. CT.	Sol'o Wilson
SURVEYOR	Sam'll Boush Jr.
PARISHES	Norfolk
MINISTER	-----
LIEUTENANT	Sam'l Boush
SORT OF TOBACCO	Arromico

NORTHAMPTON

ACRES	106,093
TITHABLES	1,044
SHERIFF	Jacob Armiger
CORONERS	Jno. Robins, James Forse, Luke Johnson
JUSTICES OF THE PEACE	Geo. Harmanson, Jno. Robins, James Forse, Tho. Marshall, Devereux Godwin, Ralph Pigot-Quorum Luke Johnson, Jacob Stringer, Tho. Savage, Jr., Severn Eyre, Matthew Harmanson, Arthur Robins, Wm. Burton, Wm. Tankred, John Potter, Gawton Hunt, Jacob Dicey, Tho. James
BURGESSES	Geo. Harmanson, Tho. Marshall
CLERK CO. CT.	Geofrey Pole
SURVEYOR	Luke Johnson
PARISHES	Hungars
MINISTER	Tho. Dell
LIEUTENANT	Geo. Harmanson
SORT OF TOBACCO	Arromico

NORTHUMBERLAND

ACRES	-------
TITHABLES	1,723
SHERIFF	Cha. Lee
CORONER	Peter Presley
JUSTICES OF THE PEACE	Peter Hack, Peter Presley, Rich'd Neale, George Ball, Tho. Hughlett, Charles Lee, Phillip Smith, Quorum. John Keen, John Shapleigh, Wm. Eustace, Sam'l Bonam, Sam'l Heath, Sam'l Blackwell
BURGESSES	Peter Presley, Geo. Ball
CLERK	Rich'd Lee
SURVEYOR	Wm. Ball
PARISHES	Fairfeild, Wiccomicco
MINISTERS	-------
LIEUTENANT	Robert Carter
SORT OF TOBACCO	Arromeco

PRINCESS ANNE

ACRES	123,612
TITHABLES	1,046
SHERIFF	Willoughby Merchant
CORONER	Jno. Moseley
JUSTICES OF THE PEACE	Edw'd Moseley, John Moseley, Jno. Cornick, Henry Chapman, Jno. Ballit***, Anth'y Walke, Cha. Beverley, Timothy Merchant, Hillary Moseley, Francis Land, Quorum. Tho. Thorrowgood, Rob't Vaughn, Wm. McClanahan, Francis,Morse, Tho. Haynes, Radolphus Malbone, Fra. Woodhouse, Jno. Thorrowgood
BURGESSES	Henry Spratt, Max. Boush
CLERK	Cha. Sayer
SURVEYOR	Sam'l Boush Jr.
PARISHES	Lyn Haven
MINISTER	Mr. Tenent
LIEUTENANT	Edw'd Moseley
SORT OF TOBACCO	Arromeco

PRINCE GEORGE

ACRES	188,231
TITHABLES	1,624
SHERIFF	Wm. Harrison
CORONERS	Rob't Bolling, Jno. Poythress, Jno. Fitzgerald,
JUSTICES OF THE PEACE	Jno. Poythress, Rob't Mumford, Rob't Hall, Rob't Bolling, Lewis Green, Bullard Herbert, Drury Stith, Fra. Epes Jr., Wm. Harrison, Quorum. John Beard, Tho. Ravenscroft, Thomas Cocke, Jno. Fitzgerald, Wm. Poythres, David Walker, James Ball, Wm. Epes Jr.
BURGESSES	Rob't Bolling, Jno. Poythress
CLERK CO. CT.	Wm. Hamlyn
SURVEYOR	Rob't Bolling
PARISHES	Bristol Port, Martin Brandon
MINISTERS	Geo. Robertson, Mr. Finney
LIEUTENANT	Matt'w Harrison
SORT OF TOBACCO	Arromeco

RICHMOND

ACRES	-----
TITHABLES	1,450
SHERIFF	Joseph Belfield
CORONER	Cha. Barbar
JUSTICES OF THE PEACE	Cha. Barbar, Tho. Griffin, John Tayloe, Wm. Fantleroy, Wm. Downman, Cha. Grymes, Quorum. Joseph Belfield, Rob't Tomlin, Jno. Metcalfe, Sam'l Peachy, Newman Brokenburgh
BURGESSES	Cha. Barbar, Tho. Griffin
CLERK CO. CT.	Martin Beckwith
SURVEYOR	Tho. Barbar
PARISHES	Sittenburn Port, North Farnham
MINISTERS	Mr. Blacknall, Jno. Garvin
LIEUTENANT	Rob't Carter
SORT OF TOBACCO	Arromeco

SPOTSYLVANIA

ACRES	145,699
TITHABLES	950
SHERIFF	Goodrich Lightfoot
CORONERS	Aug't Smith, Larkin Chew, Goodrich Lightfoot
JUSTICES OF THE PEACE	Harry Beverly, Jos. Clouder, Aug't Smith, Goodrich Lightfoot, Jno. Taliaferro, Larkin Chew, Rob't Beverly, Wm. Smith, Quorum. Thomas Chew, Wm. Bledsoe, Henry Goodloe, Edwin Hickman, John Chew.
BURGESSES	Larkin Chew, Fra. Thornton
CLERK CO. CT.	John Waller,
SURVEYORS	James Taylor, Aug't Smith
PARISHES	St. George
MINISTER	Mr. Stage
LIEUTENANT	Peter Beverly
SORT OF TOBACCO	Sweetscented

STAFFORD

ACRES	------
TITHABLES	1,800
SHERIFF	Wm. Stork
CORONER	Hen. Fitzhugh
JUSTICES OF THE PEACE	Rice Hooe, Dade Massy, Hen. Fitzhugh, Wm. Stork, Tho. Hoper, Tho. Harrison, Townsend Dade, John Fitzhugh, Quorum. French Mason, Abra. Farrow Cha. Broadwater, John Linton, Anth'o Thornton, Rice Hooe Jr., Rob't Alexander
BURGESSES	Geo. Mason, Wm. Robinson
CLERK CO. CT.	Catesby Cocke
SURVEYOR	Henry Conniers
PARISHES	St. Paul, Over Warton
MINISTERS	Mr. Steward, Alex. Scott
LIEUTENANT	Rob't Carter
SORT OF TOBACCO	Arromeco

SURRY

ACRES	228,770
TITHABLES	2,049
SHERIFF	Benj'a Edwards
CORONERS	Wm. Gray, Rob't Wynne
JUSTICES OF THE PEACE	William Brown, Hen. Harrison, John Simmons, Wm. Gray, Tho. Collier, Stith Bolling, Rob't Wynne, Arthur Allen, Quorum. Tho. Cocke, Howell Edmunds, Wm. Edwards, Benj'a Edwards, Wm. Brown Jr., John Mason
BURGESSES	Wm. Gray, Hen. Harrison
CLERK CO. CT.	John Allen
SURVEYOR	John Allen
PARISHES	Southwark, Lyons Creek
MINISTER	Mr. Cargill
LIEUTENANT	Matt. Harrison
SORT OF TOBACCO	Arromeco

WARWICK

ACRES	39,108
TITHABLES	701
SHERIFF	Wm. Cole
CORONERS	Wm. Cole, Miles Willis
JUSTICES OF THE PEACE	Miles Wills, Wm. Harwood, Nath. Haggard, Wm Cole, Tho. Haynes, Rob't Phillipson, Quorum. Jno. Langhorne, Rich'd Whitaker, Wm. Roscow, Wilson Cary, Miles Cary, Tho. Wills
BURGESSES	Wm. Cole, Wm. Roscow
CLERK CO. CT.	Ralph Gough
SURVEYOR	John Lowry
PARISHES	Warwick
MINISTER	Mr. Hewitt
LIEUTENANT	Cole Digges
SORT OF TOBACCO	Sweetscented

WESTMORLAND

ACRES	-----
TITHABLES	2,011
SHERIFF	Jno. Elliott
CORONERS	Tho. Lee, Hen. Ashton, Benj'a Berryman
JUSTICES OF THE PEACE	Benj'a Berryman, Henry Ashton, Burdit Ashton, John Chilton, Tho. Lee, Henry Lee, Quorum. Aug't Washington, Tho. Newton, Geo. Turberville, John Elliott, Wm. Lord
BURGESSES	Geo. Eskridge, Thomas Lee
CLERK CO. CT.	Tho. Sorrall
SURVEYOR	Tho. Newton
PARISHES	Coyle, Washington
MINISTERS	Walter James, Mr. DeButts
LIEUTENANT	Robert Carter
SORT OF TOBACCO	Arromeco

YORK

ACRES	69,219
TITHABLES	1,625
SHERIFF	Graves Parke
CORONERS	Henry Tyler, Law. Smith
JUSTICES OF THE PEACE	John Holloway, Henry Tyler, Law. Smith, Tho. Nelson, Archibald Blair, Graves Parke, Wm. Seldon, Wm. Starke, Quorum. Edw'd Tabb, John Blair, Matth. Peirce, Sam'l Timson, Rich'd Ambler, John Buckner, Fra. Hayward
BURGESSES	Law. Smith, Edward Tabb
CLERK CO. CT.	Phil. Lightfoot
SURVEYOR	Jno. Sclater
PARISHES	Bruton Port, York Hampton, Charles
MINISTERS	Mr. Blair, Fra. Fountain, Mr. Faulkner
LIEUTENANT	Edm'd Jenings
SORT OF TOBACCO	Sweetscented

THE PRESENT STATE OF VIRGINIA
With respect to the Colony in General 1729

The Rt. Hon'ble GEORGE, Earl of Orkney,
His Majestys Lt. Governor-General

The Honorable WILLIAM GOOCH,
Lt. Gov., Commander-in-Chief

COUNCIL and JUDGES of ye Gen'l Court

Robert Carter	John Grymes
James Blair	William Dandridge
William Byrd	John Custis
Mann Page	William Randolph
Cole Digges	Wm. Robertson, Clk. Ct.
John Robinson	Rich'd Kirkman, Clk.
John Carter	John Carter, Door Keeper to the Council

PRINCIPAL OFFICERS

COMMISARY for the Bishop of London	The Rev. James Blair
SECRETARY of the Colony	John Carter Esq.
AUDITOR of His Majesty's Revenues	Horatia Walpole Esq.
RECEIVER GENERAL of His Maj'ty's Revenues	John Grymes Esq.
Deputy AUDITOR	John Blair Esq.
ATTORNEY GENERAL	John Clayton Esq.
ADVOCATE	John Randolph
REGISTER	John Francis
MARSHALL	William Gordon

OFFICERS OF COURT OF ADMIRALTY

Robert Carter	John Carter
James Blair	John Grymes
William Byrd	William Dandridge
Mann Page	John Custis
Cole Digges	William Randolph Esq.
John Robinson	William Robertson Reg'r of the said Court

OFFICERS OF YE CUSTOMS ETC

Rich'd Fitzwilliam Esq.,
Surveyor General of the Council

Districts	Collectors	Naval Officers
Upper port James River	John Bannister	Lewis Burwell
Lower port " "	Thomas Mitchell	Wilson Cary
York	Richard Ambler Wm. Gordon, Searcher	William Robertson
Rappa:	Charles Grymes	Charles Carter
Potomack	Henry Morrison	Thomas Lee
Eastern Shore	Henry Scarburgh Griffith Brown, Surveyor	William Scarburgh

ESCHEATORS

Between York and Rappa. Rivers	John Robinson Esq.
Between James and York Rivers	William Byrd Esq.
For the Eastern Shore	Henry Scarburgh, Gen'l.
Southside James River	Samuel Boush, Henry Harrison, Gen'l

OFFICERS OF THE ASSEMBLY

Speaker	John Holloway Esq.
Chaplain	Francis Fountain
Clk. General Assembly	Wm. Robertson
Clk. House of Burgesses	John Randolph
Clk. Committee of Prop. & Grievances	Godfrey Pole
Clk. Committee of Claims	Miles Cary
Clk. Committee Courts of Justice	Benjamin Needler
Sarjant of the Mace	Philip Finch
4 Door Keepers	

GUNNERS OF THE BATTERIES

In James River	At old point Comfort at James Town	George Walker
In York River	At York Town	William Gordon
	At Gloucester Town	John Lester
In Rappa:	At Corotoman	----------
	At Toppahanock	Alexander Parker

Keeper of the Magazine at Williamsburgh — Samuel Cobbs

INDIAN INTERPRETERS

For the Pamunky and Chickahominy	Vacant
For the Nottaway, Maherin & Nansemond	Henry Briggs
For the Sapone & *****	Charles Kymbal

THE PRESENT STATE OF VIRGINIA 1729
With respect to the Counties in particular

ACCOMACK COUNTY

ACRES	225118
TITHABLES	1474
SHERIFFS	Rich'd Drummond
CORONERS	Henry Scarburgh
BURGESSES	Sacker Parker, Wm. Andrews
JUSTICES OF THE PEACE	Henry Scarburgh, Henry Custis, Edm'd Scarburgh William Burton, Rich'd Drumond, John Kendall, Henry Bagwell, Quorum. William Bevins, James Gibson, George Parker, William Andrews, Thomas Blair, Solomon Ewell, John Smith, John Custis, James Wishart, Thomas Evans.
COUNTY CLERKS	John Jackson
PARISHES	Accomack
MINISTERS	Mr. Black
SURVEYORS	Mitchell Scarburgh
COUNTY LTS.	John Custis Esq.

CAROLINE

ACRES	----
TITHABLES	----
SHERIFFS	Wm. Woodford
CORONERS	Wm. Woodford, Tho. Carr
BURGESSEs	----
JUSTICES OF THE PEACE	John Lomax, William Woodford, Thomas Carr, John Martin, Rich'd Buckner (?), Thomas Catlett, Francis Thornton, John Battaile, Quorum. John Sutton, Ambrose Madison, John Catlett, John Taliaferro, Francis Conway, Lunsford Lomax, Robert #oolfolk, Walter Chiles, Thomas Buckner, Rich'd Madison.
COUNTY CLERKS	Benj'a Robinson
PARISHES	St. Mary's, Drysdale, St. Margaret's
MINISTERS	Owen Jones, Andrew Harlow, John Brunskill
SURVEYORS	Robert Brooke
COUNTY LTS.	Henry Armistead Esq.

CHARLES CITY

ACRES	89496
TITHABLES	1082
SHERIFFS	Benj'a Harrison
CORONERS	Drury Stith, Littlebury Epes
BURGESSES	Sam'l Harwood, Jr., John Stith
JUSTICES OF THE PEACE	Drury Stith, Henry Soane, Samuel Harwood, James Maunder, Samuel Harwood Jr., Francis Hardyman, Benj'a Harrison, Quorum. John Edloe, John Soane, John Williams, James Bell, Henry Edloe
COUNTY CLERKS	Littlebury Epes
PARISHES	Westover
MINISTERS	Peter Fountaine
SURVEYORS	Robert Bolling
COUNTY LTS.	William Byrd Esq.

ELIZABETH CITY

ACRES	32772
TITHABLES	778
SHERIFFS	Joshua Curle
CORONERS	James Servant
BURGESSES	Simon Hollier, Rob't Armistead
JUSTICES OF THE PEACE	Simon Hollier, John King, Alexander McKensie, Joshua Curle, John Lowry, Jacob Walker, James Wallace, Joseph Bannister, Wilson Cary, Quroum. Thomas Mitchell, William Hunters, Merrit Sweny, John Tabb, John Brodie, Wm. Westwood
COUNTY CLERKS	Tho: Mingham
PARISHES	Elizabeth
MINISTERS	Mr. Pender
SURVEYORS	John Lowry
COUNTY LTS.	Cole Digges Esq.

ESSEX

ACRES	125598
TITHABLES	2694
SHERIFFS	James Garnet
CORONERS	John Lomax, Wm. Daingerfield
BURGESSES	Wm. Daingerfield, Salvator Muscoe
JUSTICES OF THE PEACE	Wm. Daingerfield, Reuben Welch, Thomas Waring, Salvator Muscoe, Rob't Brooke Jr., James Garbett, Quorum. William Brooke, Paul Micou Jr., Nicholas Smith, Richard Taylor, Leonard Hill Jr., Alexander Parker, Tho. Threshley Jr., John Smith
COUNTY CLERKS	William Beverly
PARISHES	South Farnham, St. Anne
MINISTERS	Mr. Latane, Mr. Rose
SURVEYORS	Robert Brooke
COUNTY LTS.	John Robinson Esq.

GOOCHLAND

ACRES	----
TITHABLES	----
SHERIFFS	Daniel Stoner
CORONERS	Wm. Mayo, Allen Howard
JUSTICES OF THE PEACE	Thomas Randolph, John Fleming, William Mayo, John Woodson, Daniel Stoner, Ren. Laforce, Tarlton Fleming, Quorum. Allen Howard, Edward Scott, George Payne, William Kabball, James Holeman
COUNTY CLERKS	Henry Wood
PARISHES	St. James
MINISTERS	-----
SURVEYORS	William Mayo
COUNTYLTS.	William Randolph Esq.

GLOUCESTER

ACRES	169069
TITHABLES	3473
SHERIFFS	John Armistead
CORONERS	Giles Cooke
BURGESSES	Francis Willis, Henry Armistead
JUSTICES OF THE PEACE	Gabriel Throgmorton, Henry Armistead, Charles Tomkies, Francis Willis, Thomas Booth, Giles Cooke, John Lewis, Thomas Sayes, Quorum. Thomas Read, Dudley Digges, Peter Whiting, John Armistead, Christopher Todd, Wm. Mountague
COUNTY CLERK	John Clayton
PARISHES	Abbingdon, Petso, Ward, Kingston
MINISTERS	Mr. Hughs, Emanuel Jones, Mr. Richards, Mr. Blacknall
SURVEYORS	Thomas Cooke
COUNTY LTS.	Mann Page Esq.

HANOVER

ACRES	268953
TITHABLES	2134
SHERIFFS	Charles Hudson
CORONERS	David Merideth, Chr. Clark, David Crawford
BURGESSES	Rich'd Meriwether, John Syme
JUSTICES OF THE PEACE	Nich. Meriwether, Charles Chiswell, Roger Thomson David Meriwether, John Syme, William Fleming, Charles Hudson, Christopher Clark, David Crawford Quorum. Peter Garland, John Anderson, James Overton, Richard Harris, Thomas Anderson, Richard Clough, John Dandridge.
COUNTY CLERK	Arthur Clayton
PARISHES	St. Pauls, St. Martins
MINISTERS	Mr. Brooke Mr. Swift
SURVEYORS	John Syme
COUNTY LTS.	Nicholas Meriwether Esq.

HENRICO

ACRES	260007
TITHABLES	2767
SHERIFFS	Joseph Royal
CORONERS	John Worsham
BURGESSES	John Bolling, Rich'd Randolph
JUSTICES OF THE PEACE	Thomas Jefferson, William Kennon, John Bedford, Francis Epes, Joseph Royal, Richard Randolph, Lewis Armistead, Dudley Digges, Richard Kennon, John Bolling Jr., Quorum. Joseph Mayo, Isham Randolph, James Powell Cocke, Wm. Worsham, Rich'd Herbert
COUNTY CLERKS	Bowles Cocke
PARISHES	Varina at Henrico, Bristol port, King William
MINISTERS	Mr. Keith, George Robertson
SURVEYORS	Francis Epes
COUNTY LTS.	William Randolph Esq.

ISLE OF WIGHT

ACRES	-----
TITHABLES	-----
SHERIFF	-----
CORONERS	-----
BURGESSES	-----
JUSTICES OF THE PEACE	Arthur Smith, William Bridger, Henry Applewhite, Joseph Godwin, Thomas Walton, Thomas Brewer, James Bean, Thomas Applewhite, Quorum. William Kinchin, Hardy Council, Wm. Wilkinson, John Edwards, Joseph Bridger, James Baker, Thomas Gerald, Nich: Williams, John Parsons.
COUNTY CLERK	James Ingles
PARISHES	Warishooke, Newport
MINISTER	Mr. Barlow
SURVEYOR	John Allen
COUNTY LT.	Henry Harrison Esq.

JAMES CITY

ACRES	87115
TITHABLES	1242
SHERIFF	Henry Power
CORONER	Edw'd Jaquelin
BURGESSES	John Eaton, Joseph Egleston
JUSTICES OF THE PEACE	John Netherland, David Bray, Lewis Burwell, Henry Powers, Quorum. Robert Goodrich, Joseph Eggleston, Alexander Irwin, Joshua Fry, Samuel Cobbs, Lewis Holland, Francis Tyler, John Eaton
COUNTY CLERK	Richard Hickman
PARISHES	James City, Bruton port, Yorkampton port
MINISTERS	William Leneve, James Blair, Francis Fountaine
SURVEYOR	William Comrie
COUNTY LTS.	David Bray Esq.

KING GEORGE (no Neck)

ACRES	----
TITHABLES	1275
SHERIFF	Tho. Vivian
CORONER	Wm. Thornton
BURGESSES	Nicholas Smith, Wm. Strother
JUSTICEs OF THE PEACE	Wm. Robinson, Nicholas Smith, William Strother, Jonathan Gibson, Joseph Strother, Thomas Vivian, Quorum. Samuel Skinker (?) Rowland Thornton (?) William Strother Jr., Jeremiah Murdock, Mar't Robinson
COUNTY CLERK	Thomas Turner
PARISHES	Hanover, Sittenburn port
MINISTERS	Mr. Edzer, Mr. Beckett
SURVEYOR	John Warner
COUNTY LTS.	Robert Carter Esq.

KING AND QUEEN

ACRES	193180
TITHABLES	2850
SHERIFF	Chr. Beverly
CORONERS	Gawin Corbin, James Taylor
BURGESSES	John Robinson, George Braxton
JUSTICES OF THE PEACE	Gawin Corbin, George Braxton, John Leigh, Richard Johnson, Wm. Todd, Robert Baylor, John Robinson, Quorum. Robert Dudley, Henry Hickman, Thomas Foster, Rich'd Beverley, Philip Todd, George Moore, Samuel Smith, John Camm, George Braxton Jr., Philip Roots, John Dixon
COUNTY CLERK	John Robinson
PARISHES	Shatton Major, St. Stephens, Drysdale Port
MINISTERS	Mr. Skaife, Mr. Donbarr, Mr. Harlow
SURVEYOR	Harry Beverly
COUNTY LTS.	Gawin Corbin Esq.

KING WILLIAM

ACRES	113376
TITHABLES	2518
SHERIFF	Wm. Claiborne
CORONER	Phil. Whitehead
BURGESSES	Phil. Whitehead, Thomas Carr
JUSTICES OF THE PEACE	George Dabney, Philip Whitehead, Augustine Moore, John Quarles, William Claiborne, Henry Fox, Leon'd Claiborne, Quorum. James Fountaine, Henry Webber, James Mason, William Cradock, John Wyatt, William West, Charles West.
COUNTY CLERK	William Aylett
PARISHES	St. John, St. Margaret port
MINISTERS	Daniel Taylor Jr., Mr. Brunskill
SURVEYOR	Harry Beverley
COUNTY LTS.	William Dandridge Esq.

LANCASTER (No. Neck)

ACRES	----
TITHABLES	1390
SHERIFF	Henry Fleet
CORONER	James Ball
BURGESSES	Edwin Conway, Charles Burges
JUSTICES OF THE PEACE	Henry West, Wm. Ball, Thomas Carter, Richard Chichester, George Heale, Edwin Conway, James Ball, Charles Burges, Charles Carter, Quorum John Seldon, Henry West Jr., William Ball Jr., Robert Mitchell, Hugh Brent, Nicho: Martin
COUNTY CLERK	Thomas Edwards
PARISHES	Christ Church, St. Mary's White Chappell
MINISTER	Mr. Bell
SURVEYORS	William Ball
COUNTY LTS.	Robert Carter Esq.

MIDDLESEX

ACRES	73940
TITHABLES	1139
SHERIFF	Matt. Kemp
CORONER	Matt. Kemp
BURGESSES	Matt. Kemp, Edwin Thacker
JUSTICES OF THE PEACE	Sir Wm. Skipworth, Bart., Roger Jones, Oliver Segar, Edwin Thacker, Matt'w Kemp, Armistead Churchill, Edm'd Berkeley, Quorum. Adam Cockburne, Henry Thacker, George Harding, Churchill Jones, Chr. Robinson.
COUNTY CLERK	William Stanard
PARISHES	Christ Church
MINISTER	Mr. Yates
SURVEYOR	Thomas Cooke
COUNTY LTS.	John Grymes Esq.

NANSEMOND

ACRES	118444
TITHABLES	1847
SHERIFF	Theo. Pugh
CORONERS	Wm. Wright, Dan'l Pugh
BURGESSES	Andrew Mead, John Lear
JUSTICES OF THE PEACE	Thomas Jordan, Charles Drury, William Wright, Thomas Godwin, John Lear, Henry Baker, John Norsworthy, John Yates, William Butler, Barnaby Kerney, Quorum. Rob't Petty, Andrew Mead, Daniel Pugh, David Ofheal John Milner, Tho. Godwin Jr., Theo. Pugh, Wm. Baker, Wm. Sumner, Thomas Swan.
COUNTY CLERK	Chr. Jackson
PARISHES	Upper Parish, Lower Parish, Chuckatuck
MINISTERS	Mr. Smith, Mr. Nicholas Jones
SURVEYOR	John Milner
COUNTY LTS.	Thomas Godwin Esq.

NEW KENT

ACRES	97326
TITHABLES	1364
SHERIFF	Wm. Kenny
CORONERS	John Scot, Rich'd Richardson
BURGESSES	Rich'd Richardson, John Bacon
JUSTICES OF THE PEACE	John Scott, John Sclater, Charles Lewis William Macon, Nich: Aldersey, William Kenney, Rich'd Richardson, Thomas Bray, Ebenezer Adams, Thomas Massie, Quorum. William Morris, Joseph Yates, Robert Lewis, John Otey, Charles Massie, Wm. Makain
COUNTY CLERK	John Thornton
PARISHES	Blisland, St. Peters
MINISTERS	Daniel Taylor, Mr. Mossum
SURVEYOR	John Syme
COUNTY LTS.	John Carter Esq.

NORFOLK

ACRES	121513
TITHABLES	1245
SHERIFF	George Newton
CORONER	Samuel Boush
BURGESSES	Samuel Boush, Wm. Craford
JUSTICES OF THE PEACE	Samuel Boush, James Wilson, George Newton, William Craford, Samuel Smith, Samuel Boush Jr., Edward Thurston, Willis Wilson, Nathaniel Newton, Quorum. Thomas Willoughby, John Lowe, Thomas Scott, William Wilkins, William Hodges, Cornelius Colbert, Matt'w Godfrey
COUNTY CLERK	Solomon Wilson
PARISHES	Norfolk Parish
MINISTER	Mr. Robinson
SURVEYOR	Maximilian Boush
COUNTY LTS.	Samuel Boush Esq.

NORTHAMPTON

ACRES	105800
TITHABLES	1033
SHERIFF	John Potter
CORONERS	John Robins, James Forse (?), Luke Johnson
BURGESSES	Thomas Marshall, Peter Bowdoin
JUSTICES OF THE PEACE	John Robins, James Forse, Thomas Marshall, Ralph Pigott, Thomas Cable, William Walters, Jacob Stringer, Quorum. Joacim Michael, Thomas Savage, Arthur Robins, William Burton, William Faukred, John Potter, Peter Bowdoin, John Custis, Mich'l Christian
COUNTY CLERK	Godfrey Pole
PARISHES	Hungars
MINISTER	Mr. Dell
SURVEYOR	Luke Johnson
COUNTY LTS.	John Custis Esq.

NORTHUMBERLAND (no. Block)

ACRES	----
TITHABLES	1572
SHERIFF	Wm. Eustace
CORONER	Peter Presley
BURGESSES	Peter Presley, George Ball
JUSTICES OF THE PEACE	Peter Presley, Richard Neale, George Ball, Charles Lee, Philip Smith, John Shapleigh, William **ard, Samuel Heath, Quorum. Samuel Blackwell, William Lowry, John Waughop, Henry Morrison, Leonard Howson, Matt'w Kenner
COUNTY CLERK	Richard Lee
PARISHES	Fairfield, Winocomoco, St. Stephens
MINISTERS	Mr. Wye
SURVEYORS	William Ball
COUNTY LTS.	Robert Carter Esq.

PRINCESS ANN

ACRES	110159
TITHABLES	1147
SHERIFF	Francis Moseley
CORONER	John Moseley
BURGESSES	Francis Land, Anthony Wall
JUSTICES OF THE PEACE	Howard Moseley, Henry Chapman, Anthony Walker, Chr. Burroughs, Hillary Moseley, Francis Land, Quorum. Thomas Haynes, John Thorogood, Francis Moseley Jr., David McClanahan, Jacob Ellegood, George Kemp, Rob't Vaughan, Solomon White Jr.
COUNTY CLERK	Charles Sayer
PARISHES	Linhaven
MINISTER	-----
SURVEYOR	Max. Boush
COUNTY LTS.	Edward Moseley Esq.

PRINCE GEORGE

ACRES	214676
TITHABLES	1795
SHERIFF	Wm. Poythers
CORONERS	John Poythers, Rob't Bolling, John Fitzgareld (?)
BURGESSES	Robert Bolling, Tho. Rawensnold (?)
JUSTICES OF THE PEACE	John Poythres, Robert Munford, Robert Hall, Robert Bolling, Lewis Green, Bullard Herbert, Drury Stith, Francis Epes Jr., William Harrison, Quorum. John Beard, Tho. Ravenscroft, Thomas Cocke, John Fitzgerald, William Poythres, David Walker, James Bell, Wm. Epes Jr., James Munford
COUNTY CLERK	William Hamlin
PARISHES	Bristol port, Martinbrandon
MINISTERS	George Robertson, Mr. Finney
SURVEYOR	Rob't Bolling
COUNTY LTS.	Henry Harrison Esq.

RICHMOND (No. Neck)

ACRES	----
TITHABLES	1839
SHERIFFS	Sam'l Peachey
CORONERS	Cha's Grymes
BURGESSES	Cha. Grymes, John Taylor
JUSTICES OF THE PEACE	Thomas Griffin, John Taylor, Wm. Fauntleroy, Wm. Downman, Charles Grymes, Joseph Bellfield, Robert Tomlin, Quorum. John Metcalf, Samuel Peasley, Newman Brockinburgh, Willoughby Newton, Tho. Wright Bellfield, John Woodbridge
COUNTY CLERK	Marma: Beckwith
PARISHES	Sittenburn port, North Farnham
MINISTERS	Mr. Beckett, Mr. Garzia
SURVEYOR	James Thomas
COUNTY LTS.	Robert Carter Esq.

SPOTSYLVANIA

ACRES	----
TITHABLES	919
SHERIFF	Edwin Hickman
CORONERS	Augustine Smith, George Lightfoot
BURGESSES	Henry Willis, Aug't Smith
JUSTICES OF the PEACE	Harry Beverly, Jeremiah Clowder, Henry Willis, Goodrich Lightfoot, John Grayson, John Talliaferro Larkin Chew, William Smith, Quorum. Edwin Hickman, Henry Goodloe, John Chew, John Graeme, Joseph Brocke, Rob't Talliaferro, John Grayson Jr.
COUNTY CLERK	John Waller
PARISHES	St. George
MINISTER	Mr. Kenner
SURVEYORS	George Home, Nath'l Claiborne
COUNTY LTS.	John Robinson Esq.

STAFFORD (NO. NECK)

ACRES	----
TITHABLES	2060
SHERIFF	Abra. Harrow
CORONER	Dade Massey
BURGESSES	Anthony Thornton, John Fitzhugh
JUSTICES OF THE PEACE	Dade Masie, Thomas Harrison, Townsend Dade, John Fitzhugh, French Mason, Abraham Harrar, Charles Broadwater, Anthony Thornton, Henry Fitzhugh, Quorum. Dennis McCarty, Elias Hose, Thomas Grigsby, John Washing, Wm. Triplett, Wm. Lynton, Peter Hedgman, Francis Awbrey
COUNTY CLERK	Catesby Cocke
PARISHES	St. Pauls, Overwarton
MINISTERS	Mr. Steward, Mr. Scott
SURVEYOR	James Thomas
COUNTY LTS.	Robert Carter Esq.

SURRY

ACRES	252240
TITHABLES	2190
SHERIFF	John Mason
CORONERS	William Gray, Rob't Wynne
BURGESSES	Henry Harrison, John Simmons
JUSTICES OF the PEACE	William Brown, Henry Harrison, John Simmons, William Gray, Robert Hoyat (?), Thomas Cocke, Lowell Edmonds, William Edwards, Benj'a Edwards, Henry Brown, Quorum. John Mason, Joseph Allen, Nicholas Cocke, Henry Brown, Richard Price, Wm. Gray Jr., Thomas Avent
COUNTY CLERK	John Allen
PARISHES	Southwark, Lyons Creek
MINISTERS	Mr. Cargill, Mr. Clarke
SURVEYOR	John Allen
COUNTY LT.	Henry Harrison Esq.

WARWICK

ACRES	39012
TITHABLES	675
SHERIFF	William Roscow
CORONER	William Cole
BURGESSES	William Roscow, Wm. Harwood
JUSTICES OF THE PEACE	Miles Wills, Wm. Harwood, Nath'l Hoggard, William Cole, Thomas Hayes, Henry Cary, Rob't Philipson, John Langhorne, Quorum. William Roscow, Wilson Cary, Miles Cary, Thomas Lewis, Anthony Armistead, John Jones, Henry Scarbrook
COUNTY CLERK	Ralph Gough
PARISHES	Warwick
MINISTER	Mr. Hewitt
SURVEYOR	John Lowry
COUNTY LTS.	Cole Digges Esq.

WESTMORLAND (NO. NECK)

ACRES	----
TITHABLES	1998
SHERIFF	William Lord
CORONERS	Thomas Lee, Henry Ashton, Benj'a Berryman
BURGESSES	George Eldridge, Thomas Lee
JUSTICES OF THE PEACE	Benj'a Berryman, Henry Ashton, Burdit Ashton, Thomas Lee, Henry Lee, Aug't Washington, Robert Carter, John Elliot, Quorum. William Lord, Wm. Aylett, Rob't Washington, Lawrence Butler, John Cooper, Daniel McCarty, Jeremiah Rust
COUNTY CLERK	George Turbervile
PARISHES	Cople, Washington
MINISTERS	Walter Jones, Mr. DeButts
SURVEYOR	Thomas Newton
COUNTY LTS.	Robert Carter Esq.

YORK

ACRES	69576
TITHABLES	1622
SHERIFF	William Stark
CORONERS	Henry Tyler, Lawrence Smith
BURGESSES	John Holloway, Lawrence Smith
JUSTICES OF THE PEACE	John Holloway, Henry Tyler, Lawrence Smith, Thomas Nelson, Archibald Blair, Rob't Armistead, William Starke, Edward Tabb, Quorum. Matt'w Pearce, Samuel Timson, Richard Ambler, Francis Hayward
COUNTY CLERK	Ri: Lightfoot
PARISHES	Bruton port, York, Hampton, Charles
MINISTERS	Mr. Blair, Francis Fountain, Mr. Staige
SURVEYOR	John Sclater
COUNTY LTS.	Cole Digges Esq.

In obedience to an order of the Rt. Hon. the Lt. Gov. & Council dated at James City, 1691, I herewith present his Hono'r and the Councill with a true schedule of what conveyances for lands are past out of the Propriet'r Office to the best of my knowledge, from the year 1669 to the year 1690.

20 Aug. 1668	Ralph Wormley Esq'r	150 acres	Rappa. County
20 Aug. 1688	Mr. Nich'o Brent	1700 acres	Stafford
20 Aug. 1688	Col. William Fitzhugh	500 acres	Stafford
20 Aug. 1688	Col. Wm. Fitzhugh	100 acres	Stafford
20 Aug. 1688	Col. Wm. Fitzhugh	200 acres	Stafford
20 Aug. 1699	Col. Wm. Fitzhugh	200 acres	Stafford

Test - Richard **Whitehead Cl. of** the **Pt's** office
Test - W. Edwards, Cl. Cou.
Exam - William Cole, Sr.

An ACCOUNT how and to whom and for what the negroes disposed for, most of them being sick and very poore.

	Pounds
3 - Mr. Henry Woodhouse, 1 Man, 1 Woman and girle	65
1 - Mrs. Sarah Moore, 1 negro youth	20
1 - Mr. John Woodhouse, 1 negro man	23
2 - John Casperew, 1 old man, a small child, sold by master	15
2 - Owen Hayes, 2 sick negroes, sold by the master	10
5 - Mr. Thomas Hodges, 5 sick negroes, not able to goe or stand	20
1 - Mr. Will Sundas, 1 sick negro	10
4 - Sick negroes that dyed at ye seaside that could not be removed	
4 - Mr. Thurston's - 4 sick dyed	
2 - Mr. Jno. Porter, a small negro girl & a sick boy that dyed carrying home	14
2 - Col. Anthon: Lawson, one young man, one old	37
4 - Mr. George Newton, 1 man, 1 woman, also 1 man with 1 eye and 1 man much burnt	65
2 - James Lennon, 1 negro boy and girle	30
1 - Mr. Will Pinkethman, 1 negro man	24
1 - Jno. Gooscott, 1 boy	20
1 - Capt. Miles Carey, 1 pretty ancient man	18
1 - Col. Tho. Milner, 1 woman	21
3 - Mr. Cope Doyly, 1 woman, 1 man, 1 girle	65
1 - Wm. Rascow, 1 negro boy	21
1 - Mrs. Izabell Spratt, 1 negro woman	20
3 - Mr. Jno. Underhill, 1 man, 2 women	69
1 - Mr. Charles Stansford, 1 woman	23
2 - Nath'l Bacon Esq., 2 negro men	44
2 - Jno. Page Esq'r., a negro woman & boy	36
2 - Mr. Tho. Pitt, a negro boy and girle	34
2 - Dr. Pond, a negro boy and girle	37
1 - Mr. Jno. Sand, Esq., a negro woman	21-10

		Pounds
4 -	Mr. Jos. Ring, 1 man, 2 women, 1 girle	72
1 -	Mr. Wm. Jackson, 1 youth	21
3 -	Mr. David Morce, 1 woman, 2 boys	55
2 -	Mr. Jos. Topping, 1 man, 1 woman	43
1 -	Mr. Travers, 1 woman	20
1 -	Capt. Rich'd Whittaker, 1 negro youth poore	15
1 -	Mr. Behethland Crew, 1 poore negro woman	16
1 -	Benj'a Brock, a poore negro boy	17-10
4 -	Madam Warner, 2 men, 2 women	80
5 -	Mr. John Buckner and Capt. John Smith for 2 negro women and 3 negro women, one of whom poore which Mr. Mathews had	100
2 -	Alex. Young, 1 man, 1 woman	41
1 -	Jno. Cooper, 1 negro woman	22
3 -	Mr. Tho. Merry, 3 poore negro women	36
1 -	Mr. Jno. Ringnall, 1 poore boy	15-10
1 -	Mrs. Mary Everett, 1 poore negro woman	14
4 -	Capt. Roger Jones, 1 man, 2 poore men, 1 woman	69
6 -	Mr. Walter Cock, 6 sick negroes 2 of them almost dead	43-10
4 -	Wm. Cole, 1 woman and child, 2 small boys	50

Presidents and Masters
COLLEGE OF WILLIAM AND MARY

(circa. 1695/6)

James Blair - President

Bartholomew Yates	Professors of	Divinity
Francis Fountain		Oriental Languages
William Dawson		Philisaphy
Alexander Irwin		Mathamaticks

Joshua Fry - Master of the Gramar Scool
John Fox - Master of the Indian Scool

A List of the Trustees, Governors and other officers and number of Scholars of

HER MAJESTIES ROYALL COLLEDGE OF WILLIAM & MARY IN VIRGINIA

July 8th 1702

Trustees, Founders & Governors appointed by the Charter:-	His Excellency Francis Nicholson Esq.
Esq's.	Wm. Cole, Ralph Wormley, Wm. Byrd, Jno. Lear
Clerks	Jam: Blaire, Jno..Farnofold, Steph: Fovace, Sam'l Gray
Gents.	Tho: Milner, Chris: Robinson, Char: Scarbrough, Jno. Smith, Benj: Harrison, Miles Cary, Hen: Hartwell, Wm. Randolph, Matthew Page
Govern's elected by virtue of the Charter	Dan'l Parke, Phill: Ludwell,Sr, Lewis Burwell, Phill: Ludwell Jr., Wm. Fitzhugh, Wm. Leigh Benj: Harrison, Wm. Basset, Arth: Allen, Tho: Barbar
Chancellor	Thomas, Lord Arch Bishop of Canterbury
President	Sam'l Blair
Rector	Wm. Byrd
School Master	Mongo Ingles
Usher	Jno. Allen
Writing Master & Register	Wm. Robinson
Scholars	29

BY THE COMMITTEE. FOR EXAMINING CLAIMS TO LAND IN PAMUNKEY NECK, AND ON THE SOUTH SIDE OF BLACKWATER SWAMP, AND TO CONSIDER OF THE MOST PROPER MEANES TO SETTLE THE NORTHERN & SOUTHERN BOUNDS OF VIRGINIA. Dated June, 1699

The Queen of the Pamunkey Indians together with the great men belonging to the said Nation setting forth that, by Severall Orders of the Generall Court there was Granted unto them a considerable quantity of Land lyeing in Pamunkey Neck, which they have a long time possessed and enjoyed. And that by the Articles of Peace made at Middle Plantation the 29th May 1677 the sd. Land was then confirmed unto them, with a clause in the said Articles that a Patent should be granted to them as is usuall to other His Maj'ties Subjects, which Patent tho' often desired by the said Indians was never yet obtained. And the said Indians thereupon complaining that Ralph Wormeley Esqr. & others in Company of the Surveyor about the beginning of June 1694 upon the sd. Petitioners Land possest by them and within one mile of their Indian Town and in Severall other places of the said Land did enter, survey, and lay out severall considerable parcells of the Pet.'s Land to their great prejudice and breach of the said Articles of Peace. And which if suffered would of necessity drive the petitioners from off their now habitation, and praying redress and that a Patent may be granted them Pursuant to the said Articles.

The same being fully weighed & Considered by the Comittee and the great men of the sd. Pamunkey Indians and Robert Peasley, their interpreter, haveing appeared personally before us, upon full heareing of what they had further to allege and due Consideration had to the Articles of Peace and 136 Act of Assembly in the printed book in which the said Articles have relation, this Comittee conceived that the fourth paragraph in the said Articles of Peace Contained ought to be kept firme & inviolable, which paragraph is as followeth:-

That for prevention of the injuries and evill conseq'ts that may arise for the future by the Violent intrusion of diverse English into & upon the Land Granted to the said Indians by the aforesaid Articles to ye great disturbance of the Peace of this His Maj'ties Colony and involving it into crime & misery. It is concluded and established that noe English shall seat or plant nearer than within three miles of any Indian Town.

And thereupon this Committee doe report:-

1. That according to the Purport intent and true meaning thereof: No English whatsoever ought to seat, plant or possess any Land in Pamunkey Neck nearer than within three miles as aforesaid of the Town where the said Indians now inhabit, that being the place whereon they were seated at the time of the said Articles and on which they have ever since continued.

2. That the said Indians have not any power or authority by colour or pretext of the said Articles or any Law or Order whatsoever to sell, lease or let out any part or parcell of the said Land within the sd. bounds other than to the posterity of their own nation.

3. That the said Land to the said Indians so as aforesaid Granted and bonded by the said Articles of Peace should be adjudged and taken to be sufficient for their habitation and reserved Lands.

4. That it would conduce much to His Maj'ties service that all other Vacant Land in the said Pamunkey Neck be held of his Maj'tie, his heirs and successors by Patent as other Lands are held on.

And whereas severall parcells of Land were by the Pamunkey Indians for good & valuable consideration leased for Ninety Nine yeares to these severall persons hereafter named which Lands by an Order of Assembly held at James City the 25th April 1679 was granted to be confirmed unto them, and that they should have the priority and first grant thereof when the same came to the King's hands. Provided always that it should not be construed and taken to give them right to any Lands granted by patent or patents before the making of 136 Act of Assembly, viz:-

To Thomas Bell a parcell of land the quantity not mentioned

Mr. John Langston Six hundred acres of land

Cornelius Dabney. Six or seven hundred acres of land

John Sexton assigned to James Turner a tract of land, quantity not mentioned

Peter Adams fifteen hundred acres of land

Ambrose Lipscome a tract, quantity not mentioned

Richard Yarborow, a tract, quantity not mentioned

George Smith six hundred acres of land

Upon due consideration whereof this Comittee doe conceive that the severall persons before named and all claimeing under them whose names are so many of them as appeared to lay their claims before this Comittee, hereafter are expressed pursuant to the P. Order of Assembly ought to be preferred before any others, viz:-

Thomas Comer his claims to one hundred acres of land in Pamunkey Neck, part of that leased to Peter Adams and by severall mean Conveyances come to his possession. As also six hundred & Seventy acres issueing out of severall former patents granted to severall persons and by sev'll mean Conveyances come to his possession.

John Haydon's claims to three hundred and seventy acres, part of the said tract purchased of Geo. Adams & quit rents paid.

Thomas Carr 150 acres purchased of Peter Adams and 400 acres purchased of James Turner, son of James Turner dec'd. and quit rents always paid.

James Adams, son of Peter Adams dec'd., 650 acres descending to him by Act of Law

John Oliver 133 acres purchased of George Adams, son of Peter Adams dec'd.

Robert Davis 280 acres by ye same title

Thomas Nichols 150 acres purchased of James Adams, son of Peter Adams dec'd.

Robert Blackwell 180 acres purchased of Anne Adams, widow of Peter Adams

Nath. West 403 acres, part of that granted to James Turner and by severall mean Conveyances come to him

Thomas Butler & his wife in behalf of the orphans of Peter Claybrook 200 acres purchased by the said Claybrook of William Turner, son of James Turner. Quit rent having been yearely paid for the same

Jane Gooch, widow, 100 acres purchased of Wm. Turner

James Terry 170 acres purchased of George Turner, son of James Turner

Thomas Ellit 130 acres by same title

James Henderson 100 acres purchased of James Turner

John Fermier 100 acres part of that granted to John Sexton

Tho. Parker 300 acres conveyed from George Smith

William Rennalls & Mary his wife in behalfe of Alexander Anderson, son of David Anderson 100 acres purchased of Geo. Smith by David Anderson

William Andrew 100 acres purchased of George Smith

Wm. Hurt Jr., 140 acres by like title

John Yarborow for himselfe and the children and devisees of Richard Yarborow

William Morris 300 acres purchased of Rich'd Yarborow

John Oakes 550 acres conveyed from Richard Yarborow

William Rawlins 800 acres purchased of Richard Yarborow

Henry Dilling in behalf of George & Douglas, orphan and heir of Robert Douglas dec'd. 200 acres purchased of Richard Yarborow

Peter White 300 acres by the same title

Andrew Mackallaster 100 acres by the same title

Thomas Hendrick 70 acres

Thomas (?) Hendrick 300 acres purchased of Richard Yarborow & John Ascough

James Dabney, Geo. Dabney, Dorothy Dabney & Sarah Dabney, devisees of Cornelius Dabney dec'd 700 acres to which is added of Low Land thereto adjoining 150aacres

Edward Bell, son of Thomas Bell dec'd, 1400 acres

Wm. Lipscome, John Lipscome and their three sisters & devisees of Ambrose Lipscome dec'd a certain tract, quantity not known, leased to sd. Ambrose

Thomas Crenshaw 150 acres purchased of Mr. John Langston

Abraham Willory 150 acres conveyed from John Sexton

Thomas Mackgehey 150 acres purchased of George Smith

James Edwards, Lewis Davis and Stephen Terry 1300 acres conveyed from Rich'd Yarborow

Philip Williams 403 acres purchased of George Turner, son of James Turner

This Committee doth report that the following claimes being with the intent & meaneing of the Proviso in the aforesd. order of Assembly mentioned & expressed and issueing out of former grants & Patents ought to be confirmed to the severall Petitioners:-

Robert King 520 acres part of a tract of land granted by patent unto William Pallam and by him assigned unto Wm. Woodward and by sd. Woodward conveyed unto Alexander King and descending from him to Robert King

Henry Maddison 270 acres purchased formerly of Mr. Samuell Oustin and afterwards confirmed by Mr. Rich'd Littlepage, being land formerly patented.

John Oustins 208 acres by the same title

Joan Drumonds 260 acres purchased by Thomas Husbands of Capt. Roger Mallory and same land purchased of Mr. Richard Littlepage, by the last Will & Testament of the said Thomas devised unto the said Joan for life and after to Jane Husbands, daughter of the said Thomas

Wm. Isbell 150 acres granted by patent to Elias Downes and conveyed to him

Benjamin Arnold about 1800 acres leased to him by the Chickahomony Indians for which he assigned to the sd. Indians in fee 600 acres of Patented Land and gave severall other valuable considerations

Roger Mallory, Thomas Mallory and Charles Mallory 2000 acres sold unto Roger Mallory Gent., dec'd by the Chickahomony Indians in exchange for other lands

This Committee also being of opinion that it will conduce much to the advancement of his Maj'ties interest and service that all Vacant Lands in Pamunkey Neck be held by Patent of the King, his heirs and successors, do thereupon conceive that the following claimes (his Maj'ties Grant to his Royall Colledge of William & Mary in Virginia being first of all complyed with & laid out) ought to be granted to the severall petitioners and they to be preferred before any other not having prior grant & entrys or Surveys, they having entree rights for and surveyed the same, and some of them thereupon beeing seated severall yeares, viz:-

John Burross 590 acres, been seated thirteene yeares

John Casar 3,000 (acres) Rights entered & surveyed

Thomas Hickman, Jane Husbands and Wm. Gough in behalfe of his son John Gough 2,200 acres (1,100 acres the one moiety thereof to Jane Husbands and John Gough by equal division, the other moiety to Thomas Hickman)

Ralph Wormeley Esq., 13,500 (acres) rights entered & Surveyed and Patent formerly granted but resignd to give precedency to ye Colledge.

Chicheley Corbin Thacker 3,500

Charles Fleming, Wm. Winston & James Dabney 3,000

Henry Fox, Gent., 1982 in three severall parcels

Edward Hill Esqr. 5060. Patents obtained the 25th October 1695 but resign'd to give preference to the Colledge

Job Howes and diverse others, the assignees & devisees of Thomas Nelson, dec'd 11,855 acres

Thomas Bray, Richard Gissedge & James Minge 3,900 acres on each side of a swamp called Goodwin's Swamp by assent of the parties thus divided: the lower part 1,340 acres to Gissedge, the middle part 1,280 acres to Minge, the upper part 1,280 acres to Bray

Richard Littlepage, sone of Richard Littlepage Gent., Dec'd. 3,160 acres entred and surveyed by Samuell Oustine and by him divised to R. Littlepage

Richard Johnson Esqr. 3,000 by order of Gen'll Court dated 25 April 1688

Edmund Jenings Esqr. 600 acres formerly granted by the Chickahomony Indians to Peter Ford & after confirmed before Sir Henry Chicheley and upon the 14th April 1688 again confirmed to the said Ford by the Lord Effingham, and by the sd. Ford conveyed to the claimer

Richard Littlepage, son of Richard Littlepage, Gent., 7,820 acres entered and surveyed 1679.

Thomas Hancock 500 acres conveyed to him by Roger Mallory

John Kinsbrow, Wm. Winston & John Longworthy granted by order of Govern'r and Councill 16th October 1685, 1,500 acres in Pamunkey and Longworthy now being dead without heirs, Kinsborow and Winston praying grant of the same upon the branches of Mangohick Creek to them and survivors, their title preferrable under the former salvos

Daniell Parke Esqr. setting forth that he surveyed 10,082 acres in Pamunkey Neck, his claime was entered upon Gen'll Court Records 3rd May 1688. (There was a dispute between Daniell Parke on the one hand and Benjamin Harrison Jr. and Jane Jones on the other regarding 600 acres said to be purchased by a George Pargiter, dec'd from the Pamunkey Indians, lived on by Pargiter for 7 years and left on his death to George Jones, late husband of Jane Jones. Evidence was given to the Committee by Mr. Gideon Macon that this information was true and that at the present time the land had been leased by covin to a Gregory Garfoot by Daniell Parke together with several negroes. The whole matter was referred to the General Assembly to decide the rightful owner)

Lewis Burwell in behalfe of his children the legataries of Nathaniell Bacon Esqr. dec'd, all the land in Pamunkey Neck lyeing between Mangohick Creek and the Devils Woodyard, being granted unto the said Nath: Bacon by order of Gen'll Court 16th October 1685

TITLES UPON INDIAN LEASES (June, 1699)

THIS COMMITTEE conceived that the following claimes and titles to Land in Pamunkey Neck haveing their ground and foundation upon Indian leases are, ipso facto, Null & Voyd as being contrary to the true Intent and meaning of the Articles of Peace and to the 136th Act of Assembly in the Printed Book. But because it conduces much to the advancement of his Maj'ties Interest and the peopleing of this his Maj'ties Colony that the said lands should be held of the King as others, and because the severall persons claimeing thereby have their immediate dependance thereupon and have made severall improvements and have a long continued & uninterrupted possession, this Committee therefore conceived that (his Maj'ties grant to his Royall Colledge of William & Mary and other the former salvo's reserved) a favourable Grant thereof may be made to them in severally, Viz:-

Robert Napier 100 acres leased to Alexander Mackdonald and assigned to him and 800 acres leased to himselfe

Matt: Mullins 150 acres leased to Thomas Ward & assigned to him

John Whitlock 150 acres by the same title

Susanna Page 1,000 acres leased to herselfe

Anthony Fuller & James Johnson 300 acres leased to them by George Pargiter

Mich: Wardrope 90 acres assigned to him by Fuller & Johnson

James Hayfeild 100 acres by the same title

John Thompson 450 acres assigned by William Clark & Marg't Clarke

Joseph Hayles, Joseph Cockerham & John Dixon 1,500 acres

Joshua Normand in behalfe of Joseph Southerland, Philip Southerland and George Southerland orphans of George Southerland 300 acres

Thomas Ware 600 acres leased to himselfe

Thomas Mackgehee 100 acres leased to Daniell Grant & conveyed to him

Philip Williams 100 acres assigned by Mackdonald

John Baker 500 acres

Edward Hackstep 550 acres leased to his mother & himselfe

Richard Gissedge 2,000 acres

John Hurt 80 acres

Francis Hill 250 acres

William Byrd, son and heir of Robert Byrd Gentl. dec'd, 1,200 acres leased to the said Robert

TITLES UPON INDIAN LEASES (Continued)

Ambrose Smith 600 acres

Ambrose Smith, John Dixon, John Hurt & Benjamin Arnold 900 acres

John Maddison & Thomas Perring 600 acres

Samuell Williams & Wm. Lea 200 acres

Sam'll Williams & Dan'll Coleman 600 acres

Thomas Spencer Sr. 250 acres

Edmund Smith & Robert Dowglas, Orphan & devisee of Rob't Dowglas, dec'd, 300 acres leased to Edmund Smith & Robert Dowglas, dec'd.

William Haynes representing that Mr. Wm. Bates about 12 years ago purchased of Capt. Roger Mallory betwixt two and three hundred acres of land in Pamunkey Neck which the sd. Mallory held by Indian title and the sd. Bates soon after departing this Country and now presumed to be dead and haveing noe Attorney here, prayed Grant for the same. This Comittee conceived the said William Haynes hath no colour of title for the same

William Leigh of King & Queen County, Gentl. representing to his Excellency that by an order of Councill dated 25th November 1682 it was directed that 4,000 acres of land should be laid out for the Rappa' Indians about the town where they dwelt. 3,474 acres were laid out but the Indians deserted the land after some time and William Leigh wished to make a survey of the land. The Comittee said this land was not in Pamunkey Neck or Blackwater and was not within their Cognizance but presumed the usual methods could be followed for takeing up the land.

LAND ON THE SOUTH SIDE BLACKWATER (June, 1699)

UPON Consideration of the Claimes and Titles presented & laid down by severall persons to land on the South side Blackwater Swamp, the Committee conceived that it is for advancement of his Maj'ties interest and service that all Vacant Lands as in Pamunkey Neck so on the South Side Blackwater Swamp should be held by Patent of the King etc. and therefore (his Maj'ties Grant to his Royall Colledge of William & Mary in Virginia being already complyed with and taken out) all persons claiming lands there by Entry & Survey and having had a long continued and uninterrupted possession shall be preferred thereto in the first place.
Those who claim by legall Entries and surveys made in the 2nd place
Nude & bare entries in the 3rd place
Seated without any Entry in the last place
PROVIDED always none of them intrench upon former Grants & Patents or Legal Entries, viz:-

Thomas Rousby, 7,400 acres entred & surveyed 1682 and ever since held in actual possession and seated with severall plantations

William Randolph Esq., 2,926 acres surveyed and patented but the Patent surrendered to give preference to the Colledge

James Minge, 2,300 acres being part of a tract surveyed for him 1683 Containing 5,972 acres and where out was taken for the Colledge by ***** pounds 3,672 acres

Benjamin Harrison Esqr. 300 acres purchased of the Weynokee Indians 1686, which hath ever since been in his actuall possession and which hereupon he hath seated

ENTRED AND SEATED

Thomas Chappell 1,000 acres

Char: Briggs 250 acres

Nathaniell Harrison and Huisha Gilliam 750 acres

Richard Halliman, Wm. Halliman & Thomas Halliman 1,150 acres

Thomas Blunt and Richard Washington 500 acres

Thomas Haynes petitioning for a Grant of 250 acres for which he entred Rights with Mr. George Williamson & seated the same and James Bynum for grant of same. The Comittee conceived Haynes to have the priority entry and to have preference

ENTRED AND SURVEY'D

James Minge & Thomas Blighton 1,660 acres surveyed 1683

James Jones 634 acres by the same title

Francis Epps 1,486 acres

William Hunt 3,200 acres

Land on the South Side Blackwater (Continued)

NUDE ENTRIES

Arthur Allen, Gent. & William Edwards, son & heir of Wm. Edwards Gent. dec'd, according to an Entry made with Mr. George Williamson, then Surveyor, dated April 20th 1696 and Joseph Wall by permission of Mr. Arthur Allen. Committee conceived the Right only to be in them who made first entry.

James Allen, Reuben Procter, George Williamson & Francis Williamson according to their severall entries made 20th April 1696

John Washington and Arthur Washington, entries made 20 April 1696

William Brown Sr., entry made for 1,200 acres

Edward Boykin according to his entry made

SEATED WITHOUT ENTRY

Abraham Evans quantity not mentioned but seated

Rich: Ham quantity not mentioned but seated

Charles Savage 200 acres seated

William Hunt and Huisha Gilliam no quantity mentioned but seated

John Cock representing to his Excellency that in June was three years he did enter with George Williamson, Surveyor, for 800 acres of Land on the South of Blackwater with Rights which the said Surveyor refused to take for that (as he said) those lands were not then opened, yet nevertheless took Entries of Thomas Blunt & Patrick Lashley for the same lands who have built and cleared thereon. The Comittee conceived the complaint groundless and that the Entryes complained of are well taken.

Thomas Blunt was given a grant for a certain parcell of land, quantity not mentioned, on the South side Blackwater, having previously not been able to get a survey on the 20th April 1696

Patrick Lashley was given a similar grant for 400 acres

Francis Poythers representing that by Patent dated 28th Sept. 1681 there was granted unto Major Francis Poythers 609 acres, 2 roods, 9 poles of Land on Blackwater which by the death of the Patentee descends to him. Comittee granted same.

Committee then stated that any hardship caused by these decisions could be examined by the Courts of the Counties at a future date to be announced, when Surveyors reports were available and decisions confirmed by His Excellency.

Pamuhkey Neck and Blackwater Land (Claims by Indians)

Drammacho Morgy a chief Ruler of the CHICKAHOMONY INDIANS petitioned that severall lands in Pamunkey Neck should, by the Articles of Peace, May 1677 belong to them and that any sales they had made of these lands should be confirmed. This was refused by the Committee who said that only land within 3 miles of the Indian Town was Indian property and that any sales or leases made by them were null and void. Except that "what lands they hold from any of his Maj'ties subjects by Exchange shall be confirmed to them, viz. that they have in exchange from Arnold and Mallory" The Indians also claimed that they gave certain lands to Peter Ford and his wife for life and as the Fords were now dead the Indians should have the lands returned. The Comittee said that as the land was confirmed to Peter Ford by Sir Henry Chicheley and afterwards by the Lord Effingham and by the said Ford sold to Edmund Jenings Esqr. therefore the said Indians have no right nor title to it.

The OCCAHAMOCK INDIANS complained that having given permission to the English to enter their lands, the English had taken it over completely and would not allow the Indians to enter or to plant or fish. This, they said, was most unjust as these were their only means of living. The Committee promised to look into this and make redress "as shall seem meet"

The NANSEMOND INDIANS complained that the English intended to take possession of land between Blackwater & Nottaway River which they claimed was upon their old Town. The Committee found that the Indians had deserted this area several years previously and therefore had no claim to it, but that no English would be permitted to seat, plant or possess within 3 miles of where the Indians now lived.

The NOTTAWAY INDIANS complained that the TUSCORURO INDIANS often came into the upper parts of the country about Appamattu where the English gave them guns, powder and shot which enabled them to hunt upon and burn up the Nottaway's ground, spoiling their hunting and that the Tuscoruro trade with the English for rum etc. and then lose these goods by play and blame the Nottaways, thus causing friction between the Nottaways and the English. They asked that the English should be forbidden to enter their territory to avoid further trouble. His Excellency directed them to decide amongst themselves what bounds they desired and let him know through their Interpreter and as to the discords he would make redress on proof of these discords.

Signed by Dionisius Wright, Clerk of the Comittee

June 2nd, 1699

This Report read and agreed to by the Councill

Signed by Ben: Harrison

This Report read and agreed to by the House of Burgesses

Signed by Wm. Randolph, Cl. House Burgesses

June 5th, 1699

A List of Patents Signed in November 1700

County	To Whom Granted	Number of Acres
New Kent	Gibbons, James	1420
"	Mackgirt, Dan'l	1168
Nansemond	Cooper, Thomas	147
"	Milner, Thomas	200
"	Drury, Capt. Chas.	209
"	Pugh, Dan'l	190
"	Pugh, Dan'l	422
Princess Ann	Sullivan, Owen	254
Nansemond	Moore, John	485
Gloucester	Davis, Edw.	300
New Kent	Nash, Robert	350
Nansemond	Werrell, Joseph	166
"	Fullerton, Robert	47
"	Milner, Francis & Marlow, Tho.	33
Norfolk	Wallis, Wm.	71
Nansemond	Jurnigan, Henry	87
Norfolk	Cherris, John	105
Nansemond	Peale, Wm.	580
Henrico	Garthright, Ephraim	165
Nansemond	Thompson, Wm.	133
"	Jones, Wm.	159
New Kent	Macon, Gideon	545
"	Major, Wm.	155
Accomack	Eyre, Thomas	200
Gloucester	Billups, George	500
Northampton	Jacob, Abr'm & Jacob, Tho.	400
Norfolk	Bush, Sam'll	1080
New Kent	Alvos, Geo.	767
Accomack	Brittingham, Wm.	96
Charles City	Crowder, Barth'o	242
York	Cary, Miles	327
King & Queen	Boughan, James	333
New Kent	Massee, Peter	300
Middlesex	Mountague, Wm.	170
Henrico	Davis, John	250
Middlesex	Thacker, Edwin	300

(Signed) E. Jenings.

A List of Patents Signed in April 1701

County	To Whom Granted	Number of Acres
Nansemond	Hookes, John	215
"	Arnold, Edw'd	89
"	Lasister, John	330
"	Speight, Wm.	203
Essex	Boughan, James	1000
Middlesex	Sandeford, John	150
Nansemond	Hill, Henry	500
Norfolk	Langley, Wm.	100
Charles City	Stith, Drury	445
Nansemond	Sewell, Wm.	746
"	Edwards, Abr.	97
"	Hunter, Wm.	240
"	Speight, Wm.	25
Norfolk	Langley, Wm.	58
Charles City	Stoakes, John	476
Warwick	Goodwin, Mathew	134
Nansemond	Brothers, John	197
Henrico	Burton, Rob't Sr.	300
Nansemond	Stalling, Nicholas	63
"	Benton, Epap (?)	360
Norfolk	Hughs, Edw'd	1234
"	Fulcher, John	569
Henrico	Woodson, John	1020
"	Perce (?), Fra:	137
"	Bolling, John	50
Nansemond	Lowry, James	43
Henrico	Pleasant, John	2294
Charles City	Bolling, Rob't	300
Pamunkey Neck in King & Queen	Rapier, Jno.	185
"	Davis, Robert	208
"	Maybank, Wm.	105
"	Winston, Wm.	1091
"	Terry, Jam:	418
Blackwater	Allen, Arth:	800
"	Edwards, Wm. & Allen, Arth:	800
"	Savaig, Char:	88
"	Harrison, Benj: Esq.	350
"	Chappell, Tho.	990
"	Briggs, Cha:	231
"	Harrison, Nath: and Gillam, Huisha	658
"	Washington, Rich:	345
"	Boykins, Edw'd	200
"	Haynes, Thos.	280
"	Lashly, Patr'k	470
"	Edwards, Wm.	1450
"	Busby, Tho:	5400
"	Harrison, Nath'l	427
"	Allen, Jam:	1400
"	Williamson, Fra:	417
"	Williamson, Geo:	770
"	Blunt, Thomas	510
"	Blunt, Thomas	159
"	Browne, Wm.	635
"	Hunt, Wm.	348
"	Dews, Wm.	344

A List of Patents Signed in April 1701 (continued)

County	To Whom Granted	Number of Acres
Norfolk	Ballentine, Geo:	200
York	Knott, Wm.	150
Pamunkey Neck in King & Queen	Mullen, Matthew	268
	Hobdey, Edward	263
	Terry, Steph'n	335
	Merriweather, Nich'o	459
	Macon, Gideon	172
	Dabney, James	500
	Dabney, Geo:	293
	Dabney, Sarah	179.2
	Anderson, Wm. et al	179.2
	Herbert, Mary	200
	Hendrick, Hance	594
	Thompson, John	537
	Gouge, Jane	80
	Carr, Tho:	546
	Fleming, Char:	1184
	Hayden, Jno.	196
	Henderson, Jam:	155
	Edwards, Jam:	854
	Cremshaw, Tho:	150
	Burrows, John	439
	King, John	211
	Hayfield, Jam:	109
	Comers, Thos.	139
	Adams, Jas.	437
	Oliver, John	146
	Littlepage, Rich:	2367
Blackwater	Evans, Abraham	127
	Ham, Richard	139
	Gillam, Huisha	348
	Blunt, Thomas	486

(Signed) E. Jenings.

A List of Patents Signed in October 1701

County	To Whom Granted	Number of Acres
Accomack	Littleton, Nathaniel	150
Henrico	Worsham, John & Patterson, Francis	924
	Cook, Thomas	628
	Taylor, Wm.	700
Essex	Meriwether, Francis	876
	Beckett, Henry	80
Middlesex	Terrell, Robert	63
	Mountague, Peter	1000
Warwick	King, Thomas	70
New Kent	Winston, Anthony	1079
	Saxon, John	1024
	Saxon, John	332
	Richardson, Jno. & Emanuel	2400
Norfolk	Richardson, Thomas	99
	Langley, Thomas	128
Nansemond	Raby, Adam	436
	Cooper, Joseph	136

A List of Patents Signed in October 1701 (continued)

County	To Whom Granted	Number of Acres
Nansemond	Lawrence, Robert	53
	Speir, James	100
Isle of Wight	Scott, Robert	130
	Denson, James	17
Pamunkey Neck in King & Queen	Hurt, Wm.	298
	Blackwell, Robert	174
	Nicholls, Thomas	183
	Maccallister, Andrew	86
	Davis, Lewis	320
	Follett, Thomas	157
	Page, Susanna	1419
	White, Peter	355
	Tremier, John	102
Rappa. or Essex	Major, John	376
S'side Blackwater	Reeves, Thomas	740
	Smelly, Robert et al	1420
	Giles, Thomas et al	678
	Pearce, George	200
Charles City	Parham, Wm.	450
	King, Henry	400
	Hunt, Wm.	4342
	Smith, Richard	550
	Irby, Edm'd	399
	Epps, Francis et al	1000
	Jones, Henry	400
	Hathorn, Robert	1400
	Jones, Wm. Sr.	600
	Poythres, John	350
	Gourd, Richard	100
	Thrower, Thomas et al	680
	Freeman, John	300
	Wynn, Thomas	200
	Buttler, John et al	450
	Cook, Thomas	1170
Henrico	Farrer, Thomas	126
Accomack	Kellam, Edward	130
Middlesex	Meacham, Edward	150

Escheat Patents Granted in October 1701

County	To Whom Granted	Number of Acres
Gloucester	Sawyer, Wm.	400
Northampton	Custis, John Jr.	100
King & Queen	Breemer, John & Jane, his wife	100
ditto	ditto	1000
Accomack	Waltham, Eliz:	650
Surry	Jordan, George	670
James City	Russell, Samuel	370
New Kent	Ryder, Mary (? Mrs.)	100
ditto	ditto	300
Gloucester	Williams, George	100
Essex	Hill, Leonard	300
	Mountague, Wm.	250
	Mountague, Wm.	700

(Signed) C.C. Thacker, Clk.

A List of Patents Signed in April 1702

County	To Whom Granted	Number of Acres
Pamunkey Neck	John Petiver	310
	Jno. Hampton	50
	Edw'd Huckstep	554
	Eliz: Ware	240
	Morris Roberts	300
	Thomas Ware	620
	Edw'd Bell	1400
	Ant'o Fuller	181
	James Johnson	110
	Wm. Andrews	100
	Matt'w Fowler	127
	Rich'd Littlepage	4886
Essex	George Loyd	694
King & Queen	Martin Slaughter	137
	James Dabney	1000
	Wm. Hurt	93
	Morris Floyd	100
	John Cesar	405
	C. C. Thacker	980
	John Whitlock	233
	Wm. Morris	366
	John Buckner	3080
	Rowland Thomas	100
Middlesex	John Smith	450
	Eliz. Musgrave	368
	John Sumers	175
	Valentine Mayo	39
	Edw'd Docker	40
	Edwin Thacker	153
	Henry Thacker	23
Blackwater	Tho: Harrison & Jno. Scott	1700
	Richard Holliman	1236
Surry	Wm. Cock	45
Henrico	Thos: Chamberlaine	509
	Nich: Hutchins	290
	Moses Wood	237
	John Jouany	77
	Wm. Soane	51
	Robert Griggs	400
	John Bolling	350
Elizabeth City	James Baker	225
Charles City	Law. Greene	203
	James Williams et al	650
Norfolk	Robert Lane	460
New Kent	John Bacon	243
Warwick	Henry Dawson	363
Gloucester	Robert Bryan	57
	John Stubbs	100
	Peter Beverley	230
Nansemond	Henry Hackley	950
	Henry Hackley	100
	John Gordon	350
	John Powell	215
Isle of Wight	Wm. West	85
	Thomas Howell	100
Accomack	Rich'd Hoffinton (?)	67

1702

A Copie of all Entreys in wt. place and by whom made since ye land on ye South Side of Blackwater has been laid open. Entr'd with me, Robert Bolling, Surv'r of Charles City County.

Name	Other Names mentioned in entry	Acres	Date
Rob't Bolling Sr.		2000	21st Sep. 1702
Capt. Wm. Hunt		2150	do.
Mr. James Minge Sr.		3250	do.
Mr. Tho: Wynn		200	do.
Capt. Jno. Poythriss Jr.		600	do.
Mr. Tho: Wynn	Jno. Green, Hathorn	600	do.
Edw: Parrum		200	do.
Wm. Handbacke	Wm. Raines	600	do.
Maj'r Charles Goodrich	Jno. Freeman	2000	do.
George Passmore	Henry Jones, Wm. Jones Sr.	500	do.
Nath'll Tatum Sr. & Jr.	Jarvis Winfield, Doboy	500	do.
Tho: Parrum	George Tilman, James Cock, Edmond Irby	200	do.
Mr. Rob't Mumford	Jno. Butler	400	do.
Mr. Rob't Mumford	Henry King	400	23rd Sep 1702
Jno. Doboy		400	do.
Wm. Mayes & Rich'd Hudson	Mr. Banister	900	24th Sep 1702
Sam'll Tatum Sr.	Nath'll Tatum Jr.	200	do.
Wm. Reives	Jno. Butler, Benja: Foster, Edw'd Chaple, James Minge	---	25th Sep 1702
Jno. Freeman		300	26th Sep 1702
George Passmore		250	3rd Oct 1702
Jno. Freeman	Rob't Bolling	500	4th Oct 1702
Jno. Leadbiter		400	10th Oct 1702
Tho: Parrum		200	do.
Nathan'll Harrison of Surry Co.	Several entries of land mentioned Col. Sam'l Brigs, Col. Randolph	---	21st Sep 1702
Hon'ble Benja: Harrison	Geo. Jordan	1200	do.
ditto	Charles Brigs	200	do.
Mr. Benja: Harrison	Capt. Wm. Hunt, Maj'r Charles Goodrich	2000	do.
ditto		2000	do.
Barnaby Mackinne	Geo. Pearce	----	do.
Rich: Parker & Wm. Edmonds	Wm. Hunt	----	do.
Tho: Bently	Geo. Jordan	150	do.
ditto	Jeremiah Ellis Sr.	250	do.
Wm. Edwards & Nath'll Harrison		---	do.
Abraham Evins	Wm. Hunt	200	do.
Howell Edmonds & Tho: Hart		---	do.
Capt. Wm. Browne	Col. Wm. Browne	---	do.
Bartholomew Andros		400	do.
Wm. Edwards		---	do.
Jno. Lawrance	Rob't Smethie, Maj'r Swann	---	do.
Capt. Luke Hansfield	Wm. Dawes	---	do.
Wm. Kinchin	Maj'r Arthur Allen	---	do.
Maj'r Arthur Allen	Wm. Dawes	---	do.
Jno. Warpoole, Rich'd Read**		---	do.
Sam'll Browne		---	do.

Land Entries for Southside Blackwater 1702 (continued)

Name	Other Names Mentioned	Acres
Rich: Washington & Benja: Evins	Jno. Williams, Jno. & Arthur Washington	--
Edward Harris	Major Allin	--
Col. Geo: Norsworthy	Fran: Williamson	--
Sam'll Briggs		300
Jeremiah Ellis		--
Wm. Cock		600
Wm. May	Wm. Williams	--
Jno. Councill		--
Hen: Briggs		--
Joseph Wall Jr.	Rich: Hains	--
Jno. Barker	Wm. Hunt	400
Jno. Owen	James Jones, Tho: Chapple, Capt. Tho: Harrison	--
Mr. Jno. Owen	Capt. Harrison	800
Tho: Blunt	Abraham Evins	--
Wm. Braswell & Rob't Scott		--
Brigman Joyner	Mr. Swann, Wm. Johnson	--
Rich: & Wm. Braswell		--
Tho: Raines	Geo: Williamson, Geo. Pearce, Barnaby Mackinne	--
Wm. Glover		150
Tho: Hunt	Rich: Washington	200
Rich: Washington & Benja: Evins	Jno. Barnes	--
Jno. Teasly	Geo. Pearce	--
Moses Showmake	Wm. Johnson, Wm. Williams	--
Rich: Holliman		--
Capt. Francis Clements		1000
Mr. James Minge Jr.		3000
Mr. James Minge		2000
Tho: Barrow	Tho: Haynes	--
Jno. Warpoole		400
Capt. Wm. Brown		650
Wm. Holliman	Edward Boykin	--
Capt. Wm. Hunt		--
Capt. Nath'll Harrison		--
Jno. Jones		--
Hen: Jones		500
Capt. Tho: Harrison		4000
Wm. Hunt	Abraham Evins	--
Wm. Rogers	Col. Browne	--
James Byneham (? Baynham)		--

Signed by Tho: Swann

LIST OF PATENTS SIGNED IN APRIL 1703

County	To Whom Granted	Number of Acres
Nansemond	Robert Poole	134
Princess Anne	John Hopkins	210
Nansemond	Nich'o Hunter	46
Nansemond	Fra. Speight Jr. & Wm. Speight Jr.	161
Nansemond	Jon'a Robinson	200
King & Queen	Thomas Pettis	36
King William	Phillip Williams	100
Nansemond	Edward Holmes	124
do.	Rich'd Lawrence	76
do.	John Duke	113
do.	Wm. Lassiter	100
York	Arthur Lunn	50
King William	William Lipscombe	300
do.	Jacob Sellars	353
King & Queen	James Taylor & Tho. Pettis	576
Blackwater Swamp	William Williams	400
King William	Nich'o Rodes	91
Nansemond	Benj'a Rogers	340
do.	Steph'n & Tho. Cowling	250
Henrico	John Robinson	881
Nansemond	Francis Milner	300
do.	Jno. Murdah	.46
do.	Rowland Gwinn	200
Upper Chippoake	Walter Cock Sr.	350
Henrico	Henry Mayes	292
Charles City	William Temple	627
Henrico	John Woodson	2700
Middlesex	Henry Thacker	77
Henrico	Matthew Branch Esq.	710
do.	John Farlar	471
Middlesex	Thomas Stapleton	125
Nansemond	Robert Rogers	234
do.	Wm. Jones Jr.	267
Norfolk	Edw'd Wood Jr.	50
Nansemond	Abraham Edward	100
do.	Joseph Cooper	276
King & Queen	Jno. Pigg	1000
Henrico	James Thweat	234
Nansemond	Andrew Ross	87
Henrico	James Thweat	223
Middlesex	Jno. Sandiford	150
New Kent	Geo. Aalves	1668
Essex	Harry Beverly	750
Isle of Wight	Arth'r Smith	500
Gloucester	Jno. Stubbs	50
King & Queen	Wm. Jones	420
King & Queen and Essex	Harry Beverly	2300
Nansemond	Richard Sanders	127
King & Queen	Francis Major	590
King William	Thomas Parker	314
Charles City	Drury Stith	680

County	To Whom Granted	No. of Acres
Henrico	Francis' Eppes Esq.	4000
Gloucester	Mordecai Cook	1200
Accomack	Rowland Savage	500
Princess Anne	Wm. Grant	150
New Kent	Jno. Snead	50
Northampton	Peirce Davis	350
Middlesex	Rebecca Mason	120
King & Queen	C. C. Thacker	130

List of Patents Signed in April 1704

Essex	Andrew Harrison	1100
Elizabeth City	Tho: Poole	474
Charles City	Robert West	298
New Kent	Francis Clark	282
Gloucester	Robert Porteus	692
Essex	Andrew Harrison	813
	John May	191
	Tho: Tinsley	1400
	Thomas Tinsley	1000
	Wm. Scott	156
	Edward Merrick	1014
	John Ridsdaile	92
	John Cook	47
	Wm. Lowry	1044
	Wm. Johnson	550
	John Coleman	1200
	Robert Brookes	650
	Thos. Gregson	37
Nansemond	James Doughty	308
King William	Wm. Bassett	1000
New Kent	Geo: Lovell	1100
York	Wm. Pattison	300
Charles City	Robert Mumford	50
Nansemond	Lewis Conner	90
King & Queen	Edward Lewis	400
	Robert Dowglass	150
Gloucester	Anne Forrest	200
New Kent	Evan Jones	442
Gloucester	Wm. Collawns	200
	Wm. Thornton	110
	Dunkin Bohannon	145
	James Ranson	40
New Kent	David Clarkson	100
	Tho: Butts	296
Charles City	Joan Liscomb	432
Essex	Clara Robinson	860
	Benj: Robinson	655
	Ann Hays	685
Accomack	Thomas Freeson	200

C. C. Thacker, Clk.

List of Patents granted for Land in Henrico County October 26th, 1704

Name	Acres
Jeremiah Benskin	324
Walter Scot	250
Rob't Eastley	315
Thomas Andrews	394
Philip Jones	13
John Parkinson	212
Tho: Jefferson	628
John Pleasants	286
John Granger	72
John Gill	235
Cha: Cozens	362
Rob't Woodson	171
Peter Renlett	200
Cha: Evans	383
Wm. Byrd Esq	3664
Wm. Byrd Esq.	507

A List of Patents for Land Signed May the Second, 1705

County	To Whom Granted	Acres
Prince George	Adam Heath	681
New Kent	Stephen Sunter	200
	Thomas Strutton	332
	Wm. Major	150
Nansemond	Henry Hackley	700
	James Collins	164
	Henry Jenkins	132
King & Queen	Timothy Conner	1420
	John Wyatt	700
	Wm. Jones	523
Henrico	Charles Evans	140
	Jno. Stewart Jr.	850
	Wm. Hatcher	550
	Allen Clarke et al	945
	Jno. Bolling et al	1100
Essex	Richard Covington et al	646
	James Boughan et al	2000
New Kent	David Bray et al	6500
	Wm. Tomlin	294
	Augustin Smith	2359
	John Talliaferro	220
	Augustin Smith	1050
	John Salmon et al	427
	John Slay et al	3288
	Wm. Tomlin et al	550
Charles City	John Hamlin	550
	Charles Evans	176
Isle of Wight	Wm. Jolly	634
James City	Wm. Barrett	55
King William	Wm. Johnson	4900
	Sam'l Williams et al	400
	Chris'r Pearson	106
	Abr. Willaroy	137
	Wm. Standard	980
Elizabeth City	Wm. Wilson	200
Princess Anne	Owen Matthews	140
Accomack	John Griffin	150
Elizabeth City	Walter Bayly	150
	Matthew Watts	50
Henrico	Robert Bolling	50
	Mary Ascough	633
King & Queen	Mary Leigh et al	200
	Mary Leigh et al	600
New Kent	John Parke	650
	Edmund Jennings Esq.	350
	Thomas Jackson	200
Northampton	Hancock Custis	50
	Anne Hall	100
	Wm. Waterfeild	200
	Joseph Benthall	33
	John Adison	150
Nansemond	Eliz'h Webb	75
	Thomas Milner	350

A List of Patents for Land Signed May 2nd 1705 (continued)

County	To Whom Granted	Acres
Nansemond	Rich'd Sumner	96
	James Copeland	300
	John Benton	93
	Wm. Sumner	76
Prince George of Surry	Benj' Evans	300
York	Edward Thomas	220

C. C. Thacker, Depty. Secty. Virg'a

List of Patents Signed in April General Court 1706

County	Acres	To Whom Granted	Surveyed By	Date
Surry	1000	Francis Clements	Arthur Allen	Mar. 18-1705/6
do.	50	Joseph Proctor	do.	Sep. 9-1705
do.	580	Wm. Cocke	do.	Mar. 19-1705/6
do.	150	Tho. Bentley	do.	Mar. 11-1705/6
do.	1000	Benj'a Harrison Esq.	do.	Mar. 12-1705/6
do.	180	Tho. King	do.	Apr. 3-1705
do.	150	Wm. Rhodes	do.	do.
do.	200	Nich'o Smith	do.	do.
Prince George	16	Rich'd Bland	Rob't Bolling	Jan. 19-1704/5
do.	43	Rich'd Bland	do.	Jan. 8-1704/5
Essex	171	Edw'd Barrow	Cha. Smith	Apr. 19-1705
do.	1234	Gawin Corbin	Deserted	--
do.	65	Tho. Merriweather	do.	--
do	103½	John Harper	--	--
do.	100	John Harper	--	--
Eliz'a City	1[illegible]	Robert Saylor	--	--
do.	274	Wm. Mallory	Wm. Lowrey	Dec. 29-1698
New Kent	1900	Dudley Digges	Deserted	--
do.	850	Roger Thomson	--	--
Henrico	1468	Charles Evans	Deserted	--
do.	570	Rich'd Cocke Jr.	do.	--
Princess Anne	447	John Carraway Sr.	Lem'll Newton	May 22-1705
do.	176	Thomas Wiles	do.	May 18-1705
Norfolk	150	William Maund	do.	May 10-1705
do.	45	Thomas Cherry	do.	Oct. 5-1705
King & Queen	211	Jane King	Deserted	--
do.	1245	John Major	do.	--
Accomack	500	Tully Robinson	Edm' Scarburgh	Sep. 28-1705
Gloucester	335	George Billops	Deserted	--
Nansemond	250	Wm. Parker	do.	--
Isle of Wight	380	Nich'o Fulgham	do.	--
Northampton	330	Tho. Smith	Edm'd Scarburgh	May 19-1704
King & Queen	546	John Hurt	Rich'd Whitehead	Mar. 27-1701
James City	130	Naz'th Whitehead	--	--
King Wm.	107	Orlando Jones	Deserted	--
Prince George	351	Robert Munford	Rob't Bolling Jr.	Jan. 23-1705/6
do.	405	John Anderson & Rob't Munford	do.	Jan. 24-1705/6
do.	1973	Col. Rob't Bolling Sr.	do.	Dec. 20-1705
Essex	145	Thomas Corbin	Harry Beverley	Dec. 28-1705
King Wm.	1091	John Kimbro	Deserted	--
Henrico	190	Worsham	Rich'd Liggon	Mar. 15-1705/6
Eliz'a City	120	Rob't Beverley	No Survey	--
King & Queen	2763	Col. James Taylor	Harry Beverly	Apr. 5-1706
Henrico	5644	Rich'd Bland	Deserted	--
New Kent	300	David Holt, Minor	By order of ye Gen'll Court renewed	--
Prince Geo.	4583	Benj'a Harrison	--	--

A List of Patents Signed October 1706

County	Acres	To Whom Granted	Surveyed By	Date
Charles City	288	Thomas Hardyway	Rob't Bolling Jr.	Nov. 23-1705
Prince Geo.	5037	John Sadler of London, Grocer and the Rev. Jos: Richardson, Clerk, husband of Elianor Richardson, Executrix of Thomas Quiny late of London, Brewer	do.	Jan. 1704/5
New Kent	200	Henry Bows	James Minge	Oct. 6-1702
Surry, Blackwater	250	Thomas Pitman Jr.	Arthur Allen	Feb. 28-1705/6
Charles City	354	John Roper	Rob't Bolling Jr.	Oct. 8-1705
Surry, Blackwater	128	Thomas Barrow	Arthur Allen	Oct. 8-1705
Surry, Northside Notoway River	446	John Barker	Thomas Swann	Dec. 7-1702
Prince Geo.	1001	John Evans	Rob't Bolling Jr.	Jan. 28-1705/6
Surry, N.side, Notoway River	530	Abra. Evans	Thomas Swann	Oct. 7-1702
Isle of Wight (Blackwater)	160	Edward Boykin	Arthur Allen	Feb. 25-1705/6
Surry, Blackwater	320	Thomas Blunt	do.	Mar. 7-1707/8
Prince Geo.	498	Thomas Wynn	Rob't Bolling Jr.	Apr. 30-1706
Prince Geo., Blackwater	347	Charles Williams	do.	Jan. 10-1705/6
Nansemond	530	William Vann	Thomas Milner	Mar. 20-1705/6
do.	42	William Spight	do.	Mar. 23-1705/6
Charles City	33	Thomas Davis	Rob't Bolling Jr.	May 17-1705
Nansemond, Blackwater	350	Robert Carr	Thomas Milner	Apr. 4-1706
Prince Geo.	333	John Poythers Sr.	Rob't Bolling Jr.	Apr. 4-1706
Essex	55½	John Parker	Charles Smith	June 13-1705
Henrico	608	Charles Hudson & John Bradley	Richard Ligon	May 3-1705/6
Nansemond	254	John Drury	Thomas Milner	Apr. 3-1706
Prince Geo.	429	Edward Richardson	Rob't Bolling Jr.	May 14-1705
King William	950	Thomas Johnson	Harry Beverly	July 23-1705
Isle of Wight, So. side of Blackwater	540	Edward Harris	Arthur Allen	Feb. 26-1705/6
Surry, S.side of Blackwater	150	Jeremiah Ellis	do.	Mar. 8-1705/6
Nansemond	143	Henry Core	Thomas Milner	Apr. 4-1706
New Kent	36	George Lovell	James Minge	Oct. 20-1705
Henrico	1150	Capt. Thomas Cocke	Richard Ligon	Apr. 29-1704
Surry, S.side of Blackwater	330	James Binam	Arthur Allen	Mar. 7-1705/6
King William	450	Samuel Normant	Harry Beverly	Aug. 22-1706
Nottaway River	2000	Maj'r Charles Goodrich	Thomas Swan	Nov. 30-1702
Essex	37	Henry Boughan	Harry Beverly	Apr. 2-1706
Prince George, Notaway River	431	John Freeman	Rob't Bolling Jr.	Dec. 17-1705
Prince George	153	Thomas Parram	do.	Dec. 17-1705

List of Patents Signed Oct. 1706 (continued)

County	Acres	To Whom Granted	Surveyed By	Date
Prince George Southside of Nottaway	219	Robert Rives	Rob't Bolling Jr.	Jan. 25-1705/6
Princess Ann	51	Dan'l Leonard	Lemuel Newton	Nov. 27-1705
Nansemond	467	John Small	Thomas Milner	Mar. 25-1706/7
Princess Ann	237	Capt. Horatio Woodhouse	Lemuel Newton	Mar. 12-1705/6
do.	100	Thomas Scott	do.	Oct. 23-1705
Essex	275	John Giddian	Charles Smith	Nov. 24-1705
do.	149½	Col. Rich'd Covington	do.	June 14-1705
do.	816	Samuel Dachimin	do.	Oct. 26-1705
Nansemond	250	Joseph Daniel	Thomas Milner	Mar. 22-1705/6
do.	54	Joseph Meredeth	do.	Mar. 19-1705/6
Surry, S. side of Blackwater	220	Thomas Halleman	Arthur Allen	Feb. 27-1705/6
do.	220	William Rogers Jr.	do.	Mar. 9-1705/6
do.	170	Benj'a Harrison Esq.	do.	Mar. 8-1705/6
do.	200	Thomas Hunt	do.	Mar. 9-1705/6
Henrico	97	Philimon Childres	Richard Ligon	Feb. 16-1704/5
do.	850	Abraham Michaux	do.	Apr. 11-1706
do.	285	Charles Evans	Lapsed from Rich'd Ligon & James Ekers Jr.	
do.	311	Francis Epps	Lapsed	
Warwick	132	Samuel Groves	do.	
do.	87	Enos Mackintosh	do.	
Essex	30	Ann Gregson	do.	
do.	37	Ann Gregson	do.	
Nansemond	60	Christopher Norfleet	Escheat Land	
do.	106	Francis Benton	" "	
do.	214	Richard Webb	" "	
do.	106	Wm. Ward	" "	
do	148	Nicholas Hunter & Elizabeth his wife in behalf of themselves & Francis Benton, an infant	" "	
do.	148	John Heslett & Sarah his wife in behalf of themselves and David Rice, an infant	" "	
do.	48	John Hare	" "	
Accomack	345	John West & Charles Bailey	" "	
York	150	William Sheldon	" "	
King & Queen	200	John Baylor	" "	
Gloucester	180	Eliz'a Collier, Edw'd Collier & Sarah Collier	" "	
Henrico	522	Anthony Tribue	Richard Ligon	Feb. 24-1705/6
Prince George	358	John Sadler, Citizen & Grocer of London & the Rev. Joseph Richardson Clerk, Husband of Elianor Richardson, Executrix of Thomas Quiny late of London, Brewer	Robert Bolling	Nov. 5-1705
Fork Mattopony River	2000	John Maddison & Henry Pigg	Harry Beverly	Mar. 23-1705/6

List of Patents Signed Oct. 1706 (continued)

County	Acres	To Whom Granted	Surveyed By	Date
King & Queen	1658	Rob't Robinson	Harry Beverly	Aug. 29-1706
On fork of Mattapony River	1525	Jno. Rogers, Peter Rogers, Edw'd Pigg, Jno. York & Tho. Gresham	do.	Mar. 26-1706/7
ditto	2000	John Pigg & John May	do.	Mar. 24-1705/6
King William	470	Ambrose Lipscomb	Harry Beverly by Order Court	Aug. 25-1706
Prince George	225	George Pasmore & John Peterson	John Bolling	Apr. 22-1706
Accomack	900	Eliz'a Scarburgh widow & Anthony West	Edmund Scarburgh	May 22-1706
do.	570	ditto	do.	do.
do.	550	Rob't Watson & David Watson	do.	May 1-1706
Henrico	280	Stephen Chaistain	Richard Ligon	Apr. 25-1706
Isle of Wight	237	John Parnell & Wm. Jolley	Thomas Swann	Nov. 19-1702
Charles City	1324	Tho. Christian & Edm'd New Jr.	Robert Bolling	Nov. 27-1705
Prince George	422	Wm. Rives	do.	Jan. 19-1705/6
Hanrico	290	Matt. Ligon & Rich'd Ligon Jr.	Richard Ligon	Mar. 15-1706
Prince George	327	Henry Michael Jr.	Rob't Bolling	Apr. 3-1706
Nansemond	443	John Hidgepath Jr.	Thomas Milner	Jan. 18-1705
New Kent	136	Nath'a West	James Minge	Oct. 26-1705
Henrico	1682	George Robertson	Lapsed Land	
King William	550	C. C. Thacker	" "	
Henrico	788	Charles Evans	Richard Ligon	Nov. 2-1705
King & Queen and Essex	3000	William Hall	Lapsed Land	
Prince George	450	Rob't Bolling Jr.	" "	
King & Queen	758	John Richards	Harry Beverly	Dec. 13-1705
New Kent	361	Jeremiah Lindsey	Escheat Land	
King & Queen	300	Roger Grigory	" "	
Essex	100	Robert Richardson	" "	
Charles City	288	Thomas Hardyway	Rob't Bolling Jr.	Nov. 23-1705
Prince George	5037	John Sadler of London, Grocer & the Reverend Jos. Richardson, Clerk, husband of Elianor Richardson, Executrix of Tho. Quiny late of London, Brewer)	do.	Jan. 1705/6
New Kent	200	Henry Bows	James Minge	Oct. 6-1702
Surry, Blackwater	250	Thomas Pittman Jr.	Arthur Allen	Feb. 28-1705
Charles City	554	John Roper	Rob't Bolling Jr.	Oct. 8-1705
Surry, Blackwater	528	Thomas Barrow	Arthur Allen	Mar. 8-1705
Surry, N'side Nottaway River	446	John Barker	Thomas Swan	Dec. 7-1702
Prince George	1001	John Evans	Rob't Bolling Jr.	Jan. 28-1705/6
Surry, N'side Nottaway River	130	Abra. Evans	Thomas Swann	Dec. 7-1702
Isle of Wight Blackwater	160	Edward Boykin	Arthur Allen	Feb. 26-1705

List of Patents Signed Oct. 1706 (Continued)

County	Acres	To Whom Granted	Surveyed By	Date
Surry, Blackwater	320	Thomas Blunt	Arthur Allen	Mar. 7-1705
Prince George	498	Thomas Wynn	Rob't Bolling Jr.	Apr. 4-1706
So. Blackwater	347	Charles Williams	do.	Feb. 18-1705/6
Nansemond	280	William Speir	Thomas Milner	Mar. 26-1706
Surry, Blackwater	200	Joseph Wall Jr.	Arthur Allen	Feb. 28-1705
Nansemond	130	William Vaun	Thomas Milner	Mar. 20-1705
do.	42	William Spight	Thomas Milner	Mar. 23-1705
Charles City	98	Thomas Davis	Rob't Bolling Jr.	Oct. 10-1705
Nansemond, Blackwater	350	Robert Carr	Thomas Milner	Apr. 4-1706
Prince George	333	John Poythres Sr.	Robert Bolling Jr.	do.
Essex	55½	John Parker	Charles Smith	June 15-1705
Henrico	608	Cha. Hudson & John Bradley	Rich'd Ligon	May 3-1705
Nansemond	254	John Drury	Thomas Milner	Apr. 4-1706
Prince George	429	Edw'd Richardson	Rob't Bolling Jr.	May 14-1705
King William	950	Thomas Johnson	Harry Beverly	July 25-1705
Isle of Wight, S'side Blackwater	540	Edward Harris	Arthur Allen	Feb. 26-1705
Surry, S'side Blackwater	150	Jeremiah Ellis	Arthur Allen	Mar. 8-1705
Nansemond	143	Henry Core	Thomas Milner	Apr. 4-1706
New Kent	36	George Lovell	James Minge	Oct. 20-1705
Henrico	1150	Capt. Thomas Cocke	Richard Ligon	Apr. 29-1704
Surry, S'side Blackwater	330	James Binam	Arthur Allen	Mar. 7-1705
King William	410	Samuel Norment	Harry Beverly	Aug. 22-1706
Nottaway River	2000	Maj'r Charles Goodrich	Thomas Swann	Nov. 30-1702
Essex	37	Henry Baughan	Harry Beverly	Apr. 2-1706
Prince George, Nottaway River	431	John Freeman	Rob't Bolling Jr.	Dec. 17-1705
Prince George	153	Thomas Parrum	do.	Jan. 25-1705/6
Prince George, S.side Nottaway	219	Robert Rives	do.	Apr. 2-1706
Princess Anne	51	Daniell Leonard	Sam'll Newton	Nov. 27-1705
Nansemond	467	John Small	Tho. Milner	Mar. 25-1706
Princess Anne	237	Capt. Horatio Woodhouse	Sam'll Newton	Mar. 12-1705
do,	100	Thomas Scott	do,	Oct. 23-1705
Essex	275	John Giddian	Charles Smith	Nov. 25-1705
do.	149½	Col. Rich'd Covington	do.	June 14-1705
Princess Anne	816	Samuel Duchimin	Charles Smith	Oct. 26-1705
Nansemond	205	Joseph Daniell	Thomas Milner	Mar. 22-1705
do.	511	Joseph Meredith	do.	Mar. 19-1705
Surry, S.side Blackwater	220	Tho. Halloman	Arthur Allen	Feb. 27-1705
do.	220	Wm. Rogers Jr.	do.	Mar. 9-1705
do.	170	Benj'a Harrison Esq.	do.	Mar. 8-1705
do.	200	Thomas Hunt	do.	Mar. 7-1705
Henrico	97	Philoman Childres	Richard Ligon	Feb. 16-1704
do.	850	Abraham Michaux	do.	Apr. 11-1706
do.	285	Charles Evans	Lapsed Land	
do.	211	Fra: Eppes	" "	

List of Patents Signed Oct. 1706 (continued)

County	Acres	To Whom Granted	Surveyed By	Date
Warwick	132	Samuel Groves	Lapsed Land	
do.	87	Enos Mackintosh	" "	
Essex	90	Anne Gregson	" "	
do	97	do	" "	
Nansemond	60	Christopher Norfleet	Escheat Land	
do.	106	Fra: Benton	" "	
do.	214	Richard Webb	" "	
do.	106	Wm. Ward	" "	
do.	148	Nicholas Hunter & Eliz'a, his wife in behalf of themselves & Fra: Benton an infant	" "	

The List of Patents continued

County	Acres	To Whom Granted	Surveyed By	Date
Nansemond	148	John Heslett & Sarah his wife in behalf of themselves & David Rice, an infant	Escheat Land	
do.	118	John Hare	" "	
Accomack	345	John West & Charles Bailey	" "	
York	150	William Sheldon	" "	
King & Queen	200	John Baylor	" "	
Gloucester	180	Eliz'a Collier, Edw'd Collier & Sarah Collier	" "	
Henrico	522	Anthony Tribue	Richard Ligon	Feb. 24-1705/6
Prince George	2208	John Sadler, Citizen & Grocer of London & the Rev. Joseph Richardson, Clerk, husband of Elianor Richardson, Executrix of Thomas Quiny late of London, brewer	Rob't Bolling	Nov. 5-1705
Fork Mattopony River	2000	John Maddison & Henry Pigg	Harry Beverly	Mar. 23-1705/6
King & Queen	1618	Rob't Robinson	Harry Beverly	Aug. 29-1706
Fork Mattopony River	1525	Jno. Rogers, Pet'r Rogers, Edw'd Pigg, Jno. York & Tho. Gresham	do.	Mar. 26-1706
Ditto	2000	Rob't Farrish, John Pigg & John May	do.	Mar. 21-1705/6
King William	470	Ambrose Lipscomb	do. by order court	Aug. 25-1706
Prince George	225	George Pasmore & John Peterson	Robert Bolling	Apr. 22-1706
Accomack	900	Eliz'a Scarburgh widow & Anthony West	Edmund Scarburgh	May 22-1706
do.	170	do.	do.	do.
do.	550	Rob't Watson & David Watson	do.	May 5-1706

County	Acres	To Whom Granted	Surveyed By	Date
Henrico	280	Stephen Chastain	Richard Liggon	Apr. 25-1706
Isle of Wight	237	John Parnell & Wm. Jolley	Thomas Swann	Nov. 19-1705
Charles City	1324	Tho. Christian & Edm'd New Jr.	Robert Bolling	Nov. 27-1705
Prince Geo.	422	Wm. Rives	do	Jan. 19-1705/6
Henrico	290	Matt'w Ligon & Rich'd Ligon Jr.	Richard Ligon	Mar. 15-1705/6
Prince George	327	Henry Mitchell Jr.	Robert Bolling	Apr. 3-1706
Nansemond	443	John Hidgepath Jr.	Thomas Milner	Jan. 18-1705
New Kent	136	Nath'a Smith	James Minge	Oct. 26-1705
Henrico	1682	George Robertson	Lapsed Land	
King William	550	C. C. Thacker	" "	
Henrico	788	Charles Evans	Richard Ligon	Nov. 2-1705
King & Queen & Essex	3000	William Hall	Lapsed Land	
Prince George	450	Robert Bolling Jr.	" "	
King & Queen	758	John Richards	Harry Beverly	Dec. 13-1705
New Kent	361	Jeremiah Lindsey	Escheat Land	
King & Queen	300	Roger Grigory	" "	
Essex	100	Robert Richardson	" "	

A List of Patents Prepared to be Signed Oct. 1706

County	Acres	To Whom Granted	Surveyed By	Date
Charles City	288	Thomas Hardyway	Rob't Bolling Jr.	Nov. 23-1705
Prince George	5037	John Sadler of London, Grocer & the Reverend Jos. Richardson, Clerk, husband of Elianor Richardson Executrix of Tho. Quiny late of London, brewer	do.	Jan. 1705/6
New Kent	200	Henry Bows	James Minge	Oct. 6-1702
Surry, Blackwater	250	Thomas Pittman Jr.	Arthur Allen	Feb. 20-1705
Charles City	554	John Roper	Rob't Bolling Jr.	Oct. 8-1705
Surry, Blackwater	128	Thomas Barrow	Arthur Allen	Mar. 8-1705
Surry, N'side Nottoway River	446	John Barker	Thomas Swan	Dec. 7-1702
Prince George	1001	John Evans	Rob't Bolling Jr.	Jan. 28-1705/6
Surry, N'side Nottoway River	130	Abraham Evins	Thomas Swann	Dec. 7-1702
Isle of Wight, Blackwater	160	Edward Boykin	Arthur Allen	Feb. 26-1705
Surry, Blackwater	320	Thomas Blunt	do.	Mar. 7-1705
Prince George	498	Thomas Wyn	Rob't Bolling Jr.	Apr. 3-1706
Prince George, Blackwater	347	Charles Williams	do.	Feb. 18-1705/6
Nansemond	280	William Speir	Thomas Milner	Mar. 25-1706
Surry, Blackwater	200	Joseph Wall Jr.	Arthur Allen	Feb. 28-1705
Nansemond	130	William Vann	Thomas Milner	Mar. 20-1705
do.	42	William Spight	do.	Mar. 23-1705
Charles City	33	Thomas Davis	Rob't Bolling Jr.	Oct. 10-1705

County	Acres	To Whom Granted	Surveyed By	Date
Nansemond, Blackwater	350	Robert Carr	Thomas Milner	Apr. 4-1706
Prince George	333	John Poythers Sr.	Rob't Bolling Jr.	Apr. 4-1706
Essex	55½	John Parker	Charles Smith	June 10-1705
Henrico	608	Cha: Hudson & John Bradley	Rich'd Ligon	May 3-1705
Nansemond	254	John Drury	Thomas Milner	Apr. 3-1706
Prince George	429	Edw'd Richardson	Rob't Bolling Jr.	May 14-1705
King William	950	Thomas Johnson	Harry Beverly	July 23-1705
Isle of Wight, S'side Blackwater	540	Edward Harris	Arthur Allen	Feb. 26-1705
Surry, S'side Blackwater	150	Jeremiah Ellis	Arthur Allen	Mar. 8-1705
Nansemond	143	Henry Core	Thomas Milner	Apr. 4-1706
New Kent	36	George Lovell	James Minge	Oct. 20-1705
Henrico	1150	Capt. Thomas Cocke	Rich'd Ligon	Apr. 29-1704
Surry, S'side Blackwater	330	James Binam	Arthur Allen	Mar. 7-1705
King William	410	Samuel Norment	Harry Beverly	Aug. 22-1706
Nottoway River	2000	Maj'r Charles Goodrich	Thomas Swann	Nov. 30-1702
Essex	37	Henry Boughan	Harry Beverly	Apr. 2-1706
Prince George, Nottoway River	431	John Freeman	Rob't Bolling Jr.	Dec. 12-1705
Prince George	153	Thomas Parrum	do.	Jan. 25-1705/6
Prince George, S'side Nottoway	219	Robert Rives	Rob't Bolling Jr.	Apr. 2-1706
Princess Anne	51	Daniell Lenard	Sam'll Newton	Nov. 27-1705
Nansemond	467	John Small	Tho. Milner	Mar. 25-1706
Princess Anne	237	Capt. Horatio Woodhouse	Sam'll Newton	Mar. 12-1705
do.	100	Thomas Scott	do.	Oct. 23-1705
Essex	275	John Giddian	Charles Smith	Nov. 24-1705
do	149½	Col. Rich'd Covington	do.	June 14-1705
do.	816	Samuel Duchimin	do.	Oct. 26-1705
Nansemond	205	Joseph Daniell	Thomas Milner	Mar. 22-1705
do.	54	Joseph Meredeth	do.	Mar. 19-1705
Surry, S'side Blackwater	220	Tho. Halleman	Arthur Allen	Feb. 27-1705
do.	220	Wm. Rogers Jr.	do.	Mar. 9-1705
do.	170	Benj'a Harrison Esq.	do.	Mar. 8-1705
do.	200	Thomas Hunt	do.	Mar. 7-1705
Henrico	97	Philimon Childers	Richard Ligon	Feb. 16-1704
do.	850	Abraham Michaux	do.	Apr. 11-1706
do.	285	Charles Evans	Lapsed Land	
do.	311	Francis Epes	" "	
Warwick	132	Samuel Groves	" "	
do.	87	Enos Mackintosh	" "	
Essex	30	Anne Gregson	" "	
do.	97	do.	" "	
Nansemond	60	Cha: Norfleet	Escheat Land	
do.	106	Francis Benton	" "	
do.	214	Richard Webb	" "	
do.	106	Wm. Ward	" "	
do.	148	Nich'o Hunter & Eliz'a his wife in behalf of themselves & Fra: Benton an infant	" "	

County	Acres	To Whom Granted	Surveyed By	Date
Nansemond	148	John Heslett & Sarah his wife on behalf of themselves & David Rice, an infant	Escheat Land	
do.	118	John Hare	" "	
Accomack	345	John West & Cha. Baily	" "	
York	150	William Sheldon	" "	
King & Queen	200	John Baylor	" "	
Gloucester	180	Eliz'a Collier, Edw'd Collier & Sarah Collier	" "	
Henrico	522	Anthony Tribue	Rich'd Ligon	Feb. 24-1705/6
New Kent	1900	Tho. Bradley & Charles Fleming	Val. Minge	Nov. 5-1706
Prince George	2208	John Sadler, Citizen & Grocer of London & the Rev'd Jos. Richardson, Clk, husband of Elianor Richardson Executrix of Thomas Quiny late of London, brewer	Rob't Bolling Jr.	Nov. 5-1705
King & Queen	255	Daniell King	Harry Beverly	July 24-1707
Fork Mattapony	1330	Francis Shackelford	Charles Smith	Apr. 11-1705
King William	200	John Waller	Mary Herbert's patent dated Apr. 25-1707 lapsed	
Essex	1071	Charles Smith	Henry Benson's patent dated Nov. 5-1675 Lapsed	
York	100	John Northern	John Underhill	Mar. 6-1666/7
Isle of Wight, Blackwater	250	James Atkinson Jr.	Arthur Allen	Apr. 4-1707
Surry, Blackwater	1400	Tho: Jamill & Joseph Lane	do.	Mar. 21-1706
Surry	260	Nath'll Harrison	do.	Mar. 5-1706
Surry, Notoway	330	William Edwards	do.	Mar. 20-1706
Prince George	964	Nicholas Overby	Rob't Bolling Jr.	July 20-1706/7
Isle of Wight, Blackwater	190	Francis Hutchins	John Allen	Nov. 15-1707
do.	3435	Barnaby Mackquiny	Arthur Allen	Sep. 25-1706
Surry, Blackwater	1120	William Hunt	John Allen	Sep. 15-1707
Isle of Wight, Blackwater	115	Sarah Reddyhoe	Arthur Allen	Oct. 23-1706
Ditto	1700	Richard Exum	do.	Apr. 9-1707
Henrico	1029	Joseph Pleasants	Richard Ligon	Oct. 30-1706
Isle of Wight, S'side Blackwater	215	Edward Jones	John Allen	July 16-1707
Surry, Blackwater	250	William Brown	do.	Oct. 9-1707
Isle of Wight	16	Richard Reynolds	do.	Aug. 16-1707
Prince George	401	Richard Hudson	Rob't Bolling Jr.	Oct. 24-1706
Henrico	577	Charles Evans	Richard Ligon	Feb. 9-1705
Isle of Wight, S'side Nottaway	445	John Simmons	Arthur Allen	Mar. 25-1707
Isle of Wight, S'side Blackwater	200	John Teasley	John Allen	Nov. 11-1707

County	Acres	To Whom Granted	Surveyed By	Date
Surry, S'side Nottaway	400	George Wyche	John Allen	Sep. 13-1707
do.	300	Joseph John Jackman	do.	Sep. 1-1707
Surry, South West Side Nottoway	50	do	do.	Nov. 21-1707
Surry, S'side Blackwater	330	John Jones	do.	Sep. 8-1707
Do.	540	Richard Parker	do.	Sep. 12-1707
Isle of Wight,	815	Nath'll Ridley	Arthur Allen	Mar. 28-1707
S'side Blackwater do.	475	Edw'd Goodson & Mat: Rushin	do.	Apr. 10-1707
Prince George	401	William Maise	Rob't Bolling Jr.	Oct. 24-1706
Henrico	365	James Legran	Richard Ligon	Mar. 8-1705/6
Isle of Wight, S'side Nottoway	360	William Gray Jr.	Arthur Allen	Mar. 19-1706
do.	140	Thomas Hunt	John Allen	Aug. 11-1707
Isle of Wight, Blackwater	245	William Kinhin	Arthur Allen	Apr. 4-1707
Isle of Wight, Blackwater	670	Barnaby Mackquiny	Arthur Allen	?
do.	545	do.	do.	Feb. 27-1706
do.	1240	Richard Washington	do.	Apr. 8-1707
do.	300	do.	do,	Oct. 25-1706
King William	670	Edmund Jenings Esq.	Harry Beverly	Feb. 24-1706
do.	3330	do.	do.	do.
Essex	66	James Boughan	do.	May 21-1707
Isle of Wight, S'side Notaway	570	William Edwards	Arthur Allen	Mar. 21-1706
do.	480	Benj'a Chapman	do.	Oct. 23-1706
Prince George, S'side Notaway	225	Robert Lanier	do.	Mar. 28-1707
Henrico	272	George Hunt	Richard Ligon	Mar. 26-1703
Isle of Wight, Blackwater	850	Richard Washington	Arthur Allen	Apr. 11-1707
do.	350	Tho: Kirby	do.	Sep. 28-1706
do.	375	Benj'a Evans	do.	Oct. 28-1706
Princess Anne	374	Thomas Ivy	Sam'l Newton	Apr. 24-1706
King & Queen	420	John Broche	Harry Beverly	Sep. 13-1706
Charles City	128	John Hunt	Rob't Bolling Jr.	Sep. 20-1706
Prince George	422	William Rives	do.	Jan. 19-1705/6
King & Queen	1618	Robert Robinson	Harry Beverly	July 8-1706
Fork Mattapony	2000	Jno. Maddison & Henry Pigg	do.	Mar. 23-1705/6
King & Queen	640	Wm. Kilping	do.	Oct. 3-1706
Prince George	225	Geo. Pasemore & Jno. Peterson	Rob't Bolling Jr.	Aug. 2-1706
Fork Mattapony	1525	Jno. Rogers, Peter Rogers, Edward Pigg, John York & Tho. Gresham	Harry Beverly	Mar. 26-1706
Prince George	64	John Hardyman	Rob't Bolling Jr.	Sep. 24-1705/6

County	Acres	To Whom Granted	Surveyed By	Date
King & Queen in Fork Mattapony	1260	Sam'l Williams & Jno. Bannister	Harry Beverly	Sep. 19-1706
Surry	185	Wm. Thomas of Isle of Wight	Arthur Allen	Aug. 5-1706
King & Queen in fork Mattapony	740	Rice Williams & Jno. Downer	Harry Beverly	--
Essex	237	Roger Preachard	do.	Sep. 7-1706
New Kent	1433	James Taylor	Val. Minge	Apr. 5-1706
Accomack	900	Eliz'a Scarburgh & Anthony West	Edm'd Scarburgh	May 22-1706
Henrico	280	Stephen Chastain	Rich'd Ligon	Apr. 25-1706
Fork Mattapony	2000	Robert Farish, John Pigg & John May	Harry Beverly	Mar. 21-1705/6
Accomack	550	Rob't Watson & David Watson	Edm'd Scarburgh	May 1-1706
do.	170	Eliz'a Scarburgh & Anth'o West	do.	May 22-1705
Henrico	2827	Fra: Epes, Rich'd Kennon, Joseph Royall, Geo. Archer	Rich'd Ligon	Apr. 2-1690
New Kent	361	Jeremiah Lindsey	James Minge	Sep. 25-1705
Eliz'a City	200	Wm. Armistead	Wm. Lowry	Nov. 26-1706
Henrico	400	Peter Dutoy	Rich'd Ligon	Feb. 10-1706/7
do.	37	Stephen Chastain	Rob't Bolling Jr.	--
Isle of Wight, Blackwater	580	John Lawrence	Arthur Allen	Sep. 26-1706
Henrico	232	Abraham S**ll*	Rob't Bolling Jr.	--
do.	130	Henry Clay	Rich'd Ligon	Mar. 18-1705/6
do.	950	Wm. Worneck	do.	Apr. 1-1706
do.	250	Stephen Mallett	do.	Oct. 20-1706
do.	138	Stephen Chastain	do.	Feb. 11-1706/7
do.	1427	Charles Fleming	do.	Aug. 11-1706
Prince George	283	Matt'w Mays, Henry Mays	Rob't Bolling Jr.	Dec. 6-1706
King & Queen	60	Timothy Conners	Harry Beverly	July 24-1707
do.	300	Roger Gregory		
Henrico	1430	Charles Fleming	Rich'd Ligon	Nov. 15-1706
Isle of Wight, Blackwater	230	Edward Stephens	Arthur Allen	Sep. 23-1706
do.	1750	Nathan'l Harrison	do.	Mar. 18-1706
Surry, Blackwater	1670	do.	do.	Mar. 5-1706
do.	510	do.	do.	Dec. 11-1706

County	Acres	To Whom Granted	Surveyed By	Date
Surry,				
Blackwater	180	Tho. Harrison	Arthur Allen	Dec. 3-1706
do.	275	Charles Briggs	do.	Nov. 7-1706
do.	830	Wm. Edmonds	do.	Nov. 23-1706
do.	180	Tho. Harrison	do.	Dec. 3-1706
do.	440	Tho. Atkins & Peter Bagley	do.	Mar. 7-1706
do.	350	Wm. Edwards	do.	Oct. 18-1706
do.	290	Sam'l Briggs	do.	Nov. 6-1706
do.	1530	Benj'a Harrison	do.	Nov. 25-1706
do.	140	James Binam	do.	Mar. 10-1706
Isle of Wight,				
Blackwater	290	Thomas Hart	do.	Oct. 22-1706
do.	200	John Wapple	do.	Mar. 12-1706
do.	1275	Wm. Edwards	do.	Oct. 16-1706
do.	500	Robert Hodge	do.	Aug. 30-1706
do.	190	Edward Boykin	do.	Apr. 4-1707
Do.	95	John Vawhan	do.	Mar. 28-1707
Do.	260	Wm. Brown	do.	May 1-1707
do.	380	John Allen	do.	Mar. 25-1707
do.	130	John Ployman	do.	Mar. 27-1707
do.	170	Rich'd Vick	do.	May 1-1707
do.	217	Joseph Wall Jr.	do.	Nov. 7-1706
do,	6365	Henry Harrison & Philip Lodwell Esq.	do.	Dec. 2-1706
do.	200	Rich'd Drake	do.	Oct. 20-1706
do.	545	Ethelred Taylor	do.	Oct. 24-1706
do.	220	Wm. Mayo	do.	Sep. 27-1706
do.	380	Benj'a Chapman	do.	Oct. 23-1706
do.	150	George Wyech	do.	Mar. 27-1707
do.	325	Philip Rayford	do.	Sep. 24-1706
do.	230	John Denson	do.	Sep. 25-1706
do.	270	Bridgman Joynes Jr.	do.	Aug. 27-1706
do.	800	Bridgman Joynes	do.	Sep. 28-1706
do.	320	Barth'o Andross	do.	Oct. 24-1706
do.	200	Rich'd Reynolds Jr.	do.	Oct. 21-1706
do.	345	Theophilus Joynes	do.	Sep. 28-1706
do.	420	James Denson	do.	Apr. 28-1707
do.	230	Thomas Drake	do.	Sep. 27-1706
do.	430	Wm. Brown	do.	Oct. 31-1706
Fork Mattapony	431	John Shackelford	Charles Smith	Nov. 3-1705
Isle of Wight,				
Blackwater	745	Wm. Brown & Tho. Blunt	Arthur Allen	Oct. 29-1706
do.	516	Francis Clements	do.	Mar. 26-1707

1710 - 1718

A LIST OF PATENTS granted for LAND in this Colony by

The Honorable Alexander Spotswood,
His Majesty's Lieuten't Governor &
Commander in Chief of this Dominion.

Acres	County	To Whom Granted	Date
47	James City	John Wade	12-12-1710
270	York	John Addiston Rogers	do.
126	Elizabeth City	George Walker	4-28-1711
200	do.	Nicholas Curle	do.
82	James City	Henry Duke Esq.	do.
500	Gloucester	John Grymes	do.
255	King & Queen	Daniel King	do.
51	Gloucester	John Smith Esq	do.
11	York	Phillip Dumford	do.
27½	York	William Moss	do.
79	Norfolk	William Miller	do.
54	Nansemond	Joseph Meredith	do.
670	King William	Edmund Jenings Esq.	6-20-1706
20	Nansemond	John Yeates & William Edwards	4-28-1711
33	Princess Anne	John Hopkins	do.
238	do.	Edward Attwood	do.
35	do.	Henry Spratt	do.
85	do.	Henry Spratt	do.
104	do.	George Kemp	do.
103	King & Queen	John Collier	do.
53	Accomack	Littleton Robins	do.
44	Nansemond	Richard Parker	do.
217	Surry, Isle Wight	Joseph Wall Jr.	do.
200	Surry	Joseph Wall Jr.	do.
103	Norfolk	William Powell	do.
79	do.	William Powell & Robert Spring	do.
206	Nansemond	William Kelley	do.
112	do.	Ephr. Peele & Joseph Peele	do.
49	Princess Anne	Lemuel Newton	do.
46½	Gloucester	John Lewis Esq., John Smith, Jno. Washington Jr.	do.
37	Essex	Henry Boughan	do.
149½	do.	Col. Rich'd Covington	do.
60	King & Queen	Timothy Conner	do.
464	Gloucester	John Spinks	do.
76	New Kent	Rob't Bradenham	do.
155	Princess Anne	Christopher Cock	do.
202	do.	John Whitehurst	do.
702	Nansemond	Elias Ballard	do.
128	do.	John Minshew	do.
294	Princess Anne	John Molbone	do.
130	Nansemond	James Lockhart, Joseph Lockhart, Benj. Lockhart, John Lockhart	4-12-1711
100	Princess Anne	David Scott Jr.	do.
752	do.	Capt. Francis Morse	do.
402	do.	Capt. Francis Morse	do.
503	Norfolk	Thomas Herbert	do.
1190	Princess Anne	Evan Jones	4-28-1711
327	Norfolk	John Joyce, Nicholas Manning, John Taylor	do.
267	Princess Anne	John Cornex	do.

Acres	County	To Whom Granted	Date
304	Princess Anne	Edw'd Lammount	4-28-1711
250	Isle of Wight	Joshua Turner	do.
352	Norfolk	William Nicholson	do.
383	Princess Anne	William Nicholson	do.
382	Norfolk	Walter Bailey	do.
1775	Princess Anne	Lewis Conner	do.
2540	do.	John Fulcher	do.
151	Nansemond	Wm. Speight Jr.	do.
165	Norfolk	John Hodges, William Powell	do.
204	Princess Anne	Thomas Corprew	do.
170	do.	John Corprew	do.
122	Nansemond	Jno. & Benj. Goodwin	do.
207	do.	Lewis Skinner	do.
195	do.	William Fryer	do.
131	do.	Edward Barnes	do.
80	do.	Robert Hooker	do.
256	do.	Henry Goodman	do.
173	do.	Wm. Crafford	do.
170	do.	Edward Arnold	do.
374	Princess Anne	Thomas Ivy	do.
51	do.	Daniel Lenard	do.
57	Nansemond	Robert Yeates	do.
188	do.	Robert Yeates	do.
347	Princess Anne	John Fulcher	do.
49	Nansemond	Tho. Duke Jr. & John Duke	do.
180	do.	Rich'd Malpas	do.
93	Norfolk	Jonah Holliday	do.
104	Princess Anne	Thomas Heath	do.
72	do.	Jno. Carraway Jr.	do.
50	do.	Francis Moore	do.
305	Norfolk	Jno. Portlock	do.
60	Nansemond	Christop'r Norflet	do.
106	do.	Wm. Ward	do.
48	do.	John Hare	do.
148	do.	John Heslett, his wife & David Rice	do.
148	do.	Nicholas Hunter, his wife & Francis Benton	do.
106	do.	Francis Benton	do.
100	James City	Frederick Jones	do.
150	York	Wm. Sheldon	do.
300	King & Queen	Roger Gregory	do.
2208	Prince George	John Sadler & Joseph Richardson, Clk.	do.
5037	do.	Ditto	do.
470	Isle of Wight	Jacob Durden	do.
160	Norfolk	Abraham Bruce	do.
300	King William	Edmund Jenings Esq.	12-19-1711
230	Henrico	Abraham Salle	do.
244	Charles City	Silvanus Stokes Jr.	do.
120	Norfolk	Margery Jackson	do.
48	York	Francis Callohill & Giles Taverner	11-20-1711
350	Nansemond	Henry Lawrence	12-19-1711
2491	New Kent	Edward Hill	do.
31	Middlesex	John Curtis	do.
300	do.	Adam Curtis	do.
583	Elizabeth City	James Wallace	do.
153	Norfolk	Joshua Curle	do.

Acres	County	To Whom Granted	Date
135	Isle of Wight	Capt. John Davis	12-19-1711
46	Middlesex	Harry Beverley	do.
393	New Kent	Silvanus Walker	do.
320	King & Queen	Guy Smith, Clk.	do.
94	Charles City	Samuel Moody	do.
85	do.	John Roach Jr.	do.
970	King William	Thomas Johnson	do.
100	do.	Charles Houchins	do.
256	do.	John Sutton	do.
150	Gloucester	William Smith	do.
250	Isle of Wight	Dr. Sam'l Brown	do.
237	Essex	Roger Preachard	do.
100	Isle of Wight	Thomas Barrow	do.
101	Princess Anne	Rich'd Williams	do.
347	Prince George	Charles Williams	do.
422	do.	Wm. Rives	do.
153	do.	Tho. Parrum	do.
237	Princess Anne	Horatio Woodhouse	do.
92	Isle of Wight	John Howell	do.
214	Nansemond	Richard Webb	do.
220	Essex	Law. Taliaferro	do.
74	Eliz. City	Wm. Hachell	do.
100	York	Jno. Northern	do.
300	Princess Anne	George Pool	do.
204	do.	Rich'd Whitehurst	do.
400	Gloucester	Anne & Mary Sterling	do.
140	Surry	Maj. Wm. Hunt	do.
190	do.	do.	do.
440	do.	Tho. Atkins & Peter Bagley	do.
128	do.	Thomas Barrow	do.
2143	King & Queen	Larkin Chew	4-26-1712
400	On the branches Mattapony River	Larkin Chew, Rich'd Buckner, Joseph Chew, John Sutton	do.
400	do.	do.	do.
531	New Kent	Edmund Jenings Esq.	do.
190	Isle of Wight	Fra. Hutchings	12-19-1711
65	Nansemond	Thomas Woodley	4-26-1712
229	do.	Thomas Goffe	do.
220	King & Queen	Larkin Chew	do.
230	do.	Justephenia & Sawyer Bennet	do.
400	Essex	Augustine Smith	do.
920	do.	William Smith	do.
367	New Kent	Stephen Sunter	do.
540	Surry	James Minge	do.
139	King William	Matthew Harris	do.
122	do.	John Higgason	do.
145	do.	George Slaughter	do.
39	do.	William Maybank	do.
83	do.	do.	do.
100	do.	Michael Walldrup	do.
183	do.	Wm. Porteus	do.
390	do.	George Shilling	do.
25	do.	John Tremere	do.
98	do.	Wm. Hendrick	do.
196	do.	Charles Oakes	do.
100	Prince George	Edw'd Goodriche	do.

Acres	County	To Whom Granted	Date
400	King William	John Waller & John Munroe	12-19-1711
438	Essex	Lawrence Smith	11- 5-1712
1071	do.	Dorothy Smith & Charles Taliaferro	do.
4020	do.	Larkin Chew	5- 2-1713
274	do.	Robert Jones	do.
315	King William	Thomas Johnson	5-13-1713
134	Elizabeth City	Joshua Curle	5- 2-1713
50	Nansemond	Elianor Roberts & John Hodges	do.
38	York	Francis Tyler	do.
315	Princess Anne	Thomas Walk	do.
187	do.	Lemuel Newton	do.
322	New Kent	Alice Field	do.
900	Accomack	Elianor Scarburgh & Anthony West	do.
170	do.	do.	do.
288	Charles City	Tho. Hardyway	do.
102	Henrico	Tarlton Woodson	do.
2300	Accomack	Arthur Upshur	do.
380	Isle of Wight	Benja. Chapman	do.
200	Henrico	Charles Evans	do.
90	King William	Orlando Jones	do.
128	Charles City	John Hunt	do.
400	Nansemond	Andrew Woodley & Thomas Woodley	do.
153	Charles City	Jeffrey Munford	do.
631	James City	Phillip Ludwell Esq.	do.
184	Norfolk	John Williams	do.
51	do,	Isaac Barrington	do.
48½	York	Henry Hayward	do.
200	Prince George	William Stainback	do.
203	Princess Anne	Jno. May	do.
180	Norfolk	Jno. Smyth	do.
90	do.	Tho. & James Simmons	do.
36	Princess Anne	George Mash	do.
18	Norfolk	Robert Spring	do.
254	Princess Anne	Wm. Brook	do.
94	do.	Tho. Moor	do.
17	Norfolk	Henry Horstead	do.
170	Isle of Wight	Richard Vick	4-26-1711
185	do.	John Pope	5- 2-1713
1020	do.	Joseph Smith	do.
400	Henrico	Wm. Sheapard & Rich'd Baker	do.
149	Essex	Tho. Peatross	do.
76	do.	Tho. Pettros	do.
79	do.	Wm. Price	do.
25	do.	do.	do.
627	do.	John Boughan & Susanna his wife	do.
100	Surry	Wm. Rookins	do.
139	Nansemond	James Weyatt	do.
300	Eliz. City	John Parsons Jr.	do.
124	do.	Charles Cellie	do.
309	Princess Anne	Thomas Scott	do.
2000	King William	Thomas Jones	8-12-1713
200	New Kent	John Meux	do.
400	Norfolk	Thomas Jolliff	do.
3000	King William	Mongo Ingles	9-23-1713
385	Middlesex	Wm. Stanard & C. C. Thacker	11-13-1713
144	Warwick	John Boucher	do.

Acres	County	To Whom Granted		Date
1663	King William	Nathan'l West		11-13-1713
296	do.	Tho. Fox		do.
200	do.	John Waller		do.
18	King & Queen	Wm. Bird		do.
175	do.	David Pritchett		do,
800	do.	Jno. Didlack		do.
3330	King William	Edmund Jenings Esq.	consideration recommended in order of Council 20th June 1706	
531	New Kent	Thomas Lankford & John Lewis		do.
1738	do.	Nathan'l West		do.
167	James City	Simon Jeffreys		do.
340	Surry	Tho. Waler		do.
1029	Henrico	Joseph Pleasants		do.
1385	do.	John Pleasants		do.
2644	King & Queen and Essex	Robert Beverley		do.
180	Isle of Wight	James Mercer		do.
100	do.	Fra. Cox		do.
170	do.	Benja. Reeks		do.
130	do.	John Ployman		do.
200	Eliz. City	Wm. Armistead		do.
50	Isle of Wight	Edward Stephens		do.
100	do.	Phillip Rayford		do.
130	do.	Rich'd Winkles		do.
75	do.	Phillip Pearse		do.
100	Surry	Fra. Stead		do.
100	Isle of Wight	Wm. Evans		do.
200	do.	Wm. Arrington		do.
65	Surry	Robert Warrin		do.
125	Isle of Wight	Fra. Mayberry		do.
200	do.	Rich'd Rennalls Jr.		do.
130	do.	Sam'l Cornwell		do.
120	Surry	Rob't Jones		do.
5½	Charles City	Jno. Stokes		do.
66	Essex	James Boughan		do.
250	Isle of Wight	Tho. Drake		do.
190	do.	Edw'd Boykin		do.
91	Nansemond	Jno. Cotton		do.
400	Surry	George Wyche		do.
250	Isle of Wight	James Atkinson		do.
9	Nansemond	John Cotton		do.
185	Isle of Wight	Cha. Jones		do.
400	New Kent	Wm. Harris		do.
100	Isle of Wight	Rich'd Blow		do.
220	do.	Wm. Mayo		do.
270	do.	Bridgman Joynes Jr.		do.
180	Surry	Tho. Harrison		do.
285	Isle of Wight	Rich'd Drake		do.
250	Surry	Wm. Raney Jr.		do.
230	Isle of Wight	Edw'd Stephens		do.
185	Surry	William Thomas		do.
517	Essex	Cath. & Elianor Proverb and Jno. Pickles		do.

Acres	County	To Whom Granted	Date
169	Essex	Tho. Merriwether	11-13-1713
149	do.	Tho. Jewell	do.
200	Isle of Wight	Law: Hunt	do.
420	do.	Jno. Drew	do.
195	do.	Henry Pope	do.
150	do.	Wm. Rose	do.
100	do,	George Smith	do.
150	do.	George Wyech	do.
164	James City	Geo. Freeman Jr.	do.
230	Isle of Wight	John Denson	do.
200	do.	Rich'd Drake	do.
350	do.	Tho. Kirby	do.
400	do.	Richard Williams	do.
275	do.	Wm. Faircloth	do.
170	do.	John Rasberry	do.
200	do.	Henry Pope	do.
225	do.	Rob't Lainer	do.
322	Nansemond	Charles Durham	do.
700	Surry	James Stanton	do.
340	Isle of Wight	John Barnes	do.
370	do.	Wm. Hickman	do.
330	Surry	John Jones	do.
500	Isle of Wight	Robert Hodge	do.
315	do.	John Hawthorn	do.
270	do.	Arnold Pew	do.
113	do.	Mr. Rich'd Renolds	do.
250	Surry	Henry Jones	do.
540	Isle of Wight	Edw'd Harris	do.
266	Nansemond	Wm. Sumner	do.
418	Surry	Wm. Rookins	do.
200	Isle of Wight	John Teasley	do.
240	do.	Capt. Jno. Allen	do.
345	do.	Theophilus Joyner	do.
350	do.	Martin Dawson	do.
158	Nansemond	John Cotton	do.
180	Surry	Tho. Harnison	do.
123	Nansemond	John Page	do.
114	do.	Edm'd Godwin	do.
325	Isle of Wight	Phillip Rayford	do.
200	Nansemond	James Howard	do.
375	Isle of Wight	Benja. Evans	do.
230	do.	Tho. Drake	do.
830	Surry	Wm. Edmunds	do.
50	James City	Joseph Wade	do.
136	Warwick	Nath'l Hoggard	do.
300	Gloucester	Thomas Cooke	do.
156	do.	do.	do.
850	Henrico	Abra. Michaux	1-27-1713
340	Isle of Wight	Abra. Brawler	11-13-1713
100	Surry	Nath'l Phillips	do.
174½	York	Wm. Row	4-30-1714
100	Henrico	John Calvert	do.
261	Prince George	James Binford	6-16-1714
100	York	Eliza. Chermeson	do.
304	New Kent	Rob't Netherlande & John Hill	do.
106	Surry	Wm. Rookins	do.

Acres	County	To Whom Granted	Date
43	Gloucester	Rich'd Parrett	6-16-1714
115	Isle of Wight	Sarah Reddyhoe	do.
140	Nansemond	John Powell	do.
90	King William	David Anderson	do.
168	James City	David Bray	do.
50	Nansemond	John Lee	do.
400	Henrico	David Pattison	do.
140	Isle of Wight	Tho. Hunt	do.
100	King William	Cole Diggs, Gent.	do.
289	New Kent	Sam'l Reynalds	do.
68	Nansemond	Wm. Sumner	do.
138	Charles City	John Cross	do.
670	Isle of Wight	Barneby Mackquiney	do.
200	do.	Thos. Jarrell	do.
500	Henrico	Henry Gill	do.
190	Isle of Wight	Nicholas Cock & George Ezell	do.
1750	do.	Nathan'l Harrison Esq.	do.
102	James City	James Thomson Sr.	do.
200	King William	Nich'o Gillington	do.
100	Nansemond	James Garner	do.
500	Henrico	William Lead	do.
18	Middlesex	Jno. Southern	do.
608	Henrico	Charles Hudson & John Bradley	do.
1427	do.	Cha. Fleming	do.
69	Nansemond	John Small	do.
400	Henrico	Peter Dutoy	do.
302	Nansemond	Richard Parker	do.
341	Henrico	John Burton	do.
350	Surry	Thomas Wiggins	do.
220	do.	Tho. Halleman	do.
100	Nansemond	Tho. Price	do.
304	James City	David Davison	do.
380	New Kent	Wm. Harris	do.
200	do.	James Smith	do.
80	Isle of Wight	Randoll Revill	do.
84	King William	William Winston	do.
54	Nansemond	Stephen Durden	do.
400	King William	Will Fleming	do.
90	Accomack	Wm. Nathan'l Bell	do.
100	New Kent	Phillip Webber	do.
200	do.	Henry Bowe	do.
36	do.	Geo. Lovell	do.
100	Surry	John Barker	do.
112	Nansemond	Adam Harrold	do.
64	do.	Henry Core	do.
245	do.	Joseph Meredith	do.
382	Henrico	James Christian	do.
320	King William	John Kembrow Jr.	do.
150	Eliz. City	Mark Johnson	do.
150	New Kent	Thomas Kersey	do.
62	Nansemond	Abra. Reddick	do.
175	do.	Joseph Thomas	do.
200	King William	Elias Downs	do.
300	do.	Jno. Kembrow Jr.	do.
595	S'side Main Branch Mattapony River	Larkin Chew	do.
171	Nansemond	John Smith	do.
150	King William	Wm. Winston	do.

Acres	County	To Whom Granted	Date
85	King William	Wm. Ford	6-16-1714
220	Surry	Wm. Rogers Jr.	do.
138	Henrico	Steph. Chastiene	do.
130	On the S'side of Blackwater & on Eastward Side of Cedar Swamp	Mary Murfrey	do.
230	Surry	John Simons	do.
445	Isle of Wight	Sam'l Harwood Jr.	do.
540	do.	William Edwards	do.
81	Nansemond	Wm. Redding	do.
400	King William	James Terry	do.
90	Nansemond	Sam'l Smith	do.
200	King William	Tho. Thomason	do.
200	do,	John Lipscomb	do.
221	Prince George	John Scott	do.
95	Surry	Joseph Seward	do.
400	James City	Robert Lide	do.
200	King William	John Crenshaw	do.
171	Nansemond	Jacob Darden	do.
320	Isle of Wight	Bartho. Andros	do.
242	King William	Thos. Preswood	do.
245	Isle of Wight	Wm. Kinlin	do.
120	do.	Wm. Edwards	do.
300	King William	Wm. Terrell	do.
490	Isle of Wight	Barneby Mackquiny	do.
278	Charles City	Rich'd Flewellen (? LLewellen)	do.
229	Henrico	Wm. Clarke Sr.	do.
300	James City	Simon Jeffreys	do.
400	Henrico	Thos. Christian	do.
427	New Kent	John Meeks	do.
240	Isle of Wight	Fra. Bressy	do.
120	do.	Isabel Havield	do.
160	do.	Edw'd Boykin	do.
100	do,	Thomas Barrow	do.
110	do.	Adam Heith Jr.	do.
140	Surry	James Binam	do.
290	do.	Sam'l Briggs	do.
225	do.	Tho. Andrews Jr.	do.
732	Henrico	Cha. Fleming	do.
370	Surry	Tho. Eldridge	do
510	do.	Nathan'l Harrison Esq.	do.
815	Isle of Wight	Capt. Nath'l Ridley	do.
260	Surry	Geo. Williams	do.
100	Isle of Wight	Henry Clarke	do.
500	King William	Jno. Sutton	do.
233	Nansemond	Wm. Bird	do.
250	Isle of Wight	Col. Tho. Godwin	do.
400	King William	Wm. Grills	do.
54	Princess Anne	Wm. Keaton	do.
48	do.	Lem'l Newton	do.
330	Surry	James Binam	do.
120	do.	Cha. Savidge	do.
104	Essex	John Long	do.
280	Henrico	Steph. Chasteane	do.
123	Charles City	Robert Loyde	do.
250	Surry	Tho. Pitman Jr.	do.

Acres	County	To Whom Granted	Date
105	Prince George	Tho. Anderson	6-16-1714
541	Henrico	Jno. Pleasants	do.
230	Isle of Wight	Charles Jones	do.
443	Nansemond	John Hedgpath Jr.	do.
500	King William	Tho. Terry	do.
758	King & Queen	John Richards	do.
60	James City	Jno. Hitchcock	do.
816	Essex	Sam'l Duchimin	do.
356	James City	Tho. Young	do.
987	New Kent	Christop'r Hudson	do.
100	Surry	Wm. Glover	do.
165	do.	Rob't Andros	do.
94	do.	Wm. Rookins	do.
577	Henrico	Charles Evans	do.
1525	Fork Mattapony	Jno. Rogers, Peter Rogers, Edwd. Pigg, John York, Tho. Gresham.	"
66	James City	Simon Jeffreys	do.
400	Henrico	Wm. Grills	do.
460	Nansemond	Andrew Ross	do.
670	Henrico	Cha. Fleming	do.
215	Isle of Wight	Edwd. Jones	do.
430	do.	Robt. Ricks	do.
280	Surry	Walter Lashley	do.
6365	Surry & Isle Wight	Henry Harrison & Phillip Ludwell Esq.	
1278	Henrico	Jno. Woodson & Charles Fleming	do.
467	Nansemond	John Small	do.
111	do.	Lewis Daughtrey	do.
190	Henrico	Antho. Rappeane	do.
553	Essex	Rich'd Covington, James Boughan, Tho. Goldman & Edw'd Goldman	do.
230	Princess Anne	Rich'd Corbett	do.
2000	King William & in fork Mattapony	John Madison & Dan'l Coleman	do.
545	Isle of Wight	Ethelred Taylor	do.
195	James City	Tho. Goldsby	do.
372	do.	Tho. Young	do.
350	Princess Anne	Wm. Robinson	do.
550	Surry	Huishea Guillam	do.
275	do.	Cha. Briggs	do.
1085	Henrico	Amos Lead	do.
1400	Isle of Wight	Tho. Jarnell Jr. & Joseph Lane	do.
100	York	Jonathan Drewitt	do.
450	Nansemond	Wm. Macclanee	do.
225	Isle of Wight	Wm. Hunter	do.
102	Essex	Rob't Richardson	do.
47	Gloucester	Tho. Read	do.
1275	Isle of Wight	Wm. Edwards	do.
4185	New Kent	Nich'o Merriwether, Wm. Merriwether & David Merriwether	do.
350	Surry	Henry Harrison	do.
440	Isle of Wight	Wm. Edwards	do.
1720	Surry	Nath'l Harrison Esq.	do.
3000	Henrico	Rich'd Grills	do.
363	New Kent	Tho. Barbar	do.
423	Charles City	Jno. Nickells	do.
240	James City	Nich'o Valentine	do.
145	Princess Anne	Grace Sherwood	do.

Acres	County	To Whom Granted	Date
360	Isle of Wight	Wm. Gray Jr.	6-16-1714
22	Norfolk	Jonas Holliday	do.
125	Isle of Wight	Jno. Kelly	do.
140	Nansemond	Tho. Daughtrey	do.
50	Accomack	Jonath. West	do.
170	Surry	Jno. Jones	do.
101	Princess Anne	Jno. Edmons	do.
1808	New Kent	Edwd. Garland	do.
380	Isle of Wight	Sam'l Harwood Jr.	do.
260	do.	Wm. Brown	do.
230	do.	Edw'd Goodrich	do.
92	Princess Anne	John May	do.
570	Isle of Wight	Wm. Edwards	do.
400	do.	Wm. West	do.
516	Surry	Fra: Clements	do.
104	Nansemond	Jno. Hare	do.
200	do.	Bryant Oquin	do.
304	do.	Rich'd Parker	do.
2730	Accomack	Matilda West	do.
29	Norfolk	Wm. Barrington	do.
200	Nansemond	Sam'l Parker	do.
230	New Kent	Edw'd Harris	do.
369	Essex	Tho. Short	do.
200	do.	Dan'll Noell	do.
53	Princess Anne	Patrick Flanagin	do.
211	Norfolk	Geo. Newton	do.
54	do.	James Wilson	do.
819	do.	Solomon White	do.
51	Princess Anne	John Jones	do.
440	Henrico	Wm. Cox	do.
28	Princess Anne	Jno. Oliver	do.
448	Henrico	Tho. Harrod	do.
230	James City	Jno. Woodard	do.
200	Isle of Wight	Mathew Marks	do.
878	Nansemond	Tho. Godwin	do.
328	Eliza. City	Tho. Allen	do.
150	Henrico	Jno. Perkinson	do.
930	Surry	Phillip Ludwell Esq.	do.
69	Warwick	Margery Whitacker	do.
277	King & Queen	John Guthrie	do.
150	Surry	Jeremiah Ellis	do.
132	Warwick	Sam'l Groves	do.
240	Isle of Wight	Walter Bayley	do.
554	Charles City	John Roper	do.
415	Isle of Wight	Henry Briggs	do.
200	Surry	Tho. Hunt	do.
270	Isle of Wight	Wm. Crumpler	do.
1700	do.	Wm. Scott Jr.	do.
475	do.	Edw'd Goodson & Matth. Rushin	do.
180	do.	Tho. Newsome	do.
280	Surry	William Jones	do.
58	Eliza. City	Jno. Hayward	11-4-1714
219	Prince George	Rob't Rives	12-16-1714
401	do.	Rich'd Hudson	do.
401	do.	Wm. Maise	do.
217	do.	Jno. Nickolls	do.

Acres	County	To Whom Granted	Date
196	Prince George	Tho. Burge	12-16-1714
142	do.	Frances Wynne	do.
300	Surry	Jno. Freeman	do.
320	do.	Tho. Blunt	do.
270	do.	Jno. Nicholls	do.
100	do.	James Macklemore	do.
150	do.	Geo. Pasmore	do.
220	Isle of Wight	Nicho. Williams	do.
350	do.	Francis Bressy	do.
1240	do.	Rich'd Washington	do.
545	do.	Barnaby Mackquinny	do.
800	do.	Bridgman Joyner	do.
237	do.	Jno. Parnell & Mary Jolly	do.
850	do.	Rich'd Washington	do.
300	do.	do.	do.
580	do.	Jno. Lawrence	do.
710	do.	Tho. Blunt	do.
150	do.	Joseph Lane	do.
143	Nansemond	Henry Core	do.
130	do.	Wm. Vaun	do.
369	do.	Joseph Ballard	do.
205	do.	Joseph Daniell	do.
378	do.	James Copeland	do.
240	do.	Tho. Howard	do.
284	do.	Tho, Page	do.
216	do.	John Coles	do.
132	do.	Tho. Lawrence	do.
38	Norfolk	John Sikes	do.
52	do.	Sam'l Crockmur	do.
182	do.	John Hunt	do.
550	do.	Wm. Godfrey	do.
153	do.	Geo. Moseley	do.
145	do.	Wm. Wallace	do.
270	Princess Anne	Jno. Corprew	do.
97	do.	Edw'd Wallace	do.
90	do.	Wm. Atwood	do.
53	do.	Jno. Ward	do.
505	do.	Jacobs Biggs	do.
103	do.	John Moseley	do.
193	do.	James Wishard	do.
159	do.	Walter Jones	do.
500	Henrico	John Ellis	do.
292	do.	Gilly Gromorin	do.
500	do.	do.	do.
174	Charles City	Joseph Bradley	do.
33	do.	Tho. Davis	do.
1320	do.	Tho. Christian	do.
197	New Kent	John Dod	do.
800	do.	Tho. Standley Sr., James Standley Tho. Standley Jr.	do.
4843	do.	George Alves	do.
308	do.	Major Smith	do.
308	do.	Will. Smith	do.
400	Accomack	Jno. Bonwell	do.
1260	King & Queen	Sam'l Williams & John Bannister	do.

Acres	County	To Whom Granted	Date
740	King & Queen	Rice Williams & John Downer	12-16-1714
100	do.	William Lea	do.
95	Warwick	Henry Hayward	do.
300	Gloucester	Mr. John Stubbs	do.
50	Essex	Nath. Fogg	do.
542	do.	James Boughan	do.
100	do.	Jno. Forgeson (Ferguson)	do.
388	King William	Frances Miles	do.
470	do.	Rich'd, Ambrose, Wm., John, Mary & Benj'a Lipscom	do.
670	Henrico	Ebenezer Adams	Dec. 23-1714
1494	do.	Rob't Woodson Jr.	do.
500	do.	Tho. Mins	do.
2497	do.	Rich'd Cock Jr.	do.
300	do.	John Farlar Jr.	do.
125	do.	Jno. Stephens	do.
2000	On Nottoaway Riv.	Francis Lightfoot	do.
15	York	John Drewry	do.
485	Nansemond	Nathan Newby	do.
20	Gloucester	Chr. Dickens	do.
149	do.	Wm..Hall	do.
?	York	Giles Taverner	do.
130	Gloucester	Richard Longest	do.
254	Nansemond	John Drewry	do.
640	King & Queen	Wm. Kilpin	do.
16	Warwick	John Read	do.
56	Essex	John Parker	do.
1024	Princess Anne	Jno. Richardson	do.
170	James City	Rob't Goodrich	do.
1001	Prince George	John Evans	do.
1034	James City	John Bush	do.
429	Prince George	John Eaton	do.
3435	Isle of Wight	Barnaby Mackquinny	do.
420	do.	Tho. Blunt	do.
480	do.	Benj'a Chapman	do.
325	do.	Wm. Brown	do.
430	do.	do.	do.
295	do.	Tho. Hart	do.
260	do.	James Jones	do.
400	King William	Jno. Buckner & Rob't Bullard	do.
2000	Fork Mattapony	Rob't Farish, Jno. Pigg, Jno. May	do.
1330	do.	Larkin Chew	do.
355	Charles City	Nich'o Cox	do.
275	King William	Wm. Duglass	do.
200	do.	Tho. Thomason	do.
1615	do.	Tho. West	do.
311	do.	Tho. Davenport	do.
112	New Kent	Nathan'l Smith	do.
178	do.	Steph. Moon	do.
430	do.	Rice Hugh	do.
170	do.	Roger Smith	do.
426	do.	Jno. Kembrow	do.
90	James City	Nich'o Moyser	do.
106	King William	Ralph Pea	do.
150	do.	Jno. Kembrow Jr.	do.
42	King & Queen	John Durham	do.

Acres	County	To Whom Granted	Date
410	King William	Sam'l Norwent (Norment)?	Dec. 23-1714
133	Henrico	Isaac Lafeit	do.
200	Surry	Tho. Pitman Jr.	do.
400	James City	Kath. Barrett	do.
180	Surry	Tho. Harrison	do.
525	Isle of Wight	Phil. Rayford	do.
250	Surry	Wm. Brown	do.
105	Nansemond	Jno. Yeates	do.
579	Accomack	Fra. Eyers	do.
543	New Kent	Paul Sears	do.
361	do.	Jer: Lindsey	do.
339	Princess Anne	Wm. Allegood	do.
324	Prince George	Jno. Gillum	do.
964	do.	Nich'o Overby	do.
620	Isle of Wight	Huishea Guillum	do.
1388	Henrico	Maj. Jno. Bolling	do.
300	Surry	William Lucas	do.
½	Eliz. City	James Burtell - (For his industry in gaining it out of the river)	Feb. 23-1714
39	Norfolk	John Conner, Joseph Curleing, Anth'o Curleing, Wm. Taylor	Aug. 16-1715
13	James City	Wm. Marable	do.
1596	Henrico	John Woodson	do.
348	do.	do.	do.
258	do.	Jno. Pleasants	do.
892	do.	Jno. Woodson	do.
1309	do.	Jno. Pleasants	do.
372	Fork Mattapony	Henry Shackelford	do.
950	Henrico	Wm. Womack	do.
350	do.	Tho. Bayley	do.
81	Prince George	Benja. Evins	do.
1343	New Kent	Edwd. Garland	do.
103	Charles City	Thos. Booth	do.
37	Essex	Harry Beverley	do.
130	King & Queen	John Wills	do.
135	Isle of Wight	Charles Parker	do.
200	Nansemond	Humph. Griffin	do.
200	Isle of Wight	Sam'l Brown	do.
400	Henrico	Tho. Watkins	do.
137	Cha. City	Benja. Evans	do.
318	Henrico	Bartho. Stavall (?)	do.
100	King William	Timo. Chandler	do.
400	Henrico	Charles Christian	do.
1433	New Kent	James Taylor	do.
540	Surry	Rich'd Parker	do.
167	Henrico	Rich'd Cox	do.
285	Charles City	Rich'd Wyatt	do.
500	Henrico	Arthur Moseley	do.
96	Norfolk	Edwd. Creckmour	do.
1900	New Kent	Charles Fleming	do.
376	Essex	Wm. Major	do.
179	do.	Rich'd Buckner	do.
280	James City	Martin Sorrell	do.
200	Norfolk	Wm. Row	do.
63	Princess Anne	Jno. Watkins	do.
222	do.	Cason Moore	do.
1330	King & Queen	John Baylor	do.

Acres	County	To Whom Granted	Date
400	**James City**	Henry Gilbert	Aug. 16-1715
531	**New Kent**	Jno. Joyner	Oct. 17-1715
500	**King William**	Michael Mixen	Aug. 16-1715
141	do.	Rob't Baylor	Nov. 1-1715
833 sq. ft.	Princess Anne Port	John Holloway gained out of Hope Creek	Nov. 8-1715
28	Charles City	Nath'l Harrison Esq.	Dec. 8-1715
180	Henrico	John Martin Part of the French refugees land	Mar. 23-1715
444	do,	John Martin	do.
133	do.	Abraham Salle	do.
155	do.	Jno. Whitloe	do.
400	do.	Wm. Whitloe Jr.	do.
550	do.	Joseph Pleasants	Aug. 16-1715
615	Isle of Wight	Joseph Holt	Apr. 30-1716
300	do.	do.	do.
200	King & Queen	Michael Guings (? Guinney) & John Sutton	May 2-1716
500	Henrico	Robert Hancock	Mar. 23-1715
452	King & Queen	Isaac Hill	do.
170	South Side Meherin River	Arthur Davis	do.
100	Isle of Wight	Wm. Kinchin	do.
85	do.	Henry Pope	do.
100	do.	Hugh Mathews	do.
150	do.	Joseph Turner	do.
85	do.	Tho. Smith	do.
50	do.	Randall Revell	do.
100	do.	Hugh Lee	do.
110	do.	Rich'd Blow	do.
150	do.	Jno. Bailey	do.
100	do.	John Vick	do.
150	do.	Tho. Joyner	do.
150	do.	Tho. Taylor	do.
65	do.	John Watts	do.
100	Isle of Wight	Wm. Wilkason	do.
225	do.	Jno. Joyner	do.
100	Essex	Francis Thornton	do.
65	Isle of Wight	Tho. Deloach	do.
80	do.	Jno. Rachell	do.
80	Surry	Jno. Mason	do.
200	do.	Joseph Wall	do.
100	do.	Geo. Booth	do.
100	do.	John Groves	do.
130	do.	John Moor	do.
200	do.	Marmaduke Brown	do.
370	do.	Tho. Jones	do.
100	do.	Christop'r Atkinson	do.
100	do.	do.	do.
100	do.	Wm. Rose Jr.	do.
95	do.	John Barlow	do.
175	Surry & Isle Wight	Arth. Kavenaugh	do.
100	Surry	Tho. Wilkason	do.
215	do.	Michael Maloon	do.
180	do.	Tho. Poythres	do.
100	do.	Cha. Gillum	do.

Acres	County	To Whom Granted		Date
61	Henrico	Peter Deitoy	part of French refugees land	Mar. 23-1715
111	do.	Peter Chastaine		do.
90	do,	Jno. Chastaine		do.
88	do.	Abra: Soblet		do.
82	Isle of Wight	Wm. Cain		do.
235	do.	Jno. Lear		do.
100	do.	Wm. Scott Jr.		do.
180	do.	Rob't Scott		do.
195	do.	Andrew Griffin		do.
90	do.	Tho. Jarrell		do.
120	do.	Tho. Carter		do.
118	do.	James Joyner		do.
80	Surry	John Rayburn		do.
100	Isle of Wight	Wm. Brown		do.
70	do.	Tho. Jarrell		do.
330	do.	Wm. Edwards		do.
350	Surry	do.		do.
90	Isle of Wight	Jno. Edwards		do.
145	do.	Wm. Ondelant		do.
145	do.	Edw'd Boykin		do.
145	do.	Abra: Stephenson		do.
100	do.	James Barnes		do.
130	do.	Wm. Brown		do.
80	Surry	James Kearny		do.
230	do.	Chichester Sturdivant		do.
100	do.	Rob't Huiment (?)		do.
100	do.	Wm. Clary		do.
200	do.	Jno. Treeman Jr.		do.
100	do.	Rob't Smith		do.
75	do.	Jno. Cotton		do.
130	do.	Nich'o Cook		do.
145	do.	Tho. Horton		do.
125	do.	Tho. Thrower		do.
140	do.	Jno. Jackson		do.
100	King William	Wm. Terrell		do.
43	Norfolk	Tho. Seikes		do.
19	do.	Wm. Taylor		do.
90	Isle of Wight	Wm. Pope		do.
390	Surry	Tho. Cook		do.
92	do.	Wm. More		do.
200	Surry & Isle Wight	Hugh Golitely		do.
100	Surry	Nich'o Patridge		do.
150	do.	James Beauford		do.
295	do.	Wm. Williams		do.
290	Isle of Wight	James Landy		do.
100	Surry	Jno. Ivy		do.
250	do.	Sam'l Clark		do.
200	Isle of Wight	Jno. Peterson		do.
250	do.	Wm. Batts		do.
150	Surry	Jarvis Winfield		do.
100	Isle of Wight	Jno. Poythres		do.
621	Essex	Jno. Sanders		do.
320	Surry	George Hamilton		do.
320	Surry	do.		do.
140	do.	do.		do.

Acres	County	To Whom Granted	Date
1250	S'side of a branch Mattapony River	Harry Beverley	Mar. 23-1715
57	Henrico	Abra: Salle - Part of French refugees land	do.
55	do.	do	do.
186	do.	Jacob Amonet	do.
221	do.	Matth. Cage	do.
133	do.	Steph. Ronno	do.
90	do.	Peter Soblet Jr.	do.
75	do.	Maryan Mallet	do.
200	do.	Jno. Lavillian	do.
133	do.	Jno. Jones	do.
85	do.	Abra: Remey	do.
230	do.	Abra: Mishuex	do.
107	do.	Antho. Mattoone	do.
163	do.	Antho. Tribue	do.
128	do.	Antho. Gevodan	do.
296	do.	Dan'l Foure	do.
133	do.	Jacob Florenoy	do.
85	do.	Abra: Remy	do.
88	do.	Peter David	do.
119	do.	James Bilband	do.
290	Gloucester	Rich'd Timberlake	do.
450	Accomack	Charles Bailey & Jno. Sparrow	do.
50	Isle of Wight	Josiah Jno. Holliman	Apr. 30-1716
317	Essex	Wm. Robinson, Nicho. Smith & John Birket	Apr. 25-1716
920	do.	Leonard Tarent	May 28-1716
3420	King & Queen	Rob't Beverley	Oct. 20-1716
76	New Kent	Charles Winfree	do.
633	do.	Nath'l West	do.
3229	Essex	Wm. Robertson	Oct. 1716
100	Surry	Charles Sledge	Aug. 14-1716
150	do.	do.	do.
100	Isle of Wight	Nehemiah Joyner	do.
75	Henrico	Joseph Callio - Part of French refugees land	Oct. 31-1716
168	do.	John Fouville	do.
66	do.	Lewis Morril	do.
52	do.	Michael Champee	do.
92	do.	John Martin	do.
59	do.	Francis Lorange	do.
33	do.	Gideon Chamboone	do.
117	do.	Moses Liveran	do.
44	do.	Isaac Parentan	do.
50	do.	Claude Gory	do.
125	do.	Steph. Mallet	do.
275	do.	John Soleager	do.
88	do.	Peter Sabotte	do.
46	do.	Francis Dupee	do.
105	do.	Isaac Parentan	do.
139	do.	Peter Morriset	do.
12	do.	Steph. Chastaine	do.
170	do.	John Forcuran	do.
43	do.	James Bilband	do.
93	do.	Steph. Buckard	do.
133	do.	Nicho. Soullie	do.

Acres	County	To Whom Granted	Date
53	Henrico	John Jones	Oct. 31-1716
107	do.	Peter Foure	do.
40	do.	John Farcee	do.
133	do.	Charles Perault	do.
88	do.	Jacob Amonet	do.
122	do.	Antho. Rapine	do.
68	do.	Isaac Lafeavour	do.
76	do.	John Painteur	do.
34	do.	Jacob Capoon	do.
58	do.	Antho. Matoone	do.
95	do.	Steph. Chastain	do.
319	do.	Tho. Hardin	do.
464	King & Queen	Henry Raynes, Wm. Howard & John Sutton	do.
100	Prince George	John Leadbiter	do.
92	Norfolk	Sam'l Boush	do.
1129	do.	Wm. Crafford	do.
97	Henrico	Philemon Childers Jr.	do.
400	Surry	Tho. Avent	do.
400	New Kent	Tho. Sharp, Clk.	do.
400	do.	do.	do.
400	do.	do.	do.
142	Nansemond	Tho. Vaughan	do.
104	do.	Jno. Murdaugh	do.
690	Henrico	Francis Epes Jr.	do.
311	do.	Francis Epes	do.
200	Surry	Jno. Roberts	do.
46	Princess Anne	Jno. Fentress	do.
400	King William	Wm. Terrell	do.
180	Surry	Jno. Mason	do.
23	Princess Anne	Jno. Attwood	do.
140	Surry	James Mathews	do.
82	Norfolk	Solomon Butt	do.
87	Princess Anne	Wm. Ashbee	do.
710	Isle of Wight	Jno. Simmons	do.
195	Surry	Tho. Tomlinson	do.
296	Princess Anne	Cason & Hen: Moor	do.
259	do.	John Bonney	do.
147	Prince George	Joseph Prichard	do.
82	do.	Wm. Gibbs	do.
226	Henrico	Geo. Hunt	do.
200	Princess Anne	Geo. Hancock	do.
353	Henrico	Geo. Floyd	do.
425	do.	John Williams	do.
480	Princess Anne	Jno. Molbone	do.
295	Isle of Wight	Jno. Denson	do.
2087	New Kent	John Higinson	do.
531	Henrico	Edwd. Curd	do.
1070	Surry	Robt. Hicks	do.
150	do.	Wm. Wyche	do.
30	Princess Anne	Jno. Pallett	do.
170	Surry	Joel Barker	do.
180	Isle of Wight	James Thweat	do.
120	do.	Tho. Holliday	do.
150	do.	Rich'd Lewis	do.
299	Prince George	Tho. Simons	do.
355	do.	Peter Wynne	do.
321	do.	Nath'l Tatum Sr.	do.

Acres	County	To Whom Granted	Date
99	Prince George	Dan'l Malone	Oct.31-1716
443	Nansemond	John King	do.
41	Middlesex	Arth'r Daneland	do.
420	Isle of Wight	James Denson	do.
320	Henrico	Jno. Bolling	Apr. 1-1717
800	Surry	Rich'd Bland	do.
672	Charles City	Charles Christian	do.
121	Nansemond	Rich'd Sanders	do.
397	do.	Abra: Odian	do.
171	do.	Elisha Ballard	do.
628	Henrico	Michell Michell	do.
118	Nansemond	Rob't Sanders	do.
400	King William	Tho. Cartwright & Eliza. Boboe	do.
420	King & Queen	Mary Broche	do.
600	King William	John Sutton, Rich'd Maulding & Tho. Terry	do.
150	Nansemond	Rob't Sanders	do.
200	New Kent	Wm. Morris	do.
18	Middlesex	Jno. Clarke	do.
165	Surry	Jethro Barker	do.
100	do.	John Barker	do.
440	Isle of Wight	Tho. Collier	do.
365	Essex	Wm. Heaberd	do.
200	Isle of Wight	Rich'd Drake Jr.	do.
431	Prince George	Jno. Freman	do.
300	King William	Wm. Terrell & Rob't Chandler	do.
151	Prince George	Abra: Heath	do.
214	Eliza. City	Tho. Wilcoks	do.
1513	New Kent	Edw'd Garland	do.
200	James City	Wm. Macklin	do.
200	Surry	Benja. Gideon	do.
85	New Kent	David Clarkson	do.
127	Nansemond	James Copeland	do.
404	do.	Wm. Ralls	do.
60	Norfolk	Rich'd Backing	do.
251	Nansemond	Wm. Ralls	do.
403	do.	do.	do.
1860	King & Queen	Jno. Madison, John Rogers, Peter Rogers, Hen. Pigg, Edw'd Pigg & John York	do.
112	Prince George	Peter Lee	do.
80	do.	Edw'd Woodleif	do.
172	do.	Sam'l Lee	do.
200	King William	Chr. Smith & Wm. Cockeram	do.
400	do.	Rich'd Mauldin	Apr. 30-1717
500	Henrico	Henry Anderson	Apr. 22-1717
300	do.	Jno. Bolling	July 15-1717
2307	do.	Tarlton Woodson	do.
275	New Kent	James Glen	do.
321	Prince George	Nath'l Tatum Jr.	do.
367	Nansemond	Jno. Ralls	do.
260	Essex	Jno. Wrideing	do.
9976	New Kent	Charles Chiswell	do.
400	Essex	James Caine	do.
395	Gloucester	Tho. Plumer	do.
17	Henrico	Rob't Burton	do.
1019	do.	Jno. Bolling	do.

Acres	County	To Whom Granted	Date
479	Henrico	Jno. Bolling, Edw'd Bowman & John Bowman	July 15-1717
439	James City	James Jennings	do.
50	Charles City	Wm. Featherstone	do.
450	King William	John Hurt	do.
165	Isle of Wight	Henry Beddingfield	do.
280	Surry	Jones Williams	do.
300	New Kent	Wm. Harris	do.
436	Essex	Joseph Waugh	do.
1093	Accomack	Tho. Gascoine	do.
267	Surry	Jno. Poythres	do.
200	do.	James Wych	do.
685	do.	Jno. Chambers	do.
104	Henrico	Hen: Wilson	do.
463	do.	Dorothy Pleasants	do.
183	Nansemond	Rich'd Conquest	do.
500	Henrico	Fran: Sassin - part of French refugees land	do.
374	Nansemond	Tho. Dawtry & Bryan Dawtry	do.
148	do.	Wm. Butler	do.
200	do.	Jno. Harrell	do.
81	do.	Wm. Whitley	do.
172	do.	Rob't Bryan	do.
171	do.	Simon Knight	do.
500	Essex	Wm. Aylett	Apr. 1-1717
346	Nansemond	Law: Baker	July 15-1717
50	Accomack	Phillip Parker & Charles Parker	do.
194	Nansemond	Joseph Cutching	do.
80	do.	John Williams	do.
97	do.	James Garnar	do.
150	do.	John Moor	do.
60	do.	James Copeland	do.
178	do.	Adam Harrell	do.
99	do.	Geo. Lawrence	do.
100	Prince George	Rich'd Deardan	do.
47	Nansemond	Elias Ballard	do.
46	Prince George	Jno. Stroud	do.
100	do.	Rob't Abernathy	do.
370	do.	Rich'd Smith Sr.	do.
100	do.	Wm. Davis	do.
100	do.	David Williams	do.
199	do.	Tho. Whood	do.
327	do.	Hen: Michell	do.
198	do.	Tho. Hobby	do.
200	do.	Thompson Stapely	do.
181	do.	Rich'd Tally	do.
54	do.	Tho. Parrum	do.
100	do.	Tho. Clay	do.
197	do.	Cha: Williams Jr.	do.
200	do.	Jno. Tucker	do.
247	do.	Tho. Jones	do.
65	do.	Wm. Pettypoole	do.
333	do.	Fra: Coleman Sr.	do.
200	do.	Jno. Ellington	do.
100	do.	Wm. Coleman Sr.	do.
289	do.	Fra: Tucker Sr.	do.
83	do.	Rich'd Smith Sr.	do.

Acres	County	To Whom Granted	Date
141	Prince George	Rob't Tucker	July 15-1717
200	Nansemond	Susan Costen	do.
206	Prince George	Wm. Rives	do.
300	do.	John Tally	do.
175	do.	Jno. Fountain & Rob't Winn	do.
64	James City	Tho. Atkinson	do.
221	Prince George	Nath'l Tatum Jr.	do.
119	do.	Wm. Caleb	do.
180	Isle of Wight	Owen Mirack - For diverse services performed towards makeing ye New Settlement for ye Saponie Indians at Christanna pursuant to a treaty with that nation it being part of that tract of land whereon ye said Indians lately dwelt which they have surrendered in exchange for a like quantity assigned them at ye aforesaid place of Christanna	
132	Isle of Wight	Francis West	Dec. 17-1717
100	do.	Jno. Baptist Curtis	do.
76	do.	Jno. Pearson	do.
100	do.	Jno. Wall	do.
54	Norfolk	Geo. Boush	Jan. 22-1717
220	Surry	Peter Mitchell	do.
1000	do.	Henry Harrison	do.
500	Henrico	Michael Johnson	do.
1000	do.	Coll. Francis Epes	do.
1790	do.	Francis Epes	do.
285	do.	Francis Epes Jr.	do.
42	do.	Wm. Kennon	do.
900	do.	Joseph Royall	do.
472	do.	Amos Lead	do.
500	do.	Godfrey Fowler & Geo. Archer	do.
230	Prince George	Shanes Raynes	do.
250	do.	Tho. Michell	do.
1530	Surry	Benja. Harrison	do.
300	do.	Amos Times	do.
250	do.	Gilbert Ivy	do.
175	do.	John Michell	do.
400	do.	Wm. Raynes	do.
385	do.	John Gaddes	do.
175	do.	Rob't Webb	do.
100	do.	Math. Sturdivant	do.
425	do.	Tho. Goodwin	do.
300	do.	Ephraim Parham	do.
190	Prince George	Rob't Mumford	do.
312	Surry	Geo. Passmore	do.
74	Princess Anne	Rich'd Iland	do.
400	King William	John Watkins	do.
390	do.	Tho. Dickason	do.
400	do.	Griffeth Dickason	do.
350	King & Queen	Bernard Paine	do.
41	Middlesex	Wm. Jones	do.
98	Essex	Frederick Coghill	do.
91	do.	Edw'd Scrimshare	do.
484	do.	Tho. Elzey	do.
214	do.	Tho. Stanton	do.
392	do.	Rob't Carter Esq.	do.

Acres	County	To Whom Granted	Date
200	New Kent	Sam'l Chamberlain	Jan. 22-1717
220	do.	do.	do.
100	Isle of Wight	James Mercer	do.
165	do.	Jno. Cain	do.
100	do.	Wm. Harris	do.
385	do.	Theop. Joyner	do.
1000	Nansemond	Doctor Hen. Jenkins	do.
100	Isle of Wight	Hen: Pendry	do.
200	Nansemond	Jno. Bizell	Jan. 24-1717
205	do.	Henry Holland	do.
247	do.	Tho. Houss	do.
366	do.	Joseph Griffin	do.
225	do.	Edw'd Arnold	do.
50	do.	John Benton	do.
83	do.	Rich'd Baker	do.
607	do.	Joseph Rogers	do.
284	do.	Edw'd Vaun	do.
296	do.	James Holland	do.
350	do.	John Small	do.
224	do.	Jno. Hare	do.
400	do.	Elias Ballard	do.
400	do.	Tho. Lawrence	do.
292	do.	Tho. Boyd Jr.	do.
97	do.	Rich'd Lawrence	do.
150	do.	Edw'd Boyt	do.
197	do.	Joseph Rogers	do.
100	do.	Rich'd Hanell	do.
100	do.	John Cole	do.
145	do.	Edw'd Roberts	do.
244	do.	Tho. Boyt Jr.	do.
275	do.	Henry Griffin	do.
338	do.	Wm. Bird	do.
280	Surry	Rob't Webb	do.
200	do.	Silvanus Stokes	do.
325	do.	Wm. Heath	do.
53	Norfolk	Matthew Mathias	do.
283	Prince George	James Baugh Jr. & Hen. Mayes	do.
101	Norfolk	Jno. Momden	do.
342	Nansemond	Tho. Nawstead & Mich'l Archer	do.
407	do.	Hump. Griffin	do.
80	Surry	Rob't Procter	do.
133	Henrico	Bartho. Dupee - part of French refugee land	Mar. 11-1717
522	do,	Antho. Trebue	Mar. 18-1717
400	do.	Stephen Sunter	do.
225	Prince George	Geo. Passmore & Jno. Peterson	do.
156	Nansemond	Jno. Coles	do.
110	Isle of Wight	Jno. Vaughan	do.
144	Surry	Jno. Nichell	do.
370	King William	Jno. Sutton	do.
400	do.	Wm. Terrell & his son, Wm. Terrell	do.
175	Prince George	Capt. Jno. Evans	do.
133	Nansemond	Hump. Griffin	do.
56	do.	Rich'd Lawrence	do.
2136	Princess Anne	Solomon White	do.
433	do.	Jno. Dawley	do.
1613	do.	do.	do.
31	Henrico	James Branch	do.

Acres	County	To Whom Granted	Date
192	Norfolk	Ambrose Shipwash	Mar. 18-1717
47	do.	Jno. White	do.
119	do.	Jno. Whitton	do.
175	Surry	Wm. Wrey	do.
200	do.	Math. Smart	do.
180	do.	John Green	do.
195	Isle of Wight	Tho. Allen	do.
215	Surry	Rich'd Fitzpatrick	do.
225	Isle of Wight	Theop. Joyner	do.
150	do.	Jacob Sumerlin	do.
90	do.	Martin Middleton - for diverse services performed towards makeing the new settlement for ye Saponie Indians at Christanna pursuant to a treaty with that nation it being part of that tract of land whereon ye sd. Indians lately dwelt which they have surrendered in exchange for a like quantity assigned them at ye aforesaid place of Christanna Dated	Mar. 18-1717
400	Isle of Wight	Edw'd Brantley do.	do.
1540	King William	Rob't Farish	Apr. 22-1718
1980	do.	Harry Beverley	do.
2200	do.	Jno. Robinson	Apr. 23-1718
535	Essex	Jno. Taliaferro	Apr. 28-1718

Truely taken this 11th June 1718

C. C. Thacker, Clk.

Land Grants made November 10th 1713

Whereas the several Proprietors of Lands within the bounds laid out pursuant to the Articles of Peace for the Pamunkey Indians, did this day attend the Governor in Council, etc. It is ordered that publication be made at the Courthouse of King William County that the following persons have made appear their Right to Land, Viz:

	Acres
Philip and George Southerland by patent dated 28th Oct 1702 granted with the consent of the sd. Indians	312
Philip Williams by patent dated 24th April 1703	100
Alexander Anderson " " 2nd Nov. 1705	24
William Andrews " " 1st April 1702	33
Heir of James Johnson " 23rd Oct. 1703	40
John Hampton " " 1st April 1702	50
George Johnson by his father's patent dated 1st April 1702	80
John Whitworth by patent dated 1st April 1702 to Thomas Ware	620
Griffin Williams by patent dated 1st April 1702 to Eliza: Ware	240
Morris Roberts by patent dated 1st April 1702	300
Jane Johnson by patent to Anthony Fuller dated 1st April 1702	162
Edward Hacksley by patent dated 1st April 1702	472
Thomas Mackgehee's patent dated 28th Oct. 1702	256
Nathaniel West by patent to Robert Napier dated 20th Oct. 1704	300
Thomas Squires by patent to John Pettiver	310
Edward Bell by patent dated 1st April 1702	590
Thomas Whitworth	200
Robert Tomms	85
William Smith	190
Ambrose Lipscomb	140
Henry Fox, now held by Mr. Micajah Perry	200
Sold out of Edward Hacksley's patent to Thomas Wood & Richard Slaughter	300
Sold out of Griffin William's patent to Valentine Winfrea	100

George Shilling and Michael Waldrobe. Their patents will be considered att the next General Council

January 24th 1723

A TRUE LIST of all the patents that have been issued for land in SPOTSYLVANIA COUNTY

PATENTEES	ACRES	DATES OF YE PATENTS
Augustine Smith	4000	May 8-1722
Edward Ripping	5000	May 26-1722
Larkin Chew	9400	June 4-1722
Larkin Chew	3800	do.
Larkin Chew	2400	do.
John Waller	1000	June 5-1722
Gawin Corbin	3000	June 6-1722
Gawin Corbin	15000	do.
John Clayton Esq. & Rich'd Hickman	40000	June 22-1722
Cole Digges Esq., Peter Beverley Esq & Wm. Robertson	12000	June 25-1722
Bartholomew Yates, Lewis Latane, Christopher Robinson, John Robinson Esq., Jeremiah Clowder, Harry Beverley, William Stanard & Edwin Thacker	24000	July 20-1722
Harry Beverley	6720	do.
Hugh Jones	5000	do.
James Taylor	5000	July 21-1712
James Taylor	8500	do.
Richard Hickman	19786	Spotswood
Edward Ripping, Richard Hickman & Ralph Gough	10000	July 23-1722
John Robinson Esq.	1850	July 25-1722
William Beverley	2500	July 27-1722
Augustine Smith	1600	Feb. 16-1722
William Hansford	400	May 14-1723
Henry Irwin	3000	May 24-1723
Larkin Chew	1600	June 12-1723
Thomas Chew	2180	do.
John Robinson Esq.	5059	June 20-1723
John Quarles	417	Sep. 30-1723
Abraham Field	800	Oct. 5-1723
Henry Webber	2000	Oct. 28-1723
Ambrose Maddison & Thomas Chew	4675	Nov. 15-1723
Augustine Moore	3462	do.
Robert Coleman	1500	Dec. 2-1723
Augustine Moore	1000	Dec. 14-1723
Harry Beverley	2084	Dec. 24-1723

Test R. Hickman, Clk. Secys. Office

EXTRACT OUT OF THE COUNCIL JOURNAL of the 23rd December 1720 of the Quantity of Land licensed to be taken up in the County of Spotsylvania

	Acres
Richard Hickman, Gent. & his partners	20000
Robert Carter Esq.	3500
Cole Diggs, Peter Beverley Esq. & Wm. Robertson Sr.	12000
William Bassett & Garvin Corbin Esq.	15000
Augustine Smith and Lawrence Smith	10000
Robert Brook Jr., Augustine Smith, Will'm Brook, Humfrey Brook and George Braxton	8000
Garvin Corbin Esqr.	3000
John Bagg****	10000
George Parker & his partners	10000

Signed by Wil: Robertson, Cl. Com.

LAND Belonging to Colo. Spotswood in Spotsilvania County

	Acres
One tract granted to Wm. Robertson by patent last day of October 1716 and conveyed to Colo. Spotswood in November following, which is called Germanna	3229
One other tract granted to Richard Hickman by patent the 2nd day of November 1719 and conveyed to Colo. Spotswood in December following, contains	3065
One other tract in the fork of Rappa. River granted to Harry Beverley by patent the 2nd November 1705 and by him conveyed to Colo. Spotswood the 22nd April 1720, contains	1920
Which three tracts of land (as I have been informed) lye together and about June or July 1722 a patent was made out in the name of Richard Hickman (in trust for Colo. Spotswood) for 28000 acres which includes these three tracts; etc. The new land contained in that patent is	19786
One other tract called the Iron-mine granted by patent the 20th February 1719 to Robert Beverley & Thomas Jones, which I have heard has since been sold to Colo. Spotswood, contains	15000
One other tract at Massaponax which was mortgaged to Messrs. Micajah Perry and Richd. Perry by one Charles Smith for 1000 years and by the said Perrys assigned to Colo. Spotswood, Thomas Jones, John Baylor & Robert Beverley the 27th April 1720, is reputed to be	3650
But Smiths widow has part of that land assigned to her for her dower and for ought I know Jones, Baylor and Beverley may yet have right to part of it	
And one other tract called Spotsylvania Company tract granted by patent the 22nd June 1722 to Thomas Jones, John Clayton and Richard Hickman in trust for Colo. Spotswood and since conveyed to him, containing	40000
Signed by Richd. Hickman	86650

The State of Colo. Spotswood's Seating, Cultivation & Improvements, which save his Lands from Lapsing, According to the Laws of Virginia.

On the Alexandria Tract containing 28000 Acres with 21 Plantations or Tenements:

The Houses have been Valued	at	9063.16.6.	
The Inclosures	at	511.17.0.	
The Orchards & Gardens	at	649. 0.0.	
The Mills with their Damms	at	1200. 0.0.	11424.13. 6.

	Acres
Which Sum of 11424.13.6d. will (by the present law) save a tract of	57123
The Stock kept thereon (being 263 head of cattle & 56 horses) will save	4650
The Cleared Land (at 30 acres per plantation, one with another) making 630 acres, will save	10500
The Fork Patent of 1920 acres has been saved by former law	1920

On the Spotsylvania Tract containing 40000 acres with 30 plantations

The Houses have been valued	at	791. 3.6.	
The Inclosures	at	435.10.4.	
The Orchards & Gardens	at	139. 0.0.	
The Slate Quarry with Bridges, Road etc.	at	150. 0.0.	1515.13.10.

Which Sum of 1515.13.10d. will save	7578
The Stock kept thereon (208 head of cattle & 45 horses) will save	4217
The Cleared Land (at 25 acres p. Plantation) making 750 acres "	12500

On the Iron Mine Tract containing 15000 acres with 6 plantations

The Houses, Furnace, Damms, Bridges etc. have been valued	at	6949. 0. 0.	
The Inclosures	at	200.14. 0.	
The Orchards & Gardens	at	38. 0. 0.	7187.14.0d.

Which Sum of 7187.14.0d. will save	35939
The Stock kept thereon (being 164 head of cattle & 12 horses)	2933
The Cleared Land (judged to be about 300 acres) will save	5000
Total of acres	142360

This valuation was carried out at Spotswood's request through his Attorney, Richard Booker, Gent., by Capt. Goodrich Lightfoot, Capt. Jeremiah Clowder, John Quarles & John Finleson, Gent'm., as authorized by a Court held on October 5th 1725

A LIST OF PATENTS GRANTED IN THE FORKS OF RAPPAHANOCK RIVER AND WESTWOOD OF SHERRANDO RIVER SINCE OCTober 1735

Patentees Names	Acres	Position & Details	Surveyed
Morgan Bryan	400		Dec. 23-1734
do.	264		Dec. 20 "
Alexander Ross	2373		Dec. 1 "
John Wilson	286		Dec. 24 "
Thomas Curtis	418		Nov. 5 "
Nathaniel Thomas	380		Nov. 3 "
Isaac Perkins	200		Oct. 10 "
John Heit Jr.	300		Nov. 28 "
Thomas Anderson	542		Nov. 29 "
John Mills Jr.	408		Dec. 13 "
John Peteate	500		Dec. 12 "
Robert Lima	294		Dec. 18 "
John Richards	500		Nov. 3 "
John Litler	448		--- 18 "
Giles Chapman	400		Nov. 12 "
James Brown	121		Dec. 21 "
Luke Emlin	125		Oct. 28 "
Morgan Bryan	450		Dec. 24 "
Francis Pincher	100		Dec. 16 "
Cornelius Cockerine	172		Dec. 22
Josiah Ballanger	500	Included in an order of Council to Ross & Bryan for 70000 acres granted Apr. 23-1735	Nov. 11/12 "
William Hogg	411		Nov. 12 1734
Benjamin Borden	850		Nov. 16 "
John Litler & James Wright	438		Nov. 15 "
John Frost	380		Sep. 25 "
Thomas Drason	205		Nov. 12 "
Thomas Branson	850		Nov. 9 "
George Hobson	937		Dec. 9 "
Morgan Bryan	1020		Dec. 27 "
Evan Thomas	1014		Oct. 18 "
John Calvert	850		Oct. 31 "
John Litler	1085		Oct. 17 "
Morgan Morgan	1000		Dec. 12 "
Hugh Parrall	466		Oct. 28 "
James Davis	1175		Oct. 10 "
Thomas Babb	600		Oct. 10 "
Edward Davis	875		Dec. 26 "
John Mills	1315		Nov. 20 "
John Peteate & George Robinson	1650		Dec. 15 "
Isaac Perkins	725		Nov. 12 "
John Hood	1175		Dec. 13 "
William Deatherage	950	In the Little Fork	Apr. 11 1735
Henry Willis	3000	In the Little Fork, 1221 acres formerly granted said Willis by severall Patents	Sep. 20 "
John Duck & Martin Duck	400	In the Great Fork	Nov. 20 "
John Rains	400	ditto	Sep. 18 "
William Tapp	1000	In the Little Fork	Sep. 11 "

Patentees Names	Acres	Position & Details	Surveyed
Frederick Pamgarer(?)	400	In the Great Fork	Mar. 18 1735
Peter Weaver	400	do.	Nov. 18 "
Tobias Wilhide & Martin Waik	400	do.	Mar. 18 "
Richard Trott	969	Do. - 650 granted June 20-1733.	Apr. 15 "
William Beverley Sr., John Randolph Jr., Richard Randolph & John Robinson	118491	On Sherrando River beyond the Mountains, not within Land Fairfax claims, it is said	May 15 1736
Benjamin Roberts	400	In the Great Fork	Jan. 21 1733
John Chisam	400	In the Little Fork	do.
William Lobb	300	In Goard Vine Fork	Dec. 26 1734
Robert Holderness	400	So. Side S.W. Mountain Road	Dec. 7 1733
Charles Curtis	400	do.	Mar. 8 "
William Pratt	400	So. Side No. Fork of Beaverdam Run	Dec. 6 "
George Teler	200	So. Side Robinson River in little fork said River	Mar. 26 1735
Edward Broadhurst	400	S.W. side Horsepen branch on S. side Mountain Road	Dec. 9 1734
George Anderson	350	Fork Robinson River	Dec. 31 "
William Edding	981	On the Mountain Road, 531 granted June 30-1736	Aug. 17 1735
James Cox	200	Among the Head Branches of Terry Run	Jan. 19 1733
Benjamin Tutt	400	At Foot of Muddy Run Mountain	Oct. 10 1735
Hancock Lee	400	On West side of Marsh Run	May 28 1734
Eusebius Stone	400	Among branches of Marsh Run	May 30 "
William Phillips	400	In fork of the Rappidanne	Dec. 26 "
do.	400	do.	do.
do.	400	do.	Dec. 10 "
Richard Tutt	300	On So. side So. Fork of Goard Vine River	Dec. 21 "
Billy Claiborne	400	Among branches Beaver Dam Run	Dec. 6 1733
James Claiborne	400	do.	Oct. 15 1734
James Cox	400	Among branches Terry's Run	Jan. 21 1733
David Phillip	200	In Fork of Rappidanne	Dec. 28 1734
Thomas Stark	200	In Fork of Robinson	July 31 1735
John Smith	400	Below the Mountain Run	Dec. 23 1734
William Rice	400	Fork of Rappidanne	Dec. 26 "
John Vawter & Philip Stogdale	580	On the Mountain Road	Nov. 8 "
Nicholas Christopher	400	In Fork Rappidanne	July 8 "
Joseph Bludwork & Conrade Amburger	400	South side of South Fork of Goard Vine River	Dec. 4 "
John Garth	400	On Branches Stantons River	Oct. 10 1735
Sam. White	100	Opeckon	Jan. 22 "
James Wight	175	do.	Feb. 3 "
James Wight	700	do.	Feb. 4 "
Walter Homes	525	do.	Feb. 4 "
George Hobson	4250	do.	Feb. 6 "
Morgan Bryan	600	do.	Feb. 2 "
Evan Thomas	164	do.	Feb. 14 "
Wm. Frost	1632	On Little Cape Capon	Feb. 10 "
John Bullaugh	210	Opeckon	Feb. 8 "

Patentees Names	Acres	Position	Surveyed
John Van Metre	400	Opeckon	Feb. 7 1735
James Anderson	366	do.	Feb. 11 "
John Reynolds & Richard Hyland	856	do.	Feb. 10 "
Owen Thomas	826	At Little Cape Capon	---
Morgan Bryan	140	Opeckon	Feb. 5 "
Thomas Anderson	800	do.	Feb. 10 "
William Chambers	213	do.	Feb. 12 "
John Pateet	400	do.	Feb. 18 "
Rob. Smith	390	do.	Feb, 17 "
Thomas Mills	410	On Little Cape Capon	Feb. 12 "
John Mills	390	do.	Feb. 13 "
Francis Thornton	1300	On the East side of Sherando	Feb, 23 "
John Sibley	293	Opeckon	Mar. 1 "
David Lewis	316	do.	Mar. 2 "
Richard Morgan	200	do.	Mar. 6 "
Jos. Hyte	100	On the West side of Sherando	Mar. 4 "
James Moore	650	On Opeckon	-- "
Stephen Owen	650	On Little Cape Capon	Mar. 5 "
Thomas Babb	166	Opeckon	Mar. 9 "
Hugh Parrell	402	do,	Mar. 10 "
John Calvert	892	do.	Mar. 29 1736
John Littler	800	do.	Mar. 30 "
John Litburn	200	do.	Mar. 3 "
Richard Carter	188	do.	Mar. 12 "
Daniel Holman	319	On North branch of Sherando	Mar. 26 "
Wm. White	100	do.	-- "
Edward Teal	261	In the Great Fork	Apr. 13 "
Richard Tutt	319	do.	Apr. 15 "
Alexander McQueen	230	do.	Apr. 16 "
William Morgan	178	do.	Apr. 30 "
John Landrum	650	do.	Sep. 17 "
Christopher Yewell	54	do.	Sep. 18 "
William DeWit	380	do.	Sep. 20 "
Malcolm McKenzie	260	do.	Sep. 26 "
Col. Henry Willis	3563	In the Goard Vine Fork	Nov. 30 "
William Watson & Wm. Poe	400	In the Little Fork	Dec. 4 "
John Picket	100	On Stanton's River	Dec. 9 "
Michael Pearson	190	do.	Dec. 9 "
Adam Banks	250	do.	Dec. 11 "
John Picket	188	do.	Dec. 13 "
Wm. Crossthwait	90	do.	Dec. 14 "
Wm. Phillips	830	do.	Dec. 15 "
Wm. Tapp	656	In the Great Fork	Dec. 16 "
Andrew Bourne	586	do.	--- "
Richard Broadus	277	do.	Dec. 17 "
Jacob Hulsclaw	540	In the Little Fork	Dec. 18 "
Jno. Chisam	400	do.	---
John Hansburger	83	In the Fork of the Robinson	Dec. 20 "
Adam Yager	100	do.	--- "
Wm. Pearse	70		Dec. 16

J. WOOD

Patentees Names	Acres	Position	Surveyed
Frederick Coblar	150	In the Great Fork	Dec. 23 1736
Lewis David Yancey	260	do.	Dec. 27 "
Goodrich Lightfoot	237	do.	---
John Tennant	225	on branches of Stanton's River	Jan. 11 "
Timothy Holdway	300	In the Great Fork	Jan. 3 "
do.	400	do.	Jan. 4 "
Philemon Cavenough	535	do.	Jan. 8 "
John Campbel	300	do.	Jan. 10 "
Capt. Robert Green	1023	In the Little Fork	Jan. 11 "
Wm. Catlet	330	In the Great Fork	--
Conrade Amburger	250	do.	Jan. 12 "
Henry Downes	236	do.	Jan. 13 "
Wm. & Peter Russell	70	do.	Mar. 25 "
Jonathan Ward	300	do.	Mar. 8 "
James Reynolds	370	do.	Mar. 10 "
Thomas Rutherford	116	do.	Mar. 11 "
Calem Price	250	do.	Mar. 22 "
Christopher Tanner	250	do.	Mar. 27 "
Capt. Robert Slaughter	300	do.	Mar. 2 1737
Charles Dewit & Rob't Green	2640	In the Little Fork	Apr. 1 "
Peter Daniel	200	In the Great Fork	Mar. 29 "

J. WOOD

A true copy and examined by us, CH. CARTER, WM. BEVERLY, W. FAIRFAX

George Richard	400	In the Goard Vine Fork	Jan. 31 1734
Wm. Lucas	200	In the No. Fork of Robinson	Feb. 5 "
Thomas Kinnerly & James Kinnerly	5756	In the Rush River	Feb, 11 "
James Kinnerly	210	On No. side Cannons River	Feb. 13 "
Robert McKay	170	On So. side Shanando	Feb. 21 "
Benjamin Allen	170	On No. branch Shanando	Feb. 26 "
do.	120	do.	Mar. 2 "
Benj: Burden	3200	On Smith's Creek	Mar. 2 "
do.	1000	On No. branch Shenando	Mar. 7 "
Robert McKay & Partners	2200	do.	Mar. 10 "
George Teter	200	Fork of the Robinson	Mar. 26 1735
John & Martin Dewitt	400	In the Great Fork	Mar. 29 "
Wm. Tapp	1000	On Indian Run	Apr. 11 "
Wm. Deatheridge	950	do.	Apr. 12 "
Rob. McKay & Partners	891	On No. branch of Shenando	June 10 "
John Wm. Hyte & Tho. Hylam	275	In the Great Fork	Sep. 17 "
John Kaines	400	do.	Sep. 18 "
Robert McKay & Partners	9860	in the Fork of Shenando	Sep. 22 "
Col. Henry Willis	1779	In the Little Fork	Sep. 26 "
Samuel Ferguson	300	In the Goard Vine Fork	Oct. 8 "
Michael Geary	100	In the Fork of the Rappidann	Oct. 9 "
John Garth	400	On Stanton's River	Oct. 10 "
Col. Henry Willis	260	On Black Walnut Run	Oct. 17 "
William Russell	1000	On Shenando	Oct. 22 "
Isaac Thomas	200	On Little Cape Capon Creek	Oct. 24 "

Patentees Names	Acres	Position	Surveyed
Thomas A**ds	255	On Little Cape Capon Creek	Oct. 25-1735
James Anderson	600	On West side of Opeckon	Oct. 28-1735
William Aldridge	650	do.	Oct. 30 "
Mary Bales	330	do.	Nov. 8 "
Benjamin Smith	415	do.	Nov. 3 "
John & Lewis Neal	640	On West side of Shenando	Nov. 4 "
William Hogg Jr.	280	do.	Nov. 5 "
Daniel Chancey	463	On West side of Opeckon	Nov. 6 "
Thomas Farmer	888	do.	Nov. 7 "
Just. Hyte	1300	On West side of Shenando	Nov. 8 "
	1200	do.	Nov. 10 "
	850	do.	Nov. 11 "
	360	do.	Nov. 12 "
	360	do.	Nov, 13 "
	450	do.	Nov. 14 "
	200	do.	Nov. 15 "
	250	do.	Nov. 17 "
	206	do.	Nov. 18 "
Ab. Hollinsworth	1250	On the West side of Opeckon	Nov. 19 "
John Calvert	689	do.	Nov. 20 "
David Lewis	516	do.	Nov. 21 "
Wm. Lucas	400	In the Great Fork	Nov. 22 "
Rob't McKay & Partners	7009	On Linwell's Creek	Dec. 1 "
	1264	On the Naked Creek	Dec. 10 "
	708	On head of Linwell's Creek	Dec. 13 "
	3060	On No. Branch of Shenando	Dec. 14 "
	7000	On So. branch of Shenando	Dec. 18 "
Morgan Bryan	600	On West side of Opeckon	Dec. 22 "
Jonathan Custis	713	do.	Dec. 23 "
John Van Metre	50	do.	Dec. 24 "
William Hogg Sr.	400	On Little Cape Capon	Dec. 23 "
Isaac Perkins	750	Opeckon	Dec. 22 "
James Wood	1125	do.	Dec. 26 "
Simon Pearson	500	do.	Jan. 14 "
Patrick Reyley	360	do.	Nov. 15 "

J. WOOD

COPIES of the RENT ROLLS of the several County's for the year 1704

ACCOMACK COUNTY

	Acres
Alexander Richards	150
Arthur Upshot	2020
Antho: West	700
Ann Simkins	1000
Arthur Donas	100
Arnell Harrison	630
Alex. Harrison	400
Alex. Bagwell	413
Anne Chew	200
Arthur Frame	500
Alex. West	550
Abraham Lambedson	100
Alex Benstone	270
Anne Blake, Widd:	120
Anne Bruxe	180
Mr. Arcado Welburn	1854
Burwell Niblitt	100
Maj. Bennit Scarbrough	521
Corneline Hermon	321
Christ: Stokly	200
Charles Scarborough	1000
Charles Leatherbony	1100
Charles Bally	959½
Charles Pywell	150
Churchil Darby	125
Charles Evill	550
Charles Champison	270
Christ: Hodey	500
Cornelius Lofton	166
Charles Stockley	170
Charles Taylor	580
Catherine Gland	217
Dorman Derby	225
Daniell Derby Sr.	300
Dorothy Littlehouse	225
David Watson	200
Delight Shield	300
Daniel Derby Jr.	125
Daniel Harwood	100
Denis More	200
Daniell Gore	3976
Col. Edm'd Scarbrough	2000
Edw'd Hitchins	170
Edw'd Turner	750
Edw'd Killam	720
Edm'd Allin	200
Edw'd Bagwell for Col. Wm. Custis	200
Edm'd Jones	800
Eliz'b Tinley	200
Edw'd Taylor	300
Edm'd Tatham	200
Edm'd Bally	800
Edm'd Ayres	1000

ACCOMACK COUNTY (Continued)

	Acres
Edw'd Miles	413
Eliz'b Mollchop	210
Edw'd Bell	101
Edw'd More	500
Edw'd Gunter	600
Edw'd Brotherton	600
Elias Blake	430
Edw'd Robins	782
Edw'd Bally	300
Elias Taylor	1500
Eliz'b Wharton	200
Mrs. Eliz'b Scarbrough	4205
Mr. Francis Mackenny	5109
Francis Rob'ts (Roberts)?	200
Francis Wainhouse	200
Francis Crofton	200
Francis Young	200
Finley Mack Wm. (Mackwilliam)?	100
Francis Ayres	300
Francis Jester	200
Francis Benstone	400
Francis Wharton	600
Geo: Anthony	100
Geo: Hastup	300
Coll. Geo: Nich'o Hack	2700
Cap't Geo. Parker	2609
Gervis Baggaly	700
Garrott Huthins (Hutchins)?	170
Geo. Parker Sea: Side	1200
Griffin Savage	650
Geo. Middleton Sr.	888
Geo. Thevit (?)	400
Geo. Pounce	400
Geo. Middleton Jr.	150
Geo. Johnson	200
Capt. Geo. Hope	900
Henry Armtrading	175
Henry Chance	445
Henry Selman	180
Henry Ubankes	400
Henry Lurton	363
Henry Stokes	208
Henry Custis	774
Henry Bagwell	412
Henry Read	350
Henry Ayres	250
Hill Drummond	483
Henry Toules	300
Henry Hickman	135
Henry Gibbins	250
Henry Truett	240
John Tounson	200
Joseph Stokley	664
Jno. Read	200
Jno. Blake	310
Joseph Ames	375

ACCOMACK COUNTY (Continued)

	Acres
Joseph Clark	200
Jno. Fisher	200
James Gray	900
Jno. Huttington	240
Jno. Legatt	300
James Lary	100
James Longue	200
Jno. Merrey	350
Jno. Milbey	500
Jno. Pratt	50
Jno. Rowell	1450
Jno. Road	110
Jno. Rowles	650
Jno. Savage Sr.	350
Jno. Charles	480
Jno. Willis Sr.	430
Jno. Willis Jr.	350
James Fairfax	900
Joseph Milby	830
John West Jr.	500
Jno. Jenkins	400
Jonathan James	150
John Rodgers	100
Jno. Collins	100
Jno. Simcocke	125
Jno. Metcalfe, Isaac Metcalfe & Sam'll Metcalfe	600
Joseph Touser	200
Jno. Stanton	200
Jno. Bally	1000
Jno. Melson	180
Jno. Barnes Sr.	657
Jno. Littlestone	200
John Nock	300
Jno. Killy	100
Jacob Morris	200
Jno. Morris	640
Jon't Ayleworth	200
James Davis	1000
Jno. Parker	200
Jno. Evans	200
Jno. Hull	200
Jno. Blockam	700
Jno. Abbott	1170
Jno. Aren (?)	234
Jno. Grey	116
Jno. Baker	400
Jno. Wharton	150
James Taylor	200
Jno. Glading	207
Jno. Loft Land	167
James Smith	756
Maj'r Jno. Robins	2700
Jno. Collins for Asban (?)	1666
James Walker	525
Jno. Whelton	90
Jno. Marshall	1666

ACCOMACK COUNTY (Continued)

	Acres
Jon't Owen	230
Jacob Wagaman	150
Capt. John Broadhurst	1100
Jno. Dyer	200
Mr. John Watts	2450
Jno. Booth	300
John Bradford	364
Ingold Cobb	150
Jno. Griffin	150
Jno. Mitchell	400
John Parker	970
James Alexander	1250
Jno. Burocke	200
James Stenferer	50
Jno. Perry	217
Jno. Drummond	1550
Jno. Carter on Fox Island	203
Jno. Warington	200
Jno. Bagwell	465
Jno. Wise Sr.	800
Jno. Wise Jr.	400
Jno. Dix	500
Isaac Dix	500
Jno. Hickman	454
Jno. Onions	200
Coll. Jno. Custis Esq.	5950
John Coslin	50
Michaell Recetts (?)	300
Mrs. Mattilda West	3600
Marke Evell (Ewell)?	250
Mary Wright	200
Nicholas Mollchops	285
Nathaniel Williams	64
Nathaniell Rattcliff	300
Owen Collenell (?)	500
Overton Mack Williams	200
Obedience Pittman	115
Peter Major	113
Philip Parker	150
Peter Rogers	167
Perry Leatherbury	1750
Peter Turlington	79
Peter Ease	250
Philip Fisher	433
Peter Chawell	250
Rob't Bell	650
Rich'd Bally Sr.	2100
Rich'd Bally Jr.	180
Rich'd Garrison	468
Roules Major	157
Roulard Savage Sr.	950
Rob't Taylor	95
Rich'd Killam	1900
Rob't Wattson	425
Rich'd Jones	500
Rob't Hutchinson	934
Reynold Badger	150

ACCOMACK COUNTY (Continued)

	Acres
Rob't West	400
Rich'd Cuttler	450
Rob't Cole	125
Rich'd Drummond	600
Rob't Stacomb	300
Rob't Norton	1050
Rich'd Grendall	350
Roger Hickman	135
Rob't Lewis	200
Rodger Abbott	450
Richard Hill	350
Ralph Justice	1050
Rich'd Hinman	1800
Rob't Davis	384
Ragnall Ayres	300
Roger Miles	200
Rich'd Bundike	773
Rich'd Kittson	1300
Rob't Bally	100
Rich'd Stanlin	150
Rich'd Flowers	200
Rich'd Price	100
Rob't Pitts	2300
Rob't Hakins	200
Rebeckha Benstone	270
Rich'd Hillaynes (?)	300
Samuell Benstone	300
Sarah Beach	300
Sillvanus Cole	250
Symon Sosque (?)	325
South Littleton Widd:	2870
Stephen Woltham	244
Steph: Warrington	400
Symon Mitchell	300
Stephen Drummond	300
Selby Harrison	50
Sollomon Evell (Ewell)?	125
Sam'l Young	50
Sarah Reyley	150
Sebastian Dellistation Sr.	500
Sebastian Dellistation Jr.	400
Shimner Wollope	2485
Sam'l Sandford	3250
Sebastian Silverthorn	150
Symon Smith	200
Sarah Coe	900
Sam'l Taylor	1232
Sarah *omis (?)	150
Sebastian Croper	600
Samuell Jester	200
Tho: Burton	600
Tho: Bud	500
Tho: Boules	300
Tho: Clark	100
Tho: Middleton	350
Tho: Stringer	600
Tho: Haule	500

ACCOMACK COUNTY (Continued)

	Acres
Tho: Taylor	100
Tho: Fockes	300
Tho: Bagwell	465
Mad'm Tabitha Hill	3600
Tho: Rose	7
Tho: Webb	50
Tho: Savage	450
Tho: Jones	100
Tho: Scott	100
Tho: Reyley	225
Tho: Tennall	150
Tho: Simpson	520
Tho: Coper	711
Tho: Miles	202
Thomas Bonwell	300
Tho: Bell Sr.	100
Tho: Bell Jr.	100
Tho: Touson Kiquosar	800
Tho: Stocklay	363
Tho: Jester	100
Tho: Smith	300
Thomas Chippin	698
Tho: Wilkinson	50
Tho: Jenkinson	374
Tho: Moore	166
Tho: Allen	700
Tho: Smith Savannah	200
Tho: Perry	232
Tho: Townson	400
Tho: Smith Gringateague	693
Lieut. Coll. Robinson	600
Wm. Robins	200
Wm. Patterson	200
Wm. Bevens	400
Wm. Mathews	400
Wm. Shepherd	200
Wm. Whett	400
Winifred Woodland	333
Wm. Andrews	300
Wm. Custis	1500
Wm. Darby	83
Wm. Fletcher	200
Wm. Killam	450
Wm. Lingoe	300
Wm. Major	130
Wm. Moores	150
Wm. Nock Sr.	800
Wm. Savage	150
Wm. Waite	110
Wm. Sill	200
Wm. Waite Jr.	600
Wm. Bradford	3500
Wm. Rogers	200
Wm. Wise	400
Wm. Finey	800
Wm. Consaloms	200
Wm. Phillips	200

ACCOMACK COUNTY (Continued)

	Acres
Wm. Parker	362
Wm. Cole	375
Wm. Merill	150
Wm. Johnson	150
Wm. Lewis	150
Walter Hages (?)	130
Wm. Chance	450
Wm. Milby	250
Wm. Nicholson	600
Wm. Burton	500
Wm. Willett	842
Wm. Hudson	270
Wm. Lewis	300
Wm. Young	194
Wm. Liechfield	154
Wm. Bunting	150
Wm. Nock Jr.	400
Wm. Lucas	300
Mary Mellochop	498
Wm. Daniell	200
Wm. Silverthorn	160
Wm. Gorman	475
Wm. White	600
Wm. Broadwater	500
Wm. Taylor	100
Wm. Williamson	600
Wm. Brittingham	538
Wm. Benstone Jr.	270
Wm. Dickens for Wm. Littleton	1050
Wm. Waite Sr.	225
Wm. Taylor	1400

Added to this Rent Roll the following lands of wch the Qt. Rents may possibly be recovered tho the owners live out of the County, viz.

Jonas Jackson	500
Rob't Andrews	500
Joseph Morris	200
Rob't Morris	200
Hillary Stringer	950
Tho: Fisher	133
Jno. Fisher	133
Tim. Coe	4100
David Hagard	130

An account of what land in ACCOMACK County the owners whereof are not dwellers -

	Acres
Tho: Preson (?) of Northampton	200
Geo: Corbin of do.	150
Joshua Fishett do.	200
Alend'r Morey of Maryland	200
Tho: Dent	500
Mr. Wm. Kendall's orphans of Northampton	2850
Mr. Hancock Lee dividing Creeks	4050
Rich'd Watters in Maryland	1057
Francis Lailor, Northampton	100
Obedience Johnson	300
Henry Smith, Aty. Southend	1000
Grattience Mitchell North.	200
Matt Tyson South****	300
Teagle Waltham Maryl'd	200
Peter Waltham New Engl'd	200
Jno. Waltham, Maryl'd	200

Jno. Wise Sherriff

A Perfect Role of the Land in MIDDLESEX COUNTY Anno Dom. 1704

	Acres
Richard Atwood	100
Richard Allin	150
Tho: Blewford	100
Mrs. Blaiss (?)	300
John Bristow	140
Rob't Blackley	100
Coll. Corbin	2260
Coll. Carter	1150
John Cheedle	50
Wm. Carter	170
Widd'o Chaney	800
Nanth: Cranke	50
Tho: Dyatt	200
John Dowie	75
Wm. Daniell	150
Henry Freeman	200
John Goodrich	50
Geo: Goodloe	50
Geo: Guest	50
Rich'd Gabriel	30
Wm. Finley	50
Wm. Gardner	100
Rob't George	180
David George	150
Widd'o Hazellwood	200
John Hoare	100
Rich'd Reynolds	50
Jno. Southerne	100
Rich'd Shurly	200
Thos. Stapleton	200
Wm. Southworth	50
Wm. Jones	300
Evan Jones	50
Esq'r Wormley Estate	5200
Wm. Churchill	1950
Jacob Briston	200
Jno. Pace	200
John Logie	300
John Price	519
Henry Perrott	1100
Rich'd Kemp	1100
Tho: Kidd	250
Francis Weeks	225
Widd'o Weeks	225
Henry Webb	100
Tho: Wood	70
Rob't Williamson	200
Tho: Lee	100
Edm'd Mickleburrough	100
Valentine Mayo	100
Wm. Montague	500
Garrett Minor	225
Marvill Mosseley	225
Joseph Mitcham	75
Minie Minor	225

MIDDLESEX COUNTY (Continued)

	Acres
Humphry Jones	150
Jno. North	200
Henry Tugill	200
Henry Thacker	1875
Thomas Tezeley	500
Charles Moderas (?)	100
Wm. Mullins	150
John Smith	700
James Smith	400
Harry Beverley	1000
George Wortham	400
Capt. Grimes	900
Sarah Mickleborough	1000
Christ'o Robinson	4000
John Vibson	100
James Daniell	150
James Curtis	300
Tho: Cranke	54
Phil Calvert	200
John Hipkins	200
Rich'd Daniell	210
Geo: Blake	100
Edw'd Williams	100
Pat. Mammon	100
Alexander Murray	250
Poplar Smith	550
Oliver Seager	380
Edw'd Gobbee	90
Henry Barnes	200
John Davis	100
Paul Thilman	300
Hugh Watts	80
Edw'd Clark	300
Charles Williams	100
Edwin Thacker Estate	2500
Thomas Dudley	200
Thomas Mackhan	200
Rich'd Paffitt	200
Tho: Stiff	100
Peter Browell	100
Tho: Blakey	100
John Robinson	1350
Roger Jones	100
John Nicholls	200
George Berwick	100
Widd'o Hanford (Harford)?	50
Widd'o Hackney	300
Wm. Kibbee	600
Ezikiah Rhodes	300
John Handiford	100
John Miller	200
Wm. Scarborow	200
Wm. Horne	75
Rob't Dudley	300
Widd'o Mason	100
Peter Chilton	100

MIDDLESEX COUNTY (Continued)

	Acres
Francis Dobson	150
James Dudley	200
Capt. Berkeley	750
Wm. Sutton	150
S'r Wm. Skipworth	350
Coll. Kemp	900
Wm. Barbee	150
Wm. Wallis	300
Adam Curtin	200
Capt. Wm. Armistead	2325

A True & Perfect Rent Roll of all the Lands held in ESSEX COUNTY this present year 1704

	Acres
Abbott, Wm.	150
Andrews, Geo.	200
Adcock, Edw'd	230
Adcock, Henry	250
Acres, James	100
Arvin, Wm.	100
Allin, Erasmus	100
Allin, Wm.	100
Ayres, Wm.	200
Acres, Wm.	200
Baulwar, James	800
Bendall, John	135
Butler, John	125
Bowers, Arthur	600
Baulwar, James	200
Beesley, (Beasley)? Wm.	100
Barron, Andrew	50
Bartlett, Tho:	100
Brown, Buskinhan	400
Beeswell, Rob't	100
Beeswell, Rob't Jr.	150
Brown, Wm.	420
Brown, Charles	1000
Buckner, Rich'd	1200
Buckner, Tho:	2000
Brill, Henry	400
Bourn, Jno.	100
Beverley, Harry	1000
Battail, John	1100
Baulwar, John	50
Booth, Widd'o	800
Butler, Jno.	100
Butcher, Jno.	150
Bendrey, Widd'o	700
Bird, Widd'o	100
Beckham, Symon	100
Brutnall, Rich'd	100
Brook, Rob't	400
Ball, Jno.	150
Brooks, James	100
Billington, Mary	200
Brooks, Peter	275
Bowman, Peter	400
Brooks, Rob't	150
Brasur, Jno.	300
Brush, Rich'd	250
Baker, Henry	350
Bradburn, Rich'd	100
Brown, Francis	150
Brown, Dan'l Jr.	150
Byrom, Henry	100
Burnett, Tho: Jr.	1000
Baughan, James Sr.	600

ESSEX COUNTY (Continued)

	Acres
Baughan, James	150
Baughan, Henry	100
Brown, Dan'l Sr.	450
Brown, Tho:	50
Blackiston, Argail	200
Burnett, John	365
Burnett, Th. Jr.	130
Bailen, Jno.	800
Brakins, ***	250
Bell, Thomas	100
Condute, Nath'l	20
Cary, Hugh	50
Connoly, Edw'd	200
Cogwell, Frederick	250
Copland, Nich'o	300
Cattlett, Jno.	1800
Covington, Rich'd	1000
Cook, John	112
Chew, Larkin	300
Crow, Tho:	300
Covington, Wm.	400
Cheney, John	200
Cheney, Wm.	700
Cole, Wm.	200
Corbin, Tho:	440
Cockin, Tho:	120
Coates, Sam'll	300
Cooper, Rich'd	100
Cooper, Tho:	100
Copland, Jno.	175
Crow, Jno.	440
Chew, Larkin	550
Cooper, Wm.	50
Compton, Wm.	50
Cox, Wm.	500
Callaway, Jos.	87
Coleman, Rob't	450
Cobnall, Symon	100
Chamberlain, Leon'd	350
Daniell, James	100
Devillard, Jacob	80
David, Tho:	150
Dudding, Andrew	230
Davis, Evans	150
Dobbins, Dan'l	550
Dressall (?), Timo'	175
Daughty, John	200
Dyer, Wm.	100
Daingerfield, Jno.	270
Daingerfield, Wm.	270
Dunn, Wm.	220
Dyer, Jeffrey	100
Day, Rich'd	100
Duke, Thomas	500

ESSEX COUNTY (Continued)

	Acres
Evans, Rice	200
Edmondson, James	500
Elliott, Alice	75
Evitt, Tho:	100
Edmondson, Tho:	700
Flowers, Isaac	250
Faulkner, Nich'o	100
Farrell, Charles	50
Franklin, Nich'o	130
Foster, Rob't	200
Foster, Jno.	200
Fisher, Jonothan	250
Fisher, Benja:	150
Frank, Tho:	175
Fullerton, James	400
Fossett (?), Wm.	100
Ferguson, Jno.	150
Faulkner, Edw'd	530
Green, George	300
Grey, Abner	350
Goulding, Wm.	200
Gannock, Wm.	2100
Gaines, Barnerd	450
Griffin, Tho:	200
Gibson, Jonathan	700
Grigson, Tho:	300
Gouldman, Francis	300
Goulding, John	200
Goulding, Edw'd	380
Good, Rich'd	200
Garnett, John	150
Glover, John	200
Hawkins, John	1066
Hinshaw, Sam'l	200
Hutton, Tho:	100
Harrison, James	400
Harrison, Andrew	300
Hilliard, Thomas	100
Hanser (?), Wm.	240
Harmon, Henry	75
Hoult, Rich'd	100
Humphrie, Joe	100
Hail, Jno.	900
Harper, John	748
Harper, Tho:	350
Hould, David	100
Hudson, Wm.	100
Hinds, Thomas	100
Howerton, Thomas	175
Hodges, Arth:	100
Howe, ###	300
Harwood, Peter	125
Harway, Tho:	1000
Hudson, Tho:	50
Hudson, Wm.	300

ESSEX COUNTY (Continued)

	Acres
Hill, Leon'd	300
Harwar (?), Sam'l	300
Jamison, David	250
Jones, Wm.	165
Jenkins, David	50
Jewell, Tho:	100
Johnson, Widd'o	300
Jones, Walter	200
Johnson, Rich'd	50
Johnson, Wm.	650
Jones, John	300
Jones, Rich'd	350
Jenkins, John	93
Jones, Wm.	300
Journey, Wm.	243
Johnson, Thomas	500
Jones, Rice	500
Key, Rob't	209
Kerby, Henry	60
Landrum, John	300
Landrum, James	100
Long, Rich'd	300
Lomax, John	2000
Loyd, George	800
Lawton, Claude	100
Little, Abraham	60
Lacy, John	100
Law, John	300
Lattame, Lewis	250
Leveritt, Rob't	100
Micon, Paul	150
Martin, John	400
Morgain, John	100
Miller, John	150
Medon, Tho:	300
Moseley, Benj'a	1100
Mottley, John	100
Morris, John	200
Moss, Rob't	180
Merritt, Tho:	124
Merritt, John	100
Munday, Tho:	500
Magton (?), David	400
Mill, Jno.	200
Moseley, Rob't	100
Mayfield, Rob't	100
Mathews, Rich'd	250
Moseley, Edw'd	550
Merriweather, Francis	3200
Moore, Fran:	175
Michaell, Jno.	200
Merriweather, Tho:	2100
Mofflin, Zach:	400
Medor, John	100
Morse, John	400
Matthews, Benj'a	200
Mountague, Wm.	850

ESSEX COUNTY (Continued)

	Acres
Newbury, Nath'l	200
Nixon, Henry	500
North, Wm.	900
Newton, Nich'o	100
Nightingall, John	200
Orman, James	300
Prosser (?), John	450
Poe, Sam'l	800
Pley (?), Widd'o	800
Parker, Jno.	250
Pitts, Jno.	200
Piskell, Jno.	300
Pain, Jno.	135
Price, Wm.	100
Petenas, Tho:	200
Powell, Honor	72
Powell, Wm.	72
Powell, Place	72
Powell, Tho:	72
Payne, Widdow	1000
Perkin, Henry	300
Pritchett, Roger	167
Paggett, Edm'd	700
Price, John	1100
Pickett, John	800
Perry, Sam'l	225
Price, Wm.	100
Quarter X't'pher Robinson	2200
Quart'r Tho: Corbin	4000
Q*** Rob't Thomas	200
Quart'r John Hay	1000
Quart!r Wm. Smith	3000
Quart!r Gawen Corbin	2000
Quart!r Peter Ransom	300
Quart!r David Gwin	950
Quart!r Wm. Upshaw	1000
Quart!r Levercone	600
Quart!r Tho: Todd	550
Ridgdall, John	300
Ramsey, Tho:	550
Rowze, Ralph	610
Rucker, Peter	500
Rowze, Edw'd	300
Royston, John	1000
Roberts, Edm'd	300
Rebs, Henry	400
Reeves, Joseph	200
Reeves, James	200
Roberts, John	50
Richardson, Rob't	200
Reymolds, James	500
Reynolds, James	500
Ransom, Peter	1200
Strange, Jno.	100
Stepp, Abra:	390
Sam'll, Anth'o (Samuel, Anthony)	300
Sail, Cornelius	73

ESSEX COUNTY (Continued)

	Acres
Salmon, John	60
Spiers, Jno.	160
Smith, Wm.	150
Stokes, Rich'd	500
Smith, Charles	3000
Sullenger, Peter	400
Sales, Widd'o	1150
Shipley, Jno.	200
Spearman, Job	300
Smith, Francis	500
Stallard, Sam'l	100
Ship, Joe	350
Short, Tho:	150
Scott, Wm.	1100
Stogell, Jno.	100
Stephens, Jno.	100
Slaughter, Phebe	352
Smith, Jno.	75
Smith, Jonas	100
Sanders, John	300
Stanton, Jno.	95
Shepherd, Jeremiah	300
Smith, Tho:	50
Shakelford, Francis	300
Sthrashley, Tho:	200
Staners, Tho:	500
Snoud, Tho:	950
Shakelford, Henry	50
Thorp, Widd'o	400
Tinsley, Tho:	111
Thacker, Sam'l	110
Tomlin, Widd'o	400
Taliaferro, Francis	1300
Thornton, Fran:	700
Tomlin, Wm.	1600
Thomas, John	100
Taliaferro, Charles	300
Thomas, Wm.	200
Taliaferro, John	2000
Turner, George	200
Tomlins, Wm.	950
Trible, Peter	100
Taylor, Rich'd	650
Tilley, Mathew	200
Venters, Barth'o	400
Virget, Job	50
Vincent, Vans	450
Wakeland, Wm.	100
Wood, Tho:	50
Winslow, Tho:	150
Winslow, Henry	100
Williams, John	450
Williams, Wm.	100
Wilson, David	50
Wilton, Richard	150
Wheeden, Edw'd	50
Ward, Widd'o	200

ESSEX COUNTY (Continued)

	Acres
Whitehorn, Widd'o	260
Wms. (Williams), Emanuell	100
Watkins, Thomas	400
Waters, John	150
Webb, James	200
Webb, John	200
Wead, Wm.	200
Wood, Tho:	300
Williamson, Tho:	100
Williamson, Wm.	100
Williamson, John	100
Webb, Robert	375
Webb, Isaac	200
Woodnatt, Henry	300
Waginer, John	400
Ward, Geo:	350
Wheeler, Tho:	250
Young, Wm.	1000
Young, Giles	100
Muscoe, Salvator	100
Moody, John	150
Maguffe, John	100
Brookins, Quart'r	250
Smith, Jno. Quart'r	1000
Newton, Henry	100
Newton, Henry	175
Nowell, Dall	400
Nowell, Widd'o	300
Garrett, Tho:	1000
Gould, Price	200
Green, Sam'l	97
Gouldman, Fran:	300
Gawdin, Wm.	100
Grimmall, Wm.	100
Gaitwood, John	400
Gaines, John	475
Sam'l Thompson	1000

Lands held in the above said County, the rents not paid and held by the severall gentlemen as followeth, viz.

John Smith, Esq'r. of Gloucester County	800	Received
Wm. Buckner of Gloucester by informations	1500	
Jno. Lightfoot, Esq'r. New Kent County	900	
Jno. Bridgate in Engl'd	700	
Rich'd Wyatt & Jno. Pettus of King & Queen County	800	
Wm. Berry of Richmond County	400	

Richard Covington.

GLOUCESTER RENT ROLLS - A Rent Roll in Petso Parish (1704)

	Acres
Capt. David Alexander	1050
James Amis	250
John Acre	100
Wm. Armistead	430
Ralph Baker	150
Martha Brooken	600
Thomas Buckner	850
Sam'l Bernard	550
Wm. Bernard	810
Rich'd Bailey	600
Mary Booker	100
Thomas Cook	350
Wm. Crymes (Grymes)?	400
Jno. Cobson	100
Rob't Carter	1102
Wm. Collone	400
Hannah Cannell	100
Benj: Clements	400
Jno. (Clarke or Cleake)	100
Wm. Cook	135
Jno. Coleman	200
Jno. Day	400
Jerim. Darnell	150
Jno. Darnell	60
James Dudley	780
Rich'd Dudley	400
Thomas Dudley	200
Thomas Dixon	300
Jno. Drumont	80
Sam'l Fowler	150
Wm. Fleming	600
Wid'o Forginson	150
Wm. Fockner	180
Jno. Grymes	1400
Susannah Grinley	200
Dorcas Green	400
Jno. Grout	300
Jno. Harper	100
Wm. Howard	300
Rich'd Hubard	100
Wm. Hansford	500
Jno. Hanes	150
Alexand'r How	120
Rich'd Hill	70
Rob't Hall	100
Rich'd Hull	250
Sam'l Howell	200
Stephen Johnson	150
Wm. Jones for Northington	530
Glebe Land	127
Jno. Kingson	400
Capt. Edw'd Lewis	1000
Rich'd Lee, Esq.	1140
Nich'o Lewis, orphan	350
Wm. Milner	900
Rich'd Minor	250

GLOUCESTER - Petso Parish (continued)

	Acres
Edw'd Musgrove	100
Hayce, an orphan	60
Eliz'b. Mastin	360
Jno. Mackwilliams	50
Rob't Nettles	300
Wm. Norman	150
Isaac Oliver	100
Dorothy Oliver	130
Jno. Pritchett	850
Jno. Pate	1100
Rich'd Price	600
Mad'm Porteous	500
Mad'm Page	550
Rob't Porteus	892
Guy Parish	100
Wm. Roane	500
James Reynolls	200
George Robinson	300
John Royston	570
Thomas Read	2000
Wm. Richards in Pamunkey	150
Jno. Shackelford	280
Edward Symons	500
Nich'o Smith	280
John Stubs	300
Thomas Simpson	280
John Smith	1300
Augustin Smith	200
Augustin Smith Jr.	500
Wm. Stanbridge	159
Wm. Thornton Sr.	525
Wm. Thornton Jr.	800
Wm. Thurston	200
Wm. Upshaw	490
Francis Wisdom	150
Thomas West	112
Thomas Whiting	450
George Williams	100
Conquest Wyatt	2200
Seth Wickins (?)	50
Walter Waters	200
Jane Wotham	60
Rob't Yard	450
Rob't Hall	250
Wm. Whittmore deserted	150
Wm. Parson orphan	100
Edw'd Stephens	70
John Kelley orphan	150

Tho: Neale

GLOUCESTER RENT ROLLS - KINGSTON PARISH

		Acres
Prose Curtis		400
Rob't Peyton		680
Rich'd Perrott		35
Henry Preston		1500
Sarah Green		200
Rob't Cully		200
Thomas Hayes		140
Andrew Bell		128
Humphrey Toy		1100
Anne Aldred		350
Dunkin Bohannah	(Bohannon)?	113½
Rich'd Hunley		50
Capt. Gayle		164
Math. Gayle Jr.		250
James Hundley		100
John Hundley		130
Philip Hundley		660
Tho: Cray		200
Hen: Knight		240
John Williams		50
Rich'd Beard		380
Timothy Hundley		300
Thomas Bedford		50
Jno. Floyd		250
John Bohannah		113½
Capt. Armistead		3675
Christopher Dixon		300
Rob't Bristow, Esq'r		900
Edw'd Gowing		100
Tho: Ryland		272
John Nevill		100
Lawrence Parrott		340
Wm. Brooks		720
Joseph Bohannah		148
Wm. Hampton		348
Widd'o Green		150
Capt. Dudley		650
Capt. Knowles		575
Capt. Tho: Todd		775
Wm. Beard		100
Wm. Tompkins		100
Henry Bolton		50
Wm. Eliott		1060
Humphry Tompkins		100
Daniel Hunton		200
Thomas Peyton		684
Rich'd Dudley		350
James Ransom Jr.		310
Tho: Peters		30
Rob't Elliott		1247
Mich: Parriott		100
Jno. Meachen Jr.		600
Caleb Linsey		140
Alexand'r Ofield		23
Mark Thomas		300
Jno. Garnet		250
Wm. Plumer		510

GLOUCESTER - KINGSTON PARISH (Continued)

	Acres
Wm. Brumley	750
Wm. Credle	50
Charles Jones	225
Rob't Sadler	50
Edw'd Sadler	20
Geo: Roberts	170
Rich'd Longest	600
Tho: Fliping	300
Charles Watters	100
Wm. Gundrey	200
Thomas Kemp	200
Tho: Allaman	842
Coll. Kemp	200
Ralph Shipley	430
George Turner	50
Coll. James Ransom	1400
Thomas Pitman	300
Rich'd Merchant	180
Widd'o Sineh (?)	300
Christopher Rispus (?)	200
Benj: Read	550
Walter Keble	550
Joseph Brooks	500
Capt. Gwin	1100
Lindsey Land	390
Thomas Garwood	77
John Callis	1000
Tho: Miggs	100
Rich'd Glascock	500
Jno. Lylley	584
Geo: Billups	1200
Rob't Singleton	650
James Foster	225
John Andrews	50
Thomas Rice	34
John Martin	200
Capt. Smith	550
Capt. Sterling	1100
John Diggs	1200
Wm. Howlett	300
Jno. Miller	100
Andrew Ripley	40
Francis Jarvis	460
Wm. Armistead	300
John Banister	650
Tho: Plumer	400
Isaac Plumer	200
James Taylor	50
Edw'd Borum	360
Widd'o Davis	300
Sam. Singleton	300
Wm. Morgan Sr.	50
Wm. Morgan Jr.	200
John Bacon	825
Henry Singleton	600
John Edwards	534
Patrick Berry	250
Anne Forrest	500

GLOUCESTER RENT ROLLS - WARE PARISH

	Acres
Thomas Poole	600
Anne Crox*on (Croxton, Croxson)?	300
Thomas Purnell	163
Nicholas Pamplin	210
Simon Stubelfield	200
Jno. Price	600
Sam'l Vadrey	400
Sam'l Dawson	350
Nathan: Burwell	600
John Dawson	780
Tho: Bacop (Bàcon)?	200
Rob't Francis	400
Walter Grewell (?)	50
Tho: Reed	400
James Shackelfield	35
Rob' t Freeman	135
Jno. Marinex	100
Isaac Valine	100
Tho: Haywood	70
Hugh Marinex	50
Leonard Ambrose	200
Philip Grady	200
Capt. Wm. Debnam	1250
James Burton	100
Jno. Spinks	300
Wm. Hurst	200
Sarah More	67
John Ray	100
Rob't Pryor	300
Christ'o Greenaway	270
Capt. Throgmorton	500
James Clark	250
Philip Cooper	200
Jno. Kindrick	100
Sam'l Simons	120
Wm. Radford	200
John Robins	900
Alice Bates	200
Jno. Easter	350
James Davison	100
Rob't Morrin	200
Anne Bray	100
Grace Easter	200
Sampson Dorrell	300
Capt. Francis Willis	3000
Thomas Powell	460
Wm. Holland	300
Capt. Cook	1500
Giles Cook	140
Wm. Jones	120
Tho: Collis	100
Philip Smith	700
Tho: Cheerman	650
Geo: More	40
James Morris	250
Abraham Iveson Sr.	1000

GLOUCESTER - WARE PARISH (Continued)

	Acres
Robert Bristow Esq'r	2050
Anthony Gregory	700
Rich'd Bailey	800
Wm. Foulcher	100
Widd'o Jeffes	216
Rich'd Dudley Jr.	300
John Buckner	900
Thomas Todd	884
John & Peter Waterfield	143
Henry Whiting	800
Mad'm Whiting	950
Jno. Goodson	150
Wm. Morris	350
Mary Lascelle	200
Peter Ransone	220
Charles Waters	200
Dororthy Kertch	220
Dorothy Boswell	1600
Rich'd Cretendon	280
Eliz'b Snelling	250
Joseph Boswell	230
John Bullard	100
Anthony Elliot	100
Wm. Armistead	100
Peter Kemp	650
Maj'r Peter Beverley	800
Ditto Tillid Lands	150
Dudley Jolley	100
Rob't Couch	100

GLOUCESTER RENT ROLL - ABBINGTON PARISH

	Acres
Mr. Guy Smith	30
James Cary	50
Wm. Sawyer	150
Edw'd Cary	100
Rob't Barlow	62
Tho: Cleaver Sworne	200
Edw'd Stevens	80
Henry Stevens	60
Chillion White	100
Jerimah Holt	350
of Ditto for Widd'o Babb	150
Rob't Yarbborrow	100
Rob't Starkey	100
Henry Seaton	170
Hugh Howard	200
Capt. Booker	1000
Jno, Stoakes	300
Jno. Dobson	400
Wm. Dobson	950
Edm'd Dobson	350
Hugh Allen	1250
George Jackson	117
Jno. Teagle	30
Widd'o Jones	45
Mary Thomas	100
Thomas Seawell	200
Benj. Lane	50
Valentine Lane	80
Jeffry Garves	33
Thomas Coleman	250
Johanna Austin	40
Major Burwell	3300
Jno. Satterwight	50
Jerimah Holt Jr.	150
Charles Stevens	75
Rich'd Roberts for wife	300
Jno. Sadler	125
James Steavens	100
Susannah Stubbs	300
Rich'd Foster	150
Henry Mitchell	50
Nathaniel Russell	550
Eliz'b Richardson	500
Wm. Camp	175
James Row	300
John Butler	100
John Smith Esq.	2000
Ditto for Rob't Bryon	400
Capt. Blackbourne	550
Peter Richeson	250
Benj. Clements	500
Thomas Graves	70
Rob't Page	175
Joseph More	150

GLOUCESTER - ABBINGTON PARISH (Continued)

	Acres
Richard Dixon	200
Eliz'b Turner	150
Owen Grathmee	250
Rich'd Woodfolk	125
Jno. Waters	50
Wm. Hilliard	80
Rich'd Heywood	100
Mary Hemingway	150
Wm. Kemp	75
Rob't Francis	104
Joshua Broadbent	200
Joseph Coleman	200
Grustam Clent	100
Philip Grady	150
Jno. Hall	125
Tho: Walker	300
Jno. Mixon	400
Tho: Sanders	450
Wm. Smith for Kittson	50
John Banister	2750
Mad'm Mary Page	3000
Jno. Lewis Esq'r	2000

Rich'd Cordell

A True Account of the Lands in King & Queen County as it was taken by Rob't Bird Sherriff in the Year 1704

	Acres
Alford, John	200
Austin, Dan'l	80
Asque, John	320
Adams, John	200
Arnold, Edw'd	150
Allin, Thomas	100
Adkinson, John	250
Austin, Thomas	100
Adamson, David	100
Anderson, Rich'd	650
Allcock, Dorothy	150
Baker, Wm.	350
Beverley, Rob't Esq.	3000
Bennett, Alexander	200
Breeding, Geo:	200
Bennett, Wm.	150
Bowles, Rob't	100
Bennett, Sawyer	150
Baylor, John	3000
Bell, Roger	150
Burford, Wm.	150
Bray, John	230
Blake, Wm.	290
Boisteau, James	900
Blake, Wm. Jr.	210
Brown, Lancelot	385
Burch, Jno.	100
Burch, Wm.	100
Brown, Tho. Blakes Land	300
Bridgforth, James	355
Bagby, Rob't	550
Banks, Wm.	1079
Bullock, John	200
Bird, Wm.	572
Breach, Jno. (Broach) ?	1200
Braxton, Geo:	2825
Blanchet, John	125
Bowker, Ralph	330
Bine, Edm'd	111
Barber, James	750
Burgess, Wm.	100
Bond, Jno.	100
Breemen, John	1100
Bland, Henry	150
Breemen, John Jr.	200
Bowden, Tho:	150
Barton, Andrew	150
Barlow, Henry	200
Baskett, John	150
Batterton, Tho:	100
Baker, James	322
Bill, Rob't	150
Bocus, Reynold	150
Bourne, George	200
Bird, Rob't	1324

KING & QUEEN COUNTY (Continued)

	Acres
Cane, Jno.	300
Chestum, Alexand'r	150
Cook, Benjamin	200
Cook, Thomas Jr.	50
Cook, Thomas Sr.	100
Cook, Jno.	50
Cleyton, John	400
Chapman, Mary	200
Cleyton, Jeremy	325
Crane, Wm.	120
Camp, Thomas	250
Carleton, Christ'o	200
Carleton, Jno.	300
Carter, Tim'o	350
Coleman, Tho:	300
Coleman, Daniell	470
Cleyton, Susannah Widd'o	700
Collier, Rob't	100
Crane, Wm.	300
Crane, Tho:	320
Chapman, John	200
Caughland, James	100
Cotton, Catherine	50
Collier, Charles	450
Collier, John	400
Collins, Wm.	350
Cammell, Alexand'r	200
Chin, Hugh	100
Conner, Tim'o	1410
Collins, James Yard	300
Corbin, Gawin	2000
Crisp, Tobias	100
Carters, ****	300
Carlton, Tho:	200
Carlton, Anne	300
Clough, George	390
Clerk & Condell both in Gloucester	1000
Widd'o Durrat	200
Day, Alexand'r & Maj. Beverley	300
Doe, Wm.	300
Dilliard, Nich'o	150
Dilliard, Edw'd	150
Dimmock, Tho:	150
Dismukes, Wm.	200
Duett, Charles	900
Didlake, James	200
Durham, John	100
Dunkley, John	380
Duson, Tho:	448
Davis, Nath'l	300
Deshazo, Peter	450
Davis, Jno.	90
Davis, Edw'd	100
Dilland, Thomas	170
Dewis, Rich'd	250
Dillard, Geo:	325
Duglas, James	275

KING & QUEEN COUNTY (Continued)

	Acres
Dayley, Owen	180
Eachols, John	220
Ellis, John	400
Eastham, George	300
Eubank, Wm.	350
Eastham, Edw'd Jr.	800
Edw'ds John (Edwards)	100
Eastham, Edw'd	100
Eastes, Abraham	200
Eyes, Cornelius	100
Emory, Ralph	100
Ellis, Timothy	350
Fonsigh, Thomas	150
Farguson, James	300
Flipp, John	80
Farish, Rob't	1400
Fielding, Henry	1000
Farmer, John	50
Fothergill, Rich'd	675
Fortson, Charles	400
Forgett, Charles	150
Fethergill, Rob't	150
Farmer, Jno. not paid for	200
Fox, Margarett not paid for	100
Gadberry, Edw'd	100
Griffin, Edw'd	100
George, Rich'd	100
Griffin, David	100
Graves, Rob't	150
Graves, Jno.	150
Gardner, Ringing	200
Gray, Joseph	200
Gilby, John	300
Gray, Sam'l	40
Gresham, Jno.	200
Gresham, Edw'd	175
Good, John	200
Gresham, George	150
Garrett, Dan'l	200
Gamble, Tho: Majors Lands	450
Gresham, Tho:	225
Graves, Jno.	150
Guttery, Jno.	230
Gregory, Frances Widd'o	700
Gough, Alice Widd'o	800
Griggs, Francis	250
Garrett, John	330
Gibson, Widd'o	200
Garrett, Rob't	200
Hand, Thomas	150
Hayle, John Esq (?)	685
Honey, James	200
Holloway, Wm.	100
Herndon, James	100
Hoomes, (Homes)? George	725
Hodges, Thomas	250
Hayle, Joseph	250

KING & QUEEN COUNTY (Continued)

	Acres
Hayle, John	100
Haynes, Wm.	494
Holcomb, Wm. Brafords Land	700
Henderson, John Thackers Land	200
Hodgson, Widd'o	200
Henderson, Widd'o	300
Henderson, Wm.	162
Housburrough Morris, Harts Land	200
Hestonley, John	100
Hill, John	200
Hendon, Wm.	70
Harris, Wm.	250
Hart, Tho:	200
Hockley, Rob't	100
Howard, Peter	300
Hardgrove, Wm.	100
Henning, Arthur	50
Hickman, Thomas	700
Hunt, Wm.	312
Hobs, Wm.	250
Hicks, Rich'd	250
Howden, Wm.	100
Howerton, Thomas	300
Holt, Joseph lives in Maryland	321
Hayward, Tho: in Gloucester	600
Jones, Tho:	150
Jones, Rob't	200
Jeffrey's, Rich'd	337
Jones, Rob't Jr.	130
Johnson, James	200
Jones, Wm.	900
King, John	150
Kallander, Tim'o	100
Kink, Anne	275
King, Edw'd	200
Knowles, Dorothy	150
King, Rob't	100
Kenniff, Darby	160
King, Daniell	200
Loveing, John	100
Lyon, Peter	250
Leigh, John	6200
Lumpkin, Rob't	400
Lee, Wm.	230
Lobb, Wm.	100
Loft, Rich'd	320
Lewis, Zachary	350
Lumpkin, Jacob	950
Lewis, David	120
Lewis, John Esq.	10100
Lewis, Edw'd	1400
Lemon, Eliz'b	100
Lynes, Rebecca	405
Levingstone, John	600
Lawrence, Matthew	210
Letts, Arthur	475

KING & QUEEN COUNTY (Continued)

	Acres
Langford, John	150
Levingstone, Jno. Sewell Land	750
Leftwitch, Thomas in Essex	75
May, John	300
Musick, George	100
Major, Jno.	250
Martin, John	300
More, Austines (?)	200
May, Tho:	300
Moore, Sam'l	100
Maddison, Jno.	500
Morris, Wm.	130
Martin, Eliz'b	400
Mackey, Sarah	177
May, John Piggs Land	200
Major, Francis	700
Mansfield, Thomas	60
Morris, Henry	100
Major, John	400
Mole (?), Nich'o	200
Marcartee, Daniell	200
Morris, Wm.	300
Mead, Wm.	300
Matthews, Edw'd	160
Martin, Cordelia Wid'o	200
Nelson, Henry	440
Neal, John	50
Nason, Joshua	200
Norman, Wm.	300
Norris, James	100
Owen, Ralph	120
Ogilvie, Wm.	300
Orrill, Lawrence	290
Orrill, Wm.	500
Ortbourne, Michaell	90
Overstreet, James	180
ditto at hand	50
Powell, Rob't	500
Prewitt, Wm.	200
Paine, Bernard	130
Pomea, (?) Francis	100
Philip, Charles	250
Pettitt, Thomas	548
Pollard, Rob't	500
Pollard, Wm.	100
Phinkett, Eliz'b	500
Pemberton, Tho:	115
Pickles, Tho:	93
Pottors, Frances Wid'o. Neales Land	100
Parke, James	200
Purchase, Geo:	580
Page, Jno.	100
Pritchett, David	225
Pigg, Henry	61
Page, John Jr.	300
Pigg, Edw'd	250
Phelps, Tho:	400

KING & QUEEN COUNTY (Continued)

	Acres
Pendleton, Philip	300
Pendleton, Henry	700
Pann, John	200
Paytons quart.	500
Pigg, John	100
Pamplin (?), Rob't	150
Pryor, Christ'o	175
Paulin, Eliz'b	175
Pate, John in Gloucester	1000
Quarles, James	300
Quarles, Dyley Zacha: Lewis Land	300
Richard, Rob't	300
Rings Quarter	1000
Robinson Daniell	100
Roger, Giles	475
Rice, Michaell	200
Richeson, Tho:	460
Richeson, Elias	180
Read, Eliz'b	550
Russell, Alexander Wyatts Land	400
Robinson, Rob't	980
Rowe, John	100
Richards, John	914
Richards, Wm.	400
Richards, Oliver	250
Riddle, Tho: Reads Land	700
Roy, Rich'd	1000
Ryley, Elias	200
Rollings, Peter	150
John the son of Rob't Robinson hold, w'th no body pays for	750
Sebrill, John	130
Stone, Mary	100
Smith in Bristoll	2800
Stone, Jno.	295
Stubbelfield, Geo:	400
Scandland, Denis	1470
Swinson, Rich'd	170
Smith, Christ'o	200
Smith, Jno. Cooper	273
Smith, Alexander	275
Seamour, Wm.	268
Sones, Tho:	150
Shepheard, Isaac	100
Southerland, Wm.	800
Shoot, Tho:	100
Shepheard, Joseph	100
Shea, Patrick	200
Southerland, Dan'l	200
Smith, Nich'o	700
Sanders, Nath'l	200
Smith, Jno. Sawyer	80
Shackelford, Roger	250
Skelton, John	100
Snell, John	150
Simpio, Charles	100

KING & QUEEN COUNTY (Continued)

	Acres
Sawney, John	113
Stringer, Marg'e	175
Spencer, Tho:	300
Sykes, Stephen	50
Smith, Francis	100
Smith, Rich'd	150
Sparks, John	200
Surly, Tho:	100
Stapleton, Tho:	200
Story, John	3000
Spencer, Katherine	600
Skipworth, Sir Wm. w'ch is not paid for	700
Stark, Tho: of London wch is not pd. for	920
Stubblefield Geo: in Gloucester	400
Smith, Austin in Gloucester	4000
Turner, Richard	200
Todd, Thomas, **Quart.**	2300
Taylor, Gaines	4000
Toy, Thomas	175
Taylor, Dan'l	70
Thomas, Rowland	610
Tunstall, Tho:	550
Todd, Rich'd	1050
Towley, John	200
Trice, James	350
Tureman, Ignatius	100
Turner, Thomas	267
Thacker, C.C.	1000
Vaughan, Cornelius	500
Vize, Nath'l	100
Uttley, John	200
Wood, James	800
Wilkinson, John	100
Wright, Tho:	300
Watkins, Wm.	137
Wiltshier, Joseph	60
Watkins, Edw'd	98
Watkins, Philip	203
White, Thomas	200
Walker, John	6000
Wilson, Benj., Wyats Land	420
Wyat, Rich'd	1843
Withy, Thomas	50
Williams, Thomas	200
Watts, Tho:	235
Ward, Sam'l	160
Watkins, Benj:	60
Watkins, Tho: Jr.	125
Williams, Eliz'b	900
Waldin, Sam'l	275
Ware, Edw'd	735
William, John	125
Ware, Valentine	487
Willbourne, Tho:	250
Wildbore, Wm.	100

KING & QUEEN COUNTY (Continued)

		Acres
Ware, Nich'o		718
White, Jerimiah		200
Whorlin, John		200
Wise, Rich'd		209
Walker, John.	Johnson's Land	1000
Wadlington, Paul not paid for being		150
York, Mathew		100

THE QUIT RENT ROLL OF KING WILLIAM COUNTY 1704

	Acres
Armsby, John	200
Alvey, Rob't	400
Andrew, Wm.	100
Abbott, Rob't	100
Arnold, Anthony	100
Arnold, Benj:	1000
Alcock, John	190
Adam, James	400
Anderson, Wm. Capt.	150
Burwell, Maj'r	4700
Bunch, Paul	150
Baker, John	250
Burges, Edw'd	150
Buttris, Rob't	400
Bibb, Benj:	100
Browne, Joseph	270
Bell, Edw'd	580
Burch, Henry	200
Burrel, Suprian	350
Baker, Tho:	100
Bobo, Eliz.	200
Bird, Wm. Maj'r	1200
Burrus, John	60
Butler, Thomas	150
Burrus, Thomas	60
Bassett, Coll.	1550
Bray, James	1400
Browne, Abraham	250
Brightwell, Eliz'b	300
Bickley, Joseph	150
Claibourne, Wm. Coll	3000
Claibourne, Tho: Capt.	1000
Claibourne, John	50
Coakes, Robert	100
Cradock, Sam'l	600
Cockram, Wm.	200
Cockram, Joseph	600
Celar, John	100
Chadwick, Wm.	150
Cathorn, John	180
Carr, Thomas	500
Chiles, Henry	700
Cranshaw, Thomas	150
Clark, Margarett	100
Coates, Wm.	50
Douglas, Wm.	200
Davis, Lewis	200
Davis, Wm.	200
Downer, John	300
Downes, Elias	300
Davenport, Davis	200
Dorrell, Sampson	5000
Davenport, Martin	100
Davis, Robert	200
Dickason, Wm.	100
Dickason, Thomas	100

KING WILLIAM COUNTY (Continued)

	Acres
Dillon, Henry	150
Dabney, James	200
Dabney, George	290
Dabney, Benja:	200
Davis, John	200
Elly, Rich'd	100
Egny, Eliz'b	100
Elliot, Thomas	480
Edward, James	350
Elliott, James	1700
Fox, John Capt.	600
Fox, Henry	2000
Finton, Francis	100
Fuller, Anthony	150
Foord, John Jr.	300
Foord, Wm.	800
Fullalove, Thomas	100
Fleming, Charles	1700
Graves, John	100
Garratt, Thomas	200
Graves, Thomas	100
Green, John	100
Gravatt, Henry	150
Goodin, Maj'r	200
Glover, Wm.	100
Herriott, George	200
Hollins, John	200
Higgason, John	350
Holderbee, Wm.	100
Holliday, Wm.	100
Hayfield, Wm.	100
Hampton, John	50
Huckstep, Edw'd	150
Hurt, Wm. Jr.	90
Hurt, Wm. Sr.	250
Hurt, John	500
Hendrick, Hans	700
Handcock, Thomas	200
Haydon, John	150
Hobday, Edw'd	150
Hill, Thomas	150
Hutchinson, Wm.	600
Hill, Francis	300
Hill, Gabriell	250
Hill, Edw'd Coll.	3000
Hayle, Joseph	200
Johns, Jane	240
Johnson, Wm.	300
Johnson, Coll.	600
Johns, Wm.	100
Isabell, Wm.	150
James, Jonathan	300
Inge, Vincent	100
Jones, Frederick	2850
Jenings, Coll.	4000
King, Robert	300

KING WILLIAM COUNTY (Continued)

	Acres
Kenlerise, Symon	200
Lee, John	20
Lypscomb, Ambrose	600
Lasy, Wm.	100
Lypscomb, Wm.	300
Littlepage, Rich'd Cap't	2600
Lypscomb, John	200
Mallory, Thomas	150
Mallory, Roger	100
Miles, Daniell	350
McGehee, Thomas	250
Marr, John	200
Morris, Wm.	440
Maybank, Wm.	100
McDonnell, John	150
Maddison, Henry	650
Merriweather, Nich'o	600
Mullone, Matthew	150
Maddison, John	300
Norment, Joseph	800
Norment, Sam'l	100
Noye, Wm.	650
Napier, Robert	100
Owens, Hugh	300
Oustin, John	350
Oakes, John	350
Oliver, John	140
Palmer, Martin	1200
Peek, John	100
Pynes, Nathaniell	1400
Pee, Thomas	400
Purlevant, Arthur	100
Powers, David	200
Pollard, Wm.	500
Pemberton, Geo:	180
Page, John	1000
Pickrell, Gabriell	100
Parks, Coll.	4500
Quarles, John	100
Reynolds, Wm.	100
Robert, Maurice	200
Randall, John	100
Ray, James	100
Rhodes, Nicholas	150
Sandlan, Nicholas	700
Strutton, Thomas	150
Street, Wm.	350
Shilling, George	300
Satterwhite, Charles	150
Slaughter, Geo:	100
Slaughter, Martin	130
Stark, John	500
Sanders, Joshua	100
See, Mathew	200
Sellers, Jacob	350
Spruce, Jeremy	150

KING WILLIAM COUNTY (Continued)

	Acres
Smith, Edm'd	150
Spencer, Thomas	600
Slaughter, John	90
Smith, Christ'o	800
Slaughter, Henry	100
Toms, Wm.	150
Towler, Matthew	150
Terry, Thomas	300
Terry, Stephen	330
Tomason, Thomas	150
Terry, James	400
Tremeer, John	100
Vickrey, Henry	450
West, Jno. Coll.	1800
Winfree, Henry	300
West, Tho. Capt.	1000
Whitworth, John	200
Whitlock, John	200
Willeroy, Abraham	550
Williams, Phillip	100
Williams, Griffith	240
Wood, Thomas	300
Whitehead, John	100
Woolsey, Jacob	130
Williams, John	150
Williams, Sam'l	600
Wright, Thomas	150
Whitbee, Robert	800
West, Nathan'l Capt.	2000
Waller, John Maj'r	800
Willis, Wm.	250
Wheelis, Joseph	130
Wormley, Madam	3000
Winston, William	170
Whitehead, Phillip	3000
Yancey, Charles	100
Yarborough, John	150
Yarborough, Richard	300
Wm. Stanard M:S	1000
James Wood K:Q	500
Zachary Lewis K:Q	450
Peter Kemp G:C	600
Wm. Beck N.K.	1600
Tho: Hickman K.Q.	550
Benj'a Clement G.C.	600
David Bray J.C.C.	1000
Job House N.K.	2000
Harry Beverley M.S.	600
Chillian White G.C.	300

A Full & Perfect Rent Roll of all the Land held of her Maj'tie in CHARLES CITY COUNTY this present year 1704 by patents etc.

	Acres
Aliat, John	100
Bradley, Joseph	200
Baxter, John	250
Bishop, Rob't	200
Bedingfield, Tho:	110
Botman, Harman	100
Burton, Henry	200
Burwell, Lewis	8000
Brooks, Rob't	150
Blanks, Richard Sr.	250
Blanks, Richard Jr.	125
Blanks, Thomas	125
Bradford, Rich'd	1397
Brown, Marmaduke	100
Bray, David	230
Cole, Rob't	80
Codell, Rich'd	100
Clark, Edw'd	962¼
Clark, Daniell	250
Clark, Joseph	230
Christian, Tho:	1273
Cock, Edw'd	350
Cock, Rich'd	975
Davis, Thomas	200
Davis, Rich'd	118
Edwards, John	287½
Epes, Littlebury	400
Epes, John	500
Ele, Sam'l	682
Evans, John	800
Floyd, Geo:	243
Folwer, Rich'd	150
Flowers, Sam'l	200
Gunn, James	250
Grosse, Edw'd	100
Hamlin, Jno.	143½
Hill, Edw'd	2100
Haynes, Nich'o	125
Harrison, Benj'a	6350
Harwood, John	100
Howard, James	200
Hattle, Shard	112
Harwood, Joseph	659
Harwood, Sam'l	350
Harwood, Rob't	312½
Hunt, Wm.	3130
Hunt, John	1500
Harmon, Eliz'b	479
Hyde, Wm.	120
Hamlin, Stephen	80
Hamlin, Tho:	254
Irby, Wm.	103
Javox, James	100
Jordin, Edw'd	100
Justis, Justinian	200

CHARLES CITY COUNTY (Continued)

	Acres
Lwlin, (Lewėllain)? Dan'l	600
Lawrence, James	100
Manders, James	100
Minge, James	1086
Mountford, Jeffry	100
Marvell, Tho:	1238
Moodie, Sam'l	82
Muschamp, John	80
New, Edm'd	100
New, Rob't	300
Owen, Wm.	100
Owen, David	100
Parker, Tho:	1667
Parish, Wm.	100
Parish, Charles	100
Parker, James	160
Parish, Edw'd	100
Parish, John	100
Roach, Jno. Sr.	630
Renthall, Joseph	270
Russell, Sam'l	253
Roper, John	220
Royall, Joseph	260
Smith, Obidiah	100
Sampson, Widd'o	211
Stith, Drewry (Drury)?	1240
Stith, John	1395
Stockes, John	176
Stockes, Silvanus Sr.	250
Stockes, Silvanus Jr.	550
Speares, Geo:	225
Tanner, Tho:	2000
Tarendine, John	150
Turner, Edw'd	195
Trotman, Anne	120
Vernon, Walter	240
Wyatt, Widd'o	800
Woodam, Tho:	100
Waren, John	54

An acc't of what Land I cannot gett the Quitt Rents the persons living out of the County

Joseph Parish at Kiquotan	100
Rich'd Smith, James City Cty.	350
Dan'l Hayley	200
Wm. Lagg, Henrico County	100

Tho: Parker, Sherrif

NEW KENT COUNTY RENT ROLL
A Rent Roll of the Lands held of her Maj'tie in the Parish of St. Peters and St. Paull Anno 1704

	Acres
Alford, John	240
Allen, Rich'd	550
Alex, (Alexander)? Abraham	100
Allen, Rob't	100
Austin	245
Austin, James	700
Amos, Fran:	100
Ashcroft, Tho:	180
Aldridge, Jno.	250
Atkinson, Jno.	300
Anthony, Mark	190
Anderson, Jno.	100
Anderson, Rob't	900
Arise, Marg't	200
Austin, Rich'd	50
Anderson, Rob't	700
Anderson, David	300
Anderson, Rich'd	200
Allen, Reynold	205
Allvis, George	325
Aron, Josiah	200
Amos, (Ames)? Nich'o	50
Allen, Daniell	250
Allen, Sam'l	150
Anderson, John	100
Ashley, Charles	100
Bourn, Wm.	140
Bray, Sarah	790
Bradbury, Geo:	100
Brother, Jno.	200
Bayley, Jno.	80
Beck, Wm, Mr.	200
Butts, (Batts)? Alice	150
Burnell, (Burwell), Mary Mrs.	2750
Bassett, Wm.	550
Ball, David	200
Baughan, Jno. Jr.	300
Bassett, Tho:	350
Blackburn, Rowland	700
Baker, Christ'o	100
Bear, Peter	100
Brooks, Rich'd	85
Burnell, Edw'd	200
Brown, Jno.	100
Bullock, Rich'd	450
Blackwell, James Jr.	200
Brooks, Rob't	45
Bulkley, Benj'a	200
Blackwell, James	950
Baughan, Jno.	100
Baughan, Joseph	100
Bostock, Jno.	100
Bostock, Wm.	80

NEW KENT COUNTY (Continued)

	Acres
Bumpus, Rob't	100
Burwell, Lewis	200
Bryan, Charles	100
Bullock, Edw'd	450
Blalock, Jno.	492
Baker, Jno.	130
Bearne, Henry	50
Bukly, (Buckly)? Jno.	225
Bow, Henry	200
Bradley, Tho:	255
Barker, Cha:	100
Bugg, Sam'l	60
Bassett, Wm. Esq.	1260
Beck, Wm.	433
Beare, Joseph	150
Barrett, Christ'o	60
Baughtwright, Jno.	250
Bad, Sam'l	150
Banks, Andrew	50
Baker, Rich'd	80
Bowles, John	500
Bunch, John	100
Burnett, Jno.	150
Barnhouse, Rich'd	1600
Barbar, Tho:	500
Burkett, Tho:	41
Bates, Edw'd	50
Breeding, John	300
Brower, Mary	100
Bassett, Wm. Esq.	1100
Bradingham, Rob't	150
Baxter, James	90
Cotrell, Rich'd	200
Clarkson, David	200
Crump, Stephen	60
Crump, Wm.	330
Clopton, Wm.	454
Chandler, Rob't	160
Crump, Rich'd	60
Cambo, Rich'd	80
Crawford, David Jr.	400
Crawford, David Mr.	300
Chambers, Edw'd	235
Clerk, Edw'd	282
Collett, Tho:	100
Clark, Christ'o	300
Cocker, Wm.	1000
Case, Hugh	100
Carley, Rich'd	80
Chiles, Henry	700
Cook, Abraham	200
Crump, James	150
Crump, Rob't	150
Clough, Capt.	80
Chandler, Wm.	300
Chandler, Francis	150
Cordey, Tho:	150

NEW KENT COUNTY (Continued)

	Acres
Curnell, Andrew	330
Croome, Joell	600
Crutchfield, Peter	400
Chesley, Wm.	500
Crutchfield, Jr.	400
Carlton, Wm.	140
Chambers, George	100
Cox, Wm.	350
Dolerd, Wm.	50
Dennett, John	350
Durham, James	100
Dumas, Jerimiah	250
Deprest, Rob't	350
Dodd, John	300
Dabony, James	320
Davis, Eliazar	375
Duke, Henry Esq.	325
Dibdall, Jno.	800
Darnell, Rachell	100
Duke, Henry Esq.	170
Davis, John	80
Davenport, Mest (?)	125
Daniell, John	150
Eperson, John	120
Elmore, Tho:	300
Elmore, Tho: Jr.	100
Ellison, Garratt Rob't	520
England, Wm.	490
Elderkin, John	300
Elmore, Peter	100
English, Mungo	500
Ellis, Wm.	100
Finch, Edw'd	300
Foster, Joseph	800
Forgeson, Wm.	507
Fleming, Charles	920
Francis, Tho:	150
Freeman, Wm.	200
Fenton, Widd'o	270
Feare, Edw'd	200
Fisher, Wm.	100
Goodger, Jno.	200
Green, Edw'd	200
Gibson, Tho:	370
Garrat, James	375
Gonton, Jno.	250
Glass, Jno.	150
Graham, Tho:	250
Gleam, Jno.	300
Giles, Jno.	120
Gentry, Nich:	250
Garland, Edw'd	2600
Glass, Anne	150
Granchard, Tho:	480
Greenfield, Fran:	80

NEW KENT COUNTY (Continued)

	Acres
Gillmott, Jno.	150
Gawen, Phillip	50
Gillmott, Rich'd	150
Glassbrook, Rob't	400
Gadberry, Tho:	200
Gill, Nich'o	222
Gotling, Wm.	460
Goodring, Alexander	100
Gills, John	100
Guridge, Rich'd	225
Herlock, John	320
Hilton, Jno.	300
Hughs, Jno.	180
Huberd, Jno.	827
Howle, Jno.	150
Howle, Jno. Jr.	100
Hughs, Rob't	966
Harris, Edw'd	100
Harris, Tho:	100
Hawes, Haughton	850
Harris, John	146
Hill, Jno.	250
Hester, Fran:	300
Horsley, Rowland	250
Horman, Rob't	300
Hughes, Rees	400
Hill, Sam'l	300
Holled, Sam'l	100
Harrellton, Paul	360
Hatfield, Wm.	318
Harris, Wm.	125
Harris, Benj'a	100
Horkeey, John	800
Hainy, John	280
Haiselwood, Jno.	200
Haiselwood, Tho:	50
Hockiday, Wm.	300
Holdcroft, Henry	95
Hogg, Mary	140
Harmon, Wm.	350
Hogg, Jno. Jr.	260
Harris, Wm.	100
Hopkins, Wm.	200
Howes, Job	300
Hight, John	100
Hankins, Charles	340
Harris, Wm.	150
Harris, Rob't	75
Handey, Wm.	150
Hogg, Wm.	200
Haselwood, Rich'd	100
Harlow, Tho:	230
Hutton, Geo:	150
Jackson, Tho:	500
Izard, Fran:	1233

NEW KENT COUNTY (Continued)

	Acres
Jarratt, Rob't	1600
Johnson, Mich'l	40
Jones, John	100
Johnson, Wm.	265
Jones, Jane	200
Johnson, John	100
Johnson, Edw'd	150
Jennings, Rob't	100
Jones, Frederick	500
Joh (n)es, John	100
Jeeves, Tho:	100
Jones, Francis	200
Jones, John	100
Jones, Evan	500
King, Eliz'b	300
Kembro, Jno.	540
Kembro, Jno. Jr.	150
Keeling, Geo:	1500
Lightfoot, John Esq'r	3600
Littlepage, Rich'd	2160
Lesplah, Peter	100
Lestrange, Tho:	200
Liddall, Geo. Coll.	100
Lawson, Nich'o	200
Levermore, Phill	1000
Lewis, John Esq.	2600
Lawson, John	50
Lewis, John	375
Lovell, Geo:	920
Lovell, Charles	250
Leak, Wm.	280
Logwood, Tho:	100
Lacey, Wm.	500
Lacey, Tho:	100
Luke, Jno.	150
Lochester, Rob' t	80
Lewis, Tho:	115
Lee, Edw'd	120
Lochester, Edw'd	80
Law, James	100
Laton, Reubin	100
Linsey, Joseph	1150
Linsey, Wm.	50
Lane, Tho:	100
Millington, Wm. Jr.	450
Mitchell, Stephen Jr.	75
Millington, Wm.	200
Moss, Sam'l	200
Mitchell, Tho:	300
Meanley, Wm.	100
Mims, Tho:	200
Mitchell, Stephen	200
Moor, Pelham	125
Martin, Tho:	100
Martin, Martin	150
Morris, Rob't	245
Moss, Tho:	430

NEW KENT COUNTY (Continued)

	Acres
Morgan, Edw'd	50
Moon, Stephen	70
Major, Wm.	456
Murroho, Jno.	100
Moon, Jno.	250
Mason, Tho:	300
Martin, John	400
Masey, Peter	100
Madox, John	300
Martin, Wm.	230
Martin, James	100
Moss, James	720
Moon, Thos.	65
McKing, Alexander	170
McKoy, Jno.	300
Merridith, Geo:	400
Melton, Rich'd	290
Morreigh, John	110
Menfield, John	210
Mills, Nich'o	300
Mask, Jno.	411
Medlock, John	350
Moon, Edw'd	65
McKgehe, Wm.	131½
Merriweather, Nich'o	3327
Mage, Peter	450
Mitchell, Wm.	512
Marr, Geo.	100
Moor, Anne	75
Mutray, Tho:	382
Mirideth, James	270
Mohan, Warwick	850
Muttlow, (Mattlow)? James	150
Morgan, Matthew	210
Morris, John	450
Markham, Tho:	100
Moxon, Wm.	100
Mackeny, Eliz'b	250
Meacon, Gideon	270
Nucholl, James	300
Neaves, James	150
Nonia, (Nonice)? Rich'd	100
Norris, Wm.	100
Osling, John	150
Otey, John	290
Oudton, Matt	190
Page, John Jr.	400
Park, John	200
Pease, John	100
Philip, Geo.	100
Penix, Edw'd	200
Plantine, Peter	240
Pendexter, Tho:	1000
Pyraul, James	150
Pullam, Wm.	575
Purdy, Nich'o	200
Page, Mary Mad'm	3450

NEW KENT COUNTY (Continued)

	Acres
Perkins, John	120
Paite, Jerim.	220
Pasley, Rob't	300
Perkins, Wm.	305
Pait, John	1500
Petever, Tho:	100
Pittlader, Wm.	147
Pickley, Tho:	281
Pittlader, Tho:	295
Porter, John	100
Petty, John	2190
Park, Coll.	7000
Purly, John	100
Raglin, Evan	300
Raglin, Evan Jr.	100
Raglin, Thos	100
Ross, Wm.	150
Richardson, Henry	300
Raymond, James	80
Reynold, Tho:	355
Reyley, Jno.	100
Reynolds, Jonah	50
Rhoads, Charles	175
Reynolds, Sam'l	820
Rice, Tho:	300
Redwood, John	1078
Rule, Widd'o	50
Richardson, Richard	890
Russell, John	550
Richardson, John	1450
Richard, Eman'l	1250
Round Tree, Wm.	100
Randolph, Widd'o	100
Styles, John	200
Smith, Nath'l.	82
Sanders, Wm.	40
Spear, Rob't	450
Sanders, James	60
Scott, John	300
Scrugg, Rich'd	100
Strange, Alexander	450
Smith, Wm.	110
Scrugg, Jno.	50
Snead, Tho:	200
Sunter, Stephen	478
Symonds, Josiah	100
Sanders, John	130
Stephens, Wm.	100
Stanley, Tho:	150
Sandidge, Jno.	100
Sprattlin, Andrew	654
Snead, John	75
Smith, James	80
Sexton, Wm.	80
Sims, Jno.	1000
Smith, Roger	300

NEW KENT COUNTY (Continued)

	Acres
Sherriff, Henry	100
Salmon, Thomas	50
Sanders, Tho:	75
Symonds, George	125
Stamp, Ralph	625
Stanup, Capt.	1024
Stanup, Rich'd	325
Shears, Paul	325
Stepping, Tho:	350
Slater, James	700
Tony, Alexander	170
Tovis, (Tevis)? Edm'd	100
Turner, Henry	250
Turner, Wm.	250
Turner, Geo:	400
Thorp, Tho:	200
Thurmond, Rich'd	131½
Tucker, Tho:	700
Turner, James	50
Thompson, James	100
Tully, Wm.	200
Turner, Geo. Jr.	200
Tate, James	160
Town, Eliz'b	100
Thomasses Orphans	500
Tinsley, Cornelius	220
Tyler	100
Tinsley, Tho:	150
Tinnell, Wm.	400
Taylor, Tho:	25
Tinsley, Jno.	130
Tapp, Jno.	110
Tynney, James	150
Tynney, Alexand'r	210
Thompson, Capt.	2600
Tyney, Thom:	190
Taylor, Joseph	150
Taylor, Lemuell	212
Taylor, Thomas	350
Twitty, Thomas	200
Upshend, Jon	60
Vaughan, Wm.	300
Vice, Amen	50
Venable, Abr:	100
Venable, John	200
Vaughan, John	250
Vaughan, Vincent	410
Wintby, Jacob	250
Winfry, Charles	100
Waddell, Jno.	40
Walker, Wm.	650
Walton, Edw'd	150
Wilson, Jno.	200
Waddill, Wm.	375
Warring, Peter	88
Wingfield, Tho:	150
Weaver, Sam	100

NEW KENT COUNTY (Continued)

	Acres
Wyatt, Alice	1300
West, Nath:	6370
Webb, Mary	200
Wilmore, Jno.	200
Webster, Joseph	80
West, Giles	200
Wharton, Tho:	270
Willis, Fran:	134
Waddy, Sam'l	150
Willford, Charles	200
Waid, James	250
White, Jno.	320
Wood, Henry	100
Woody, Symon	50
Woody, John	100
Winstone, Antho'	310
Winstone, Jane	850
Woody, James	130
Winstone, Sarah	275
Watson, Theophilus	325
Woodson, Jno.	600
Walton, Edw'd	450
Wood, Walter	100
Watkins, Wm.	50
Wilkes, Joseph	250
Williams, Clark	300
Willis, Stephen	500
Williams, Tho:	100
Worrin, Rob't	300
Woodull, James	200
Walker, Capt.	400
Wilson, James	60
Wheeler, John	75
Williams, Wm.	100
White, John	190
Yeoman, John	50
Yeoell, (Jewell or Ewell)? Judith	150

Quit Rents Y't hath not been p'd this year viz.

Richardson, Matt	200
Wm. Wheeler	150
Coll. Parker	300

James Mosie (?) Sherriff

THE RENT ROLL of the Land in JAMES CITY COUNTY 1704

	Acres
Adkinson, Tho:	50
Adkinson, Henry	250
Armestone, Joshua	50
Adams, Anne	150
Argo, James	200
Abbitt, Francis	100
Aperdon, Wm.	80
Allen, Rich'd	540
Baker, Jno.	100
Bentley, Jno.	125
Bell, Edw'd	75
Burwell, Lewis	1350
Beckitt, Tho:	60
Bray, James	3500
Bryon, Jno.	100
Bingley, James	100
Bonham, Jno.	50
Brown, James	250
Bower, Wm.	50
Broadnax, Wm.	1683
Bayley, Wm.	100
Black, Geo:	200
Bush, Jno.	800
Ballard, Tho:	100
Bray, David	5758
Burton, Ralph	200
Blankitt, Henry	100
Brand, Rich'd	125
Breeding, Jno.	100
Bruer, Shackfield	350
Blackley, Wm.	142
Barratt, Wm.	305
Barron, Tho:	100
Blankes, Henry	650
Bagby, Tho:	180
Barnes, Francis	200
Brackitt, Tho:	150
Browne, Wm.	1070
Buxton, Sam'l	300
Bimms, Christ'o	300
Ballard, Wm.	300
Boman	90
Benge, Rob't	60
Center, Jno.	100
Clark, Wm.	1100
Charles, Phil.	200
Capell, Tho:	200
Cearley, Wm.	450
Clerk, Rob't	300
Clerk, Sarah	200
Cole, Rich'd	80
Cooper, Tho:	60
Cook, Rich'd	75
Cosby, Charles	250
Crawley, Rob't	460
Cryer, Geo.	100

JAMES CITY COUNTY (Continued)

	Acres
Cobbs, Ambrose	350
Cock, Jonathan	250
Cowles, Thomas	675
Dormar, Jno.	100
Drummond, Wm.	150
Deane, Jno.	150
Duckitt, Abraham	290
Danzee, Jno. Jacob Coignan	4111
Deane, Tho.	80
Deane, Wm.	100
Drummond, Jno.	700
Deane, Tho.	150
Duke, Tho.	750
Davey, Francis	778
Doby, Jno.	300
Duke, Henry Jr.	1000
Davis, Geo.	50
Duke, Henry Esq'r	2986
Elerby, Eliz'b	600
Edmunds, Eliz'b	175
Eggleston, Joseph	550
Eglestone, Benj'a	1375
Fearecloth, Tho.	277
Farthing, Wm.	50
Fraysee, Jno.	250
Fox, Wm.	50
Fovace, Stephen	150
Fish, Jno.	100
Freeman, Geo.	197
Furnbush, Wm.	400
Flanders, Francis	350
Goodrich, Benj'a	1650
Gwin, Jno.	100
Ganey, Tho.	60
Guilsby, Tho.	300
Graves, Joseph	250
Goss, Charles	171
Goodall, Jno.	400
Geddes	476
Gill, Jno.	100
Green, Tho.	50
Gregory, Nich'o	50
Green, Wm.	100
Ginnigs, Phill.	400
Gibson, Gibey	150
Goodman, John	275
Goodwin, Rob't	150
Grice, Aristotle	700
Greene, Tho.	500
Hudson, Wm.	50
Herd, Zeph.	100
Hadley, Dyonisia	100
Hall, Jno.	50
Harvey, Geo.	1425
Howard, Jno.	25
Hughes, Geo.	250
Harfield, Mich.	50

JAMES CITY COUNTY (Continued)

	Acres
Hudson, Geo.	100
Hudson, Leonard	170
Hood, Jno.	250
Harris, Wm.	140
Hamner, Nich'o	500
Henley, Leonard	300
Hooker, Edw'd	1067
Higgins, Jno.	75
Henley, Jno.	100
Holiday, Tho.	250
Hitchcock, John	100
Holoman, James	150
Hubert, Matt.	1834
Handcock, Rob't	300
Haley, James	310
Hook, Mich.	260
Hill, Tho.	310
Hatfield, Rich'd	100
Hilliard, Jerimah	225
Hilliard, John	200
Hopkins, John	120
Hunt, Wm.	1300
Hix, John	115
Harrison, Wm.	150
Hawkins, John	200
Hix, Joseph	100
Harrison, Benj'a Jr.	100
Inch, Jno.	30
Jones, Fred.	300
Inglis, Mungo	1300
Jenings, Edm'd Esq.	200
Jaquelin, Edw'd	400
Jeffry, Tho.	60
Jackson, Eliz'b	200
Jackson, Rich'd	150
Jeffry, Matt.	100
Johnson, Anth'o	100
Jones, Wm.	50
Johnson, Jno.	260
Jones, Wm.	115
Jordan, John	1000
Knowstarp	150
Lawrence, Rich'd	250
Ludwell, Phil. Esq'r	6626
Laffoon, John	75
Lund, Thomas	100
Lillingtone, Benj'a	100
Lidie, Rob't	500
Loftin, Corneles	200
Lightfoot, Phil.	1650
Lightfoot, Jno. Esq'r	250
Love, Jno.	100
Loftin, Corneles Jr.	200
Liney, Wm.	55
Mookins, Roger	160
Macklin, Wm.	300
Marston, Wm.	150

JAMES CITY COUNTY (Continued)

	Acres
Morris, Edw'd Jr.	100
Manningaren	150
Marston, Tho.	1000
Martin, Rich'd	150
Maples, Tho.	300
Mattlow, Jno.	170
Morris, James	800
Mores, David	170
Myers, Wm. Jr.	100
Mountfort, Tho.	600
Morris, Jno.	195
Marble, Geo.	135
Mallard, Paynes	100
Merryman, James	300
Morecock, Tho.	700
Meekings, Tho.	175
Marraw, Dennis	30
Major, John	100
Norrell, Hugh	328
Nicholson, Jno.	144
Nicholls, Henry	100
Nailer, Wm.	300
Omooney (O'Mooney)? Mary	126
Prince, George	50
Page, John	1700
Page, Mary	900
Pigot, Benj'a	90
Pall, Wm.	450
Parker, Tho.	1650
Peper, Stephen	100
Phillips, Jno.	300
Pattison, Alex.	100
Perkins, Charles	320
Philips, Edw'd	100
Philips, Wm.	300
Pearman, Wm.	300
Pearman, Jno.	200
Pendexter, Tho.	550
Parish, Tho.	100
Pattisson, Tho.	200
Parke, Dan'l Esq'r	1800
Pattison, Catherine	150
Rhodes, Randall	50
Ryder, Mary	350
Rhodes, Francis	100
Rovell, Jno.	50
Revis, Wm.	150
Russell, Sam'l	350
Stafford, Mary	210
Sanders, Jno.	50
Sprattley, Jno.	350
Smith, Christ'o	450
Short, Jno.	90
Smallpage, Rob't	190
Santo, Rob't	100
Smith, Jno.	114
Slade, Wm.	80

JAMES CITY COUNTY (Continued)

	Acres
Soane, Henry	750
Sykes, Barnard	1012
Selvey, Jacob	50
Sharp, Jno.	800
Shaley, Jno.	150
Simes, Wm.	650
Sorrell, Mary	500
Sherman, Eliz'b	500
Tinsley, Edw'd	100
Tinsley, Rich'd	100
Tomson, James	100
Thackson, John	289
Tyery, Wm.	1590
Thurston, John	500
Thomas, Wm.	150
Tyler, Henry	730
Tullett, John	625
Thomas, Hanah	100
Thomson, Henry	150
Twnie (Twine)? Tho.	100
Thomas, Jno.	250
Vaughan, Henry	1900
Udall, Matthew	50
Verney, Wm.	50
Vaiding, Isaac	300
Weathers, Tho.	130
Wood, Rich'd	130
Whitaker, Wm.	320
Ward, Tho.	100
Weldon, Sarah	100
Whaley, Mary	200
Winter, Tim'o	250
Wilkins, Sam'l	170
Wright, Sam'l	100
Williams, Matt.	75
Walker, Alex.	500
Williamson, John	120
Walker, David	150
Walker, Alex. Jr.	2025
Warberton, Tho.	190
Weldey, Geo.	317
Wragg, Tho.	500
Wooton, Jno.	150
Willson, Jno.	140
Wilkins, Tho.	600
Wood, Edw'd	300
Wood, Tho.	200
Walker, David	100
Ward, Rob't	800
Wright, Mary	175
Woodward, Lanslett	50
Woodward, John	650
Woodward, Geo.	350
Woodward, Sam'l	350

JAMES CITY COUNTY (Continued)

	Acres
Waid, Henry	150
Waid, Edw'd	150
Young, Rob't	350
Young, Thomas	350
Benj'a Sholtwater of York County	300
Tho. Sorrell	200
Mary Neshamah of the Blackwater	168

A RENT ROLL of all the Land in YORK COUNTY in 1704

	Acres
Wm. Jackson	200
Matt. Pierce	100
Jno. Latin	150
Rob't Cobbs	100
Francis Sharp	100
Geo. Baskewyle	350
Rich'd Gilford	100
Jos. Frith	50
Wm. Jones	70
Nath. Crawley	384
Tho. Crips	750
Wm. Davis	200
Lewis Barnee (Barnes)?	80
Arthur Lun	50
Jno. Bates	669
Jno. Serginton	150
Wm. Taylor	100
Rich'd Page	150
Wm. Jorden	580
Jno. Lynes	150
Alex. Banyman	50
Wm. Cobbs	50
Mary Whaley	550
Henry Tyler	180
Rich'd Kendall	150
Wm. Hansford	300
Nich'o Sebnell	150
David Stoner	50
Ralph Hubbard	50
Wm. Harrison	50
Jno. Wyth	100
Tho. Hill	930
Tho. Vines	200
Morgan Baptist	100
Phil. Deadman	75
Bazill Wagstaff	127
Wm. Allen	117
Rob't Read	750
Jos. Mountford	307
Roger Boult	100
Edw'd Fuller	70
Tho. Jefferson	100
Henry Duke	25
Jno. Hansford	100
Rob't Peters	160
Jno. Morland	100
Wm. Lee	350
Rich'd Burt	200
John Eaton	170
Rob: Starke	250
Rob't Harrison	200
Jno. Morris	125
James Bates	117
Eliz'b Jones	94
Edw'd Young	100
Rob't Green	200

YORK COUNTY (Contd)

	Acres
Tho. Fear	100
Edward Thomas	223
John Loyall	100
Stephen Pond	200
Wm. Wise	850
Cornelius Shoehorn	100
Joseph White	750
Daniell Park Esq'r	2750
Tho. Fear Jr.	130
Orlando Jones	450
Ambrose Cobbs	163
Henry Dyer	50
Wm. Davis	100
Wm. Buckner	302½
Tho. Barber	600
Eliz'b Tindall	60
Dudley Diggs	1350
Wm. Hewitt	150
Mary Collier	433
Charles Collier	684
Tho: Hansford	75
Geo. Browne	150
Wm. Gibbs	50
Wm. Pekithman	650
Jno. Smith	150
Baldwin Matthews	1300
Jno. Daniell	200
Seamor Powell	130
Jno. Lewis Esq'r	300
Wm. Timson	2000
Jno. Page	490
Jos. Benjafield	80
Tho. Stear	60
Stephen Fovace	565
Edw'd Jenings Esq'r	850
Eliz'b Archer	370
Wm. Coman	50
Eliz'b Hansford	100
Sam'l Hill	25
Jno. Henderson	50
Tho. Buck	350
Lewis Burwell	2100
Rob't Crawley	400
Rob't Hyde	200
Rob't Harrison	250
Jeffry Overstreet	50
Tho. Overstreet	50
John Myhill	52
Mary Roberts	25
Benj'a Stagsdall	50
Tho. Wade	375
Jos. Walker	615
Jno. Sanders	100
Mongo Inglis	400
Tho. Holyday	100
Jno. Williams	100

YORK COUNTY (Continued)

	Acres
Antho. Sebrell	50
Rob't Jones	100
James Cansebee	200
Rich'd Booker	200
James Morris	100
Henry Adkinson	82
Rob't Jackson	150
Anthony Robinson	183
Hannah Lamb	50
James Calthorp	900
Tho. Boulmor	265
Peter Pasque	12
Jno. Chapman	70
Jno. Pond	112
Sarah Tomkins	250
Rob't Kirby	200
Tho. Kirby	270
Edw'd Curtis	200
Jno. Forgison (Ferguson)?	200
Wm. Row	902
Jno. Hunt	550
Wm. Taverner	100
Armiger Wade	424
Rich'd Dixon	490
Edm'd Jenings Esq'r	1650
Jno. Persons	300
Tho. Nutting	375
Peter Manson	150
Rich'd Slaughter	275
James Persons	350
Tho. Roberts	450
Jno. Toomer	335
Dan'l Taylor	225
Rob't Hayes	220
Henry Andros	274
Jno. Wells	750
Rob't Curtis	250
Tho. Cheesman Sr.	1800
Jos. Potter	25
Hen. Heywood	1300
David Holyday	600
John Northern	130
Jno. Doswell	367
Isaac Powell	100
Symon Staice	200
Jno. Drewutt	200
Rob't Topladie	100
Jno. Potter	93
Lewis Vernum	150
James Slaughter	250
Tho. Burnham	50
Jno. Doswell Jr.	100
Rob't Shields	400
Wm. Wilson	50
Owen Davis	247
Tho. Walker	100
Rich'd Nixon	150

YORK COUNTY (Continued)

	Acres
Henry Clerk	100
Elias Love	25
Wm. Howard	100
Jno. Sanderver	100
Jno. Cox	50
Tho. Gibbins	100
Tho. Hind	100
Tho. Cheesman Jr.	600
Wm. Browne	200
Jno. Rogers	650
Jno. Moss	150
Jno. Lawson	100
Nich'o Phillips	150
Wm. Sheldon	750
Jno. Wayman	100
Tho. Edmonds	150
Lawrence Smith	1700
James Paulmer	150
Wm. Gurrow	150
Peter Goodwin	400
Rob't Snead	50
Edw'd Crawley	150
Wm. Gordon	150
Jno. Hilsman	75
Jno. Wright	100
Jno. Gibbons	50
Eliz'b Goodwin	1200
Sam'l Cooper	150
Jno. Frips	150
Tho. Wooton	150
Edw'd Moss	759
Rebecha Watkins	100
Wm. Whitaker	1800
Hampton Parish	200
Bruton Parish Glebe	300
Rob't Ivy he living in James City Cty. and no tenn't on Land	100

Wm. Barbar, S(heriff) Y(ork) C(ounty)

A TRUE & PERFECT RENT ROLL of the Land in ELIZABETH CITY COUNTY for the year 1704

	Acres
Coll. Wm. Wilson	1024
Mr. Wm. Smelt	150
Mr. Pasque Curle	300
Mr. Nich'o Curle	950
Coll. Dudley Diggs	216
Sam'll Pearce	100
Mary Jenings	250
Mark Powell	184
Wm. Davis	42
Jno. Skinner	50
Tho. Baines	50
Wm. Latham	90
Tho. Tucker	60
Matthew Smell	100
Charles Cooley	200
Jno. Chandler	150
Wm. Umpleet	25
Charles Tucker	240
Tho. Allin	227
Wm. Williams School	600
Wm. Williams of himself	260
Mrs. Bridgett Jenkins	100
Christ'o Davis	25
Wm. Spicer	60
Tho. Hawkins	270
Jno. Bowles	360
Jno. Theodam	100
Barth'o Wetherby	300
Jos. White	200
Cap't Henry Royall	750
Rob't Bright Sr.	100
Tho. Naylor	100
Geo. Cooper Sr.	100
Tho. Needham	100
Cha. Cooper	100
Wm. Dunn	100
Charles Jenings	225
Sam'll Davill	100
Paltey Davill	100
Francis Rogers	200
Tho. Babb of Selden	300
Rich'd Honsley (Hensley)?	90
Sarah Nagleer	230
Henry Dunn	50
Peter Pearce	50
Moses Davis	150
Mich. Breltuen (?)	100
Henry Robinson	200
Christ'o Copeland	340
Tho. Faulkner	50
Mr. James Wallace	1300
Mr. Bertram Servant	418
Rob't Taylor	50
Joseph Harris	50
Wm. Robinson	50
Wm. Boswell	220

ELIZABETH CITY COUNTY (Continued)

	Acres
Wm. Winter	70
John Lowry of Selden	110
Edw'd Roe	100
Henry James	100
Rich'd Rowtton (?)	50
Tho. Poole	1200
John Wheat, Land	66
Geo. Bell	80
Widd'o Ballis	350
Geo. Walker	325
Mr. Rob't Beverley	777
Jno. House (?)	157
Jno. Bushell Jr.	150
Roger Masnibred	50
John Sheperd	210
Wm. Minsor	150
Edw'd Lattimore	190
James Baker	225
Tho. Tucker	60
Jno. Cotton	50
Mark Johnson	400
Maj'r Wm. Armistead	460
Coll. Anth'o Armistead	2140
Daniell Preeday	50
Matthew Watts	454
Bryan Penny	50
Giles Dupra	150
Jno. Bayley	415
Mary Simmons	200
Jno. Parish	50
Anth'o Griggs	50
Abr. Parish	100
Mark Parish	200
Benj'm Smith	650
Tho. Nobling of Archer (?)	212
Wm. Mallory	200
Widd'o Croashell	100
Charles Powers	400
Rob't Chadwill of Jno. Young	440
Sam'll Fingall	333
Frank Savoy	50
Mr. Edw'd Nichills (Nichols)?	600
Jane Nichols	50
John Francis	25
James Priest	50
Simon Hollier	200
Mr. Tho. Gebb	630
Mr. Rich'd Booker	526
Mr. Wm. Lowry	526
Mr. Merry or Mrs. Dunn	500
Wm. Haslyitt	100
Cap't. Augustine More	285
John More	250
John Passones	780
Rebeckha Morgan	50
Tho. Roberts	250

ELIZABETH CITY COUNTY (Continued)

	Acres
Mr. John Turmer (Turner) ?	50
Henry Lais	50
Cap't Henry Jenkins	300
Mr. Francis Ballard of Seldon	460

Henry Royall Sherriff

A True & Perfect Rent Roll of the Land that is held in
WARWICK COUNTY 1704

	Acres
Maj'r Wm. Cary	300
Mr. Nedler, Plantacon	80
Rob't Hubbert	101
Wm. Harwood	625
Rich'd Glanville Orphans	165
Wm. Hubbert	200
Henry Gibbs	315
Wm. Hewitt	150
James Hill	135
John Golden	50
Tho. Harwood	575
Jno. Harwood	704
Cap't Tho. Charles	100
Hump. Harwood	400
Matthew Wood	300
Edw'd Joyner	60
Coll. Dudley Diggs	4626
Eliz'b Lucas	800
John Hillard	74
Edw'd Loftes	60
Wm. Rowles Orphans	150
Sam'll Hatton	225
Isaac Goodwin	225
Geo. Robinson	70
Seymon Powell	250
John Dawson	300
Wades Orphans	100
Henry Dawson	200
John Bowger	100
Joseph Cooper	200
Rob't Rob'ts (Roberts)	60
Geo. Burton	330
Cap't Mills Wells	425
Roger Daniell Orphans	196
Jno. Hansell	100
Emanuell Wells	325
Eliz'b Wells Widd'o	155
Widd'o Lewelling	100
Wm. Wells	615
Elias Wells	50
Widd'o Pierce	155
Tho. Haynes	850
John Scarsbrook	850
Francis Jones	150
Matthew Jones	750
Jno. Read	875
Mr. Brewer Land	1350
Mr. Henry Cary	670
Langhorne Orphans	602
Coll. Coles Orphans	1350
Peter Jones	150
Sam'll Crew Orphans	150
Sam'll Symons	173
Mrs. Eliz'b Whitaker	600

WARWICK COUNTY (Continued)

	Acres
John Cannon	75
John Linton	75
Rich'd Cough	60
Coll. Miles Cary	1960
Mr. John Mallhote	61
Rowland Wms. (Williams)	171
Rob't Chapell	150
James Chapell	100
Edward Powers	200
James White	40
Peter Sawers Orphans	95
Wm. Cotton	143
James Cotton	70
John Croley	100
Stephen Burgess	128
Widd'o Yorgen	60
Geo. Jackson	193
Sarah Rainshaw	125
Rich'd Wooton	243
Sam'll Hoggard	120
James Floyd	100
Fr. Rices Orphans	200
Mr. Nath. Hoggard	270
Widd'o Chappell	321
Tho. Ascow	50
Garrett Ridley	300
Sam'll Ranshaw	238
Charles Stukey	86
Jos. Naylor	100
Jos. Russell	150
Charles Allen	295
Wm. Newberry	100
John Turner	100
Wm. Smith	150
Eliz'b Holt	150
James Browne	150
Henry Royall	246
Edw'd Rice	375
Tho. Blackistone	75
Mark Noble	215
James Reynolds	75
John Holmes	200
Sam'll Duberry	200
Edw'd Powers	200
Jno. Hatton Orphans	93
Wm. Towland	25
Tho. Merey	3613 or ? 363
Wm. Braley	150
Cope Doyley	500
Nath Edw'ds (Edwards)	100
Sam'll Groves	490
Croucher Orphans	50
Henry Whitaker	60
Woodman Land	200
Wm. Cook	29
Jno. Tignall	392
Tho. Mountfort	890

WARWICK COUNTY (Continued)

	Acres
Joseph Mountfort	558
James Priest	50
Abr. Cawley	80
Wm. Jones	20
Edward Davis	200
The County Land	150
Denbigh Prh. Gleeb	130
Mulberry Island Gleeb	50
Tho. Hansford	75
Mr. Rascows Orphans	1195
Tho. Hansford (never pd.)	75

Patents out of the County

Jno. Trevillian	248
Holman Orphans	200

Robert Hubberd Sherriff

PRINCESS ANNE COUNTY RENT ROLL 1704

	Acres
John Carraway	180
Tho. More	100
Henry Chapman	250
Geo. Poole	1085
James Whithurst	600
Tho. Morris	63
Tho. Joy	600
Thomas Scott	100
Geo. Smith	250
Tho. Hife	200
Rich'd Smith	200
Tho. Hattersby	90
Tho. Jolley	150
Mich. Ventres	450
Cap't Blomer Bray	270
James Mecoy	200
Francis Bond	264
Edw'd Wood	50
Jno. Morrah	200
Alex'd Morrah	200
Ruth Woodhouse	450
Horatia Woodhouse	525
Joseph White	330
Jon. Basnett	250
Owen Wills	100
Mr. Wm. Corneck	1974
Jno. Oakham	390
David Scott	600
Jno. Keeling	2000
Adam Keeling	500
Humphry Smith	50
Jno. Holise (?)	130
Capt. Wm. Crawford	2650
Rich'd Williamson	450
Edw'd Trantor	180
Jno. Sherland	800
Rob't Rany	70
Edw'd Old	450
Coll. Lemuell Mason	650
Mr. Francis Emperor	400
James Kemp	681
Bartho. Williamson	400
Symon Hancock Jr.	200
Geo. Batten	150
Matth. Brinson	250
Mr. Edw'd Mosely Sr.	1000
Wm. Martin	200
James Joslin	100
Alex'd Lilburn	500
James William	100
Mr. Henry Spratt	1736
Symon Hancock Sr.	300
Tho. Walk	298
Jno. Kemp	340
Randolph Lovett	100
Edw'd Davis	200

PRINCESS ANNE COUNTY (Continued)

	Acres
Jno. Sammons	150
Eliz'b Edw's (Edwards)	50
Mr. Benj'm Burroughs	800
Jno. Moncreef	140
Matt. Pallett	600
Wm. Thurston	290
Lancaster Lovett	1850
Rob't Cartwright	260
Jno. Cartwright	100
Math. Macklahan	100
Adam Thorowgood	700
Henry Walstone	800
Edw'd Land	400
Tho. Hall	400
Wm. Catherill	150
Doct'r Browne	600
John Richardson	1000
Rob't Richmond	1000
Tho. Benson	225
Lewis Pervine	800
Edw'd Attwood	400
Wm. Moore	414
Mr. Henry Woodhouse	3000
Tully Emperor	300
Jno. Godfrey	170
Wm. Dyer	700
Edw'd Cooper	200
Wm. Ship	300
Jno. Buck	250
Peter Mallbourn	280
Benj'm Rob'ts (Roberts)	100
Cap't Jno. Gibbs	3100
Sarah Sanford	1200
Henry Harrison	300
James Lemon	1500
Wm. Wallsworth	100
Wm. Caps	1050
Jacob Taylor	80
Steph. Pace	50
Adams Hayes	1360
Wm. Chichester	400
Rob't Dearemore	514
Cap't Francis Morse	1300
Patrick Anguish	150
Tho. Brock	400
Wm. Brock	100
Jno. Sullivant	200
Frank Sheene	300
Jno. Acksted	400
Charles Hendley	100
Duke Hall	70
Job Brooks	150
Jno. Brooks	100
Tho. Turton	110
Peter Crosby	250
Jno. Pisburn	314

PRINCESS ANNE COUNTY (Continued)

	Acres
James Sherwood	200
Edw'd Cannon	550
Rich'd Capps	100
John Doley	640
Matthew Mathias	80
Mr. James Peters	889
John Owens	190
Josias Morris	900
Tho. Mason	140
Wm. Wishart	200
Jno. Russell	300
Stephen Sall	250
Timothy Denniss (?)	100
Geo. Walker	425
Wm. Ashby	100
Charles Griffin	216
Symon Franklin	100
Alice Thrower	125
James Wishart	225
Rich'd Draught	500
Doct!r Wm. Hunter	80
Mr. Jon'tn Sanders	203
Wm. Grinto	650
Henry Fittzgerreld	200
Coll. Anth'o Lawson	3100
Cap't Jno. Thorowgood	1000
Rob't Thorowgood	940
Henry Suthern	690
John Wharton	850
Joseph Doller	150
Jno. Biggs	600
Tho. Lurrey	100
Tho. Walker	820
Adolph Swaine	450
Edw'd Mustin	100
Geo. Bullock	300
Jno. Leggett	400
Mark Tully	300
Wm. Walstone	400
Mark Powell	550
Eliz'b Nicholls	500
Hugh Hoskins	50
Wm. Burrough	50
Wm. Warren	100
Cap't Hugh Campble	800
Geo. Worrington	400
James Tully	400
Wm. Lovett	1300
Wm. Grant	150
Tho. More	100
Rich'd Whithurst	350
Cap't Tho. Cocke	800
John Comins	175
Tho. Griffin	200
Tho. Spratt	600
Jno. Russell	150

PRINCESS ANNE COUNTY (Continued)

	Acres
James Heath	550
David Duncon	100
Daniell Lane	350
George Fowler	600
John Booth	350
Giles Collier	500
Jacob Johnson	1700
Alex'd Willis	150
Rich'd Bonny	2000
Mr. James Doage	784
Anth'o Barnes	200
Jno. Macklalin	100
Tho. Etherington	108
Jno. James	328
Wm. Woodhouse	300
John Mayho	160
Joseph Penny	35
Tho. Penny	650
Mr. Argoll Thorowgood	1000
Cap't Wm. Moseley	600
Jno. Moseley	325
Wm. Smith	180
Wm. Symmons	400
Adam Forguson	120
Benj'm Cummins	200
Jno. Elkes	500
Patrick White	1250
Rich'd Jones	200
Evan Jones	600
Mich. Jones	200
Rich'd Wicker	300
Henry Snaill	250
Mr. Sam'll Bush	550
Mr. Tully Robinson	500
Jno. Briberry	50
Wm. Moseley	50
Cap't Christ'r Merchant	400
Rich'd Cox	50
Matt. Godfrey	150
Thomas Tully	600
Hector Denby	600
Tho. Keeling	700
Wm. More	100
Tho. Cason	550
Sarah Jackson	600
Jacob More	200

Henry Spratt

An Alphabeticall List of the Quit Rents of NORFOLK COUNTY 1704

	Acres
Ashley, Dennis	150
Avis, Widd'o	50
Adam, Wm.	100
Alexander, John	300
Barrington, Wm.	100
Bartee, Rob't	150
Bull, Rob't Sr.	1050
Blanch, Wm.	100
Bond, Wm.	200
Brown, Widd'o	270
Bruce, Abr.	1010
Brown, Wm.	100
Bowers, Jno.	166
Bolton, Wm.	212 or 2102?
Bryon, Roger	200
Bayley, Walter	290
Bruce, Jno.	300
Bishop, Wm.	100
Bull, Henry	1500
Bucken, Wm.	410
Babington, Tho.	150
Babington, Jno.	150
Babington, Rich'd	50
Burges, Geo.	200
Butt, Rich'd	1840
Brown, Edw'd	300
Bigg, Tho..	100
Balingtine, Alexander	300
Balingtine, Geo.	510
Bull, Tho.	2200
Bramble, Henry	100
Blake, Arthur	200
Bolton, Rich'd	700
Branton, John	330
Bacheldon, Joseph	300
Bruh (Bush)?,, Sam'l Maj'r	1628
Balingtine, Wm.	60
Bowles, Henry	330
Cartwright, Peter	1050
Cooper, Wm.	150
Cooper, Jno.	150
Cramore, Geo.	100
Carling, Walter	50
Carling, Joseph	200
C**ch, Rich'd	1050
Chaney, Widd'o	600
Cuthrell, Going	470
Crekmore, Edw'd	800
Cartwright, Widd'o	800
Corprew, Jno.	650
Corprew, No.	650
Crekmore, Jno.	750
Caswell, Widd'o	350
Colley, Jno.	100
Cottell, Tho.	200
Conden, Tho.	390

NORFOLK COUNTY (Continued)

Name	Acres
Conner, Lewis	2200
Carney, Jno.	100
Carney, Rich'd	100
Collins, Wm.	100
Crekmore, Edm'd	690
Charleton, Jno.	50
Cutrell, Tho.	150
Chapman, Rich'd	50
Churey, Tho.	100
Churey, Jno.	150
Dixon, Jno.	300
Davis, Wm. Sr.	250
Davis, Wm.	158
Dresdall, Rob't	318
Davis, Tho.	332
Desnall, Wm.	100
Davis, Edw'd	300
Dalley, Henry	1524
Dalley, Wm.	156
Davis, Tho.	340
Denby, Edw'd	100
Daniell, Hugh	100
Etherdge (Etheridge)?, Tho. Cooper	75
Etherdge (Etheridge)?, Tho. B.A.	50
Etherdge (Etheridge)?, Tho. Sr.	34
Etherdge (Etheridge)?, Tho. Jr.	33
Etherdge (Etheridge)?, Edw'd	66
Etherdge (Etheridge)?, Wm.	250
Etherdge (Etheridge)?, Wm. Jr.	80
Etherdge (Etheridge)?, Marmeduke	525
Edmonds, John	50
Ellis, Wm.	200
Etherdge (Etheridge)?, Edw'd Cooper	200
Estwood, Tho.	170
Estwood, Jno.	75
Etherdge (Etheridge)?, Edw'd Sr.	33
Edw'ds (Edwards), John	250
Etherdge (Etheridge)?, Charles	75
Evans, Abigall	100
Furgison, Tho.	100
Freeman, Jno.	190
Freeman, Alexander	750
Foster, Henry	1000
Ferbey, Jno .	500
Fulsher, Jno.	1396
Godfry, Waren	350
Godfry, John	1470
Godfry, Matthew	450
Grefon, Jno.	700
Garvin, Dan'l	50
Guy, Jno.	110
Givins, Wm.	350
Gilligann, Ferdinando	180
Gilligann, John	200
Gaines, James	150
Gaines, John	50
Guy, James	100

NORFOLK COUNTY (Continued)

	Acres
Horbett (?), Thomas	150
Hayes, Wm.	200
Harris, John	110
Holyday, Jno.	440
Hodges, Joseph	50
Hoges, Tho.	407
Hoges, John	526
Hollowell, Jno. Sr.	524
Hollygood, Tho.	100
Hollowell, Jno.	200
Holsted, Henry	633
Hollowell, Joseph	1280
Holsted, John	350
Hues, Edw'd	1404
Hullett, Jno.	300
Hodges, Roger	109
Hodges, Tho.	50
Hodges, Rich'd	375
Harvey, Rich'd	265
Handberry	300
Hollowell, Elener	1550
Herbert, Jno.	400
Hargrave, Benj'm	250
Hartwell, Rich'd	150
Henland, Jno.	800
Ivey, Geo.	496
Jackson, Symon	720
Ives, Tim'o	400
Ives, Tim'o Jr.	100
Ives, John	434
Johnston, John	275
Johnston, Morcey	275
Jolef, Tho.	200
Joyce, Jno.	200
Jolef, Jno. Jr.	300
Jenings, Henry	100
Jolef, Jno. Sr.	840
Kaine, Rich'd	50
Langley, Wm.	487
Langley, Tho.	878
Loveney, James	100
Luelling, Edw'd	315
Luelling, Rich'd	200
Lovell, Widd'o	740
Low, Henry	191
Lane, Rob't	460
Ludgall, Matthew	250
Levima, John	510
Lenton, Wm.	150
Mercer, Tho.	600
Maning, Tho.	97
Maning, Nich'o	260
Manes, Joseph	73
Matthias, Matthew	100
Miller, Wm.	1090
Miller, Jno.	200

NORFOLK COUNTY (Continued)

	Acres
Miller, Widd'o	100
Murden, Widd'o	2000
Miller, Tho.	1050
Maund, Wm.	200
Maning, Jno. Sr.	300
Miller, Joseph	882
Mecoy, Dennis Sr. & Jr.	160
Monan, James	100
Mufrey, Alex.	800
Maning, Jno. Jr.	100
Moseley, Widd'o	300
Miller, Widd'o Land	200
Mason, Tho.	125
Mason, Lemuell	400
Mason, Tho.	653
Mason, Geo.	300
Mockay, Adam	400
Newton, Geo.	1119
Nicholson, Jno.	160
Nash, Tho.	50
Nichoson, (Nicholson)? Henry	320
Nash, Rich'd	100
Nicholson, Wm.	300
Norcott, Tho.	273
Outlaw (?), Edw'd	208
Owens, Wm.	650
Odyan, Wm.	200
Pearce, Wm.	200
Peters, Widd'o	698
Portlock	360
Porter, Sam'll	100
Prescot, Moses	1200
Philpot, Rich'd	200
Powell, Rich'd	100
Powell, Lemuell	246
Powell, Wm.	624
Perkins, Wm.	50
Patison, Rob't	350
Roberts, Jos.	100
Robert, Sam'll	800
Rose, Rob't	385
Rose, Jno.	150
Richardson, Tho.	379
Spring, Rob't	98
Spivey, Matt.	600
Smith, John	127
Scott, Tho.	400
Smith, Rich'd	600
Smith, John	200
Silvester, Rich'd	1280
Smith, John Sr.	1200
Sikes, Walter Sr.	550
Sikes, Jno.	200
Sugg, George	408
Sugg, Wm.	200
Sayer, Francis	600
Smith, Humphry	100

NORFOLK COUNTY (Continued)

	Acres
Standbro, Jno.	40
Stanley, Rich'd	200
Sharples, Henry	100
Sugg, Joseph	300
Symons, Thomas	166
Symon, James	200
Sparrow, Wm.	350
Tucker, Wm.	100
Thornton, Fbancis	200
Thurston, Matthew	100
Theobald, James	140
Thellaball, Widd'o	600
Tuker (Tucker)?, Rich'd	100
Tuker,(Tucker)?, Tho.	280
Taylor, Jno.	100
Taylor, Rich'd	75
Tully (? Tilly), Jno.	165
Tarte, Elezar Sr.	300
Taylor, Andrew	222
Tuker, (Tucker)?, Jno.	400
Tart, Alice	300
Tarte, Elezar Jr.	595
Taylor, Wm.	265
Trigoney, Henry	200
Velle, Moriss	335
Walice, Tho.	150
Weston, Edw'd	100
Willoughby, Tho. Coll.	3200
Weshart, John	150
Woodly, Rob't	350
Williams, John	125
Wilder, Mich.	200
Watkins, Tho.	190
Williamson, Jno.	750
Whedon, Jno. Jr.	100
Willoughby, Tho. Cap't	660
Whedon, Wm.	200
West, John	500
Watson, Rob't	80
Wallis, Rich'd	250
Wallis, Jno.	135
Wallis, Wm.	450
Whithurst, Rich'd	150
Whithurst, Wm.	150
Wilkins, Wm.	200
Williams, John	200
Whedbey, Geo.	200
Worden, James	400
Wilson, James Jr.	200
Wilson, Lemuell	300
Wilson, James Coll.	2800
Woodward, Henry	280
Whedon, Jno. Jr.	320
White, Patrick	500
Willis, John	470

NORFOLK COUNTY (Continued)

	Acres
Weldey, Dorothy	25
Ward, Jno.	320
Wakfield, Tho.	40
Wilden, Nath.	100
Wooding, Tho.	170
Wood, Edw'd	100
Watford, Joseph	97
Ward, John	400
Wright, Wm.	574
Wright, James	216
Wadborn, Mich.	500
Wms (Williams), Jane	400
Webb, Mary	100
Worminton, John	200
Wilden, Francis	100
Weddick, Henry	343
New discovered land	1615

An Acc't of the Land belonging to such persons out of the County and also others out of the Country.

Coll. Cary	
Tully Robinson	
James Daves	
Rob't Berrey	95
Jno. Bennett	33
Coll. Nasareth	400
Cornelius Tullery	150

James Wilson, Sherriff

A Compleat List of the Rent Roll of the land in NANSEMOND COUNTY in Anno 1704

		Acres
John Murdaugh		300
Jno. Duke		113
Tho. Duke Jr.		930
Edw'd Roberts		250
Paul Pender		240
Tho. Duke		400
James Fowler		440
Rob't Baker		50
Isaac Shetto		100
Edw'd Shetto		200
Anth'o Gumms		50
Francis Shetto		100
Wm. Parker		100
Francis Parker		170
Tho. Parker		300
Jno. Small		100
Moses Hall		95
Edw'd Beamond		550
Rich'd Parker		514
Cap't James Jossey	(Jessey)?	550
Wm. Sanders		200
Jno. Sanders		165
Tho. Mansfield		60
Wm. Woodley		390
Andrew Bourne		200
Gilbert Owen		120
Wm. Sanders Jr.		165
Cap't John Speir		500
Cap't James Reddick		943
James Griffin		500
Nich'o Stallings		965
John Stallings		250
Rich'd Stallings		165
Elias Stallings Jr.		250
Joseph Baker		740
Wm. Jones		500
Rob't Roundtree		245
John Roundtree		475
Geo. Spivey		200
James Spivey		600
James Knight		300
Jno. Gorden		330
Edw'd Arnold		80
James Mulleny		500
Tho. Docton		200
Wm. Britt		400
Nath. Newby		850
Elias Stalling		470
Rob't Lassiter		850
Patrick Wood		200
Wm. Thompson		133
Jonathan Kitterell		300
Adam Rabey		586
Jno. Powell		758

NANSEMOND COUNTY (Continued)

	Acres
John Reddick	300
Henry Copeland	150
Thomas Davis	250
John Smith	100
Tho. Harrald	652
Rich'd Baker	40
Sam'll Smith	230
Wm. Hood	200
Tho. Roundtree	350
Henry Hill	175
Jno. Larkham	500
Wm. Vann	100
Joseph Cooper	267
John Harris	600
Francis Copeland	513
Eliz'b Price	150
Wm. Hill	150
Tho. Spivey	200
Jno. Campbell	400
Jno. Morley	100
Jos. Rogers	15
Jno. Cole	814
Tho. Harrald	100
Christ'o Gawin Jr.	20
Daniell Horton	200
Wm. Bruin	300
Peter Eason	400
Anne Pugh	2300
Benj'm Blanchard	130
Tho. Norfleet	500
John Odum	50
Tho. Gough	150
Hugh Gough	150
Epapap Boyne	100
Henry Baker	375
Christ'o Gwin	1010
James Speirs	200
Epaphra Benton	250
Wm. Eason	180
Andrew Brown	25
Wm. Horne	100
Rob't Reddick	200
Henry Hackley	210
Tho. Roberts	30
Abr. Reddick	400
Jno. Parker	240
Rich'd Barefield	900
John Benton	660
Jno. Pipkin	100
Jos. Brady	250
Christ'o Dudley	200
Tho. Norris	100
Tho. Wiggins	100
Patrick Lawley	50
Rob't Warren	110

NANSEMOND COUNTY (continued)

	Acres
Rich'd Odium	50
Tho. Davis	340
Tho. Barefield	100
John Eason	150
Jeremiah Arlin	250
Jno. Perry	870
Jno. Drury	87
Joseph Booth	987
Cresham Cofield	350
Rich'd Sumner	600
Edw'd Norfleet	200
Jno. Norfleet	600
Edw'd Moore	250
Tho. Moore	200
James Lawrey	40
James Daughtie	400
John Wallis	150
Rich'd Sanders Jr.	100
Wm. Byrd	300
James Howard	700
John Brinkley	430
Rob't Horning	80
Wm. Speirs	200
Sarah Exum	150
Jno. Larrence	175
Nich'o Perry	200
Sampson Merridith	400
Coll. Tho. Milner	1484
Joseph Merridith	250
Thomas Kinder	160
Henry King	300
Joseph Hine	150
Wm. King	140
Julien King	700
Mich. King	80
Cap't Tho. Godwin Jr.	697
Henry Lawrence	200
Jno. King	1000
Rich'd Hine	200
Cap't Fra. Milner	479
Benj'm Nevill	475
Eliz'b Marler	80
Wm. Keene	200
Jno. Symmons	678
Hen. Johnson	150
Jno. Darden	500
Wm. Everett	150
Wm. Pope	890
Joseph Worrell	270
Tho. Jernegan Jr.	135
Rich'd Lawrence	200
Jonathan Robinson	400
Rob't Yates	150
Tho. Odium	20
John Barefield	300

NANSEMOND COUNTY (Continued)

		Acres
John Raules		600
Thomas Boyt	(Boyd)?	400
Tho. Vaughan		200
Jno. Parker		300
Rich'd Green		200
Elisha Ballard		300
Sam'll Watson		200
Francis Spight		400
Joseph Ballard		200
John Oxley		100
Benj'm Rogers		600
Rob't Rogers		300
Hen. Jerregan		200
Jno. Stansell		500
Henry Jenkins		400
Cap't Wm. Hunter		800
Jno. Moore		200
Rich'd Moore		250
Edw'd Homes		300
Fra. Cambridge		100
Wm. Ward		200
Jno. Rice		140
Wm. Battaill		800
Wm. Spite		500
Abr. Oadham		520
Jacob Oadham		20
Jno. Lee		100
Wm. Macklenny		200
Rob't Coleman		1400
Jno. Bryan		200
Wm. Daughtree		100
Jno. Copeland		600
Jno. Butler		200
James Butler		75
Tho. Roads		75
Wm. Collins		1220
Jno. Hodgpath		700
Jno. Holland		700
Rob't Carr		200
Wm. Walters		600
Rob't Lawrence		400
Wm. Bryon		350
Lewis Bryon		400
James Lawrence		100
Wm, Catlin		100
Joseph Gutchins		250
Geo. Lawrence		400
Lewis Daughtree		100
Tho. Rogers		50
Jno. Rogers		200
Henry Core		50
Edw'd Cobb		200
Rich'd Taylor		300
Rob't Brewer		200
Wm. Osburne		200
Tho. Biswell		400

NANSEMOND COUNTY (Continued)

	Acres
Jno. Catlin	200
Rich'd Folk	100
Thomas Parker	100
Peter Parker	140
Wm. Parker	140
Rich'd Hine Jr.	200
Stephen Archer	200
Charles Roades	800
Henry Roades	100
James Collings	300
Henry Holland	400
Wm. Kerle	325
Joseph Holland	100
Jno. Thomas Jr.	100
Jno. Thomas	275
Tho. Mason	350
Edward Mason	150
Jno. Sanders	150
Mich. Brinkley	200
James Moore	400
Henry Blumpton	1500
Jno. Symmons	100
Jeremiah Edmonds	70
John Gay	200
Phillip Aylsberry	100
James Copeland	390
Jno. Brothers	460
Rich'd Creech	200
Rich'd Bond	90
Tho. Handcock	30
James Knott	1050
Wm. Edwards	150
Robert Elkes	175
Edw'd Price	140
Jane Belson	100
Wm. Staples	210
Rob't Montgomery	150
John Moore	100
Cap't Edm'd Godwin	800
Thomas Wakefield	150
Godfrey Hunt	360
Henry Wilkinson	250
Nich'o Dixon	200
Geo. Keeley	650
Rich'd Taylor	300
Anne Coefield	300
Joseph Hollyday	1000
Mr. Jno. Braisseur	400
Tho. Best	160
Alex'd Campbell	500
Cap't Charles Drury	570
Tho. Drury	75
Luke Shea	650
John Babb	500
Abraham Edwards	400

NANSEMOND COUNTY (Continued)

	Acres
Rich'd Sanders	500
Anth'o Wallis	80
Dan'll Sullivan	100
Joseph Ellis	290
Nich'o Hunter	190
Rich'd Webb	200
John Hare	190
Christ'o Norfleet	400
Jno. Hoslep	148
Francis Benton	200
Cap't Wm. Sumner	275
Eliz'b Syke	100
Anne Hare	600
Jno. Porter	450
Edw'd Welsh	100
Jno. Winbourne	400
Paul Pender	200
Mich. Cowling	100
John Cowling	100
Rowland Gwyn	75
Andrew Ross	150
Jno. Ballard	400
Benj'm Montgomery	910
Tho.-Corbell	200
Jno. Yates	400
Jno. White	150
Geo. White	50
Jno. Bond	150
Wm. Hay	100
Henry Bowes	600
Wm. Sevill	85
Jno. Hambleton	200
Robert Jordan	850
James Howard	25
Ruth Coefield	110
Jno. Chilcott	100
Jno. Rutter	80
Tho. Rutter	75
Wm. Rutter	75
Cap't Barnaby Kerney	460
Tho. Cutchins	150
Rob't Lawrence	130
Sam'll Cahoone	240
Jno. Iles	220
Tho. Sawyer	180
Wm. Outland	400
Coll. Geo. Northworthy	650
Coll. Tho. Godwin	810
Caleb Taylor	200
Tho. Carnell	320
Rich'd Bradley	250
Jno. Corbin	300
Wm. Sykes	150
Maj'r Tho. Jorden	700
Rich'd Lovegrove	150
Tho. Davis	144

NANSEMOND COUNTY (Continued)

	Acres
Sam'll Frimmer	160
Henry Bradley	500
Jno. Clarke	25
Margarett Jorden	200
Wm. Elkes	100
Humphrey Mires	150
James Dard	100
Widd'o Hudnell	45
Wm. Grandberry	300
Isreall Shepherd	200
Benj'm Small	100
Anne Grandberry	75
Charles Roberts	50
Rich'd Silator	300
Rob't Murrow	320
Eliz'b Peters	334
Tho. Jones	200
Eliz'b Butler	200
Coll. Smith Bridges	500
Jno. Larrance	200
Tho. Jarnegan Jr.	165
Tho. Jarnegan Jr.	600
Wm. Drury	80
Wm. Butler	120
Henry Jenkins	860
Edw'd Bathurst	250
Tho. Houssler	200
Edw'd Streater	200
Wm. Duffield	50
Charles Tho. (Thomas) Jr.	50
Jno. Blessington	150
Ursula Goodwin	100
Tho. Atwell	440
Wm. Peale	180
John Lambkin	50
James Murphree	160
Rob't Peale	275
John Peters	368
James Peters	340
John Wakefield	50
Rich'd Wynn	890
James Lockhart	800
John Keeton	2000
Jno. Murrow	200

Persons living out of county and other yt. will not pay or give acc't

Capt. Tho. Lovett
Cap't Jno. Wright
Fra. Parker Jr.
Tho. Macom
Jno. Wright
Wm. Lapiter
Jno. Lapiter
Capt. Luke Haffield
Mrs. Eliz'b Swann

A List of her Maj'tys Qt. Rents in the ISLE OF WIGHT COUNTY 1704

	Acres
Jno. Atkins	200
James Atkinson	400
Wm. Exam	1440
Wm. Brown	150
Francis Exam	200
Rich'd Bennett	70
James Briggs	200
Ph. Bratley	200
Abr. Drawler	200
Jno. Branch	45
Francis Branch	50
Edw'd Brantley	175
Jno. Brantley	364
Edw'd Boykin	1100
Geo. Barloe	80
Jno. George	200
Tho. Carter	700
Reubin Cooke	250
Jno. Clarke	850
Tho. Cook	300
Wm. Clark	600
Edw'd Champion	600
Jno. Dowles	150
Peter Deberry	100
Thomas Davis	100
Jno. Davis	250
Peter Hayes	600
Christ'o Hollyman	400
Rich'd Hardy	700
Tho. Holyman	150
Jno. Harris	365
Silvester Hill	925
Roger Hodge	300
Arthur Jones	900
Edw'd Jones	250
Rich'd Jones	250
Jno..Johnson	890
Roger Ingram	300
Matt. Jorden	1950
Tho. Newman	360
Geo. Readick	790
Francis Lee	100
Ph. Pardoe	100
Jno. Parsons	155
Geo. Moore	400
Jno. Mangann	100
Rob't Mongo	400
Henry Martin	200
Jno. Murray	650
Francis Rayner	80
Jno. Richardson	150
James Sampson	1200
Jno. Stevenson	150
Tho. Sherrer	200
Wm. Thomas	250

ISLE OF WIGHT COUNTY (Continued)

	Acres
Tho. Tooke	1228
Tho. Throp	350
Baleaby Terrell	100
Peter Vasser	230
Jno. Williams	600
Geo. Williamson	2735
Fra. Williamson	2035
Tho. Wood	50
James Lupe	45
Eliz'b Reynolds	100
Jno. Sejourner	240
Rob't Hoge	60
Andrew Woodley	770
Arthur Allen	1800
Henry Baker	750
Rubin Prockter	250
Tho. Howell	100
Nath. Whitby	170
Jane Hakins (?)	600
Jno. Mongo	100
Natt. Ridley	200
Jno. Bell	200
Wm. West	250
Charles Goodrich	80
Jno. Britt	350
Jno. Barnes	200
Henry Geldman (?)	1000
Jno. Waltham	450
Charles Edwards	400
Wm. Exam	150
Maj'r Lewis Burwell	7000
Henry Applewaite	1500
Tho. Pitt	300
Jno. Pitt	3400
Mary Benn	675
Rob't Clark	450
Anth'o Holliday	860
Wm. Westrah	450
Eliz'b Gardner	100
Jno. Gardner	246
Jno. Turner	950
Anth'o Foulsham	100
Anne Williams	150
Edw'd Harris	240
Jno. Cotten	200
Tho. Joyner	1400
Jno. Lawrence	400
Tho. Mendue (?)	200
Wm. Mayo	300
Jno. Garland	100
James Bryan	1200
Wm. Keate	200
Jno. Browne	100
Francis Sanders	100
Jno. Rogers	200

ISLE OF WIGHT COUNTY (Continued)

	Acres
Hodges Council	420
Hardy Council	760
Tho. Reeves	600
Wm. Crumpler	580
Bridgman Joyner	1100
Eliz'b Swan	600
Tho. Jones	700
Arthur Whitehead	250
Tho. Allen	150
Jeremiah Exam	300
Nich'o Casey	550
Jno. Giles	1150
Alex'd Connell	200
Jno. Rutter	300
Godfrey Hunt	600
Wm. Trygell	100
Tho. Jorden	207
Benj'a Jorden	150
Jno. King	300
Wm. Wilkinson	200
Tho. Grace	160
Wm. West	50
Jno. Penny	300
Rob't Richards	100
Tho. Northworthy (?)	1000
Geo. Green	250
Jno. Dauer	100
Phil. Pearce	500
Wm. Best	100
Humphrey Marshall	600
Tho. Brewer	200
Wm. Smith	2100
Sam'll & Wm. Bridger	12900
Wm. Williams	100
Rich'd Ratcliffe	380
Joshua Jordan	150
Dan'll Sandbourne	180
Nich'o Houlghan	780
Mary Marshall	200
Joseph Godwin	250
Joseph Bridger	580
Henry Pitt	700
James Barron	300
Arthur Smith	3607
Robert Brock	400
Wm. Godwin	400
Hugh Braley	1000
Henry Turner	350
Tho. Wooten	963
Rich'd Reynolds Esq'r	853
Rich'd Reynolds	746
Jno. Parnell	400
Benj'm Deall	467
Theo. Joyner	595
Jno. Jordan	100
Henry Wiggs	506

ISLE OF WIGHT COUNTY (Continued)

	Acres
Wm. Body	1375
Arthur Purcell	750
Jno. Portens	100
Wm. West	690
Simon Everett	1100
Walter Waters	150
John Jordan	150
John Nevill	433
Rob't Colman	1500
Wm. Green	150
Mary Cobb	150
Robert Edw'ds (Edwards)	150
Anne Jones	100
Abraham Jones	600
John Jones	200
Rich'd Lewis	100
Henry Dullard	100
Tho. Williams	100
James Mercer	100
Pooll Hall	350
Jno. Howdee	100
Tho. Lovett	100
Geo. Anderson	150
Daniell Nottiboy	100
Henry Wilkinson	350
Jno. Watkins	200
Tho. English	100
Tho. Page	103
Francis Davis	200
Rich'd Braswell	100
Rob't Johnson	2450
John Minshea	300
Wm. Pryan	200
Wm. Dawes	400
Nich'o Tyner	300
Isaac Ricks	700
Rob't Scott	300
Jno. Roberts	950
Wm. Duck	180
Rob't Lawrence	400
Jno. Denson	200
Rob't Smelly	600
Francis Bridle	250
Roger Failton	237
Tho. Bullock	100
Wm. Murphy	600
Tho. Powell	100
Widd'o Glyn	390
Jno. Pope	250
Tho. Gayle	200
Wm. Powell	200
Rich'd Hutchins	300
Hen. Bowman	100
Henry Pope	557
John Wms. (Williams)	971
Hen. Sanders	700

ISLE OF WIGHT COUNTY (Continued)

	Acres
Jno. Selloway	900
Jno. Bardin	100
Phill. Rayford	650
Phill. Pearse	500
Jno. Tenseley	150
Geo. Northworthy	1176
Rob't Rich'ds (Richards)	450
Tho. Bevan	100
Wm. Hunter	150
Tho. Wheatley	400
Rich'd Wilkinson	150
James Bragg	500
Jno. Portens	300
Tho. Harris	350
Edw'd Harris	100
Nich'o Askew	80
Ambrose Hadley	100
Widd'o Powell	480
Tho. Jones	100
Tho. Underwood	100
Rob't King	300
Tho. Giles	880
Lewis Smelly	550
Wm. Smelly	280
Godfrey Hunt	600
Edmund Godwin	400
Wm. Wms. (Williams)	1000
John Wilson	1200
John Bryan	200
John Askew	100
Sam'll Bridger	200
Roger Nevill	200
Coll. Godwin	600
Jacob Durden	500

Rent Roll of All the Land held by Her Maj'te in SURREY COUNTY 1704

	Acres
Allin, Arthur Maj'r	6780
Andrews, Barth'o	375
Avery, Jno.	150
Atkins, Tho.	80
Averett, Jno.	120
Atkinson, Rich'd	100
Andrews, Tho.	190
Andrews, Rob't	130
Andrews, David	225
Baker, Henry Coll.	850
Bruton, James	500
Bennett, James	200
Bland, Sarah	1455
Browne, Jno.	600
Benbridge, Geo.	200
Bighton, Rich'd	590
Bell, Jno.	180
Berham, Rob't	650
Blake, Wm.	200
Browne, Edw'd	200
Buicham (Bincham)? Jno.	100
Benett, Rich'd	200
Baker, Sarah	50
Briggs, Sarah	300
Barter, Joell	100
Briggs, Sam'll	300
Blico, Christ'o	50
Brigs, Charles	331
Brigs, Henry	100
Bentley	180
Blackbun (Blackburn)? Wm.	150
Blunt, Tho.	1355
Bookey, Edw'd	180
Browne, Wm. Coll.	2510
Browne, Wm. Capt.	398
Bineham, James	157
Bullock, Mary	100
Barker, Jno.	1160
Bayley, Peter	100
Barker, Jery	420
Bunnell, Hezickiah	150
Bougher, Phill.	100
Baile, Jno.	250
Bayley, Edw'd	350
Chapman, Benjamin	500
Cockin, Wm.	100
Cocker, Jno.	900
Crafort, Rob't	1000
Crafort, Carter	100
Chambers, Wm.	50
Clark, Jno.	100
Cook, Eliz'b	200
Carriell, Tho.	100
Clements, Jno.	387
Clarke, Jno.	100

SURREY COUNTY (Continued)

	Acres
Cook, Eliz'b	200
Carriell, Thomas	100
Cleaments, Jno.	387
Clark, Rob't	400
Checett, James	50
Cotten, Walter	257
Cotten, Tho.	257
Collier, Jno.	350
Collier, Joseph	40
Cock, Wm.	630
Cock, Walter	875
Cooper, James	100
Clements, Fran.	600
Collier, Tho.	550
Cardenscaine, Obedience	200
Dicks, James	400
Davis, Arthur	460
Drew, Tho.	800
Drew, Edw'd	600
Delk, Roger	190
Davis, Arthur	50
Dean, Rich'd	100
Davis, Nath.	157
Edward, Wm. Mr.	2755
Evans, Anth'o	200
Edw'd, John (Edward)	470
Elliott, Wm.	250
Edw'd (Edward), Howell	300
Ellis, James	180
Edmund, Wms.	100
Ellis, Edward	30
Ellis, James	170
Ezell, Geo.	150
Ellis, Jere.	50
Evans, Abrah.	150
Flake, Rob't	200
Foster, Anne	200
Ford, Geo.	100
Flood, Walter	820
Flood, Tho.	150
Ford, Elias	200
Flemin, Lawrence	360
Foster, Christ'o	500
Foster, Wm.	100
Ferisby, Benj'm	170
Gray, Wm. Cap't	1750
Gray, Wm. Jr.	1050
Grimes, Hustis	100
Gwalney, Wm.	400
Gray, Jno.	200
Gwalney, Wm.	225
Goodman, Wm.	200
Gillham, Hinche	658
Griffin, John	200
Gully, Rich'd	50
Gray, Wm.	100
Green, Edw'd	200

SURREY COUNTY (Continued)

	Acres
Green, Rich'd	260
Harrison, Benj'm Coll.	2750
Harrison, Nath.	2177
Hunt, Wm.	4042
Holt, Eliz'b	1450
Holt, John	150
Holt, Tho. Cap't	538
Holt, Wm.	630
Harris, Wm.	150
Hart, Henry	725
Humfort, Hugh	150
Hancock, John	60
Hart, Robert	600
Humphrey, Evan	70
Hollyman, Mary	290
Harde, Tho.	900
Hill, Rob't	200
Holloman, Rich'd	480
Hargrove, Bryan	100
Humfort, Wm.	50
Hill, Syon (Symon)?	300
Holloman, Tho.	450
Heath, Adam	200
Harrison, Dan'll	70
Ham, Rich'd	75
Heart, Tho.	750
Hyerd, Tho.	50
Hunt, Wm.	696
Horne, Rich'd	100
Hollingworth, Henry	60
Howell, Wm.	50
Jackman, Jos. John Mr.	2980
Jones, James	1000
Jarrell, Tho.	115
Jarrett, Charles	615
Judkins, Sam'll	100
Judkins, Wm.	100
Jurdan, Geo.	620
Jarrett, Fardo	630
Johnson, Wm.	360
Johnson, John	350
Jurdan, Rich'd	350
Kigan, Mary	200
Killingworth, Wm.	60
Knott, Wm.	300
Ludwell, Phill. Coll.	1100
Lancaster, Rob't	100
Lacey, Mary	100
Lang, Mary	77
Lane, Tho.	200
Lane, Tho. Jr.	200
Laughter, Jno.	300
Laneere, Geo.	300
Lasley, Patrick	520
Lucas, Wm.	315
Matthew, Edm'd	50
Merriell, Geo.	250

SURREY COUNTY (Continued)

	Acres
Moorland, Edw'd	225
Macon, Eliz'b	300
Mallery, Francis	147
Merrett, Matt.	60
Middleton, Tho.	100
Moss, Wm.	100
Moreing, John	695
Mierick, Owen	250
Newson, Wm.	225
Newson, Rob't	250
Newitt, Wm.	330
Norwood, Rich'd	80
Nicholl, Geo.	150
Nichols, Rob't	230
Noeway, Barefoot	150
Norwood, Geo.	330
Park, Mary	100
Pittman, Tho. Jr.	100
Phillips, John	270
Price, Jno.	340
Petteway, Eliz'b	650
Pulystone, Jno.	1400
Parker, Rich'd	269
Phelps, Humphrey	100
Pully, Wm.	300
Procter, Joshua	660
Persons, John	830
Phillips, Wm.	300
Pettfort, Jno.	200
Pettfort, Wm.	50
Randolph, Wm. Coll.	1655
Ruffice, Eliz'b	3001
Reynolds, Rob't	150
Richardson, Joseph	300
Reynolds, Eliz'b	150
Reagon, Francis	200
Roads, Wm.	150
Rollings, Gregory	106
Read, Wm.	450
Rose, Rich'd	100
Rachell, Geo.	70
Rowling, Jno.	476
Rokings, Wm.	596
Roger, Wm.	450
Scat, Joseph	295
Sims, Geo.	200
Secoms, Nich'o	800
Savage, Charles	358
Stringfellew, Rich'd	75
Suger, Jno.	250
Sewards, Anne	300
Sharp, Tho.	70
Sewins, Thomas	400
Steward, John	200
Smith, Rich'd	200
Savage, Mary	263

SURREY COUNTY (Continued)

	Acres
Smith, Tho.	750
Swann, Wm.	1800
Shrewsbury, Joseph	260
Shrewsbury, Francis	820
Savage, Henry	200
Short, Wm.	400
Scarbro, Edw'd	150
Scagin, Jno.	100
Simmons, Jno.	1300
Shrewbury, Tho.	566
Stockly, Rich'd	100
Smith, Tho.	380
Thompson, Sam'll	3104
Tooker, Henry Maj'r	700
Tayler, Ethelred	538
Thorp, Joseph	250
Tyous, Tho.	400
Taylor, Rich'd	77
Vincent, Mary	187
Wright, Thomas	100
Williams, Charles	100
Wall, Joseph	150
Williams, Wm.	300
Ward, Tho.	100
Wall, Joseph Jr.	150
Warren, Allen	300
Warren, Thomas	1040
Watkins, Rich'd	1345
Williams, Roger	150
Webb, Robert	340
Wattkins, John	1160
Warren, Robert	150
Welch, Henry	100
Warrick, John	80
Wilkinson, Matthew	200
Wiggins, Tho.	300
Waple, Jno.	300
Witherington, Nich'o	100
Will, Roger	78
White, Charles	136
Young, John	300

Aprill 19th 1705. Errors Excepted (?) Jos. Jno. Jackman Sher.

Persons denying payments for Lands held in this County viz Cap't Tho. Holt as belonging to

Tho. Ben*es Orph.	950
Mrs. Mary White	280

Lands held by persons living out of the County

Cap't Jno. Taylor	850
Mrs. Sarah Low	500
Mr. Jno. Hamlin	100
Cap't Tho. Harrison	530

SURREY COUNTY (Continued)

Barth'o Clement One Tract of Land he living in England the quantity unknowne.

Jo'n Davis One Tract, Living in Isle of Wight

Geo. & River Jorden one Tract denys to pay Qt. rents for it and no persons living thereon.

There is one Bray Living in Warwick has a small tract Land.

A True and Perfect Rent Roll of all the Lands held of her Maj'tie in HENRICO COUNTY, Aprill 1705

	Acres
Andrews, Thomas	396
Arcoutch, Mary	633
Archer, Jno.	335
Adkins, Jno.	125
Archer, Geo.	1738
Aldy, John	162
Akins, James Sr.	200
Asbrook, Peter Sr.	200
Akins, James Jr.	218
Allin, Widd'o	99
Byrd, Esq'r	19500
Bolling, Rob't	500
Bolling, John	831
Bevill, John	495
Branch, X'to	646
Blackman, Wm.	175
Bridgwater, Sam'll	280
Bowman, John Jr.	300
Bowman, Edw'd	300
Branch, Benj'm	550
Brown, Martha	893
Bullington (Billington)? Benj'm	200
Bowman, Len.	65
Bullington	144
Bevell, Essex	200
Baugh, John	448
Baugh, James	458
Burton, Isaac	100
Bottom, John	100
Bayley, Abr.	542
Brooks, Jane belonging to Wm. Walker, New Kent	550
Braseal, Henry	200
Braseal, Henry Jr.	300
Burton, Rob't	1350
Burgony, John	100
Branch, James	555
Burrows, Wm. & Wm. Blackwell, New Kent	63
Branch, Thomas	540
Bailey, Thomas	251
Branch, Matthew	947
Burton, Wm.	294
Bullington (Billington)?, Rob't	100
Broadnax, J.C.C.	725
Beverley, Rob't	988
Cheatham, Tho.	300
Cox, Batt	100
Cox, John	150
Cox, George	200
Chamberlaine, Maj. Tho.	1000
Childers, Abr. Sr.	368
Cannon, John	108
Cox, Wm.	300
Childers, Ab. Jr.	100
Clark, Wm.	333
Clark, John	300

HENRICO COUNTY (Continued)

	Acres
Cox, Rich'd	300
Cardwell, Tho.	350
Chezdall, Roger	200
Cock, Wm.	1535
Cock, Rich'd Sr.	2180
Childers, Philip Sr.	50
Childers, Philip	300
Childers, Tho.	300
Carter, Theod.	75
Cock, Cap't Thomas	2976
Couzine, Charles	362
Clark, Alanson	604
Cock, James	1506
Curd, Edw'd	600
Cock, Rich'd CCC	476
Cock, Jno.	98
Dison (Dixon)?, Nicholas	150
Dodson, Wm.	100
Douglas, Charles	63
Edw'd (Edward) Tho.	676
Entroughty, Derby	200
Ealam, Rob't	400
Ellis, John	217
East, Tho. Sr.	475
East, Tho.	554
East, Edw'd	150
Epes, Cap't Fred.	2145
Evans, Charles	225
Ealam, Martin	130
Epes, Isham; Epes, Fra. Jr., Each 444½ acres	889
Field, Peter Major	2185
Farrar, Cap't Wm.	700
Farrar, Tho.	1444
Farrar, Jno.	600
Fowler, Godfrey	250
Ferguson, Robert	230
Ferris, Wm.	50
Franklin, James Sr.	250
Franklin, James Jr.	786
Ferris, Rich'd Sr.	550
Farmer, Henry	100
Forrest, James	138
Forrest, John	150
Fetherstone, Henry	700
Farloe, John Sr.	100
Farloe, John Jr.	551
Faile, John	240
Gilley, Grewin Arrian	2528
Gee, Henry	435
Good, John Sr.	600
Gaithwaite, Sam'll	50
Gaithwaite, Ephraim	163
Granger, John	472
Gill, John	235
Good, Sam'll	588
Gower, James, Grigs Land	500

HENRICO COUNTY (Continued)

	Acres
Hill, James	795
Holmes, Rich'd	100
Harris, Tho.	357
Harris, Tim'o	250
Hill, Rosam'd	1633
Hobby, Lawrence	500
Hatcher, John	215
Haskins, Edw'd	225
Hatcher, Edw'd Sr.	150
Hunt, Geo.	200
Hughs, Edw'd	100
Hancock, Sam'll	100
Holmes, Thomas	50
Hambleton, James	100
Hutchins, Nich'o	240
Hatcher, Benj'm Sr.	250
Hatcher, Wm. Jr.	50
Hobson, Wm.	150
Hatcher, Wm. Sr.	298
Hatcher, Henry	650
Hancock, Robert	860
Harris, Mary	94
Hall, Edw'd	184
Herbert, Mrs.	1360
Hudson, Rob't	281
Jones, Hugh	934
Jefferson, Thomas	492
Jones, Philip	1153
Jorden, Henry	100
Jamson, (Jameson)? John	225
Jackson, Ralph	250
Kennen, Eliz'b	1900
Knibb, Sam'll	209
Knibb, Solomon	833
Kendall, Rich'd	400
Liptroll, Edw'd	150
Lewis, Wm.	350
Lester, Dareus	100
Ladd, Wm.	70
Ligon, Eliz'b Widd'o)	
Ligon, Mary Widd'o)	1341
Laforce, Reu.	100
Lockett, James	50
Lownd, Henry	516
Lockitt, Benj'm	104
Ligon, Rich'd	1028
Ligon, Hugh	150
Mann, Rob't	100
Matthews, Edw'd	330
Moseby, Edw'd	150
Mosely, Arthur	450
Nunnally, Rich'd	70
Osbourne, Tho.	288
Owen, Tho.	68
Perkinson, John	622
Perrin, Ann	500
Pleasants, John	9669

HENRICO COUNTY (Continued)

	Acres
Parker, Wm.	100
Parkins, Nich'o Sr.	500
Pledge, Jno.	100
Powell, Rob't	150
Peice, (Peirce)? John	130
Pleasant, Jos.	1709
Porter, Wm.	305
Peirce, Wm.	175
Peirce, Francis	312
Paine, Thomas	300
Portlock, Eliz'b	1000
Pew, Henry	350
Pattram, Fra.	778
Pride, Wm. Sr.	1280
Polland, Tho. Sr.	130
Perkinson, Seth	50
Pinkitt, Wm.	192
Pinkitt, Tho.	300
Pattison, Joseph	500
Porter, John	100
Polland, Tho. Jr.	235
Polland, Henry	235
Pinkitt, John	215
Robertson, Geo.	1445
Regsdaill, Godfrey	450
Rawlett, Peter	164
Russell, Charles	200
Rowlett, Wm.	200
Rowen, Fra.	148
Robertson, John	415
Rouch, Rachell	300
Robertson, Thomas	200
Russell, John	93
Royall, Joseph	783
Redford, John	775
Randolph, Coll. Wm. including 1185 acres swamp	19465
Steward, Jno. Jr.	902
Scott, Walter	550
Soane, Cap't Wm.	3841
Stanley, Edw'd	300
Snuggs, Charles	400
Sewell, Wm.	59
Smith, Humphrey	40
Sharp, Rob't	500
Stovoll, Barth'o	100
Skerin, Widd'o	75
Steward, Daniell	270
Smith, Obadiah CCC	200
Stowers, Wid'o	200
Sarrazin, Stephen	120
Tancocks Orphans	1230
Trent, Henry	224
Turpin, Thomas	491
Turpin, Philip	444
Turpin, Tho.	100
Turner, Henry	200

HENRICO COUNTY (Continued)

	Acres
Taylor, Tho.	475
Tanner, Edw'd	217
Traylor, Edw'd	100
Totty, Tho.	260
Traylor, Wm.	730
Vedon (Voden)?, Henry	100
Woodson, John	4060
Wms (Williams), Rob't	300
Woodson, Rob't Jr.	1157
Ward, Rich'd	300
Watson, John Sr.	1603
Walthall, Wm.	500
Walthall, Henry	832
Whitby, Wm.	215
Watkins, Henry Sr.	100
Webb, John	100
Watkins, Tho.	200
Woodson, Rich'd	180
Woodson, Wid'o	650
Williamson, Tho.	1077
Webb, Giles	7260
Wood, Tho.	50
Watkins, Wm.	120
Watkins, Jos.	120
Watkins, Edw'd	120
Ward, Seth	700
Wood, Moses	100
Wilkinson, Jos.	75½
Wilkinson, John	180
Worsham, John	1104
Womack, Abr.	560
Willson, Jno. Sr.	1686
Willson Jno. Jr.	100
Walthall, Rich'd	500
Wortham, Geo.	100
Wortham, Charles	90
Womack, Wm.	100

Out of wch (total acres) must be deducted these quantities of Land following viz:

Tancockes Orphans Land	1230
Allens Orphans Land	99

An Acc't of Lant y't hath been concealed:

John Steward Jr.	2
Tho. Jefferson	15
Tho. Turpin	10
Hen. Gee	10
Steph: Sarrzen	10
Mr. Lownd	1
James Atkins Sr.	32
Matt. Branch	10
James Franklin	360

HENRICO COUNTY (Continued)

An Acc't of Land yt. hath been concealed (continued)

James Hill	50
Rosemond Hill	33
John Bullington	44
Benj'a Lockett	4
John Russell	23
Charles Douglas	13
Col. Randolph Carles Swamp Land	1049

A Rent Roll of all the Lands held in the County of PRINCE GEORGE for the Year 1704

	Acres
Tho. Anderson	450
Wm. Aldridge	160
Mr. Charles Anderson	505
Rich'd Adkinson	200
Tho. Adams	250
Matt. Anderson	349
Henry Ally	390
Wm. Anderson	235
Jno. Anderson	228
Henry Anderson	250
Rob't Abernathy	100
Jno. Avery	100
Rich'd Bland	1000
Rob't Birchett	375
Arthur Biggins	200
James Benford	461
Jno. Barloe	80
Charles Bartholomew	600
Philip Burlowe	350
Nich'o Brower	100
Jno. Bishop Sr.	100
Jno. Bishop Jr.	100
Isaac Baites	360
Tho. Busby Cap't	200
Wm. Batt	750
Coll. Byrd Esq.	100
Edw'd Birchett	886
Coll. Bolling	3402
Edw'd Browder	100
Matus Brittler	510
Jno. Butler	1385
Andrew Beck	300
Henry Batt	790
Wm. Butler	283
Tho. Blitchodin	284
Tho. Curiton	150
Hen. Chammins	300
Cap't. Clements	1920
Wm. Clannton	100
Rob't Catte	100
Barth'o Crowder	75
Tho. Clay	70
Jno. Coleman	200
Geo. Crook	487
Francis Coleman	150
Jno. Clay	350
Wm. Coleman Jr.	100
Geo. Crooker	30
James Cooke	750
Rob't Carlill	100
Jno. Clerk	83
Rich'd Clannton	100
Stephen Cock for Jones Orph	2405
Tho. Daniell	150
Roger Drayton	270

PRINCE GEORGE (Continued)

	Acres
Joseph Daniell	50
Jo'n Doby	500
Geo. Dowing	100
Wm. Davis	100
Jno. Duglas	300
Rich'd Darding	500
Christ'o Davis	50
Tho. Dunkin	136
Rob't Ellis	50
Jno. Epes Sr.	530
Wm. Epes Sr.	750
Jno. Epes	300
Wm. Epes	633½
Edw'd Epes	500
Littlebury Epes	833½
Benj'm Evans	700
Tho. Edw's (Edwards)	250
Dan. Epes	200
Jno. Evans	800
Jno. Ellis Jr.	400
Jno. Ellis Sr.	400
Mary Evans	400
Peter Evans	270
Cap't Fred. Epes	226
Jno. Freeman	300
Wm. Frost	50
Jno. Foundaine	350
Rob't Fellows	418
Eliz'b Flood	100
Benj'm Foster	923
Jno. Field	100
Jno. Green	125
Rich'd Gord	100
David Goodgame	479
James Gresthian	363
Maj'r Goodrick	900
Tho. Goodwin	150
Hubert Gibson	250
Rich'd Griffith	335
James Griffin	100
Charles Gee	484
Charles Gillam	200
Hugh Goelightly	500
Lewis Green	149
Wm. Grigg	200
John Gillman	1000
John Goelightly	100
Coll. Hill	1000
Dan'll Hickdon	280
Rob't Harthorn	213
Jno. Hamlin	1484½
Coll. Harrison Esq.	150
Ralph Hill	175
Wm. Harrison	1930
Wm. Heath	320
Edw'd Holloway	100
Rob't Hobbs	100
Jno. Hobbs Sr.	250

PRINCE GEORGE COUNTY (Continued)

	Acres
Edw'd Holloway Sr.	620
Jno. Hobbs	100
James Harrison	200
Gilbert Haye	200
Rich'd Hudson	75
Gabriell Harrison	150
Rob't Hix	1000
Joseph Holycross	84
Isaac Hall	450
Jno. Howell	185
Tho. Howell	25
Mrs. Herbert	3925
Jno. Hixs	216
Rich'd Hamlin	240
Tho. Harrison	1077
Eliz'b Hamlin	250
Wm. Helme	100
Jeffry Hawkes	125
Adam Heath	300
Jno. Hill	160
Jno. Hardiman	872
Justance Hall	614
Wm. Jones Jr.	230
Wm. Jones Sr.	600
Henry Jones	200
Robert Jones	241
Edw'd Irby	800
Nich. Jarrett	700
James Jackson	80
Adam Ivie	200
Tho. Jackson	60
James Jones Sr.	1100
Henry Joye	450
Peter Jones	621
Rich'd Jones	600
Ralph Jackson	110
Joshua Irby	200
John Jones	350
Rich'd Kirkland	300
John King	50
Henry King	650
Arthur Ravanah	60
Eusebius King	100
John Livesley	300
Sam'll Lowey	100
Jno, Lumbrey (?)	400
Jno. Leenoir	700
Mrs. Low	70
Sam Lowey for Neth**l Orph.	498
Tho. Lewis Sr.	200
Hugh Liegh	762
Francis Leadbetter	100
Jno. Leadbetter	400
Wm. Low	1584
Wm. Madox	190
Rob't Munford	339
James Minge Sr.	500

PRINCE GEORGE COUNTY (Continued)

	Acres
Matt. Marks	1500
Sam'll Moody	328
Francis Mallory	100
Dan'll Mallone	100
Jno. Mayes	365
Rich'd More	472
Henry Mitchell Sr.	100
Jno. Mitchell	170
Wm. Mayes	763
Edw'd Murrell	100
Tho, Mitchell Jr.	100
Peter Mitchell	305
Henry Mitchell Jr.	200
Francis Maberry	347
James Matthews	100
Jno. Martin	200
Rich'd Newman	120
Walter Nunnaley	299
Nich'o Overburry	809
Jno. Owen	25
Geo. Pasmore	330
Francis Poythres Sr.	1283
Joseph Pattison	200
Geo. Pail	246
Nathan'll Phillips	150
Jno. Price	50
Wm. Peoples	150
Eliz'b Peoples	235
Joseph Perry	275
Rich'd Pigeon	524
Thomas Potts	200
Joseph Pritchett	50
Jno. Petterson	373
Geo. Pace	1000
Ephram Pakham	300
Tho. Poythres	616
David Peoples	60
Grace Perry	100
Jno. Poythres Jr.	916
Jno. Petterson	428
Mr. Micajah Perry	600
Jno. Roberts	316
Nath. Robinson	100
Roger Reace Jr.	100
Henry Read	75
Roger Reace Sr.	100
Wm. Reanes	250
Francis Raye	300
Jno. Reek	50
Wm. Rachell	100
Timothy Reading Sr.	460
Jno. Riners	200
Edw'd Richardson	300
Coll. Randolph	226

PRINCE GEORGE COUNTY (Continued)

	Acres
Matthew Smart	100
Wm. Standback	150
Tho. Symmons	566
James Salmon	477
Wm. Savage	150
Wm. Sandborne	70
Jno. Scott	300
Martin Shieffield	150
James Smith	67
John Stroud	60
Rich'd Seeking (?)	100
Wm. Sexton	50
James Seedaker	710
Chichester Sturdevant	214
Daniell Sturdevant	850
Rich'd Smith	550
Jno. Spaine	118
Matthew Sturdivant	150
Cap't Stith	470
Maj'r Henry Tooker for ye Merch'ts in London	4600
Geo. Tilliman	446
Jno. Tilliman	530
Wm. Tomlinson	400
Adam Tapley	977
Cap't Jno. Taylor	1700
Mich. Taburd	150
Maj'r Tooker	181
Rob't Tooker	400
Rob't Tester	170
Joseph Tooker	200
Wm. Temple	100
Jno. Thornhill	350
Jno. Taylor	100
Nath. Tatham Jr.	200
Sam'll Tatham Sr.	100
Sam'll Tatham Jr.	195
Henry Talley	639
Rich'd Turberfield	140
Francis Tucker	100
Nath. Tatham Sr.	501
Jno. Thrower	250
Tho. Thrower	150
James Taylor	306
Sanders Tapley	300
Tho. Tapley	300
James Thweat Sr.	715
James Thweat Jr.	100
Eliz'b Tucker	212
Tho. Taylor	400
Edw'd Thrower	150
Jno. Vaughan	169
Sam'll Vaughan	169
Nath. Urvvin (Irvin)?	150
Dan'll Vaughan	169

PRINCE GEORGE COUNTY (Continued)

	Acres
James Vaughan	169
Rich'd Vaughan	309
Wm. Vaughan	309
Tho. Vinson	550
Nich'o Vaughan	169
Jno. Woodlife Sr.	644
Wm. Wallis	200
Jno. Wichett	250
Cap't Jos. Wynn	860
Jno. Woodlife Jr.	750
Jno. Winningham Jr.	200
Rich'd Wallpoole	625
Jno. Womack	550
Cap't Tho, Wynn	400
Jno. Wall	233
Tho, Winningham	100
Eliz'b Woodlife	844
Rich'd Worthern (?)	1600
Rich'd Winkley	450
Cap't Nich'o Wyatt	250
Valentine Williamson	250
Hurley Wick	600
Wm. Wilkins	900
Francis Wilkins	150
Rob't Winkfield	107
Jarvis Winkfield	100
Henry Wall	275
Jno. Wilkins	150
James Williams	1436
Geo. Williams	210
Jno. White	150
Edw'd Winningham	100
Sam'll Woodward	600
Donnell Young	383
John Young	200

Wm. Epes Sherriff

Orphans Land which is refused paying Quitt Rents for viz:

Mr. Jno. Bannister orphans of Steph. Cock	1970
Cap't Henry Bates orph. of father and mother Mrs. Mary Bates	1200
Cap't Henry Randolph orph. of Cap't Giles Webb	129
Morris Halliham orph's of Rob't Rives	200
Crockson Land formerly of & who it belongs to now I cannot find	750

The Rent Roll of NORTHAMPTON COUNTY for the Year of our Lord God 1704

	Acres
Andrews, Rob't	300
Andrews, Andrew	100
Addison, John	350
Abdell, Tho.	125
Abdell, Jno.	200
Abdell, Wm.	125
Alligood, John	300
Angell, James	100
Alligood, Henry	100
Bullock, Geo.	100
Borer, Geo.	150
Brown, Tho.	1862
Benthall, Joseph Sr.	793
Benthall, Joseph Jr.	50
Branson, Francis	100
Bateson	200
Billot, Jno.	400
Bell, Geo.	400
Billott, Wm.	100
Brower, Jno.	50
Blackson, Jno.	100
Brooks, Jeane	110
Beadwine, Jno.	200
Benthall, Dan'll	258
Baker, Jno.	400
Brichouse, Geo.	2100
Cob, Sam'll	130
Coape, Wm.	200
Custis, Jno. Coll.	3400
Collier, Barth'o	150
Carpenter, Charles	240
Cox, Jno.	500
Church, Sam'll	143
Cleg, Jno. Sr.	204
Cleg, Henry	204
Carvy, Rich'd	100
Cowbry, Josiah	167
Cormeck, Mich.	200
Clerk, Jno.	100
Corban, Geo.	250
Clerk, Geo.	833
Caple, Nath.	100
Callinett, Jno.	100
Crew, John	300
Costin, Francis	275
Custis, Maj'r John	3250
Custis, Hancock	50
Chick, Tho.	100
Dowing, Jno.	70
Dewy, Geo.	300
Dewy, Jacob	100
Delby, Margery	450
Dowty, Rowland	150
Dunton, John	170
Denton, Tho.	400
Dowman, John	100

NORTHAMPTON COUNTY (Continued)

	Acres
Dullock, John	100
Dunton, Tho. Sr.	120
Dunton, Tho. Jr.	120
Dunton, Wm.	420
Dunton, Benj'm	220
Duparks, Tho.	90
Davis, Jno.	850
Danton, Joseph	120
Dixon, Michaell	460
Eshon, Jno.	600
Evans, Jno.	200
Edmunds, David	500
Evans, Tho.	300
Esdoll, Geo.	100
Eyres, Tho.	1133
Eyres, Nich.	325
Eyres, Cap't Jno.	774
Eyres, AnneWid'o	733
Esdoll, Edw'd	100
Fisher, John	637½
Francisco, Dan'l	150
Fisher, Tho.	637½
Foster, Rob't	150
Fabin, Paul	60
Frost, Tho.	100
Frank, Jno.	500
Floyd, Charles	378
Frostwater, Geo.	200
Frizell, Geo.	140
Frostwater, Wm.	200
Fitchett, Joshua	100
Floyd, Berry & Matthew	555
Gogni, David	150
Gill, Rob't	200
Gascoyne, Rob't	125
Gascoyne, Wm.	525
Greene, Jno. Sr.	2200
Giddens, Tho.	227
Grice, Peter	200
Godwin, Devorix	600
Gostogan, Tho.	100
Gullding, Charles	200
Griffith, Jeremiah	345
Griffith, Benj'm	200
Hill, Francis	100
Henderson, John	250
Haggaman, Isaac	750
Harmanson, Jno.	1600
Harmanson, Henry	1250
Hanby, Charles	25
Hanby, Rich'd	75
Hanby, Dan'll	50
Hanby, John	150
Harmonson, Cap't Wm.	308
Harmonson, Geo.	1586
Harmonson, Tho.	400

NORTHAMPTON COUNTY (Continued)

	Acres
Hawkins, Jno. Sr.	66
Hawkins, Jno. Jr.	66
Hawkins, Gideon	66
Hunt, Groton	485
Hunt, John	440
Hunt, Tho.	290
Hall, Francis Widd'o	340
Johnson, John Sr.	250
Johnson, John Jr.	100
Johnson, Jacob	350
Isaacs, John Jr.	100
Joynes, Maj'r	150
James, Joan Widd'o	250
Johnson, Obedience Cap't	400
Johnson, Tho, Jr.	75
Johnson, Tho. Sr.	400
Jackson, Jonah & John	625
Joynes, Edm'd	200
Joynes, Edw'd	200
Johnson, Jeptha Sr.	50
Jacob, Phillip Sr.	350
Johnson, Jeptha Jr.	200
Johnson, Obedience & Jeptha Sr.	250
Johnson, Edm'd	400
Jacob, Rich'd	200
Jacob, Abraham	50
Kendall, Wm.	2410
Knight, John	200
Lawrence, John	120
Lailler, Luke	100
Lucas, Tho.	100
Lewis, Rob't	100
Littleton, Susannah Wid'o	4050
Luke, John	400
Marshall, Geo.	250
Marshall, Jno.	250
Maddox, Tho.	1500
Mickall, Yeardly	400
Matthews, John	275
Major, John	390
Map, John	50
Moore, Matthew	175
Moore, Matthew	275
Mackmellien, Tho.	300
More, Gilbert	225
Morrianie, John	119½
More, Jno.	545
More, Eliner	175
Nicholson, Wm.	600
Nottingham, Wm.	150
Nottingham, Joseph	150
Nottingham, Rich'd	350
Nottingham, Benj'm	300
Nelson, John	100
Only, Clement	200

NORTHAMPTON COUNTY (Continued)

	Acres
Odear, John	100
Parramose, Tho.	400
Preson, Tho.	600
Powell, Frances Widd'o	1225
Palmer, Sam'll	1562
Pyke, Henry	150
Powell, John	636 1/3
Pittett, Tho.	300
Pittett, Justian	200
Pittett, John	275
Powell, Sam'll	200
Paine, Daniell	150
Piggott, Ralph	1368
Read, Thomas	150
Rascow, Arthur	100
Ronan, Wm.	150
Roberts, Jno.	200
Richards, Lettis	150
Robins, Jno. Maj'r	1180
Robins, Littleton	1000
Rabishaw, Wm.	55
Roberts, Obedience	260
Robinson, Benjamin	250
Shepherd, Jno.	200
Smith, Joseph	250
Smith, Sam'll	150
Smith, Jno.	200
Savage, Tho.	450
Smith, Tho.	400
Smith, Abrah.	300
Seady, Anth'o	120
Scot, Widd'o	750
Smith, Rich'd minor	300
Scot, Geo.	100
Smith, Rich'd	99
Scot, Jno.	100
Scot, Henry	800
Scot, David	800
Smith, Peter	450
Sanders, Rich'd	100
Swan, John	800
Shepherd, Tho.	140
Sanders, Eustick	100
Sanderson, John	676
Savage, John	410
Stringer, Hillary	1250
Savidge, Cap't Tho.	1600
Savidge, Elkington	750
Scot, Wm. Sr.	153
Straton, Benj'm	745
Smith, Geo.	133
Stockley, Jno. Sr.	370
Shepheard, Widd'o	830
Seamore, John	200

NORTHAMPTON COUNTY (Continued)

	Acres
Tilney, John	350
Tryfort, Barth.	147
Teague, Simeon	100
Turner, Rich'd	50
Teague, Tho.	200
Tankard, Wm.	450
Tanner, Paul	148
Webb, Henry	100
Wills, Thoma (?)	300
White, John	400
Wilson, Tho.	250
Westerhouse, Adryean Sr.	200
Walker, John	300
Ward, Tho.	120
Walter, John	400
Waterfield, Wm.	200
Warren, John	525
Warren, Argoll	350
Widgeon, Rob't	100
Wilkins, Jno.	150
Webb, Edw'd	200
Wilcock, Jno.	200
Warren, James	50
Waterson, Wm.	855
Warren, Rob't	190
Water, Lt. Col. Wm.	700
Webb, Charles	133¼
Willett, Wm.	2650
Waterson, Rich'd	150
Wilkins, Argoll	150
Walter, Eliz'b Widd'o	100
Warren, Joseph	50

Land not paid for viz:

Gleab: formerly Cap't Foxcrofts	1500
John Maj'r at Occahannock	200
Hogbin not being in Virg'a	100
Tho. Smith	300
Tho. Marshall, orphan	75
Jno. Rews not in Virg'a	100

Wm. Robertson, Clk.

PERSONAL GRIEVANCES of divers Inhabitants within his Majesties Colony of Virginia. Dated 9th November 1676

Alexander Walker complaining and proving that 23 hogsheads of sweet scented tobacco were seized by ye Rt. Hon'ble Sr. Wm. Berkeley.

Henry Jenkins complaining that Sr. Wm. Berkeley seized 22 head of cattell.

Otho Thorp. His wife forced from home and set on the Trenches by Bacon. 27 servants carried away, 1200 pounds sterling plundered by the rebels.

Mr. Thomas Grendon of Charles City County, Merchant. Several servants, Oxen, Sheep, Silver Plate etc. to the value of 500 pounds sterling and 9 hogsheads of tobacco carried away by Lt. Col. Edward Hill.

Thomas and William Dudley, sonnes to Wm. Dudley Sr. of Peankytank in the County of Middlesex, lately deceased. Stating that their father was forced during Bacon's rebellion to administer the oath imposed by Bacon but did so unwillingly and was pardoned by the Governor after the rebellion. Nevertheless 15 hogsheads of tobacco was seized for the use of Sir Wm. Berkeley. Test - Gregory Walklate, Hen: Hartwell.

Mr. John Page on behalf of John Jeffryes of London Esqr. 63 pipes of Fiall wine lost in James Towne during rebellion.

Anne Hunt, widow of William Hunt of Charles City County, decd. The husband having been active in the rebellion, according to false reports, all the estate was seized without "Endictment or Tryall"

Nicholas Prynne, Master of the Ship Richard and Elizabeth of London, Concerning goods shipped to William Hunt from Alderman Booth & Comp'y of London to the value of 265 pounds sterling. Said Prynne gave Bills of Lading and Lt. Col. Edward Hill seized the goods on the death of Hunt.

Thomas Palmer, Carpenter. Built a house for Thomas Hansford, who was executed as a Rebell. Debt for house was 3800 lbs. of Tobacco. Hansford's wife paid Palmer 7 hogsheads of tobacco but this was seized by the Gov'r.

Warrant to Sheriffe of Surry Countie to seize sheep of Robert Kay. Sa'l Swann, Vice Comrs.

Sandes Knowles of Gloster County, Planter. Was forced to take Bacon's oath but was pardoned by Governor. Major Robert Beverly seized petitioner 3 negroes and 5 English servants and goods to the value of 400 pounds sterling. Deposition on petitioner's behalf by Henry Singleton.

Wm. Howard. Stating that Mr. Robert Beverly entered his house on a pretext of searching for Howard's son-in-law, John Harris, who was in Bacon's army and seized servants and goods to the value of 500 pounds sterling. The Order given in the case also mentions cases of Mr. Richard Clerk and George Seaton.

John Deane of James City County, Planter. Confessing that he took Bacon's oath and asking for Pardon. Complains that 4 hogsheads of tobacco was seized by Mr. William Hartwell.

Personal Grievances against William Hartwell, Servant to the Governor

John Williams of James City County, Planter. "Imprisoning him 10 days and forcing him by hard usage to a Composicion of 2 hoggsheads of Tobacco & 6 Barrells of Indian Corne to the value of 16 pounds sterling".

Thomas Bobby. Imprisoned and forced to pay 500 lbs. Porke, 200 lbs. Bacon and 100 lbs. Butter etc.

Nicholas Toope. "Imprisoned 5 weekes and forced to give a bill for 20 paire of shoos etc."

John Johnson and James Barrow. Imprisoned and forced to pay 10,000 shingles.

William Hoare. "Imprisoned 10 dayes, cattell & Hoggs taken. 10,000 lbs. of Porke demanded by Hartwell to save his life" (Confessed also by James Gery, the Governor's serv't)

Edward Lloyd, a Mulatto. Imprisoned, goods seized and wife frightened whilst in labour and died. Forced to pay Capt. of the Guard 400 lbs. of tobacco.

Thomas Glovers. Imprisoned 5 weeks & forced to give a horse for his discharge, value 1200 lbs. tobacco. Petitioner was advised by Mr. Ballard to serve under Bacon.

Andrew Godeon. Imprisoned "ten dayes untill he passed an obligacion for five moneths worke".

William Rowland. Pressed into Bacon's service, imprisoned and forced to pay 8,000 lbs. of tobacco for his enlargem't.

Thomas Lushington. Against Hartwell for imprisoning the Pet'r, stripping his Clothes from his Backe and taking his Papers out of his Pocket.

Note, These severall Complts. agt. Hartwell were for Imprisonment of persons after the Country was reduced to Obedience, without any Warrant, that could be by him produced or proved, but the pretence onely of having the Governor's verbal order, or Col. Ballard's; and that the Governor received the severall Composicions before complain'd of and not Hartwell.

Petition of Richard Clarke. Was seduced into the late unhappy Rebellion but did no wrong etc. But armed men under the command of "Roger Potter & Bryan Smith came to the Pet'rs. house and thence in company of Wm. Hartwell, Richard Auborne and Samuel Mathews took Fower English servants, Seaven Negro slaves, six hoggsheads of tobacco and all the Petrs. household goods etc. amounting to at least 400 lbs. sterling" Two English servants and 7 negroes are in possession of Major Robert Beverly.

George Seaton. All his goods, value 150 pounds sterling seized by Major Robert Beverly.

Sands Knowles. 3 negro slaves, 1 shallop, 5 English servants and other goods seized by Robert Beverly.

Complaints presented by John Berry and Francis Mirgson.

A LIST of the Names of those Worthy Persons whose Services and sufferings by the late Rebell Nathaniel Bacon Jr. and his Party have been reported to us most Signal and eminent during the late unhappy troubles in Virginia Etc.

The Right Hon'ble Sir Wm. Berkeley, then Governour of Virginia who suffered much in his person and estate.

Sir Henry Chicheley, imprisoned by Bacon. He was employed on the Indian Expedition and was on the point of subjecting them when his orders were countermanded by the Governor.

Col. Nathaniel Bacon, the elder, kinsman of the Rebell Bacon. Plundered by the Rebell Bacon of goods to the value of at least 1,000 pounds ster. He tried to stop the rebellion by offering Bacon the Rebell part of his estate.

Col. Philip Ludwell. Plundered in his owne estate and some orphans.

Col. Augustine Warner, Speaker of the House of Burgesses in late Assembly.

Mr. Thomas Ludwell, Secretary of Virginia

Col. Daniel Parkes. Plundered of at least 1,500 pounds sterling

Col. William Cole, who was one of the Council.

Col. Jos: Bridger, who helped to overcome the rebels in the South Part of James River

Col. Nicholas Spencer. Fought well against rebels

Mr. Ralph Wormely. Lost 500 pounds sterling

Col. Christopher Wormley. Lost 500 pounds sterling.

Capt. Walter Whitaker. Imprisoned after Bacon's death.

Major Richard Lee, was one of the Council and was imprisoned etc.

Col. Thomas Ballard and Lt. Col. Edward Hill. Lost considerable amounts.

Major Robert Beverly, Clerk of the Assembly. Suffered loss by rebellion but also plundered a great deal, on his own account.

Col. Mathew Kemp. Suffered much by the rebels.

Mr. Arthur Allen, lost at least 1,000 pounds sterling.

Col. Wm. Claiborne, the elder and his sonnes.

Capt. Otho Thorpe. Lost a lot and also had to make a composicion of 200 pounds sterling for his Pardon for signing a Paper extorted by menaces by Giles Bland etc.

Mr. Philip Lightfoot, Col. John Smith, Major Lawrence Smith.

Col. John West, Major John Lewis, both imprisoned by rebels

Mr, John Ascough, Mr. Henry Whiting, Mr. Humphrey Gwyn - great sufferers

Mr. Richard Whitehead, Mr. Edmond Gwynne, Mr. Thomas Royston, Dr. Cumes. Suffered by plundering and imprisonment.

Mr. Charles Roan. House burnt down etc. after Bacon's death by a party of rebels commanded by Gregory Walklate.

Mr. Thomas Deacon, Major John Burhham - imprisoned by rebels.

Major Powell - wounded at James Towne

Major John Page & Mr. John Bray, lost estates

Col. John Leare, lost much & was first to report on conditions after rebellion.

Col. Charles Moryson. Furnished Sir Wm. Berkeley with provisions etc.

Capt. William Diggs, son to Mr. Edward Diggs deceased. Fought Hansford, one of the chief rebels.

Inhabitants, Sufferers by the burning of James Towne:-

Col. Thomas Swanne, Major Theoph: Hone, Mr. Will: Sherwood and the orphan of one Mr. James, house burnt down by the rebell Lawrence.

In Accomack, Persons of Particular Eminence who suffered were these

Col. Stringer, Col. Littleton, Mr. Foxcraft, Major Juniper and Major Gen'll John Custis - his house was Sir Wm. Berkeley's headquarters.

THE GOOD QUEEN OF PAMUNKEY suffered greatly and particularly mourns the loss of her Rich Matchcoat

Major Robert Bristow, now of Tower Street, London.

Bonds taken to the Kings use for seizing delinquents Estates
Dated July 18th 1677

	Pounds penalty
Bond from James Barrow for the estate of John Turner	40
Bond from Mary Young and Wm. Wilkinson for estate of Tho. Young	100
Bond from Nicholas Wyatt & Geo. Middleton for estate of Wm. Rookings, died in prison before execution	300
An Engagement without penalty from Lemuel Mason, Francis Sayer and Robert Bray, Com'rs for Lower Norfolke for Carvers Estate	
A Bond from Naomy Scarbrough, widow & relict of Wm. Scarbrough, & Rob't Lee of Surry County	200
A Bond from Lidia Cheesman & John Scarsbrooke for estate of Edm'd Cheesman dec'd.	500
A Bond from Rob't Spencer & Thomas Jordan for estate of John Whitson, executed	150
Bond from James Willis & Thomas Douglasse both of Charles City County for estate of Rob't Jones, tryed & sentenced to dye but not Ex'ted	500
Bond from Eliz: Hansford & Charles Hansford for estate of Thomas Hansford, dec'd.	200
Bond from Charles Wilford & *** Loughes for estate of Tho. Wilford, dec'd.	100
Bond from James Whaley & Bryan Smith for estate of Tho. Whaley	100
Bond from Frances Iles, widow of John Iles, and John Watts of Isle of Wight County for estate of ye late husband	200
Bond from Eliz: Bacon, Tho. Grendon & John Pleasants for estate of Nathaniel Bacon Jr.	500
Bond from Margaret Page & Robert Spring for estate of Henry Page	100
Bond from Elianor Groves & Thomas Barlow, both of Isle of Wight County, for estate of Wm. Groves	100

Signed by Tho. Ludwell.

SURVEY OF THE DONBARTON FRIGAT - January 29th 1690

Wee ye Subscribers by Order of Capt. Rowe, Comander of their Maj'ties Shipp Donbarton, this day made a survey of ye sd. Shipp, & wee doe finde her as followeth, etc. etc.

Signed by: Edward Lassells
Cuthbert Dodsworth
Thomas Pollard
William Harwood
Cor: Purnell

Certified a true copy by Fr: Nicholson

SUITS BROUGHT TO THE GENERAL COURT 10th July 1693

William Randolph Esq., Att. Gen'l vs. Thomas Ballard
Joseph Wring & William Buckner
Thomas Maddox & Daniel Neech
John Washingtain (Washington)
Robert Peyton, Tho. Todd &
Peter Beverley
Daniel Parke Esq.
Gawin Corbin
Thomas Martin
William Wilson
James Howell
James Jones
Richard Nusum
Richard Nusum & Thomas Martin
Richard Lee Esq.
Lewis Conners Executor
Samuell Traverse Executors
John Mans Executors
Lewis Burwell
Bertram Servant
Christopher Robinson Esq.,
his executors
Thomas Loyd
Thomas Loyd & David Gwynn
Bertram Servant
Wm. Sherwood Esq.
John Dyer & Thomas Ballard
John Coifeild
Gawin Corbin
John Grymes
William Crawford
Willis Wilson

Fra: Nicholson.
E. Jenings, Dep. Sec'ty

THE NAMES OF PERSONS AS COMMANDED TO SUPPLY VACANCYES IN THE COUNCIL THE 22nd JULY 1693

William Cole
John Armstead
Richard Johnson
Edward Portue
Lewis Burwell
Matthew Page
Robert Carter
Dudley Diggs
William Randolph
John Lloyd
Lawrence Smith
Anthony Lanson

All which are Noted Inhabitants or Planters of the best Estates and all of them sometimes Justices of the Peace and in other principall Imployes.

THE NAMES OF THE PERSONS TO SUPPLY VACANCYS IN THE COUNCILL APRIL 20, 1696

Peter Armistead
Lawrence Smith
William Randolph
Dudley Diggs,
Robert Carter
John Custis
Mathew Page
Lancelott Bathurst
William Tayloe
Peter Beverley
Lewis Burrell (Burwell)?
Benjamin Harrison Sr.

Are Principall Inhabitants & good Estates in the Country

To His Edc'y Edm'd Andros, Kn. to His Majesty
Lt. & Gov'r Gen'rl of Virginia

The Humble Address of ye Clergy of Virginia
at a General Meeting at James City
June 25th, 1696

James Blair, Commissary

Cope Doyley	And: Monro
James Solater	Ch. Anderson
William Williams	Jo'n Monro
Henry Pretty	Francis Ferdyce
Joseph Holt	Jonathan Saunders
Geo. Robinson	And: Cant
John Ball	John Alexander

James Wallace

NAMES OF PERSONS TO SUPPLY VACANCIES IN THE COUNCIL

10th april 1697

John Armstead	Mathew Page
Lawrence Smith	Lancelot Bathurst
William Randolph	William Taylor
Dudley Diggs	Peter Beverly
Robert Carter	Lewis Burrell
John Curtis	Benjam'n Harrison Sr.

Are Principal Inhabitants
and Good Estates in ye Country.

Edm'd Andros.

A List of The Present Members of His Majestys Council in Virginia, With the Distances they live from Williamsburg to which place they never come but when sent for; the General Courts and Courts of Oyer and Terminer excepted.

	Miles
Mr. Diggs	20
Mr. Robinson	45
Mr. Grymes	30
Mr. Custis, in Town	
Mr. Lightfoot	12
Mr. Taylor	50
Mr. Lee	54
Mr. Dunwiddie (Dinwiddie)?	46
Mr. Burwell	10
Mr. Fairfax	150

A List of Gentlemen fitt to succeed to Vacancies

The Rev'd Mr. Wm. Dawson, in Town - Bishop of London Comisary
Mr. John Lewis 18

These two I have recommended to your Lordship.

Mr. Benj'a Harrison
Mr. John Robinson Jr.
Mr. Cha. Carter
Mr. Rich'd Randolph
Mr. John Bowling
Mr. Will. Nelson)
Mr. Beverly Randolph)
Mr. John Taylor Jr.)
Mr. Mann Page)
Mr. Carter Burwell)

The last five are young Gentlemen; the others live some forty, some fifty, and Mr. Carter one hundred miles from hence; nor are there any Persons nearer qualified for that station.

Approximate date 1745

TO THE KINGS MOST EXCELL'T MAJ'TIE

Dread Soveraigne,

Wee noe Sooner heard the Joyfull news of that Peace Soe Long desired in Europe & Soe hon'ble to the English Nation w'ch under God was Chiefly owing to yo'r Maj'ties unimitable valour & Wisdom but wee did according to our allegiance & duty congratulate Yo'r Maj'ties happy and wonderful Success in perfecting that greate & Glorious Work as also yo'r Maj'ties Safe Returne to yo'r own people after the many hazards of a Long & bloody Warr, And the fresh advice wee have since received of yo'r Maj'ties perfect health & Welfare & of the happy union & Agreem't w'ch is between yo'r Maj'tie & yo'r Parliam't in England for both w'ch wee have heere in this yo'r Maj'ties Province Solemnized, Publick Dayes of Thanksgiving as in duty bound to God and yo'r Maj'tie makes & presumes to Lay this Second Address at yo'r Royall Feet. etc.

Signed By:

His Maj'ties Councill	Judges of the Provincial Court	Grand Jury
Henry Jowles, Chan:	Robert Smith	Phillip Lynes, Foreman
Charles Hutchins	Thomas Tasker	Charles Greenberry
Thomas Tench	John Thompson	William Comigys
John Addison	James Keetch	Ambrose Kinamont
Thomas Brookes	Richard Hill	Charles Filder
James Frisby	John Hammond	John Rawlins
	John Hawkins	Charles Beaven
		John Emerson
		Ephraim Wilson
		William Myls
		Thomas Kilman
		Humphry Tilton
		Thomas Atterberry
		William Watts
		Peter Watts
		Aaron Tunison

Fr: Nicholson

Approximate date 1697

Petition to Francis Nicholson,
Comander in Chief of Maryland

Dated September 5, 1698

(Concerning various Scandalous and Defamatory rumours spread by Jno. Cood)

Signed By: Justices Rob't Smith, Jno. Hamond, Rich'd Hill
Tho. Tasker, Tho. Staly, Jno. Pollard, Jno. Hawkins

Further petition signed by:

Justices: Rob't Smith, Tho. Tasker, James Keoch, Jno. Hamond,
Jno. Pollard, John Sampson, Rich'd Hill, Tho. Staly,
John Hawkins.

Grand Jury: Wm. Turls, And'w Parker, Rich'd Jones, Tho. Coursey,
Sam'll Gaylard

Jury: A. Miller, Gabriell Parrot, Wm. Roland, Gilbert Clarke,
Edw'd Groom, Jno. Hurst, Lane Todd, John Duvole, Hugh Riley,
Cornelius Howard, Char: Hammond, John Willoughby,
Phill: Lines (or Lewis), Foreman, Elias Kirry,
Sam'll Holdsworth, John Holdsworth, Thomas Jones,
George Layfield, Geo. Plater, Wm. Dent, Rob't Goldsborough,
Wm. Bladen, Sam'll Watkins,

A True Copy: W. Bladen, Cl. Com'e.

Further petition signed by:

Grand Jury: Wm. Turls, Henry Hardy, Tho. Rieves, And'w Parker,
Sam'll Handy, Sam'll Howard, Chr: Beanes, Rich'd Jones,
Jacob Gibbson, Rob't Fenes, Abra: Taylor, Jno. Wiatt,
Tho. Homewood, Wm. Hollis, Jno. Manping, Tho. Coursey

Justices: Rob't Smith, Rich'd Hill, Tho. Tasker, John Pollard,
James Keoch, Jno. Thompson, Jno. Hamond, Jno. Hawkins,
Tho. Staley.

Jury Elected Regarding the Building of the Capital City of Williamsburg by an Act of the General Assembly at James City - 27th April, 1699

"Wee, the Jury etc. etc."

Dated under our hands and sealed this 8th day of September 1699

Joseph Ring, Foreman	John Hockaday
Warwick Mohun	Wm. Browne
Robert Read	Peter Crutchfeild
Alex: Walker	Wm. Pinkethman
Jeremiah Laundey	John Frayser
Lanc't Smith Jr.	Alex: Walker Jr.

1699. The **COLLONELS** and Commanders in Chief. The Lieutenant Collonels and Commanders in Chief, the Lieutenant Collonels and the Majors of the **MILITIA** in the Severall Counties in this his Maj'ties Colony and Dominion of Virginia are as followeth -

HENRICO COUNTY

William Byrd, Esq., Coll. & Commander in Chief
William Randolph, Lieut. Coll.
Peter Feild, Major

CHARLES CITY COUNTY

Edward Hill, Esq., Coll. & Commander in Chief
Edward Hill Jr., Lieut. Coll.
Charles Goodrich, Major

SURRY COUNTY

Benjamin Harrison, Esq. Coll. & Commander in Chief
Henry Tooker, Major

ISLE OF WIGHT COUNTY

Samuell Bridger, Lieut. Coll. & Commander in Chief
Henry Baker, Major

NANSEMOND COUNTY

George Bosworthy, Lieut. Coll. & Commander in Chief
Thomas Swan, Major

PRINCESS ANNE COUNTY

Anthony Lawson, Lieut. Coll. & Commander in Chief
John Thorowgood, Major

NORFOLK COUNTY

Lemuel Mason, Lieut. Coll. & Commander in Chief
James Wilson, Major

ELIZABETH CITY COUNTY

Wm. Wilson, Lieut. Coll. & Commander in Chief
Anthony Armistead, Major

WARWICK COUNTY

Miles Cary, Lieut. Coll. & Commander in Chief
William Cary, Major

JAMES CITY COUNTY

Philip Ludwell Jr., Coll. & Commander in Chief
Henry Duke, Lieut. Coll.

YORK COUNTY

Edmund Jenings Esq., Coll. & Commander in Chief
Thomas Ballard, Lieut. Coll.
William Buckner, Major

NEW KENT COUNTY

John Lightfoot Esq., Coll. & Commander in Chief
Joseph Foster, Lieut. Coll.
William Bassett, Major

KING & QUEEN COUNTY
William Leigh, Coll. & Commander in Chief
Joshua Story, Major

GLOUCESTER COUNTY
Matthew Page, Esq., Coll. & Commander in Chief
James Ransome, Lieut. Coll.
Peter Beverly, Major

MIDDLESEX COUNTY
Ralph Wormeley Esq., Coll. & Commander in Chief
Matthew Kemp, Lieut. Coll.
Robert Dudley,, Major

ESSEX COUNTY
Ralph Wormeley, Esq. Coll. & Commander in Chief
Wm. Moseley, Lieut. Coll.
John Catlett, Major

LANCASTER COUNTY
Robert Carter, Coll. & Commander in Chief
Joseph Ball, Lieut. Coll.

NORTHUMBERLAND COUNTY
Robert Carter, Coll. & Commander in Chief
George Cowper, Lieut, Coll.
Rodhann Kenner, Major

RICHMOND COUNTY
Richard Lee Esq., Coll. & Commander in Chief
George Taylor, Lieut. Coll.
Thomas Lloyd, Major

WESTMORELAND COUNTY
Richard Lee Esq., Coll. & Commander in Chief
Willoughby Allerton, Lieut. Coll.
Francis Wright, Major

STAFFORD COUNTY
George Mason, Coll. & Commander in Chief
Thomas Owsley, Major

ACCOMACK
Charles Scarburgh, Coll. & Commander in Chief
Edm'd Scarburgh, Lieut. Coll.
Richard Bayley, Major

NORTHAMPTON
John Custis, Coll. & Commander in Chief
Nathaniel Littleton, Lieut. Coll.
William Watters, Major

CLERGY: A List of Parishes, Ministers and Tithables July 8, 1702

COUNTY	PARISHES	MINISTERS	TITHABLES
ACCOMACK	Accomack		
CHARLES CITY	Bristol Port	Geo: Robinson	
	Westopher	Chas: Anderson	606
	Martin Brandon)		135
	Weyonoke)	Jam's Bushell	363
ELIZABETH CITY	Elizabeth City	James Wallace	479
ESSEX	South Farnham	Lewis Latone	
	Sittenburnport	Barth: Yates	
	St. Mary's	Wm. Andrews	
GLOUCESTER	Petsoe	Eman'l Jones	
	Abbington	Guy Smith	
	Ware	James Clarke (? Cocke)	
	Kingson (Kingston)		
HENRICO	Verino al Henrico	Jacob Ware	709
	Bristoll port	Geo: Robinson	518
	King Wm. parish	Ben De Joux	
JAMES CITY	Wallingford		
	Wilmington	Jno. Gordon	139
	James City	James Blaire	308
	Martin's Hund'd	Step'n Fovace	93
	Bruton port	Cope-Doyly	In York
ISLE OF WIGHT	Warwick Creek	Tho: Sharpe	304
	Newport	And'w Monroe	537
KING & QUEEN	St. Stephens	Rolp. Booker	783
	Stratton Maj'r	Edw'd Portlock	
LANCASTER	Christ Church	And'w Jackson	508
	St. Mary		
	(White Chappell)	Jno. Carnagie	433
MIDDLESEX	Christ Church	Rob't Yates	
NANSEMOND	Upper Parish		
	Lower Parish		
	Chuckatuck		
NORFOLK	Eliza: River	Wm. Rudd	707
NEW KENT	Blisland		526
	St. Peters	Jam's Booker	801
NORTHUMBERLAND	Fairfeild	Jno. Farnifold	
	Wicocomoco	Jno. Urqhart	
NORTHAMPTON	Hungars	Pet'r Collier	712
PRINCESS ANN	Linhaven	Solom'n Wheatly	674

List of Parishes, Ministers and Tithables July 8, 1702 (continued)

COUNTY	PARISHES	MINISTERS	TITHABLES
RICHMOND	St. Mary's		
	Sittenburn port	Barth: Yates	
	North Farnham	Pet'r Kippax	
SURRY	Southwarke	Alex: Walker	552
	Lyons Creek		
	at Lawns	Tho: Burnet	327
STAFFORD	St. Paule		346
	Overwharton	Jno. Frazier	518
WARWICK	Mulberry Island		204
	Denby		278
WESTMORELAND	Cople (?)	Jam's Brechin	
	Washington		480
YORKE	Bruton port	Cope Doyly	581
	Hampton	Steph: Fovace	
	York }		
	Charles }	James Slater	
KING WILLIAM	St. John	Jno. Monroe	803

By: E. Jenings

Jam: Blair, Comissary to ye Lord Bishop of London

Perog'n (?) Cony, Chaplaine to his Excellency

TO HER MOST EXCELLENT MAJESTY ANNE BY THE GRACE OF GOD QUEEN OF ENGLAND SCOTLAND FRANCE IRELAND AND VIRGINIA, DEFENDER OF THE FAITH

The most Humble Address of Your Majesties most Loy. and Dutifull Subjects, the Inhabitants of Stafford County, in your ancient Colony & Dominion of Virginia. Memorial.

Your Sacred Majesties Dutifull
Subjects and Servants

Robert Alexander
John Washington
Mathew Thompson
Richard Hassacar
Wm. Bunbury
Thomas Harrison
George Mason
Moses Lynton
John West
John West Jr.
John Peake
G. Mason
Will: FitzHugh
Benj. Colclough
Tho. Lund
Giles Travers
Alex. Waugh
Thomas Pillson
Edward Hart
Charles Ellis
Philip Alexander
George Anderson

Recorded in the Secretaries Office

E. Jenings.

1702

TO THE QUEENS MOST EXCELLENT MAJESTY

THE HUMBLE ADDRESS OF THE GRAND JURY FOR THE BODY OF YOUR MAJESTIES COLONY AND DOMINION OF VIRGINIA

May it Please your Majestie.
Memorial (Death of late Soveraign William the Third)

----- That your Majesty may live to enjoy a Long and happy Reigne over us.

Peter Beverly, Foreman	Wm. Fitzhugh
Miles Cary	Ja: Westcomb
Wm. Robinson	Jno. Deane
Jno. Washington	Wm. Jones
Geo. Eskeridge	Charles Curtis
Wm. Randolph	Henry Brereton
John Major	Richard Bland
Wm. Small	Geo. Glasuck
Wm. Cary	Henry Scarburgh
Wm. Wilson	John Walker
Rich'd Bally	David Clarkson
Edm'd Scarburgh	William Hansford

Record'd in y'r Secret'l Office

Dated ? 1702

TO THE QUEENS MOST EXCELLENT MAJESTY

THE HUMBLE ADDRESS OF THE OFFICERS CIVIL AND MILITARY OF PRINCESS ANN COUNTY IN THE DOMINION OF VIRGINIA.

Civill Officers

Ben'o Burrough
Edw'd Moseley
Adam Thorowgood
Tho. Lawson
Henry Spratt - Sheriff
Solomon White
John Richardson
John Moseley, Clk. Ct.
Henry Chapman - Sub Sheriff

Coll. & Comd'r in Chief

Edw'd Moseley

Lieut. Coll

Plomer Bray

Major

Adam Thorowgood

Captains

Henry Spratt
Horatio Woodhouse
John Moseley
O. Coke
Henry Chapman

Lieutenants

James Davis
Tully Smith
Wm. Smith
Edw'd Moseley Jr.

Circa 1702

REQUEST TO GOVERNOR FRANCIS NICHOLSON TO HAVE A REFUGEE BROUGHT IN BY THE EMPEROR OF PISCATOWAY AND PUNISHED

Robert Alexander	G. Mason
Edward Barton	Math. Thompson
Thomas Baxter	Rich'd Fassaker
Giles Vandinsteal	Philip Buckner
Hugh Kneton	William Williams
John Waugh Jr.	John Washington
Tho's Norman	Robert Collson
John Simson	David Laughan

These are all true copies - Hen: Nicholson

Date July 1699 ?

VIRGINIA JAMES CITY July 1, 1699

These 15 Gentlemen are persons every way qualified to be of his Majesty's Hon'ble Council here, and therefore humbly recommended by ---------

Lewis Burwell
Robert Carter
William Leigh
John Curtis (Custis) ?
William Willson
Lawrence Smith
Mih'l Carey
Philip Ladwell (Ludwell)?
William Randolph
Joseph Ring
Wm. Churchill
Wm. Fitzhugh
Wm. Basset
James Ranson
John Lewis

TO HIS ROYALL HIGHNESS GEORGE PRINCE OF DENMARK
LORD HIGH ADMIRAL OF ENGLAND

The humble Petition of Several Merchants of London Trading to Virginia & Maryland. Humbly Sheweth,
That there are now about eighty sail of Merbhants Ships in Virginia and Maryland, as also several others fitting out for the said Places, for the security whereof, Wee humbly pray that a Convoy may be appointed to depart England by the last of January, with orders to bring home all such Ships as shall be loaden in the said Plantations by the 30th June. If any Ships should not be then ready to come away for England Wee humbly pray that some of the men of Warr may have instructions to stay for the said Ships until the 14th August next or that Directions may be given the Govenours (of the said Plantations) That no Ship be detained there by Embargoe.

And your Petitioners shall ever pray etc.,

Ri: Levett	James Booth
Wm. Lone	Francis Lee
E. Haistwell	George Hatley
Peter Paggen	George Packson
Isaac Millner	Cuthb't Jones
Benj'a Hatley	Joseph Jackson
Francis Levett	Tho. Cary
David Dennisse	Tho. Haistwell
Peregrine Browne	Geo. Livingston
Rob't Dunckley	Humphrey Bett
John Brown	Geo. Nelthorpe

(Not Dated) Circa 1702

GRAND JURY FOR GENERALL COURT OCTober 1716

David Bray
Reub'n Welch
Cha: Chiswell
Miles Cary
Thos. Jones
John Armistead
Wm. McClenahan
Thos. Nelson, Foreman
J. Pratt
Jer: Clowder
W. Dandridge
John Story
Richard Sayer
Fran: Lightfoot
Aug'n Moor
Wil: Robinson

True Copy compared with the original by
Wil: Robertson, Cl. Com.

A SCHEME SETTING FORTH HOW THE COUNCIL OF VIRGINIA STAND RELATED TO ONE ANOTHER (un-dated) ? 1716

Edmund Jenings, not related to any of the Council
Robert Carter, ditto
James Blair, marryd Mr. Harrison's sister, who has been dead some years
Phillip Ludwell marryd Mr. Harrison's sister
John Smith, not related to any of the Council
John Lewis, ditto
William Byrd marryd Mr. Ludwell's niece who is now dead
William Basset marryd Mr. Ludwell's Half-niece
William Cock not related to any of the Council
Nathaniel Harrison's sister marryd Mr. Ludwell,

Man Page not related to any of the Council
Edmund Berkley marryd Mr. Ludwell's Half-niece who is now dead

A List of Gentlemen Fitt to Supply Vacancies in Councell

Wm. Dandridge Esqr. Recomended by his Grace the Duke of Montagu, is an English Gent. of a plentiful fortune, and of many good qualities, & having the interest of so great a nobleman to back his pretensions, I place him first in this list.

John Custis Esqr. of a great estate in this Colony whose Ancestors have been of the Councell, he is little ally'd to any of the present Councellors, his many qualifications render him fit for that board.

**m's (Jam's)? Jones Esqr. is an English Gent. long residing here where hee has acquired a very considerable estate, he is ev'ry way qualified for the place, and has no affinity to any among the Councell.

(Hen)ry Armstead Esqr. ev'ry way qualified for being admitted among the Councell, I place him last, in expectation that one of the four Councellors now sitting, who are all nearly ally'd to him in blood, may dye before it comes to his turn

These are all I can think of att present fitt to bee recomended, they are persons of intire loyalty and affection to His Majestie, and I pray your Lds'pps to think this number sufficient to supply any vacancies that may speedily happen in the Councell.

(Signed) Hugh Drysdale

Circa 1722

List of Naval Officers, Collectors and Receivers June 8, 1699

Upper district James River:	Philip Lightfoot, Collector Nathaniell Harrison, Navall Officer and Receiver of the Virginia duties
Lower district James River:	Peter Hayman, Collector William Wilson, Navall Officer & Receiver
Yorke River:	William Buckner, Collector Miles Cary, Navall Officer & Receiver
Potowmock River:	Nicholas Spencer, Collector Hancock Lee, Navall Officer & Receiver
Northumberland County:	Isaac Allerton, Navall Officer & Receiver
Westmorland County including Yeocomoco River: In Stafford County including Upper Matchotucks River:	Rice Hoe, Navall Officer & Receiver
On the Eastern Shoar:	Henry Scarburgh, Collector John Custis, Navall Officer & Receiver

List of Naval Officers and Collectors April 20, 1700

Collectors	Naval Officers
Henry Scarburgh	Richard Lee
Edward Hill Jr.	Robert Carter
W. Allerton	John Custis
P. Heyman	Miles Cary
Wm. Buckner	Wm. Wilson
	Nathan: Harrison

Court present at Elizabeth City County Courthouse May 13th, 1700

Edward Hill Esqr., Judge of the Court of Admiralty

Mathew Page Esq.
Mr. Anthony Armistead
Mr. Thomas Barber
Mr. Thomas Ballard
Mr. Will'm Buckner
Mr. Humph'y Harwood
Mr. Will'm Cary
Mr. Will'm Ruscow

List of Grand Jury present May 14th, 1700

Miles Cary
Tho. Gibbins
John Goodwin
Barte: Wethersby
Edw'd Latimer
Woodridge Westwood
William Dunne
Joshua Curle

Henry Jenkins
Rich'd Dunbar
Thomas Gray
Chr: Copeland
John Bushell
Charles Tucker
Thomas Allen
Will Spicer

James Baker
Rich'd Routon
John Fadam
Will'm Davis
Thomas Faulkner
John Hixon
Joseph White

Jury elected to try John Houghing, a Pirate, May 1700

William Lowry
Coleman Brough
Jasco: Curle
Augustine Moore

Math'w Watts
Henry Royall
Philip Johnson
John Cooper

Robert Taylor
Rich'd Hursley
Geo: Cooper
Tho. Baylis

List of deponents appearing May 15th, 1700

Samuel Harrison
Joseph Wood
Tho. Murry
Wibur Scawly
John Limpany
Rob' Lurbie
Rob' Fox
John Collins

Joseph Man
Dan'l Blewit
Geo: Livingston
Edw'd Grey
Samuel Harris

Robert Hatton
John Saviere
Joseph Revell
Thom: Statler (Slatler) ?
Jacob Moreland
John Staples
Samuel Crutchfeild
Joseph Forest, a Quaker

Samuel Taylor
Rowland Thomas
Edm: Ashfeild
Isaac Herring
Joseph Bigger

Grand Jury elected May 16th, 1700

Cha: Jennings
John Hunt
Nich's Curle
Joshua Curle
Worlich Westwood
Thomas Heyres
Sam'll Daniell
Gabr'll Dunne
Henry Dunne
Will'm Dunne
John Ferguson
Henry Lewis
Robert Bright
John Miller
John Bushell (Rushell) ?
John Chaundler
Henry Barnes
Tho. Faulkner
Tho. Hawkins

Jury elected to try Francis Delamere, a Pirate, May 16th, 1700

William Armistead
Wm. Hutson
John Smith
Tho. Grey
John Sheppard
Cr: Copeland
Henry Robinson
Rich'd Freed
Fran: Rogers
Jam: Baker
Rich: Routen
Thomas Needham

List of Prisoners belonging to the Shipp Indian King on board the pirate shipps at the time of her engagement with His Maj'ties Shipp Shoreham. Given in Court May 16th, 1700

Edward Whittaker
Balwin Mathews
Sam'l Browne
John Slyfoot
John Shipman
Lewis Andrewes
John Smith
Henry Heard
Geo. Livingston

Dispersed to other shipps:

Sam'l Crutchfeild
Peter Shaw
Geo. Simmons
Morgan Cary
John Looft
Geo. Wray
Wm. Woolgar
Rich: Appleby
John Bell
John Jolly
Sam'l Stapleton
John North
Michael Martin
James Kelleby
James Sinclear
Fran: Warrell
Sam: Baker
Tho: Loyall
Rog'r Steevens
Joshua Atkinson
James Wall
Geo: Hocketts
John Stanley
Math'w Clayson
Coert Coertson
Cha: Pond

A List of men on board the Friendship of Belfast when taken by the pyrate shipp:

Hans Hammell, the Master - killed

John Calwell
Joseph Bigger
Robert Jordan
Sam'l Stewart
Joseph Chigston
James Pringle
John Pringle

These 7 were in the Friendship and in the boat when the Shoram fought the Pyrates

Robert Dayziell
Thomas Watt
And'w Davison
John Webb
Dav: Lime
James Manking

These six were on board the Shoram when she fought the Pyrates

John Galt, Prisoner on board the Pyrate Shipp.

A List of ye French Refugees 1700

Pierre Delorme and his wife
Marguerite Sene and her daughter
Magdalaine Mirtle
Jean Videau
Tertulien Sebuet, his wife and two children
Pierre Lauret, Jean Roger
Pierre Chastain, his wife and five children
Philippe Duvivier
Pierre Nace, his wife and their two daughters
Francois Cleu, Symon Sardin
Soubragon and Jacques Nicolay
Pierre du Toy, Abraham Nicod
Pierre Mallet, Fragou Coupet
Jean Oger, his wife and three children
Jean Saye
Elizabeth Augeliere
Jean and Claude Mallifaut with their ***
Isaac Chabanas, his son and Catharine Bomard
Etienne Chastain, Adam Vignes
Jean Menager and Jean Lesnard
Etienne Badouet, Pierre Morriset
Jedron Chamboux and his wife
Isaac Faury and Jerome Dumas
Joseph Bourgoian, David Bernard
Jean Chivas and his wife
Jean Tardieu, Jean Moreau
Jaques Roy and his wife
Abraham Sablet and his two children
Quintin Chasalain and Michal Roux
Jean Guichet, his wife and three children
Henry Cabanis, his wife and one child
Jaques Sayre, Jean Boisson
Francois Bosse, Jean Fouchie
Francois Saffin, Andre Cochet
Jean Gaury, his wife and one child
Pierre Gaury, his wife and one child
Jaques Hulyn, his wife and four children
Pierre Perrat and his wife
Isaac Sanetier, Jean Parransos, his sister
Elie Timson, his wife and Elizabet Tignal
Antoine Twichard, Jean Boarru and Jean Bouchet
Jaques Boyer, Elizabet Mingot
Catharine Godnat, Pierre la Cougon
Jean and Michel Cautepie, his wife and two children
Jaques Bronet, his wife and two children
Abraham Moulin and his wife
Francois Billet, Pierre Corante
Etienne Gudvin, Rene Massendau
Francois du Tastie, Isaac Avery
Jean Parmentier, David Thonitier and his wife
Moyse Leuveau, Pierre Tillou
Marie Leusque, Jean Constantin
Claud Bardon, his wife
Jean Imbert and his wife
Elizabet Fleury, Loys du Pyn
Jaques Richard and his wife
Adam and Marie Prévost
Jaques Vivas and his wife

List of French Refugees (continued)

Jaques Brousse, his child
Pierre Covau, Louys Bon
Isaac Fordet, Jean Pepuy (?)
Jean Gaillard and his son
Anthonie Matton and his wife
Isaac Lueadou and his wife
Louys Orange, his wife and one child
Daniel Taune and two children
Pierre Cupper, Daniel Roy
Magdalain Gigon, Pierre Gielet
Jean Jovany, his wife and two children
Pierre Ferner, his wife, one child
La Vifue Faure and four children
Isaac Arnaud and his wife
Pierre Chatasnier, his wife and his brother
Jean Fouasse, Jaques Bibbeau
Jean March, Catharine Billot
Marie and Symon Jouidon
Abraham Minot
Timothy Moul, his wife, one child
Jean Savin, his wife, one child
Jean Sargenton, his wife, one child
Claude Philipe and his wife
Galnel Stuster, Pierre de Come
Helen Trubyer

59 women or girls
38 Children
108 Men
205 persons. Mess'rs de la Muce and de Sailly Fout

in all 207 persons

Virginia, James Town, July 31, 1700

This is a true copy.

Olivier de la Muce, Ch. de Sailly

Received of ye hon'ble Marquis de la Muse & Char. de la Sailly ye summe of nine hundred fourty five pounds in full for ye passage of two hundred and five people aboard ye ship Mary Ann bound for Virginia.
I say received this 19th April 1700. - Geo. Hawes

Witness - Alexander Clerrer

Virginia, James City, July 31st 1700

This is a true copy.

Olivier de la Muce, Ch. de Sailly

This is a true copy, the original being in the custody of Fr. Nicholson

List of French Refugees at Manican Town
March 6th 1701/2

Mallet
Champagne
Moullins
Tariy
Chastain
Dutout
Nicod
Joanny
Minot
Gorry
Billebo
Tanure
Parrantes
Levraux
Tillion
Voye
Baret
Gorry Lejeune
Panctie
Amonet
Morisett
Rapme
Chambon
Perru
Maton
Cabany
Breusse
Guerran
M. Chastain
Cornu
Imber
Jean Saye
Soullie
Vigne
Guerrin
Petit
Verasse
Chatagne
Sassin
Dutart
Torin
Bernard
Richard
Soblet
Morell
Bollard
Cantipie
Fonville
Hugo
Theodore
Roux
Robert
Malaut
Le Febure
Martin
Trion
Bossard
Blouet
Michell
Picot
Villain
Menetruere
Remy
Givaudan
Bening
Chabran
Malarde
Caillou
La Veifre
Le Toix
Sobriche
Massan
Gonthier
Clapier
Joseph
Broke
Castige
Mazel
Marche
Richer
Preriot
Samuel
Lucadon
Durand
Passeur
Du Clos
Bognan
Hugon
Giraut
La Goufaut
Vaillant
Faisant
Mr. Aubrey
Mr. de Joux
Mr. Philippe
Verry
Mr. Sale

Land allocated to the French Refugees at Manican on October 26th, 1704 totalled:

10,033 Acres, 3 Roods, 19 Poles

TO THE QUEENS MOST EXCELL'T MAJESTY

The humble Address of the Clergy of Virginia
April 22 1703

James Blair, Comiss.

Geo. Robertson	James Clark
Bar. Yates	James Sclater (Slater)?
Rich'd Squire	Solomon Wheatty
Dan. Taylor	Edw'd Portlock
Peter Kippax	John Monro
Tho. Edwards	Lewis Latane
John Gordone	Arthur Tillyard
Thomas Sharpe	William Rudd
And. Monroe	Charles Anderson
Guy Smith	James Boisseau

To the Right Hon'ble the Lords Commissioners of
Trade and Plantations

A Memoriall

Of the Merchants and Planters Trading to Virginia and Maryland on behalf of themselves and many thousands of the inhabitants whose effects we have now ready to send for their Cloathing of which all our advices direct a speedy suply - being an answer to a memoriall presented to his Royall Highness and recommended to your Lordships concerning a sailing of your Convoy to Virginia and Maryland ------- --------- We therefore humbly Pray

Phill. Ludwell	Jos. Hopkins
Tho. Lane	Micajah Perry
Thomas Corbin	John Hyde
Robert Wise	Francis Willis
Tho. Wharton	Richard Perry
Wm. Madgwicke	Thos. Loyd
Robert Porteus	Tim. Keyser
Jon'a Scarth	Jon'a Matthews
Ed'w Rhodes	John Goodwin
Edw'd Warner	Ben'a Wooley

Date ? April 10, 1703

HER MAJESTY' S COLONY AND DOMINION OF VIRGINIA

ORDER OF COUNCIL BEARING DATE OF 17th of JUNE 1703

County	Field Officers	Captains
Gloucester		Wm. Dehnam Rich'd Booker Tho. Todd David Alexander Jno. Gwyn Wm. Smith
Essex	Wm. Catlett, Lt. Coll. Edw'd Mosely, Major	Cha. Smith Wm. Tomlin Rich'd Covington Edw'd Goldman Edw'd Rowzee Tho. Grigson Ja: Boughan Rob't Coleman
Lancaster	Hon'ble Robert Carter Esq., Collonel Jos. Ball, Lt. Coll. Wm. Lister, Major	Henry Fleet Wm. Ball Tho. Pinkard Rich'd Ball Sam'll Fox Wm. Heard
Stafford	Geo. Mason, Collonel Rice Hooe, Lt. Col. Wm. Fitzhugh, Major	Cha. Ellis Geo. Anderson John West Edw'd Mountjoy Tho. Harrison
Richmond	Wm. Tayloe, Collonel George Taylor, Lt. Collonel David Gwyn, Major	Charles Barber John Tarpley Wm. Robinson / Alex Donaphan Wm. Barber Tho. Beal Henry Brereton John Craske Fra: Slaughter Wm. Underwood
Westmorland	Hon'ble Rich'd Lee Esq. Col. Wm. Addison, Lt. Col. Francis Wright, Major	Charles Ashton Henry Ashton B. Berryman Tho. Atwell Gerard Hiatt Alex'r Sprue Andrew Monro Rich'd Cradock Jno. Bushrod

County	Field Officers	Captains
Northumberland	Hon'ble Robert Carter, Esq., Collonel Geo. Cooper, Lt. Coll. Rod'm Konnor, Major	Leon'd Howson Tho. Winder Jno. Howson Tho. Crallee Chr. Neal Rich'd Haynie Peter Presley Philip ***** Maurice Jones Edm'd Sanders Peter Hack
York	Hon'ble Edm'd Jenings Esq., Collonel Tho. Ballard, Lt. Coll. Wm. Buckner, Major	Wm. Timson Tho. Chesman Dan'l Taylor Baldwin Manton Philip ***** Lawrence Smith Tho. Nutting
Middlesex	Coll. Gawin Corbin	Lt. Geo. Wortham Jno. Smith Lt. Tho. Blakey Henry Parrot Rob't Daniel
Surry	Henry Tooker, Major	The troop late Capt. Harrison Wm. Brown Tho. Holt Wm. Gray Lt. Tho. Lane

Virginia Admiral Court
October 20, 1703

TO HIS EXCELLENCY FRANCIS NICHOLSON, ESQ.
HER MAJ'Y L'T. GOVERN'R OF VIRGINIA.

The humble Address of the Grand Jury for the Body of this Colony and Dominion of Virginia

Wm. Tayloe, Foreman
Rodham Kennor
James Taylor
Wm. Aylet
Sam'l Bridges
Rich'd Wyat
Jno. Story
Ant'o Holliday
Wm. Jones
Edwin Thacker
Henry Fox

Tully Robinson
Geo. Nich'o Hack
Phill. Lightfoot
Wm. Bridger
Jno. Waller
Wm. Fox
Harry Beverly
Hen: Duke Jr.
Jno. Frayser
Hugh Norvell
Jno. Custis Jr.
Wm. Hansford

A Petition dated February 25th, 1706.

To The Queen's Most Exc't Majesty

The humble Petition of several Merchants, Planters and Manufacturers of Tobacco, on behalf of Themselves and Others.

Joseph Woolfe
Godfrey Webster
Benjamin Statley
George Nelthors
Heneage Robinson
Alexander Spranger
Thomas Meux
Richard Perry
Humph: South
John Browne
William Clayton
Thomas Johnson
Isaac Millner
Sam. Deane
John Browne
Ia: Wayte
Tim: Keyser
Arthur Bailey
James Bray
Thomas Nisbett
William Dawkins
Francis Lee
Baet: Young
John Goodwin
Thomas Wharton
Rand. Knipe
John Glover
Hen: Van Som
John Hester
Tho: Ellis
Tho: Webster

John Hyde
John Linton
Thomas Coutts
Micajah Perry
Robert Dunckley
Francis Willis
Tho: Lanes
Benjamin Bradly
John Cooper
Benjamin Way
John Burridge
Henry Offley
Thomas Wych
Thomas Guy
Jos: Dash
Rob: Wise
James Wagstaffe
Deane Cock
Benjamin Maxen
Henry Phibb
Heritage Lenken Jr.
Io. Searth
John Askew
Abraham Coleman
Ric'd Russell
Joseph Lacy
John Shackerly
Robert Seymour
John Travres
Ric'd Harney
Jos: Locke
Ric'd Wilkinson
Joseph Bagnall
Edw'd Stevens

COPY OF THE GRAND JURYS UNANIMOUS ADDRESS, UPON THE GOVERNORS CHARGE, PRESENTED OCTOBER 19th 1720

To the Honble. Alexander Spotswood, His Majesties Lieutenant Governor and Commander in Chief of the Colony and Dominion of Virginia, etc.

Jon. Perkins	Aug. Moore, Foreman
Henry Power	Daniel Stoner
Christo: Jackson	Mich'l Archer
Harry Beverley	G. Eskridge
Jon. Brown	Tho: Bray
Reub'n Welch	Benja: Weldon
J. Thornton	Graves Parke
Geo. Newton	Wm. Thornton
Tho: Jones	W. Dandridge
Jno. Taliaferro	Joh: Robinson
	Sam'l Smith

A LIST OF WHAT SHIPPS HAVE ARRIVED IN THIS DISTRICT from ye 6th Nov'br to this 10th March 1692

Shipps Names	What Place	Masters Names
Olive Branch	London	Rich'd Hobkins
Joseph	Bristoll	Jno. Whiteing
Williams	Bristoll	W'm. Freth
George	Foey	James Denbow
Richard	Bristoll	Wm. Gething
Bark Tryall	Boston, N. England	Jacob Warren
Francis	Plym'o.	Jno. Foreman
Brigandin Exon	Boston, N. England	Edw'd Citty
Phenix	Whitehaven	Tho. Masten
Barbados Merch't	Liverpoole	Cuthbr. Sharpless
Montjoy	Bristoll	Ja: Scott
Orange	Bideford	Dan'll Perryman
Bar(n)stable	Barstable	Jno. Strange
Assurance	Bristoll	Jno. Moore
Unity	Lyme	Tho. Thomas
George	Bristoll	Jos. Whiteing
A Brigandine	Bristoll	Jno. James.

AN ACCT. OF SHIPPS IN THE DISTRICT OF YORK RIVER Not Cleared this 9th May 1692

Shipps Names	Masters Names
Tho. & Francis	Cr: Bushill
Rich: & Sarah	Tho. Granes
Hampshire	Nich'o Daniell
Mary	Jno. Wynn
Barnadiston	Wm. Norrington
Dan'll & Jane	Rob't Ransom
Jeffryes	Tho. Arnall
John	Wm. Cann
Dan'll & Henry	Hugh Bickford
Rappa: Merch't	Jno. Harle
The Lambert	Jno. Clow (Nose)?
Rob't & Sam'll	Math: Trim
Adventure	Peter Tedder
Providence	Sam'll Scrutton
Friendly Society	Habk: Wells
Susanna	Rich'd Laycock
Friendship	Goldsmith Arnall
Constant Thomas	Jno. Richardson

A LIST of Shipps Cleared out of Rappa: District 1692

Ships Names	What Place	Masters Names
Robert	Londonderry	Natha: Davis
Olive Branch	Liverpoole	Jno. Marshall
Submission	Liverpoole	Edmd. Ball
Freeman	Whitehaven	Geo. Ribton
Francis	Bristoll	And'w Gifford
Ann	do.	Sam'll Lugg
Sarah & Susannah	do.	Jno. Chapman
Concord	do.	Wm. Attwood
Factor	do.	Hans (? Hen.) Totterdale
Dispatch	do.	Jacob Morgan
Michaell	do.	Israell Loyd
Allathear	do.	Cha: Heyden
Bengall	do.	Adam Mantri**
Comfort	do.	Tho. Cooper

SHIPPS REMAINING TO BE CLEARED

Hopewell	Bristoll	Tho: Warner
Mary	do.	Nath: Yourner
Margarett	do.	Allis Ashley
Effingham	London	John Purvis
America	do.	Antho: Gesper
Providence	do.	Rich'd Dyer
Owners Goodwill	do.	Jno. Hooke
Bonnaventure	do.	Rog'r Myers
Stephen & Edward	do.	** Showell
Jane	Belfast	Rob: Murra
------	Plymo'	-- Pickford
Industry	do.	Phil'p Harwood

An Account of Shipps yt. have been loaded in Lower District James River

Ships Names	What Place	Masters Names
True Love	London	Joakin Pagett
Biscay Merch't	"	Luke Lopdell
Hannah	Bristoll	Jno. Read
Tyger	do.	Rice Jeoffryes
Merch: Adventure	London	Tho. Webber
Swan	Exon	W'm. Coggan
Eagle	London	Henry Weston
Maryl'd Merch't	Bydeford	Tho: Conibeare
Martha & Mary	Fowy	Jno. Waymouth
Robert	Bristoll	Wm. Morgan

An Account of Shipps yt. are in ye Lower District James River 1692

Ships Names	Masters Names	From
Delaware Merch't	Benja: Holt	Pensylvania
Parragon of Topsham	Jno. Tillenore	Exon
Resolution of Hull	Matthew Hearon	Hull
Expectation of Bristoll	Wm. Jones	Bristoll
Ann & Mary of London	Richard Tibbotts	London
Mary of London	James Fidler	do.
Benjamin of London	Fredk. Johnson	do.
Hope of Bristoll	Edw'd Dobey	Bristoll
Sarah of Bristoll	Jos: Learl	do.
Pinke Blessing of London	Gilbert Knott	London
Seaflower of Poole	Thomas Clour	Poole
Providence	Jno. Evans	Plymouth
Fortune of Plymo'	Phillip Wilnecke	do.

A List of Shipps in the Upper District of James River, bound for England

Shipps Names	Masters Names
Perry & Lane	Capt. Cr: Morgan
John	Capt. Sam'll Dodson
Hopewell	Capt. John Rudds
Samuell	Capt. John Harrison
Ketch Crane	Capt. Wm. Pennell
London Armes	Capt. Fr: Fisher
John	Capt. Rich'd Boswick
Mary of Dartmo'	Capt. Tho: Prettejohn

Gone for London:

John Jane of Plymo'	Capt. Rob: Tufton of New England
William	Capt. Rob: Lurting

9th May 1692, Virginia

A List of Shipps Entred & Clear'd in ye District of Rappahanock from ye 21st June 1691 to ye 5th July 1692. Ralph Wormeley, Coll'r

Ships Names	Masters Names	Ships Names	Masters Names
Robert	Natan'll Davis	Olive Branch	Jno. Marshall
Concord	Wm. Atwood	Submission	Edm'd Ball
Francis	And'w Gifford	Speedwell	Rob't Perry
Dispatch	Jacob Morgan	St. Thomas	Hen: Sutton
Factor	Hen: Totterdale	Own: Good Will	John Purviss
Comfort	Thos. Cooper	Own: Good Will	John Hooke
Sarah & Sussannah	Jno. Chapman	Bonadventure	Roger Myres
Michaell	Israell Loyd	Steph: & Edward	Thos: Laywell
Allathea	Charles Hayden	America	Anthony Tester
Anne	Sam'l Z(?)ugy	Mayflower	Bartho: Whitehorne
Bengall Merch't	Adam Mainbrew	Freeman	George Ribton
Margarett	Ellis Ashby	Jane	Robert Morra
Hopewell	Thos: Warner	Rebecca	Paul Bickford
Providence	Jno. Evans		

A List of Shipps Entred & Cleared in ye District of Potomack from 17th Sept. 1691 to 17th June 1692. Col. Christopher Wormley Coll'r

Ships Names	Masters Names	Ships Names	Masters Names
Barnstable Merch't	John Stroncye	Unity	Thos. Thomas
Orranyo (Orange)?	Dan'll Berryman	Barbados Merch't	Cuthbert Sharpless
Joseph	Jno. Whiteing	Katherine	John Gunry
Wellcome	Wm. Froke	Tryall	Jacob Warren
Richard	Wm. Gething	Briggandine	Edw'd Lilley
George	Josh: Whiting	Francis	Jno. Foreman
Mount Joy	James Scott	Three Brothers	Jno. Martin
Assurance	John Moore	Adventure	Charles Bligh
Joane	Hugh Parker	Lyon	Lewis Spry
Constant Love	Thomas Opie	Jno. of	
Attendance	John James	Stonehouse	Jno. Topsham
Margarett	Stephen Clarke	Olive Branch	Wm. Selwood
George	James Donbowe	Agreement	Rob't Hutching
Olive Branch	Rich'd Robins	Lyon	Jno. Crompton
		Phenix	Thos. Musten

A List of the Merchant Shipps bound to England under ye C-------
of their Maj'ties Shipp Assurance, Capt. Idaac Towneing, Comm'r
July 17th, 1692

Comand'rs Names	Shipps Names	Tonnage
Rob't Murrer	Jane of Belfast	25
John Lard	Wm. & John	100
Stephen Clarke	Margarett	80
Tho. Willis	Friends Agreement	80
Jno. Crompton	Lyon	80
John Martin	3 Bros. of Plymo'	40
Rob: Edgcomb	Jane of Plymo'	40
Nicho: Smith	New Hopewell	180
Jno. Harris	James & Benja.	220
Deane Cook	James & Eliza:	120
Bartho: Watts	Globe	200
Fra: Fisher	London Armes	200
Rich'd Beswick	John of London	200
Lewis Spry	Lyon	50
Thos. Thomas	Unity	100
Benja: Holt	Dellaway Merch't	70
Edw'd Tarleton	Dolphin	28
Tho: Lurting	Josiah	200
Ja: Gundry	Katherine	60
Sam'll Dodson	John	300
Tho: Green	Richard	120
Edw'd Burford	Abraham & Frances	300
Wm. Penn	Amity	100
Wm. Perry	James	240
Jno. Rudds	Hopewell	300
X'pher Morgan	Perry & Lane	350
Jnthe: Taylor	William from Carolina	70
Abra: Wildes	Maryland Merchant	120
Tho: Sutton	Concord	150
Jos: Scotting	Jno. & Thomas	200
Jno. Howell	The Shield	150
And: Carder	Friendshipp	100
Tho: Graves	Rich: & Sarah	170
Tho: Warner	Hopewell	300
Paul Bickford	Rebeccah	50
Jno. Carne	George	120
Jno. Lane	Isabella	90
Goldsmith Arnall	Friendshipp	350
Tho: Arnall	Jeffryes	450
Jno. Tanner	Old Hopewell	180
Jno. Burford	May Flower	140
Wm. Norrington	Barnadiston	400
Abra: Wildes	Dilligence	200
Tho: Prettyjohn	Mary	80
Fred: Johnson	Benjamin	200
Wm. Thapson	John	35
Wm. Lovell	Jno. & Francis	100
Jno. Moore	Assurance	150
John Evans	Providence	70
Wm. Jones	Expectation	150
Tho: Opie	Constant Love	150

Comand'rs Names	Shipps Names	Tonnage
Wm. Roberts	Reserve	80
Hugh Parker	Jane	40
Jno. Lord from Jamaica	Jamiaca Planter	200
Jno. Harris	Jno. & Susannah	130
Mathew Horne	Resolution	200
Cha: Bligh	Adventure	140
Wm. Sellwood	Olive Branch	100
Rich: Hind	Hope	70
John Fillmore	Parragon	60
John Harle	Rappa: Merchant	200
Hugh Bickford	Dan'll & Henry	200
Tho: Cullin	Ebenezar	50
John Wyn	Mary	200
Rob: Ransone	Dan'll & Jane	200
Math: Trimm	Rob't & Samuell	300
Tho: Proeman	Henry	200
Sam'll Scrutton	Providence	140
Tho: Sewell	Stephen & Edw'd	150
Nicho: Dan'll	Hampshire	350
Wm. Cann	John	130
Antho: Gester	American	180
Jno. Strange	Barnstable Merchant	75
Rich'd Tibbott	Ann & Mary	200
Jno. Nore	Adventure	250
Rich'd Laycock	Susannah	150
Jno. Purvis	Effingham	400
Roger Myers	Bonadventure	300
Jno. Luke	Resolution	80
Jno. Hooke	Owners Goodwill	100
Habakkuk Wiles	Friendly Society	300
Ja: Scott	Mountjoy	70
Sam'll Phillips	Baltimore	200
Geo: Phillips	Jno. & Margarett	200
Jos: Leech	Sarah of Bristol	250
Ellis Ashby	Margarett	180
Tho: Finds	John	150
John Vicary	Two Sisters	45
John Stephyns	Ruth	150
Tho: Maddox	Rob't & Andrew	60

Signed on July 17th 1692 by Fr: Nicholson

List of Shipps and Vessells Entering York River
from 29th September to 25th December 1698

TRYALL OF BRISTOLL	Briganteen, built Virginia 1697, 70 Tons Abraham Lewis, Master John Stephens, Wm. Smith, Edward Harford, John Jones, Owners.
VIRGINIA MERCHANT OF BRISTOLL	Ship, built Virginia 1696, 200 Tons Walter Bayly, Master Wm. Swimmer, Sir Wm. Danes, Abraham Elton, Anthony Swimmer, Jno. Swimmer, John Day, Henry Swimmer, Owners.
DUBARTUS OF NEW ENGLAND	Sloop, built New England 1697, 25 Tons Robert Starkey, Master Jno. Coleman, Andrew Belcher, Owners

List of Shipps and Vessells Cleared in York River
from 29th September to 25th December 1698

HAPPY JANE OF VIRGINIA	Sloop, built Virginia 1696, 20 Tons George Hayes, Master Seth Wickens, Owner

List of Shipps and Vessells Entering York River
from 25th December 1698 to 25th March 1699

PENSILVANIA MERCHANT OF LONDON	Built Pensilvania 1697, 250 Tons Sam'll Harrison, Master Micajah Perry, Thomas Byfield, Rich'd Haynes, James & Benja. Braines of ye Pensilvania Co., Owners

List of Ships Entered & Cleared in York District
from 25th March 1698 to 25th March 1699

ENDEAVOUR	Sloop, built Pensilvania, 7 Tons Jos. Kirle, Master
HAPPY JANE OF VIRGINIA	Sloop, built Virginia, 20 Tons John Cooke, Master
DOLPHIN	Briganteen, built New England, 25 Tons John Price, Master

List of Ships Entering York River
from 25th March to 24th June 1699

OLIVE BRANCH OF EXON	Square Stern, built New England 1691, 75 Tons Isaac Goswill, Master Abraham Goswill, Jno. Oliver, Nich'o Glanvill, Isaac Goswill, Owners
NATHANIEL OF VIRGINIA	Sloop, built Virginia 1681, 10 Tons Jno. Cooke, Master Edmund Jenings Esq., Owner

List of Ships Cleared In York River
from 25th March to 24th June 1699

VIRGINIA MERCHANT	Square Stern, built Virginia 1697, 40 Tons Walter Baily, Master Arth. Bailey, Rich'd Willis, Fra' Willis, Ben' Hatley, James Howell, Owners

List of Ships Entering in Lower District James River
from July 10th to December 25th 1699

FRIENDS ADVENTURE	Square Sterned, built New England 1698, 30 Tons Joseph Buckley, Master Rob't Emms, Tho. Lasher, Sam'll Lewgir, Sam'll Philips, Owners
SQUIRRELL OF BRISTOLL	Briganteen, built Virginia 1697, 50 Tons Thomas Ward, Master Wm. Swymmer, Jno. Day, Owners
VIRGINIAN OF LONDON	Square Sterned, built Virginia 1695, 200 Tons Charles Bartellett, Master Daniel Parks, Robert Roane, Henry Bartellett, Owners
LYON OF BRISTOLL	Square Sterned, built Virginia 1695, 250 Tons Rob't Bailey, Master Sir Wm. Danes, Wm. Swymmer Esq., Abram Elton, Jno. Swymmer, Rob't Bailey, Lewis Connor, Owners
ROANOAKE MERCHANT OF PHILADELPHIA	Sloop, built Philadelphia, 20 Tons Nich'o Jones, Master Coll. Quary, Owner
FRIENDSHIP OF BELFAST	Square Sterned, Plantation built, 60 Tons Wm. Pringle, Master Wm. Rainey, Moses Jones, Jno. Black, Jno. Eules, Jno. Rainey, Wm. Pringle, Owners.

(Collector - P. Hymen)

List of Ships Cleared in Upper District James River
from 18th July to 9th November 1699

VIRGIN OF VIRGINIA	English Briganteen, built James River 1698, 40 Tons Thomas Goodwin, Master Rich'd Bland, John Taylor, Elizabeth Hamlen, John Hardiman, Owners

(Collector - Philip Lightfoot)

List of Ships Entered in Rappahanock River
from 6th May to 6th August 1699

SUSANNAH OF PLYMOUTH	Briganteen, built New England 1693, 30 Tons Tho. Carne, Master Jonath' Dipford, Gregory Barker, Cha. Appleby, Owners
RICHARD OF N. CAROLINA	Shallop, built N. Carolina, 1693, 4 Tons Richard Sanderson, Master and Owner

List of Ships Cleared in Rappahanock River
from 22nd May to 22nd August 1699

RACHELL OF BRISTOLL — Square Sterned, built New England 1697, 80 Tons
George Ebbery, Master
Erasmus Dole, Owner

DEBORAH OF PENSILVANIA — Built Pensilvania 1697, 13 Tons
Gilbert Wood, Master
Edmund Baxter, Owner

List of Ships Entering in Potomack River
from 24th June to 29th Sept. 1699

PANTHER OF BRISTOLL — Hackboat, built in Potomack River 1699, 220 Tons
Thomas Warner, Master
Jno. Cook Sr., Jno. Hawkins, Wm. Clark,
John Sommers, Edw'd Thurston, Owners

(Naval Officer - Rich'd Lee)

List of Ships Entering in Rappahanock River
from 7th October 1699 to 1st Jan. 1700

WILLIAM & ANN OF LONDON — Square Sterned, built Maryland 1699, 60 Tons
Rich'd Cheney, Master
Wm. Cooper, Antho. Stratton, Tho. Stark,
Rich'd Bailey, Ja. Denus, Jno. & Tho. Cardonnell,
Geo. Ford, Hen: Harbin, Tho. Arundell, Wm. Nephew,
Jno. King, Jno. D***, Owners

(Collector - G. Corbin)

List of Ships Entering in Potomack River
from 21st Dec. 1699 to 25th March 1700

MACHOTICK MERCHANT OF BRISTOLL — Ship, built Virginia 1699, 200,Tons
William Adams, Master
Rich'd Franklyn, Thomas Anthony & Compa. in
Bristol, Owners

POTOMACK GALLEY OF BRISTOLL — Square Sterned, built Virginia 1699, 100 Tons
Rich'd Benford, Master
Jno. Bubb, Michael Pope & Compa., Merchants
in Bristol, Owners

WILLIAM & ORION OF BRISTOLL — Square Sterned, built Maryland 1692, 50 Tons
Jeffery Baily, Master
Sir John Duddleston, Wm. Attwood & Company,
Merchants in Bristol, Owners

WILLIAM & ANN OF FOWY — Square Sterned, built Virginia 1699, 180 Tons
John Stepp, Master
Wm. Williams, Jonathan Tingcomb & Co., Owners

RICHARD OF BRISTOLL — Square Sterned, built Virginia 1699, 50 Tons
Rich'd Pope, Master
Sir John Duddlestone & Co., Owners

List of Ships Entered & Cleared in Upper District Potomack
from 29th May 1699 to 30th January 1700

LOYALTY	Built Barnstable, 40 Tons Thomas Garrat, Master
POTOMACK SAILOR OF BRISTOLL	Square Stern, built Virginia 1699, 75 Tons Philip Yoe, Master

(Certified by Willo' Allerton)

List of Ships Entering Inwards in Lower District Potomack
from 21st June 1699 to 18th May 1700

MARTHA OF NORTH CAROLINA	Sloop, built N. Carolina 1698, 6 Tons Cornelius Benington, Master Thomas Pollick, Owner
PANTHER OF BRISTOLL	Hackboat, built Virginia 1699, 220 Tons Tho. Warner, Master John Cook Sr., John Hawkins, Nm. Clerk, Jno. Summers, Ed: Thurston, Owners
DANIEL & ELIZABETH OF JERSEY	Square Stern, built Salem 1699, 60 Tons Rich'd Janverin, Master Daniel Janverin Sr. and Jr., Owners
WILLIAM & ANN OF FOWY	Square Stern, built Potomack District 1699, 180 Tons Jno. Steap, Master Wm. Williams, Jonath: Tingcomb, Jno. Steap, Nath'll Tingcomb, Charity Scott, Owners

(Certified by Peter Hack, D. Coll'r)

List of Ships Entering Potomack River
from 24th June 1699 to 24th June 1700

GLOSTER OF BRISTOLL	Square Stern, Plantation built, 160 Tons Elisha James, Master

(Certified by Rich'd Lee Esq., Naval Officer)

List of Ships Entering in Upper James River
from 28th December 1699 to 17th April 1700

DOVE OF MARYLAND	Shallop, built Maryland 1699, 9 Tons Richard Booker, Master William Edmondson, Owner
FRIENDSHIP OF NEW ENGLAND	Ship, built Charles Town, 70 Tons John Ballott, Master Andrew Belcher, Tho. Carter, Dan'll Oliver, John Coleman, Jonathan Dows, John Ballott, Owners

(Examined by Edward Hill, Collector)

List of Ships Entering Lower District James River
from December 25th 1699 to March 28th 1700

JAMES OF BARNSTAPLE	Square Stern, built Virginia 1698, 60 Tons Wm. Browning, Master James Kimpland, Nicholas Glass, John Crabb, Andrew Carden, John Strange, Owners
JANE & MARGARET OF LONDON	Square Stern, built Rhoad Island 1694, 60 Tons Peter Gullian, Master Capt. Willis Wilson, Roger Jones, Benja: Harrison, Owners
PRIZE OF HARWICH	Built Virginia 1697, 150 Tons James Jackson, Master Capt. Willis Wilson, Mr. Wm. Roscon, Owners

List of Ships Entered in York River District
from 24th June 1699 to 25th March 1700

JAMES OF VIRGINIA	Shallop, built N. Carolina 1688, 4 Tons James Calthrop, Master & Owner
TRYAL OF BRISTOLL	Brigantoon, built Virginia 1697, 70 Tons Abraham Lewis, Master John Stevens, Owner
ANN OF NEW ENGLAND	Ketch, built New England 1699, 30 Tons Robert Starke, Master Andrew Belcher, Owner
RICHARD & MARY OF BRISTOLL	Square Stern, built Virginia 1699, 200 Tons Philip Franklyn, Master Richard Franklyn, Owner
PHENIX OF BRISTOLL	Round Stern, built Virginia 1698, 200 Tons William Jones, Master Charles Harford, Owner
ROBERT OF SOUTH CAROLINA	Square Stern, built Bermudas 1696, 70 Tons Jno. Bridges, Master Robert Daniel, Owner

List of Ships Entered in Rappahanock District
from 11th November 1699 to 25th March 1700

SARAH OF BRISTOLL	Square Stern, built Virginia 1694, 200 Tons Jno. Miller, Master Sir Jno. Duddlestone, Exec'r of John Bubb Esq., Sir Wm. Danes, Henry Bradley, Jacob Beal, James Wallis, Mich'a White, Ja: Hartwell, Wm. Attwood, Jno. Miller, Owners
SWALLOW OF BOSTON	Sloop, built New England 1696, 25 Tons Wm. Burroughs, Master John Foster, Nath'll Hinksman, Jos. Souter, Wm. Burroughs, Owners

List of Ships Entered in Rappahanock District from 11th November 1699 to 25th March 1700

PROVIDENCE OF MARYLAND	Sloop, built Choplank, Maryland 1698, 30 Tons Timothy Baily, Master Rob't Ungle, Wm. Morrison, Rob't Grandy, Wm. Edmundson, Owners
HANNAH OF MARYLAND	Shallop, built Maryland, 2 Tons James Papoones, Master William Whittington, Owner
DISPATCH OF BRISTOLL	Square Stern, built Virginia 1696, 60 Tons Peter Saxby, Master Richard Franklyn, Wm. Smith, Jno. Jones, Abram Loyd, Edward Hartford, Cha: Hartford, Jno. Stevens, Jno. Scandrett, Tho: Anthony, Ja: Freeman, Francis Rogers, Cornelius Serjeant of Bristol, Matthew Jones of London, Owners
SUSANNAH OF PLYMOUTH	Briganteen, built New England 1693, 30 Tons Thomas Carne, Master Ja: Bleigh, Henry Carne, T** Mangels, Gregory Barker, Hugh Deptford, Mary Chandler, Owners
JUDITH OF RAPPAHANOCK	Square Stern, built James City, Va. 1697, 120 Tons Jno. Good, Master John Smith, Wm. Armistead, Rob't Carter, Tho. Mountjoy, Owners

(Certified by Rob't Carter, Naval Officer)

List of Ships Entering In Upper District James River from 17th April 1700 to 22nd July 1700

JAMES CITY OF VIRGINIA	Sloop, built New England 1696, 42 Tons Wm. Davie, Master Benja: Harrison Esq., Wm. Edwards, Owners
BETTY	Built N. Carolina, Plantation Cutter, 5 Tons Sam'll Swan, Master and Owner
ASSURANCE	Plantation Sloop, built James Town 1693, 40 Tons Jacob Williams, Master Wm. Byrd Esq., Wm. Randolph, Fra: Epps, Micajah Low, Owners
VIRGIN	Brigantine, built "in this country" 1698, 40 Tons Thos. Goodwin, Master John Hamlin, Jno. Taylor, Rich'd Bland, Jno. Hardiman, Owners
FRIENDLY SOCIETY OF LONDON & VIRGINIA	Weight 60 Tons. John Hudley, Master

List of Ships Entering in York District from 25th March 1700 to 24th June 1700

HENRY AND JOHN OF VIRGINIA	Sloop, built 1697, 35 Tons John Bannister, Master & Owner
BLACKWATER	Sloop, built Virginia 1697, 20 Tons Robert Peyton Jr., Master Robert Peyton Esq., Owner
NATHANIEL OF VIRGINIA	Sloop, built 1682, 10 Tons John Cook, Master Edmund Jenings Esq., Owner
ADVENTURE OF NORTH CAROLINA	Sloop, built 1697, 10 Tons Thomas Payn, Master Benja: Tulle, Owner
ENDEAVOUR OF SOUTH CAROLINA	Brigantine, built New England 1696, 30 Tons William Clay, Master Joseph Blake Esq., Owner
HOPE OF NORTH CAROLINA	Plantation Shallop, built 1697, 4 Tons David Blake, Master and Owner
SAMUEL OF NORTH CAROLINA	Plantation Shallop, built 1690, 3 Tons Rich'd Sanderson, Master Henry Slade, Owner
TRYAL OF NORTH CAROLINA	Plantation Shallop, built 1694, 4 Tons Cornelius Jones, Master and Owner
FRIENDS ADVENTURE	Square Stern, built Boston 1698, 70 Tons Michael Cole, Master New Pennsylvania Company, Owners
VIRGINIA MERCHANT OF BRISTOL	Ship, built Virginia 1696, 250 Tons Walter Bailey, Master Anthony Swimmer etc., Owners
INDIAN KING	Square Stern, built Virginia 1699, 550 Tons Edw'd Whitaker, Master Daniel Park Esq., Owner
INTEGRITY	Square Stern, built Biddiford 1676, 60 Tons James Norman, Master Thomas Mountfort, Owner

(Collector - Wm. Buckner)

List of Ships Entering In Rappahanock District from 25th March to 25th June 1700

ST. JOHN BAPTIST	Square Stern, built New England 1695, 60 Tons Nicholas French, Master Thomas Hind, Bartho: Conley, Ignatius Conley, Owners.

List of Ships Entering Rappahanock River
from 19th February to 24th June 1700

ELIZABETH OF LIVERPOOL	Square Stern, built Maryland 1698, 350 Tons Gilbert Livesey, Master Gilbert Livesey, Tho. Johnson Sr. and Jr., Jonas Kenion, Owners
SUSANNAH	Briganteen, built New England 1693, 90 Tons Tho. Carne, Master Jonath' Dipford, Gregory Barker, Cha: Appleby, Owners
FRIENDSHIP OF BELFAST	Square Stern, built New England 1698, 60 Tons Hans Hammill, Master Wm. Rainy Sr., Moses Jones, Jo: Black, Jno. Eales Jno. Rainy, Wm. Rainy Jr., Owners
EXPECTATION OF BRISTOLL	Briganteen, built James City 1698, 100 Tons Christopher Scandrett, Master Abra: Loyd, Chas. Harford, Jno. Scandrett, Edw'd Harford, Cornelius Sergant, Thomas Anthony, Ja: Freeman, Ja: Rogers, Wm. Smith, Jno. Jones, Rich'd Franklyn, Matthew Jones, Jno. Stephens, Owners

List of Ships Clearing Lower District James River
from March 25th to June 5th 1700

VIRGINIAN	Square Stern, built Virginia 1695, 200 Tons Charles Bertelett, Master Daniell Parks, Esq., Robert Roane, Henry Bertelett, Owners

List of Ships Cleared Outwards in Upper District Potomack
from 27th February to May 1700

MARY & SIBILLA OF EXON	Square Stern, built Biddiford, 50 Tons Henry Rogers, Master

List of Ships Entering Inwards in Accomack
from 1st January to 8th April 1700

LIVER OF LIVERPOOL	Square Stern, built in Accomack 1699, 120 Tons Rob't Moone, Master Bryan Blundal, Jno. Cleaveland, Wm. Basnett, Lewis Jenkins, Rob't Moone, Owners
TRIALL OF BOSTON	Built Newhaven, Connecticut 1699, 20 Tons Jno. Collins, Master Jno. Turner, Owner

(Certified by Jno. Custis, Naval Officer
for Eastern Shores)

List of Ships and Vesells Entered in Rappahanock River from 24th June to 25th December 1700

RACHEL OF JERSEY	Square Stern, built Charlestown 1699, 70 Tons John Vincent, Master Charles Lehardy, Cha: Pointestre, Philip Pipon, Philip Patriach, Elie Dumaresq, John de Carterel, Geo. le Brun, Jno. Vincent, Owners
NUPTIALL OF MARYLAND	Shallop, Plantation built, 4 Tons John Edgar, Master and Owner
ELIZABETH OF MARYLAND	Shallop, Plantation built, 2 Tons Rich'd Dennis, Master

List of Ships Entering Inwards in Upper District James River from 22nd July 1700 to 25th March 1701

VIRGIN	Brigandine, built Virginia 1698, 40 Tons Jos: Nosworthy and Thomas Goodwyn, Masters John Taylor, David Bray, James Bray, Owners
JAMES CITY	Sloop, built New England 1696, 40 Tons Wm. Davie, Master Benja: Harrison Esq., William Edwards, Benja: Harrison Jr., Owners
COCK	Square Stern, built Virginia 1692, 35 Tons Lazarus Watts, Master Jno. Addiss, James Cock, Henry Ceane, Thomas Cock, Owners
DOLPHYN	Sloop, built New England 1694, 15 Tons Edw'd Johnson, Master Robert Sneed, Owner
DOLPHIN	Sloop, built New England 1697, 25 Tons Nath'll Coffin, Master James Coffin, Richard Gardner, Owners
PRINCES FEATHER	Sloop, built Maryland 1695, 20 Tons Chas. Johnson, Master P'r Paggen, James Booth, Jno. Cary, Eliza' Claphamson, Isaack Millner of London, Owners
WILLIAM AND JANE	Square Stern, built New England 1699, 130 Tons Wm. Harding, Master William Harding, Jr., Thomas Coppin, William Harding Sr., Melitia Holder, Fred' Jones, James Taylor of London, Owners
WILLIAM AND MARY	Pinck, built Hull 1691, 100 Tons Rich'd Plowman and X'pher Hunt, Masters Samuell Boush, William Byrd, Micajah Lowe, Owners
NICHOLSON	Square Stern, Prize condemned Virginia 1698, 110 Tons Ephraim Breed, Master Wm. Byrd Esq., William Randòlph, Francis Epps, Owners.

List of Ships Entering Inwards in Upper District James River from 22nd July 1700 to 25th March 1701

MARY GOLD	Square Stern, built Maryland 1695, 60 Tons Benja' Reed, Master Jno. Davie, Owner
FRANCIS	Sloop, built Maryland 1695, 20 Tons Rich'd Bradford, Master Peter Pagan, Ja: Booth, John Cary, Eliza' Claphamson, Isaac Milner, Owners
WESTOPHER	Sloop, built Virginia 1693, 40 Tons Thom' Goodwin, Master Wm. Bird Esq., Coll. Wm. Randolph, Capt. Fra' Epps, John Chiles, Owners

List of Ships Clearing Outwards from Upper District James River from 25th March to 6th June 1701

HOPE	Built New York 1695, 60 Tons Abr' Carter, Master James Cock of Plymouth and Wm. Cawford of Virginia, Owners

List of Ships Entered Inwards in Upper District James River from March 18th to April 20th 1701

MERCY OF NEW YORK	Sloop, built 1696, 10 Tons Christopher Hoogland, Master Jno. Laroux, Owner

List of Ships Clearing Outwards from Upper District James River from March 6th to March 26th 1701

VIRGIN	Briganteen, built Virginia 1698, 40 Tons Joseph Nosworthy, Master Jno. Hamlin, Jno. Taylor, Rich'd Bland, Jno. Hardiman, Owners.

(Certified by Nath'll Harrison, Coll'r)

List of Ships Entering Inwards in Lower District James River from 17th November 1700 to 6th June 1701

VIRGINIAN OF LONDON	Square Stern, built Virginia 1698, 140 Tons Charles Bartellet, Master Danield Parke Esq., Owner
KETCH SPEEDWELL OF SALEM	Square Stern, built Boston 1697, 30 Tons Tho: Miller, Master Wm. Hurst, Owner
WILLIAM AND ANN OF FOWY	Shipp, built Virginia 1699, 180 Tons Tho: Michell, Master Wm. Williams, Jonathan Tingcomb, Nath'll Tingcomb, Jno. Stepp, Charity Scott, Owners.

List of Ships Entering Inwards in Lower District James River
from 17th November 1700 to 6th June 1701

GEORGE AND MARTHA OF VIRGINIA	Square Stern, built Nansimond County 1699, 100 Tons Benjamin Chapman, Master Geo. Nosworthy, Owner
WILLIAM OF VIRGINIA	Square Stern, built Ireland seized in James River and registered James City 1698, 70 Tons Wm. Bosell, Master Wm. Bird Esq., Capt. Willis Wilson, Mr. Tho: Ward of Barbados, Owners
RICHARD OF CAROLINA	Rounde Sterne, built Carotuck 1695, 4 Tons Obadiah Rich, Master Obadiah Rich, John Hopkins of Appamatux in Virginia, Owners

List of Ships Entering Inwards in Lower District James River
from 6th June to 29th September 1701

AMITY OF JAMAICA	Square Stern, built Road Island 1696, 10 Tons Richard Rivers, Master John Smith, Major Cha' Hobby, Owners

(Certified by Geo. Luke, Collector)

List of Ships Clearing Outwards in Lower District James River
from 3rd January to 6th June 1701

JANE AND MARGRITT OF LONDON	Square Stern, built Rode Island 1694, 60 Tons Peter Guillum, Master Capt. Wilson, Roger Jones, Benjamin Harrison, Owners

List of Ships Clearing Outwards in Lower District James River
from 6th June to 29th September 1701

WILLIAM AND MARY OF LONDON	Pink, built in Hull, Reg. Virginia 1700, 100 Tons Nathaniell MaClonaham & Rich' Plowman, Masters
DRISTER	Sloop, built Maryland, 8 Tons Edward Green, Master Robert Plumsten, Owner
CONSTANT JANE OF BARBADOS	Square Stern, built New England 1700, 50 Tons John Jones, Master George Pearse, John Jones of Bristoll, Owners

List of Ships Clearing Outwards in Lower District James River
from 6th June 1700 to 26th March 1701

DOLPHIN	Built Westerfield, Reg. New York 1699, 16 Tons Wm. Davison, Master & Owner

(Certified by Wm. Wilson, Navall Officer)

List of Ships Clearing Outwards in Lower District James River
from June 5th 1700 to March 26th 1701

FRIENDS ADVENTURE OF NEW YORK	Built Philadelphia 1696, 12 Tons William Laurien, Master John Corbett, Owner
SUSANNAH OF BELFAST	Briganteen, built New England 1694, 50 Tons Thomas Lovell, Master & Owner

List of Ships Clearing Outwards in Lower District James River
from March 26th to July 26th 1701

SUSANNAH OF ROANOAK	Square Stern, built New England 1699, 25 Tons Jno. Tucker, Master Col. Wm. Wilkenson, Jno, Tucker, Owners
SHOREHAMS PRIZE	Square Stern, foreign built, 150 Tons Henery Wilkee, Master King Ge*** Prize Ship

List of Ships Entered in York District
from 24th June 1700 to 25th March 1701

DOLPHIN OF BOSTON	Round Stern, built Salem 1696, 30 Tons Sam Boyes, Master Samuel Lillir, Owner
SUPPLY OF BOSTON	Sloop, built Guford, New England 1696, 30 Tons Wm. Marshal, Master Robert Bransdon etc., Owners
THOMAS OF VIRGINIA	Sloop, built 1700, 10 Tons Thomas Todd, Master & Owner
TRYAL OF BRISTOL	Briganteen, built Virginia 1697, 70 Tons John Chaplin, Master John Stephens, Owner
BEGINING OF BOSTON	Sloop, built Charlestown 1700, 45 Tons Henry Thornton, Master Daniel Ballard, Owner
BLACKWATER OF VIRGINIA	Sloop, built 1699, 20 Tons James Sellwood, Master Robert Peyton, Owner
PROVIDENCE OF VIRGINIA	Built 1695, 7 Tons John Trevilian, Master George Stokes, Owner

(Certified by Wm. Buckner, Coll'r)

List of Ships That Have Entered York District from 25th March to 8th June 1701

ADVENTURE OF NORTH CAROLINA	Sloop, built 1697, 10 Tons Richard Sanderson, Master Benjamin Tulle, Owner
CONTENT OF MARYLAND	Sloop, built 1698, 10 Tons Thomas Allen, Master Rich'd Bennett Esq., Owner
MARTHA OF VIRGINIA	Sloop, built 1699, 25 Tons John Paynter, Master Lewis Burwell, Owner
SALISBURY OF BRISTOLL	Square Stern, built Virginia 1699, 200 Tons Thomas Mountjoy, Master Thomas Mountjoy etc., Owners

List of Ships That Have Entered York District from 8th June to 14th November 1701

MARTHA OF NORTH CAROLINA	Built 1698, 6 Tons James Damerel, Master Thomas Pollock, Owner
DOLPHIN OF VIRGINIA	Ketch, built Salem 1696, 30 Tons Samuel Boyes, Master Edmund Jenings Esq., Owner
DOLPHYN OF MARYLAND	Sloop, built 1700, 10 Tons William Parker, Master Charles Ratcliff, Owner
ENDEAVOUR OF SOUTH CAROLINA	Briganteen, built New England 1696, 30 Tons William Clay, Master Joseph Blake Esq., etc., Owners
HARRIS OF MARYLAND	Sloop, built 1700, 6 Tons Henry Fielding, Master James Harris, Owner
MERRIMACK OF NEW ENGLAND	Ketch, built Newberry, New England 1699, 30 Tons Thomas Miers, Master Samuel Allen, Owner
DOLPHYN OF VIRGINIA	Built Virginia 1696, 4 Tons Phillip Hunings, Master & Owner
SQUIREL OF BRISTOLL	Briganteen, built Virginia 1697, 50 Tons Thomas Ward, Master William Swimmer Jr. etc., Owners

List of Ships Entering Inwards Rappahanock District
from 24th June to 29th September 1701

FRIENDLY SOCIETY OF LONDON — Pink, 60 Tons
Thos. Couch, Master
John Goodwin, Jona' Matthews of London,
Wm. Chürchill, Robert Carter of Virginia, Owners

List of Ships Cleared in York River District
from 8th June to 14th November 1701

CONSTANT JANE OF BARBADOS — Sloop, built Portsmouth, New England 1700, 50 Tons
Samuel King, Master
George Peers etc., Owners

(Certified by Miles Cary, Naval Officer)

List of Ships Entering Inwards Rappahanock River
from 25th December 1700 to 25th March 1701

WILLIAM AND MARY OF GUERNSEY — Square Stern, built Boston 1700, 70 Tons
Peter Bonamy, Master
Wm. Merchant, Tho: Merchant, Rob't Holey,
Jno. Gruchie, Leonard LeMesurier, Peter Tupper,
Andrew Bonamy, Owners

JOHN BAPTIST OF LIVERPOOL — Square Stern, built New England 1695, 60 Tons
John Gore, Master
Levnius Hueston, Tho: Hind, Jno. Cockshutt,
Richard Geldart, Owners

List of Ships Entering Inwards Rappahanock River
from 25th March to 24th June 1701

RICHARD OF CORRATUCK — Shallop, built Pasquotank 1693, 4 Tons
Richard Sanderson Jr., Master
Richard Sanderson Sr., Owner

WILLIAM AND MARY OF MONSERAT — Sloop, built Charlestown 1700, 16 Tons
David Brenton, Master
Wm. Garrish, Elias Horsell, Owners

List of Entry's Inwards in Potomack Lower District
from 9th October 1700 to 9th April 1701

ANNE OF JERSEY — Built Boston 1699, 110 Tons
Tho: Denton, Master
Moses Corbet, James Corbet, Tho: Durell,
Cha: Pendextre, Elias Dumaresq, Cha: Hilgrove,
Philip Fall, Philip Patriarch, Philip Dauvergne,
James Lempreere, Amice Dauvergne, Owners

(Certified by Peter Hack, Naval Officer)

List of Ships Entered in Upper District Potomack
from 19th October 1700 to 27th March 1701

HESTER OF BRISTOLL — Square Stern, built Maryland 1697, 160 Tons
Elisha James, Master
Abra: Hook, Elisha James etc., Owners

List of Ships Entering Potomack River
from 6th May to 29th September 1701

CONCORD OF VIRGINIA	Briganteen, built 1699, 42 Tons Mark Cullum, Master Fra: Wright, Owner
LITTLE JOHN	Ship, built Virginia 1696, 60 Tons Jacob Martin, Master Jno. Scott, Owner

List of Ships Entering Inwards in Port Accomack
from November 1700 to March 1701

DOLPHIN OF NEW ENGLAND	Sloop, built Connecticut 1697, 20 Tons Joseph Soleman, Master Jno. Foster, Sam' Lilly, Rob't Howard, Sam' Philips, Rich'd Walters, Rob't Gibbs, Wm. Clark, Owners
ANN & SARAH OF PENSILVANIA	Sloop, built New Jersey, 12 Tons Jno. Hogg, Master Jno. Hogg, Elias Hogg, Owners
PRIMROSE OF NEW YORK	Sloop, built Rhode Island 1700, 30 Tons Andrew Deupuy, Master Ben: Faneuil, Abra' Turtlelott, Owners
MARY & SARAH OF NEW YORK	Built East Jersey 1698, 14 Tons Jno. Trent, Master Lewis Kinkead, Owner
HOPEWELL OF PENSYLVANIA	Built Rhode Island 1689, 8 Tons Jno. Huling, Master Jno. Crends (?), Owner
ROBERT & SARAH OF NEW HAMPSHIRE	Built Kittery, Main 1700, 20 Tons Jno. Hollicom, Master Robert Elliot, Owner
ANNE & ELIZABETH OF LIVERPOOL	Sloop, built Northampton County 1701, 16 Tons Edward Tarlton, Master Jno. Cleavland, Wm. Basnett, Brian Blundell, Lewis Jenkins, Robert Moon, Owners

List of Ships Entering Rappahanock River
from 29th Sept. to 25th Dec. 1701

LYON OF BRISTOLL	Square Stern, built Virginia 1694, 250 Tons Robert Bayly, Master Wm. Swymmer Esq., Sir Wm. Daines, Abraham Elton, Jno. & Anthony Swimmer, all of Bristoll, Lewis Conner of Virginia, Owners
SWALLOW OF BOSTON	Sloop, built 1696, 25 Tons Wm. Burrows, Master John Foster, Nathaniel Hinkman, Joseph Souter, Wm. Burrows, Owners

List of Ships Entering Rappahanock River
from 29th Sept. to 25th Dec. 1701

HARRISON OF LONDON	Square Stern, 220 Tons John Harrison, Master John Harrison, Ben: Bradley, Arthur North, Tho: Wych, Roger Jones, John Thompson, Will Bird, Robert Bolling, Benj: Harrison, Henry Hartwell, Will Wilson, Owners

List of Ships Entering Inwards in Lower District James River
from 25th March to 16th July 1702

GEORGE & MARTHA OF VIRGINIA	Square Stern, built 1699, 100 Tons Jno. Wright, Master Col. George Nosworthy, Owner
VIRGINIAN OF LONDON	Square Stern, built Virginia 1695, 200 Tons Charles Bartelett, Master Rob't Roane, Hen: Bartellett, Dan'll Park, Owners

List of Ships Entering in Upper District James River
from 25th March to 16th July 1702

WILLIAM	Built Virginia 1698 Wm. Boswell, Master Mme. Jane Wilson, Tho: Ward, Owners
HOPEWELL OF PHILADELPHIA	Square Stern, built 1701, 25 Tons Timothy Davis, Master Tho: Masters, Jno. Claypole, Rich'd Janny, Owners

List of Ships Entering Inwards in Lower District Potomack
from 25th March to 25th June 1702

SWALLOW OF NEW ENGLAND	Sloop, built 1696, 25 Tons Timothy Burbank, Master John Fawster, Nath'll Hinksman, Jos. Souter, Wm. Burroughs, Owners
ELIZABETH & HANNAH OF VIRGINIA	Square Stern, built Coan, Virginia 1701, 30 Tons Charles Bligh, Master Major Rodham Kenner, Owner
VIRGINIA MERCHANT OF BRISTOLL	Square Stern, built Virginia 1696, 250 Tons Walter Bayley, Master William Swymmer Esq. & Company, Owners
VIRGINIA MERCHANT OF WAYMOTH	Square Stern, built Virginia 1701, 80 Tons Thos. Lanthorn, Master James Gould, David Arbuthnot, Owners
VIRGINIA DOVE OF BIDIFORD	Square Stern, built Virginia 1699, 100 Tons Sam'll Ellis, Master Thomas Smith, Owner.

(Certified by Peter Hack, Collector and
Richard Lee, Naval Officer)

List of Ships Entering Inwards Lower District Potomack
from 29th July 1701 to 25th March 1702

GOOD INTENT — Square Stern, built New England, 60 Tons
Humphrey Scammon, Master
Wm. Pepperell, Owner

HESTER — Square Stern, built Maryland 1696, 160 Tons
Elisha James, Master
Elisha James, Abra: Elton etc., Owners

List of Shipps & Vessells Entering Inwards Lower District James River
from 29th September, being Michaelmass Day, 1701 to Christmass Day,
ye 25th Decem'r and from thence to Lady Day, ye 25th March 1702

DILIGENCE OF PENSILVANIA — Sloop, built 1693, 8 Tons
Sam'll Harriot, Master
Sam'll Carpenter, Sam'll Harriot, Owners

ENDEAVOUR OF BOSTON — Square Stern, built Charleston 1701, 25 Tons
Tobias Green, Master
John Forster, Esq., Mary Edwards, Geo. Hallet,
Rich'd Shale, Owners

SARAH OF MARYLAND — Square Stern, built Pensilvania 1700, 12 Tons
George Marchant, Master
Rich'd Bennett, Owner

List of Ships & Vessells Entering Inwards Lower District James River
from 25th March to 10th July 1702

WILLIAM OF VIRGINIA — Square Stern, built Ireland, 70 Tons
William Boswell, Master
Wm. Bird, Willis Wilson, Tho: Ward
in Barbados, Owners

BETTY HOPE OF PENSILVANIA — Square Stern, built Pensilvania, 10 Tons
John James, Master & Owner

JOHANNA OF GOSPORT — Pink, built Hampshire, Reg. Annapolis 1699, 100 Tons
Richard Burbridge, Master
Wm. Stafford, Tho: Jackson, Owners

TRYALL — Sloop, built Virginia 1692, 6 Tons
Joseph Ming, Master
Henery Lysill, Owner

FORTUNE OF PENSILVANIA — Sloop, built Sussex, Reg. Philadelphia 1702, 25 Tons
Abraham Celkeet, Master
Sam'll Holt, Jas: Vanleaur, Owners

List of Ships Entering Inwards in Lower District James River
from July 26th 1701 to March 26th 1702

JANE & MARG'T OF LONDON — Square Stern, built Rhode Island 1694, 60 Tons
Peter Guillum and George Hart, Masters
Capt. W. Wilson, Mr. Roger Jones, Benja: Harrison,
Mr. Ed' Bidw't, Owners

List of Ships Entering Inwards Upper District James River from March 25th to July 10th 1702

LIXBOA MERCHANT OF BIDEFORD	Square Stern, built Anapolis 1697, 80 Tons Joseph Smith, Master Wm. Brookes, Jos: Gulstone, of Lixboa, William Brookes of Appledore, John Benson, Owners
WESTOVER OF VIRGINIA	Sloop, built Virginia 1693, 40 Tons Tho: Goodwyn, Master Wm. Byrd Esq., William Randolph, Jno. Chiles, Owners
NICHOLSON OF VIRGINIA	Square Stern, foreign made free, 110 Tons Eph' Breed, Master William Byrd, William Randolph, Fra' Epps, Eph' Breed, Owners
VIRGIN OF VIRGINIA	Briganteen, built 1698, 40 Tons Jas: Norsworthy, Master Capt. Jno. Taylor, Owner

List of Ships Entered and Cleared in Accomack District from 12th July 1701 to 20th March 1702

SWALLOW OF BOSTON	Sloop, built 1696, 25 Tons Wm. Burrows, Master Wm. Burrows & Company, Owners

List of Ships & Vessells Entered in Rappahanock River from 25th December 1701 to 25th March 1702

ANN OF BOSTON	Ketch, built Boston 1699, 30 Tons Nathaniell Cary, Master Andrew Belcher, Owner
PROVIDENCE OF DUBLIN	Pink, foreign made free, Reg. Va. 1701, 160 Tons Wm. Liggatt, Master Robert McKerrell, Owner
LEVER OF LEVERPOOL	Square Stern, built Virginia 1699, 80 Tons John Farrer, Master Bryan Blundall, Jno. Cleveland, Wm. Basnett, Lewis Jenkins, Robert Moon, Owners
FRANCIS OF BIDEFORD	Square Stern, built Crabb point in Chester River, Mariland 1697, 50 Tons John Hartnell, Master John Smith, Owner
JOHN BAPTIST OF LIVERPOOL	Square Stern, built New England 1695, 60 Tons John Gore, Master Levinus Hueston, Tho: Hinde, John Cockshutt, Richard Geldart, Owners

List of Ships Entering Inwards in Upper District James River from 6th June 1701 to 23rd April 1702

JAMES CITY OF VIRGINIA	Sloop, built New England 1696, 40 Tons William Davy, Master Benja. Harrison Esq., Benja. Harrison Jr., Will: Edwards, Owners
MARGARET	Sloop, built New Jersey 1698, 20 Tons Jacob Vantilbrough, Master & Owner
DOLPHIN OF NANTUCKET	Sloop, built New England 1697, 20 Tons Nath' Coffin, Master Rich'd Gardiner, James Coffin and others, being inhabitants of Massachusetts Bay in New England, Owners
WILLIAM AND MARY OF BOSTON	Brigantine, built New England 1693, 35 Tons Tho: Sill, Master Benj: Alford, Andrew Belcher, Owners
LYON OF BOSTON	Square Stern, built New England 1701, 125 Tons Jonathan Dows, Master Andrew Belcher, Ben: Alford, Jno. Portland, Giles Dyer, Tho: Palmer, Sam: Phillips, Jonathan Dows, Owners

List of Ships Entering Inwards in Rappahanock River from 25th March to 24th June 1702

ABRAHAM OF BRISTOLL	Square Stern, built Maryland 1698, 100 Tons John Street, Master Abraham Hood, Rich'd Bagley (Baylie)? Edward Jones, John Street, Owners
MARY OF LONDON	Sloop, built New England 1699, 30 Tons Geo. Lawson, Master & Owner

List of Ships Entering Inwards in York River from 14th November 1701 to 25th March 1702

HAPPY RETURN OF BOSTON	Square Stern, built New England 1699, 22 Tons William Hunter, Master Robert Brisco etc., Owners
EXPECTATION OF BRISTOLL	Square Stern, built Virginia 1698, 150 Tons William Lavercombe, Master Charles Harford Jr., etc., Owners
WILLIAM & ORION OF BRISTOLL	Square Stern, built Maryland 1692, 50 Tons Thomas Warner, Master Sir John Dudlestone Bart. etc., Owners
PHENIX OF BRISTOLL	Round Stern, built Virginia 1698, 200 Tons Christopher Scandrett, Master Charles Harford Jr. etc., Owners
POTOMACK FACTOR	Square Stern, built Virginia 1699, 75 Tons John Waldron, Master Sir Richard Crump etc., Owners

List of Ships Entering Inwards in York River
from 25th March to 10th July 1702

TRYALL OF NORTH CAROLINA	Plantation Shallop, built 1694, 4 Tons Thomas Pett, Master Cornelius Jones, Owner
INDIAN KING OF VIRGINIA	Square stern, built Virginia 1699, 550 Tons Edw'd Whitaker, Master Daniel Parke Esq., Owner
DOLPHIN OF VIRGINIA	Ketch, built Salem 1696, 30 Tons Samuel Boyes, Master Edmond Jenings Esq. etc., Owners
RICHARD & MARY OF BRISTOLL	Pink, built Virginia 1699, 200 Tons Philip Franklin and John Good, Masters Rich'd Franklyn etc., Owners
TRYALL OF BRISTOLL	Briganteen, built Virginia 1697, 70 Tons John Chaplin, Master John Stevens, Owner
RESERVE OF NORTH CAROLINA	Sloop, built Boston 1701, 15 Tons John Ingram, Master William Wilkinson etc., Owners
PHENIX OF ANTIGUA	Sloop, built Charles Town 1700, 40 Tons Peter Mannering, Master William Thomas, Owner

List of Ships that have Entered in Rappahanock District
from 25th March to 24th June 1702

ANN OF NORTH CAROLINA	Shallop, built Pascotanck 1701, 10 Tons Rich'd Prince, Master Francis de la Mare, Owner
TURTLE OF BARBADOS	Sloop, built Providence 1698, 10 Tons John Dibbs, Master & Owner
SPEEDWELL OF MARYLAND	Sloop, built Maryland 1695, 5 Tons Daniel Hilliard, Master Robert Bradley & Co., Owners
LETTICE OF RAPPAHANOCK	Sloop, built Virginia 1699, 40 Tons Symon Young, Master John Loyd Esq., Owner

List of Ships Clearing Outwards from Accomack District
from 5th November 1701 to March 31st 1702

EXCHANGE OF NEW YORK	Square Stern, built Connecticut 1696, 35 Tons Jno. Price, Master Jno. Price, Jonathan Atwater, Owners

List of Ships Clearing Outwards from Accomack District
from 5th November 1701 to 31st March 1702

EXCHANGE OF MAIN	Built Pipatoway 1697, 15 Tons Francis Plaisted, Master Wm. Pepperill, Owner
DOLPHIN OF NEW ENGLAND	Built Hartford, Connecticut, 25 Tons Henry Tew, Master Wm. Clark, Ferdinand Clark, Henry Tew, Owners
JOANNA OF BOSTON	Built Boston 1699, 40 Tons Michael Gill, Master Jno. Buck, Joseph Buckly, Owners
SEAFLOWER OF BOSTON	Sloop, built Massachusetts 1701, 30 Tons Benj: Bucklin, Master Abraham Bligh, Jno. Cutler, Jno. Marshall, Owners

(Certified by John Custis, Navall Officer)

List of Ships Clearing Outwards in Lower District James River
from 29th Sept. 1701 to 25th March 1702

SARAH OF PLYMOUTH	Sloop, built Virginia 1701, 25 Tons Jno. Worden, Master Jas: Blight, Owner

List of Ships Clearing Outwards in Lower District James River
from March 25th to July 10th 1702

JONATHAN & MARY OF VIRGINIA	Square Stern, built Virginia 1699, 30 Tons Thomas Tanner, Master James Fowler, Jonathan Mathews, Owners
WILLIAM & MARY OF VIRGINIA	Square Stern, built Virginia 1702, 150 Tons Thomas Carly, Master Tho: Godwin, Owner

(Certified by Wm. Wilson, Naval Officer)

List of Ships Clearing Outwards in Lower District James River
from 25th March to 10th July 1702

HAMPTON OF VIRGINIA	Square Stern, built Williamsburg 1702, 40 Tons Thomas Goodwin, Master Thomas Preeson, Owner

List of Ships Clearing Outwards from Rappahanock River
from 25th March to 24th June 1702

WEYMOUTH OF BRISTOL	Rob't Colbard, Master

List of Ships Cleared Outwards in Upper District James River
from March 25th to July 10th 1702

HOPE OF PLYMOUTH	Sloop, built New York 1695, 75 Tons Abra' Carter, Master James Cocke, Wm. Crawford, Owners.

List of Ships Cleared Outwards in Rappahanock River
from June 17th 1702 to _________

SPEEDWELL OF MARYLAND	Sloop, built Manokin River 1685, 8 Tons Daniell Hilliard, Master John Cobb, Owner

List of Ships Entering & Clearing in Potomack River
from 29th Sept. 1701 to 25th March 1702

VIRGINIA MERCHANT OF VIRGINIA	Square Stern, built Virginia 1701, 80 Tons Tho: Linthorne, Master James Gould, David Arbuthnot, Owners
LITTLE JOHN OF BRISTOLL	Square Stern, built Virginia 1696, 60 Tons Samuell Wiatt and Jacob Martin, Masters Jacob Martin, Owner

(Certified by Rich'd Lee, Naval Officer
and Peter Hack, Deputy Collector)

List of Ships Cleared in Yorke River District
from 25th March to 10th July 1702

SQUIRREL OF BRISTOLL	Briganteen, built Virginia 1697, 50 Tons Thomas Ward, Master Wm. Swimmer Jr. etc., Owners
TRYALL OF BRISTOLL	Briganteen, built Virginia 1697, 70 Tons John Chaplin, Master John Stephens etc., Owner

List of Ships Cleared in Yorke River District
from 8th June 1701 to 25th March 1702

ENDEAVOUR OF SOUTH CAROLINA	30 Tons William Clay, Master

List of Ships Clearing Outwards in Upper District James River
from 24th February to 24th July 1703

JAMES CITY	Sloop, built New England 1696, 40 Tons Richard Brand, Master Benja' Harrison Esq., Benja. Harrison Jr., Wm. Edwards, Owners
DOVE	Briganteen, built Boston 1702, 60 Tons Nich' Bowes, Master Edward Bromfield, Edmund Knight, Nath'l Breeding, David Peabody, Nich' Bowes, Owners
HOPE	Sloop, built New York 1695, 75 tons Abram Carter, Master Wm. Crawford, James Cock, Owners
GOATLY FRIGAT	Built Virginia, 150 Tons Jonathan Wicker, Master Sarles Goatly, Rich'd Haynes, Steph' Goatly, John Newton, Wm. Bearly, Rich'd Swadlin, Jona' Wicker, Owners

(Edward Hill, Coll'r)

List of Ships Entered & Cleared in Lower District James River
from 25th March 1702 to 25th March 1703

UNITY OF NEW ENGLAND	Tho. Church, Master, 40 Tons
FISHER OF BOSTON	Jno. Wright, Master, 30 Tons
DOVE OF NEW ENGLAND	Fra' Peabody, Master, 16 Tons
*** and LEWSEY OF VIRGINIA	Tho: Parrott, Master, 50 Tons

(Certified by George Luke, Collector)

List of Ships Clearing Outwards in Lower District James River
from April 23rd to September 25th 1703

TRUSLOW OF BARBADOS	Square Stern, Plantation built 1698, 15 Tons Robert Tristam, Master Benja' Bullard, William Kirkham, Tho: Ward, Owners
BETTY OF BERMUDAS	Plantation built 1701, 25 Tons Thomas Priddon, Master William Jooll, Thomas Lawson, Owners
JONATHAN AND MARY OF VIRGINIA	Square Stern, built New York 1697, 30 Tons James Fowler, Master James Fowler, Jonathan Matthews, Owners
UNITY OF PENSILVANIA	Square Stern, plantation built, reg. at Williamsburgh 1703, 30 Tons William Lloyd, Master M't McClenan, Owner
GEORGE & MARTHA OF VIRGINIA	Square Stern, plantation built 1699, reg. at James Citty, 60 Tons John Wright, Master George Norsworthy, Owner
MIRIAM REBECCA OF BERMUDAS	Sqare Stern, plantation built, 30 Tons Edward Seares, Master Sam'll Smith, Richard Tribe, Owners
TRYALL OF PENSILVANIA	Square Stern, plantation built, reg. at North Carolina 1700, 6 Tons Jos' Miner, Master Rob't Quarry, Owner
FRIENDSHIP OF PHILADELPHIA	Square Stern, plantation built, 25 Tons George Wilson, Master William Trent, Joseph Pidgeon, Rob't French, Owners
SARAH OF CONNECTICUT AND PHILADELPHIA	Sloop, plantation built, reg. Phil. 1702, 20 Tons Sam'll Harrison, Master William Trent, Joseph Pidgeon, John Moore, Owners

(Certified by William Wilson, Naval Officer)

List of Ships and Vessels that have been Cleared in Rappahanock River from 24th June to 29th Sept. 1703

RESERVE OF NORTH CAROLINA	Sloop, built Boston 1701, 15 Tons Jno. Ingram, Master William Wilkinson, Owner
FISHER OF NEW ENGLAND	Ketch, built Boston 1701, 30 Tons John Pitts, Master Cyprian Southack, James Obern, Owners
JOHN OF PENSILVANIA	Square Stern, built New York 1703, 8 Tons Wm. Allen, Master William Allen, Tho. Clark, Owners
JOSEPH & SARAH OF NEW PROVIDENCE	Square Stern, built 1701, 40 Tons Rob't Miers, Master Joseph Groves, Rich' Tolliafero, Owners
SWALLOW OF BOSTON	Square Stern, built 1696, 25 Tons Timothy Burbanck, Master John Foster, Nath'll Hinksman, Wm. Burrows, Jos. Souter, Owners
JANE & BETTY OF PHILADELPHIA	Square Stern, built New Jersey 1702, 8 Tons Wm. Wade, Master Phillip Harwood, Edward Smout, Wm. Wade, Owners

(Certified by Richard Chichester, Collector)

List of Ships Clearing Outwards from Accomack River from 2nd March to 25th September 1703

SEAFLOWER OF BOSTON	Sloop, built Mass. 1701, 30 Tons Dan'll Marchall, Master Abra' Bligh, Jno. Cutler, Jno. Marchall, Joseph Appleton, Owners
DOLPHIN OF NEW England	Square Stern, built Connecticut 1701, 25 Tons Hen: Tew, Master Wm. Clark, Fardinado Clark, Hen: Tew, Owners
ENDEAVOUR OF NEW ENGLAND	Built New England 1698, 45 Tons Francis Mahomy, Master John Hunkins, Tho' Jeffrey, Owners
HAMPTON OF VIRGINIA	Built 1701, 40 Tons Rich' Whitherington, Master Tho' Preesen, Owner

(Certified by Hen: Custis, Naval Officer)

List of Ships Entered & Cleared in York River District from 12th March to 16th October 1703

ANN OF NORTH CAROLINA	Sloop, built 1701, 10 Tons William Fillet, Master Francis de la Mare, Owner

List of Ships Entered & Cleared in York River District
from 12th March to 16th October 1703

TRYAL OF NORTH CAROLINA	Sloop, built 1694, 4 Tons Cornelius Jones, Master & Owner
INDIAN KING OF VIRGINIA	Square Stern, built 1699, 550 Tons Edward Whitaker, Master Daniel Park Esq., Owner
DOVE OF BOSTON	Square Stern, Reg'd 1702, 16 Tons Thomas Faddom, Master William Cole, Owner
TWO BROTHERS OF NEW PROVIDENCE	Sloop, built 1699, 8 Tons Abraham Carle, Master Thomas Williams, Owner
SUSANNA OF NORTH CAROLINA	Sloop, built New England 1699, 25 Tons John Tucker, Master & Owner
MARY OF BIDDIFORD	Built Maryland 1691, 60 Tons Thomas Cantrell, Master John Smith, Owner
RICHARD & MARY OF BRISTOLL	Square Stern, built Virginia 1699, 200 Tons John Chaplyn, Master Richard Franklyn etc., Owners
PHENIX OF BRISTOLL	Round Stern, built Virginia 1698, 200 Tons Chr' Scandret, Master Charles Harford Jr. etc., Owners
VIRGINIA MERCHANT OF BRISTOLL	Square Stern, built Virginia 1696, 250 Tons Walter Bayley, Master Anthony Swimmer etc., Owners
SALISBURY OF BRISTOLL	Square Stern, built Virginia 1699, 200 Tons William Adams, Master Richard Franklyn etc., Owners

(Certified by Miles Cary, Naval Officer)

List of Ships Entering Inwards Uppdr District James River
from 24th July to 29th September 1703

DOVE	Sloop, built Maryland 1700, 7 Tons Robert Dale, Master Michael Holland, Owner
OTTER OF CAROLINA	Sloop, built 1702, 10 Tons Walt' Craddock, Master Frederick and Tho' Jones, Owners

List of Ships Clearing From Rappahanock River
from 24th June to 29th Sept. 1703

DILIGENCE OF PHILADELPHIA	Square Stern, built 1693, 8 Tons Walter Needham, Master John Staples, Owner
HAPPY RETURN OF MARYLAND	Ketch, 45 Tons, Reg'd Annapolis 1703 Thos. Woolsley, Master Joshua Sweetnam, Owner

List of Ships Entering Rappahanock River
from 25th March to 24th June 1703

BATCHELORS ENDEAVOUR OF MARILAND	Sloop, built 1701, 6 Tons James Diamond, Master & Owner
EXPECTATION OF BRISTOLL	Square Stern, built Virginia 1698, 150 Tons Tho' Hodges, Master Charles Harford, Jno. Jones, Abra. Lloyd, Edw'd Harford, Jno. Scandrett, Francis Rogers, Owners
ANN OF BARBADOS	Square Stern, built Philadelphia 1700, 45 Tons Henry Edey, Master Abell Bond, Jno. Farmer, Owners

(Certified by G. Corbin, Naval,Officer)

List of Ships Entering Inwards in Potomack District
from 25th January to 29th September 1703

JOSIAH AND BETTEY	Pink, built Salem 1689, 50 Tons Josiah Nowell, Master Mr. Henry Coan, Thomas Gowing, Edw' Billing, Owners
MARY & SARAH OF BRISTOLL	Square Stern, built Boston 1699, 140 Tons Isaac Knight, Master Mr. Tho' Cole, Hugh Hayward, Richard Dolson, Elisha James, Isaac Dighdon, Owners
ELIZABETH & HANNAH OF VIRGINIA	Square Stern, built 1701, 30 Tons Phillip Rodgers, Master Major Rodham Kenner, Owner
CONCORD	Briganteen, built Potomack 1699, 42 Tons Rich'd Kenner, Master Fra' Wright, Rod' Kenner, Jno. Crawley, Owners
JOHN	Square Stern, built Maryland 1697, 70 Tons Rob't Read, Master Rob't Burridge, Robert & Eliz' Fowler, Owners
HESTER	Square Stern, built Maryland 1697, 300 Tons Jno. Richardson, Master Elisha James, Abra' Hooke etc., Owners

List of Ships that have Entered in York River
from 12th March to 16th October 1703

UNITY OF BRISTOLL — Sloop, built New England 1701, 28 Tons
Francis Bond, Master & Owner

FISHER OF PHILADELPHIA — Smack, built 1703, 8 Tons
Joseph Kirle, Master & Owner

WILLIAM & ELIZABETH OF LONDON — Square Stern, built New England 1695, 230 Tons
Henry Drake, Master
William Lone, Owner

BLACK THORN OF BOSTON — Sloop, built New England 1694, 30 Tons
Robert Starke, Master
Benjamin Golloy (Gallop)? Owner

BETTY OF BRISTOLL — Round Stern, built New England 1701, 70 Tons
Anselm Hollyday, Master
Joseph Coysgarne, Owner

List of Ships Entering in Potomack Upper District
from 24th July 1703 to 22nd May 1704

JOHN — Square Stern, built Chester, Mary'd 1697, 70 Tons
Rob't Reade, Master
Jno. Buridge Esq. & Compa., Owners

LITTLE JOHN — Plantation built, 60 Tons
Samuell Wiatt, Master
Jacob Martin, Owner

ELIZABETH & HANNAH OF VIRGINIA — Briganteen, built Coan 1701, 30 Tons
Rich'd Kenner, Master
Major Rodham Kenner, Owner

(Certified by W. Allerton and Peter Hack, Coll'rs)

List of Ships that have Entered & Cleared in Accomack District
from 22nd September 1703 to 28th April 1704

MARY OF BOSTON — Built New England 1702, 20 Tons
Jno. Bowdoin and Dan'll Marshall, Masters
John Bowdoin, Owner

LIVER OF LIVERPOOL — Square Stern, built Virginia 1699, 80 Tons
Bryan Blundall, Master
Bryan Blundall, Jno. Cleveland, Wm. Basnett, Lewis Jenkins, Rob't Moone, Owners

(Certified by Hen: Custis, Naval officer)

List of Ships Entered & Cleared in Accomack District
from 27th Sept. 1703 to 1st May 1704

LOGWOOD OF BOSTON — Sloop, built 1702, 20 Tons
Sampson Shore, Master. Sam' Lilly, Owner

ELIZABETH OF JAMES RIVER — Sloop, built Norfolk 1702, 10 Tons
Zeboth Collings, Master & Owner

(Certified by Hen' Scarburgh, Coll'r)

List of Ships Cleared from Upper District James River from 22nd September 1703 to 22nd May 1704

TWO BROTHERS OF NEW ENGLAND	Sloop, built 1703, 35 Tons Sam'll Waters, Master Wm. Partridge Esq., etc., Owners
ENDEAVOUR OF CAROLINA	Sloop, foreign, reg'd 1703, 20 Tons Jacob Allen, Master Abram Eves, George Logen, Owners
SARAH OF PENSILVANIA	Sloop, built Connecticut 1699, 20 Tons Wm. Hughes, Master Benj' Wright, John Dilworth, Jno. Jones, Owners
EXETER MERCHANT OF EXON	Square Stern, built New England 1694, 250 Tons John Wilcox, Master Micajah Perry, Tho' Lane, Rich'd Perry, Nicholas Hutchings, Ann Lyle, Stephen Derick, Owners

(Certified by Edward Hill, Collector)

List of Ships Entering Inwards Lower District James River from 25th September 1703 to 25th May 1704

BENJAMINE & MARY OF BERMUDA	Square-stern, plantation built, reg'd in Bermuda 1701, 20 Tons Soloman Seares, Master Benjamin Edinson, Jonathan Smith, Owners
MARY OF PHILADELPHIA	Sloop, built Pensilvania 1702, 4 Tons James Wilson, Master
ANN OF VIRGINIA	Sloop, Reg'd Williamsburgh 1703, 20 Tons William Lloyd, Master Nath'll McClenahan, Owner
WILLIAM OF VIRGINIA	Square Stern, built Ireland, Reg'd at James Town 1698, 60 Tons William Bosell, Master William Wilson, Thomas Ward, Owners
CONSTANT ALLICE OF PHILADELPHIA	Square Stern, built Pensilvania 1701, 50 Tons Henry Young, Master James Coutts, Edw'd Shippe, Lancelot (?) Coutts, Owners
SPEEDWELL OF PENSILVANIA	Square Stern, built Annopolis 1702, 4 Tons Thomas Raymond, Master Thomas Tench, Owner
HOPE OF PLYMOUTH	Square Stern, built New York 1695, 60 Tons Joseph Howell, Master, James Cock, Wm. Craford, Owners
NICHOLSON OF VIRGINIA	Square Stern, built Virginia 1703, 90 Tons Ebenezer Payne, Master, Samuell Bridger, Owner

List of Ships Entering Inwards Lower District James River
from 25th September 1703 to 25th May 1704

TWO BROTHERS OF VIRGINIA	Square Stern, built 1703, 90 Tons William Davie, Master Jos' Godwin, Owner

(Certified by William Wilson, Collector & Naval Officer)

List of Ships that have Cleared in York River District
from 16th October 1703 to 22nd May 1704

ELIZABETH OF NEW YORK	Sloop, built 1702, 15 Tons Wm. Nieuwenhuysten, Master & Owner
WILLIAM & MARY OF BERMUDA	Sloop, built New Providence 1701, 30 Tons John Dill, Master Joseph Dill, Owner
JAMES OF NEW YORK	Sloop, built New England 1698, 10 Tons James Beard, Master & Owner
BENEDICT OF MARYLAND	Briganteen, built 1702, 30 Tons John Pitt, Master Thomas Enals, Owner
LEVET OF LONDON	Square Stern, built Hampton 1696, 440 Tons Thomas Bagwell, Master Arthur Bayly, Owner

(Certified by Wm. Buckner, Collector,
and Miles Cary, Naval Officer)

List of Ships that have been Cleared in Rappahanock River
from 25th March to 24th June 1704

SWALLOW OF BOSTON	Sloop, built New England 1696, 25 Tons Timothy Burbank, Master Wm. Burroughs, Jno. Foster, Owners
SWAN OF NEW ENGLAND	Briganteen, built 1701, 30 Tons Wm. Fellowes, Master John Burnham, Owner
JOHN BAPTIST OF LIVERPOOL	Square Stern, built New England 1695, 60 Tons John Goare, Master Levinus Hueston, Thomas Hind, John Cockshutt, Richard Geldart, Owners
MANSFEILD OF LONDON	Square Stern, built New England 1696, 340 Tons John Burford, Master Jonathan Mathews, John Goodwin, Nicholas Goodwin, Abraham Holditch, John Baker, Jeremia Johnson, Owners
RICHARD & WILLIAM OF LONDON	Square Stern, built Virginia 1695, 200 Tons Thomas Matticks, Master Sir Rich'd Levett, Wm. Loane, Francis Levett, Robert Rowin, Owners

List of Ships that have been Cleared in Rappahanock River
from 25th March to 24th June 1704

MAYFLOWER OF VIRGINIA	Square Stern, built 1700, 40 Tons Isaac Knight, Master John Foster, Isaac Knight, Elisha James, Hugh Hayward, Owners
HANNAH & KATHERINE OF LIVERPOOLE	Briganteen, built Virginia 1704, 60 Tons Thomas Hughes, Master Thomas Hughes, John Hughes, Richard Nicholls, Owners
SPEEDWELL FRIEND OF NEW ENGLAND	Square Stern, built New England 1704, 20 Tons Tho' Lanyon, Master Jno. Northey Sr., David Northey Jr., Sam'll Northey Jr., Owners
PROVIDENCE OF NORTH CAROLINA	Shallop, built Virginia 1701, 5 Tons Jno. Brock, Master James Cole, Owner

List of Ships Entering Inwards in Rapphanock River
from 29th September to 25th December 1703

CHICHESTER MERCHANT OF PENSILVANIA	Square Stern, built 1702, 24 Tons James Loring, Master Wm. Bawler, Jer' Collett, Jno. Vanlire, Jos' Laddon, Randolph Janny, Owners
JOHN OF PENSILVANIA	Sloop, reg'd Philadelphia 1703, 8 Tons Samuell Stewart, Master William Allen, Owner
THOMAS & ELIZABETH OF LONDON	Square Stern, built New England 1694, 200 Tons Rich' Archer, Master Thomas Ogden Sr. and Jr., Wm. Horsepoole, Thomas Robinson, Thomas Steeres, Gerrard Elwes, Sarah Castells of London, Owners

List of Ships Entering Inwards in Rappahanock River
from 25th December 1703 to 25th March 1704

MULBERRY OF NEW YORK	Square Stern, 15 Tons Wm. Smith, Master Wm. Smith, Thos. Crosthwaite, James Bacon, John Canyon, Wm. Harris, Owners
MARY OF PHILADELPHIA	Square Stern, 15 Tons Sam'l Bucknall or (Bicknall)?, Master Geo. Claypoole, Sam' Bicknall, John Redman, John Day Jr., John Coysgarne, Thos. Paxton, Owners

List of Ships Entered & Cleared in Accomack River from 19th June 1705 to 8th August 1706

JOHN & DEBORAH OF NEW ENGLAND	Ketch. Joseph Wallis, Master
JOHN & ELIZABETH OF VIRGINIA	Briganteen William Hurst, Master

List of Ships Entered & Cleared Lower District James River from 20th Oct. 1705 to 22nd August 1706

TWO BROTHERS OF VIRGINIA	90 Tons Jos' Sledge, Master
NICHOLSON OF VIRGINIA	90 Tons Geo. Sparrow, Master
FELIX OF MARYLAND	30 Tons Tho. Haymand, Master
GREYHOUND OF PHILADELPHIA	12 Tons Edw'd ****, Master
SPEEDWELL FRIEND OF BOSTON	20 Tons David Northey, Master
ELIZABETH OF NEW YORK	30 Tons, Mich'l Fulton, Master
LOYALTY OF VIRGINIA	20 Tons Tho' Priddon (?), Master
HENRY & ELIZABETH OF PHILADELPHIA	4 Tons Henry ***, Master
DOLPHIN OF NEW YORK	16 Tons, Wm. Moyen, Master
NEW SPEEDWELL OF PHILADELPHIA	25 Tons Jacob Howard, Master
RICHARD & MARY OF S. CAROLINA	18 Tons Mich'l Stephens, Master
ENDEAVOUR OF BOSTON	40 Tons Benj' Andrews, Master
ANN OF VIRGINIA	20 Tons Henry Lamsey, Master
DOVE OF BOSTON	35 Tons, John Ela, Master
BRIDGWATER OF PHILADELPHIA	15 Tons Tho' Jacobs, Master
HOPEWELL OF PHILADELPHIA	6 Tons Mat' Gibson, Master

List of Ships Entered & Cleared York River
from 24th June 1705 to 22nd August 1706

INDUSTRY OF PHILADELPHIA	Sloop, 8 Tons Edward Thruston, Master
JOHN AND BETTY OF VIRGINIA	Briganteen, 20 Tons Joseph Thomas, Master
HOPE OF NORTH CAROLINA	Sloop, 4 Tons Sam'll Payn, Master
DOLPHYN OF NORTH CAROLINA	Sloop, 8 Tons Thomas Miller, Master
TRYALL OF NORTH CAROLINA	Sloop, 4 Tons Cornelius Jones, Master
RUTH OF NORTH CAROLINA	Sloop, 10 Tons Joseph Ming, Master
FORTUNE OF PHILADELPHIA	Sloop, 25 Tons Thomas Lindsay, Master
PEARL OF PHILADELPHIA	Sloop, 25 Tons Edward Tyler, Master
THOMAS AND MARY OF PENSILVANIA	Sloop, 10 Tons Edw'd Wills, Master
LITTLE HANNAH OF PHILADELPHIA	Sloop, 12 Tons Robert Wright, Master
MACK JACKS ADVENTURE OF VIRGINIA	Sloop, 20 Tons James Gregson, Master
MARY OF PHILADELPHIA	Sloop, 8 Tons Thomas Lindsay, Master
DOLPHYN OF NEW ENGLAND	Sloop, 10 Tons Ezekiell Andrews, Master
SEA HORSE OF BOSTON	Ketch, 30 Tons Joshua Pickman, Master
ELIZABETH & GRACE OF N. CAROLINA	Sloop, 20 Tons Jos' Reding, Master
ELIZABETH OF BOSTON	Square Stern, 90 Tons David Robertson, Master
GLOSTER OF VIRGINIA	Briganteen, 50 Tons Jona' Yeates, Master
RUTH OF N. CAROLINA	Sloop, 10 Tons John Porter Jr., Master
FRIENDSHIP OF VIRGINIA	Sloop, 28 Tons Benjamin Dyer, Master

List of Ships That Have Cleared in South Potomack District from 29th August 1705 to 22nd August 1706

VIRGINIA DOVE	Square Stern, built Virginia 1699, 100 Tons Samuel Elliss, Master Thomas Smith, Owner
AFRICA OF LYME REGIS	Built Boston 1701, Wm. Read, Master Jno. Burridge Esq., Nath' Gundry, Owners
JOHN OF LYME REGIS	Square Stern, built Maryland 1697, 70 Tons Rob't Read, Master Jno. Burridge Esq. & Company, Owners
PHENIX OF BRISTOLL	Built Virginia 1698, 200 Tons Chr' Scandrett, Master Cha' and Edw'd Harford etc., Owners
MARY & SARAH OF BRISTOLL	Built Boston 1699, 140 Tons Peter Balyne, Master Hugh Hayward, Elisha James, Owners
WILLIAM & ORIANA OF BRISTOLL	Built Maryland 1691, 50 Tons Rob't Edwards, Master Sir Jno. Dudlestone etc., Owners
ELIZABETH OF WEYMOUTH	120 Tons Daniel Williams, Master Francis Russell, Jno. Addis, Owners

List of Ships Entered & Cleared in Rappahanock District from 24th June 1705 to 24th June 1706

LITTLE GEORGE OF PENSILVANIA	Sloop, 25 Tons Jacob Howard, Master
WILLIAM & FRANCIS OF RAPPAHANOCK	Round Stern, 45 Tons Tho' Eastum, Master
MARY OF NEW YORK	Sloop, 25 Tons Geo. Milbourne, Master
RICHARD & MARY OF S. CAROLINA	Square Stern, 18 Tons Christopher Hall, Master
GREYHOUND OF CARROTUCK	3 Tons Benja' Tulle, Master
WILLIAM OF POCOMOKE	10 Tons Tho. Wharton, Master

A LIST OF BONDS TO HIS KINGS MAJ. RECEIVED FROM HIS SEVERAL COLLECTORS OF HIS MAJ. COLLONIES IN VIRGINIA MAY 2, 1698

Ships Names	Masters Names	Securities Names	Proceeding
Catherine	Matthew Williams	James Howell	Dismissed
Edward & Francis	Thomas Mann	John Mann	Pending
Peyton	George Walker	Rob't Peyton, P. Beverly, Tho. Todd	Dismissed
Sussex	William Wrett	Thomas Ballard	Pending
Rappahanock	John Harle	Daniel Park	Pending
Begining	Daniel L. Britton	Jos. Ring, Wm. Buckner	Dismissed
Glocester	John Sled	Lewis Burwell	Pending
Virginian	Edward Whittaker	Daniel Park	Dismissed
William & Mary	Joseph Lewis	Gawen Corbin	Pending
William & Mary	Joshua Sledd	Richard Lee	Pending
Concord	George Panter	Thomas Meriden	No suit brought
Catherine	Robert Price	Thomas Loyd	Pending
Expedition	William Webb	Jno. Dyer, Tho. Ballard	Suit not yet brought
William & John	Moses Jones	Wm. Edmondson, Robert Bennet	Pending
Speedwell	Dan'l Jenifer of St. Thomas	Willis Wilson	Pending
John & Margaret	William Esterson	William Wilson	Dismissed
Friendship	John Wilson	John Coefeild	Suit not yet brought
Speedwell	Edward Bally	Bertram Servant	Pending
Two Brothers	John Jarret	Thomas Loyd	Pending
Nansemond Frigate	John Cox	Wm. Sherwood	Pending
Batchelors Delight	Tho. Bentley	Lewis Conner	Pending
Cock	John Sanders	Thomas Cock	Pending
Adventure	Price Henstone	Wm. Crawford	Pending
John & Sarah	Richard Crocket	Christopher Robinson	Pending
Two Brothers	Wm. Clark	Jno. Loyd, Tho. Loyd	Pending
Catherine	John Scott	Tho. Loyd, David Gwyn	Pending
Token	John Tench	John Miller, Gawen Corbin	Dismissed
Mary & Ellery	Thomas Carpenter	Richard Nusum	Pending
Advice	William Nicholas	John Griffin	Pending
William & John	Moses Jones	Geo. Neal, Tho. Martin	Dismissed
Mary	Thomas Farmer	Richard Nusum, Tho. Martin	Pending
Jeremiah	Robert Redhead	Sam'l Traverse	Pending
Linajos (?)	Richard Taliafero	John Grymes	Pending
Jane	Robert Ransone	Daniel Clark	Pending
Edward & Mary	Joshua Sledd	John Mann	Pending
William & Sarah	Thomas Meech	Dan'l Meech, Tho. Maddux	Judgment 371 pounds
Salisbury	Thomas Lawrence	John Washington	Judgement 1000 pounds
Society	John West	John Jones, James Jones	Pending

Wm. Randolph, Attor. Gen'l.

Petition of Severall Masters and Com'drs. of Ships
Now Rideing at Anchor at Riquotem Road.

Dated 20th June 1701

(This petition states that the Masters are anxious to set sail for England but have no convoy and requests that Capt. Edward Whitaker, Commander of the Indian King, be appointed Comm'r in Chief)

Edwd. Burford	Dan'l Dunlop	Nicho: Hump'ry	Jo'n Jane
John Burford	Tho: Granes	Tho: Preeson	Rich'd Scott
John Goar	Ralph Beamy	Deane Cock	Natt: Tincomb
John Walker	Mich'l Staple	Wm. Braded	Rich'd Biswick
Hump'y Bellow	Jos: Bewley	Tho: Longman	Rob: Blackstone
Sam'l Bowman	Tho: Opy	Wm. Guy	John Turner
Ja: Norman	Jo'n Boyd	Jo'n Blenham	J. Bezeley
Jos'ua Whiting	Bellengham West	Jo'n Souden	Jo'n Banbury
Fra: Whiteside	Steph: Atkinson	Jo'n Coterill	Fra: Jackson
Rich: Franklin	Fra: Whiteside	Sam'l Ellett	Jo'n Paniter
Jo: Jeffryes	Pe'r Senhouse	Jo'n Thomas	Hen: Brown
Rich'd Tregian	Benj: Selvester	Wm. Selwood	Wm. Scott
Ric: Wilkinson	Abra: Carter	Steph: Robins	Rich'd Hankin
Rob't Bayley	Edw'd Ellis	Hugh Rockett	
	Peter Bonamy		

The Seconds in these following Words:

Capt. Deane Cock, Capt. Nicho: Humphry. Wee whose names are under written do become humble suitors to yr. Ex'cy to appoint the above mentioned Comand'rs to be seconds to the Comd'r in Chief.

(The names that follow are the same as the above list but with a few additions and some alternative spellings, viz:

Jo'n Temer, Mich'l Stapell, John Tanner, Rich'd Spracklin, Peter Blackstone, John Cotterill, Ste: M'Kinyon, John Bleckern, Benja' Sillvester, John Lowden, John Drew, Jos: Royall, Ralph Beams, Tho: Opie.

A List of the Names of the Masters of Ships who agreed to obey the orders of Capt. Nevill & Capt. Passenger. 1701

Sam'l Bowman
John Jane
John Boyd
Edw'd Burford
Hen: Brown
Pet'r Bonamy
Tho: Longman
Peter Senhouse
John Goar
Tho: Preeson
Belling: West
Jos: Bezeley
Tho: Opie
Sam'l Ellis
Hugh Rockett
Jo'n Paniter
Rich'd Wilkinson
John Drane

Peter Blackstone
John Walker
Rich'd Scott
Ste: Robins
Fra: Whiteside
Ste: Atkinson
Rich'd Biswick
Ralph Beams
John Cotterill
Da: Dunlop
Jos: Jeffryes
James Norman
Josua Whiting
John Thomas
Wm. Selwood
Natt: Milner
Abra: Carter
Jos: Royall

Mich'l Stapell
Tho: Granes
John Burford
John Tanner
John Blenkern
Natt: Tincombe
Rich'd Hankin
Hump'ry Bellow
Wm. Broaded
John Souden
Rich'd Spracling
Fra: Jackson
John Banbury
Rich'd Tregian
Benj: Silvester
Benj: Reed
Robert Bayley
Edw'd Ellis
Wm. Scott

A List of Merch'tmen who have rec'd instructions from Capt. Nevill, Comand'r of his Maj'ties Ship Lincoln

Ships Name	Masters Name	Ships Name	Masters Name
Eliz'th & Judy	Ste: Atkinson	Edw'd & Mary	John Coterill
York Merch't	Rob't Beames	Wm. & Anne	Natt: Tincombe
Hopewell	Rich'd Scott	Josia	John Sowden
Young James	Ste: Robins	Mountjoy	Wm. Guy
Wm. & Mary	Pet'r Boraby	Sarah	Jos: Jeffryes
Chichester	Jo'n Boyd	Trasby	John Jane
Ann	Benj: Silvester	Nassaw	Rich: Tregian
Supply	Pet'r Blackstone	Bristoll	Bellingham West
Mary	D. Dunlop	Martha Sloope	John Panister
America	Tho: Granes	Bristoll Pink	John Thomas
John	Rich'd Biswick	Indian King	Edw'd Whitaker
Batchelours		James &	
Endeavour	Hump: Bellow	Elizabeth	Deane Cock
Harriss	Rich'd Hankin	Hartwell	Nicho: Humfrey
Eliza. & Mary	John Burford	Marygold	Benj: Read
Sarah Mary)		Adventure	Tho: Opie
Hopewell)	Mic'l Stapell	Chatherine	Hugh Rockett
John	John Tanner	John Baptist	John Goar
Industry	John Blenkern	Augustine	R. Wilkinson
Providence	Jos: Bezeley	America	Wm. Broaded
Deptford	Rich: Spracling	Lyon	Rob't Bayley
Hope	Abra: Carter	Integrity	Ja: Norman
Brittannia	John Drewe	Providence	Jos: Royall
Damond	John Banbury	Ben & Hester	Jos: Whiting
Daniel	Wm. Selwood	Throughgood	Wm. Scott
Gloster	Edw'd Ellis		

A Map of Virginia Showing Rappahanock & Potomack Rivers dated 1737 or later

Rappahanock River (Left Bank)

Stingray Point, Col. Churchills, Parrots Creek, Capt. Robinsons, Col. Grymes, Urbanna, Col. Corbins, Weeks Point, Clift by Mill Creek, Jones Point, Bowlers Warehouse, Lowry's Point, Col. Robinson's, Piscatoway, Hoskin's Creek, Hobb's Hole, Capt. Dangerfield, Col. Beverley's, Payne's Island, Barrows Marsh, Medases Bay, Port Tobacco Bay, Madam Lomax, Taliaferro's Creek, Roy's Warehouse, Presser's Creek, Passitank, Wier Creek, Harrison's Creek, Conway's Warehouse, Snow Creek, Nussoponax Run, Newpok'n, Mr. ***sons, Fredericksburg, Golden Run

Rappahanock River (Right Bank)

Fleet's Island, Nahtepoysen Creek, Musket Point, Secretary Carter's, Old house Creek, Corotoman River, Courthouse, Col. Ball's, Chownings Point, Nesum's Creek, Fairweather Creek, Mrs. Burgess, Deep Creek, Mud Creek, Moratico Creek, Col. Tarpley's, Capt. Griffins, Farnham Creek, Capt. Barbers, Totuskey, Capt. Tomlins, Mr. Rusts, Courthouse, Maj. Fantleroys, Col. Tayloe's, Rappa. Creek, Naylor's Hole, Charles B**ser Dams, Pepetick Creek, Bray's Church, Thatchers, R***** dam, Furnace, Murdock Creek, Poltridge, Chingateague, Long's ferry, Doctor Turner's, Gibson's Warehouse, Nanzemoxon Creek, Courthouse, Nanzemond, Dowty's Creek, Omen Creek, H**ws Creek, Pye Creek, Lamb Creek, Muddy Creek, Little Falls Run, Capt. Berryman's, Clayborns, Fallmouth, Fa**s Run.

Between the mouths of Rappahanock & Potomack Rivers

Fleetsbay Creek, Indian Creek, Bluff Point, Oyster Creek, Dividing Creeks, Ingrams Bay, Mill Creek, Great Wicocomoco River, Kenners Creek.

~~Un-dated~~ map of Virginia (continued)

Potomack River (Left Bank)

Smith's Point, Little Wicocomoco, Hacks herring run, Hulls Creek, Presly's Creek, Cod Creek, Coan River, Cherry Point, Yeocomoco River, Yeocomoco Point, Sandy Point, Rotank Creek, Lower Machotick Creek, Herds Creek, Ponds, Ragged Point, Coles Point, Machotick River, Mattox's Point, Kingcopsco Point, White Point, Nominy River, Smart's Creek, Poor Jack Creek, Carriomen Creek, Hollis's Creek, Table of Poplars, Blackstones Isle, Hollis's Cliffs, Pope's Creek, Bridges Creek, Mattox's Creek, Munro's Creek, Attopin Creek, Ducking stool Point, Upper Machotick, Dodson's creek, Mathias Point, Chotank Creek, Matomkin Point, Tickle's Hole, Boyd's Hole, Col. Fitzhugh's, Pasbitansy Creek, Courthouse, Potomack Creek, Accokick, Marlbrough, Aquia Creek, Brents mill-bridge, Mr. Scot's, Chapawamsick, Quantico Creek, Cockpit Point, Powel's Creek, Freestone Point, Neapsco Creek, Occoquon Bay, Courthouse, Pohick & Accotinck Creeks, Dogue Creek, Capt. Washington's, Little Hunting Creek, Hunting Creek.

Potomack River (Right Bank)

Point Lookout, Smith's Creek, St. Mary's River, St. George's Island, Piney Point, Britain's Bay, Clements Bay, Wecocomoco River, Cedar point, Mr. Phil'p Lee's Landing, Popes Creek, Portobaco Creek, Nangemie Creek, Maryland Point, Chepomoxon, Matawoman, Piscatoway Creek, Swan Creek, Broad Creek.

Top Section of ~~Un-dated~~ Map

Rappahanock River, continued to Fork

Left Bank - Motts Run, Barrowsford

Right Bank - Horsepen run.

~~Un-Dated~~ Map of Virginia (continued)

The Great Fork (Rappahanock River, South Branch) Left Bank

Hunting Run, Indian Ford, Wilderness Run, Flat Run, Germanna Ferry, Russel's Run, Rackoon Run, Jacks Ford, Boyles Run, Blew-water Run, Thornton's River, (Road), Conway's Run, Conways River, Pocosax Fork.

Great Fork (Right Bank)

Lightfoots Run, Dragoon Run, Brooks Run, Blew cowslip run, Cedar run, Little Cedar run, Robertson River, Beautiful run, Bever dam run, Darbys run, Maple run, Brockers run, Elk Run, Jacksons mill, Stauntons River, Garth run, Jonas's run.

The Little Fork (Rappahanock River, North Branch) Left Bank

Stanley (?) Mill, *** run, Beverleys Ford, Yew Hills, Gourd vine fork, Red***k Mountains.

Little Fork (Right Bank)

Richland run, Deep run, Rocky run, Summerduck run, Horseford, Marsh run, Tinpot run, Hedgmans River, Carter's run, Happy Creek Gap, Happy Creek, Fork of Shenandoah, Indian run, Willis's mill run, Battle run, Battle Mountains, Cannons run, Rushy River,

Potomack River, Left Bank

Hores Creek, Ocoquon (River), Crooked Bridge, Goose run, Dorrels run, Town run, Elk run, Champs run

Potomack River (Right Bank)

Sandy run, Bull run, Broad run, Kettle run, Slaty run, Cedar run.

Shenandoah River

Col. Carter, Manasses Run, Fiery Mountain

A MAP OF THE NORTHERN NECK IN VIRGINIA

The Territory of the Right Honorable Thomas, Lord Fairfax

Situate betwixt the Rivers Potomack and Rappahanock, according to a late Survey. Drawn in the year 1737 by Wm. Mayo. Receiv'd Novbr. 28th 1737 with Maj'r Gooch's Lett'r dated the 19th August 1737

Starting At The Mouth of the Rappahanock River, Left Bank:-

Stingray, Churchil, Robinson, Grymes, Urbana Creek, Corbin, Weeks Point, Jones Point, Bowlers Warehouse, Lowry, Robinson, Piscatoway Creek, Hoskins Creek, Hobs's Hole Warehouse, Dangerfield, Edmundson, Tayloe, Beverley, Rain's Island, Vaughan, Layton's Warehouse, Brooke, Hankins, Roy, Micoud, Port Tobacco Creek, Mitchams Creek, Lomax, Goose Creek, Tailaferro's Creek, Thowle, Roys Warehouses, Prossers Creek, Stanhope, Moon Swamp, Robinson, Passitank Creek, Catlet, Buckner, Wier Creek, Battle, Conway's Warehouse, Thornton, Snow Creek, Talipferro, Nassaponax Creek, Spotswood, Newpost, Grayson, Williams, Fredricksburg, Thornton, Falls, Falls Run, Golden Run, Motts Run, Tubal Works, Rocky Run

Fork of the Rappahanock (The Great Fork), Left Bank:-

Hunting Run, Wilderness Run, Kat Run, Germanna, Russells Run, Mountain Run.

South Branch of the Rappahanock Called Rappid Anne (Left Bank)

Orange Courthouse, Tods Branch, County Road, Baylors Run, Blue Run, Brooks Run, South River, Offals Branch, Conway, Barnets Run, Conway's River, Pocoson Fork

Fork of the Rappahanock (The Great Fork) Right Bank - Fox Run

South Branch of Rappahanock Called Rappid Anne (Right Bank)

Ferry, Draggon Run, Potato Run, Raccoon Fork, Cedar Run, Little Cedar Run, Robinson River, Smiths Run, Beverdam Run, Darby's Run, Maple Run, Elk Run, Stantons River, Stanton, Jones River.

Map of The Northern Neck in Virginia (Continued)

Starting at the Mouth of the Rappahanock River, Right Bank

Windmill, Muskette Point, Muskette Creek, Carter, Curotoman, Ball, Nesum's Creek, Arms's Creek, Fairweather's Creek, Burges, Teagne's Creek, Well's Creek, Deep Creek, Ball, Mud Creek, Morahico Point, Morahico Creek, Tarpley, Griffin, Tarpley, Hornby, Suggitt, Richardson's Creek, Totaskey, Barber, Adcokick Point, Tomlins, Fantleroy, Tayloe, Rappahanock Creek, Fantleroy, Churchil, Fantleroy, Morton, Beaver Dam, Charles, Pepetick Creek, Warehouse, Gray's Church, Robinson, Bover Dam, Bristol Furnace, Tutt, Pitman's Landing, Murdock's Creek, Randal, Fetherstones Island, Chingotiague Creek, Long's Ferry, Turner, Gibson's Warehouse, Skinker, Nantz*moxon Creek, Lomax, Dowty's Creek, Omen Creek, Hard's Creek, Richards, Pye Creek, Champ, Lambs Creek, Doniphon, Hackley, Strother, Muddy Creek, Thornton, Kenyon, Ball, Washington, Newton, China's Run, Berryman, Strother, Clayburn's Run, Fitzhugh, Falmouth, Fall's Run, Jacobs Run, Rockopin Run, Barrow's Ford

Hedgman's River or The North Branch of the Rappahanock (Right Bank)

Rich Land Run, Deep Run, Summerduck Run, Kinner, Little Summerduck Run, Persimmon Run, Ludwel, Marsh Run, F(?)ormans Ford, Ludwel Run, Hedgman, Chambers, Kindal, Great Run, Pope, Carters Run

Hedgman's River (Left Bank)

Stanton, Wheatly, Field, Mountain Run, Carter, Hebards Run, Ruffens Run, Hopper, Bever Dam Run, Carter, Negro Run, The Marshy Fork

Cannon's River, Fork of Hedgman's River (Right Bank)

Ingram Run, Miles Run, Willis, Crooked Run, Duncan, Battle Run, Rush River, Long Run, Thornton.

Cannon's River (Left Bank)

Beverley, Muddey Run, Spring Run, Gourd Vine Fork, Ashley

A Map of the Northern Neck in Virginia (continued)

Starting at the Mouth of the Potomack River (Right Bank) - Maryland

Point Lookout, Smith's Creek, St. Mary's River, St. George's Island, Piny Point, Britain's Bay, Clements Bay, Blackstone's Island, Wecocomoco River, Cedar Point, Pope's Creek, Port Tobacco Creek, Nangernie Creek, Mary Land Point, Chepomoxen Creek, Matawoman Creek, Crane Island, Pascatoway Creek, Swan Creek, Broad Creek, Addison, Eastern Branch, Goose Creek, Watson, Mason's Island, Rock Creek, McGee's Ferry, The Great Falls, Sawmil Creek, Dutchman's Island, Sinigar Creek, Broad Run, Little Manockasy, Manockasy River, Little Creek, Muddy Branch, Calvin, Falls, Undietum Creek, Spurgeant, (Waggon Road to Philadelphia), Shepheard, Chaplain, York, Roan, Moor.

Coast Between Rappahanock and Potomack Rivers' Mouths

Indian Creek, Bluff Point, Dividing Creek, Ingram's Bay, Great Wecocomoco River, Little Wecocomoco River

Starting at the Mouth of the Potomack River (Left Bank)

Smith's Point, Herring Run, Herring Pond, Herring Creek, Hull's Creek, Prestly's Creek, Coan River, Yeocomoco River, Sandy Point, Potank Creek, Lower Machotick Creek, Ragged Point, Cole's Point, Machotick River, Kingcopuco Point, Nomony Bay, Nomony River, Smart's Creek, Poor Jack Creek, Curritomen Creek, Holles's Creek, Holles's Cliffs, Pope's Creek, Bridge's Creek, Mattox Creek, Monroe's Creek, Attopin Creek, Upper Machotick Creek, Dodson's River, Chotank Creek, Matomkin Point, Boyds Hill, Paspatansy, Patomack Creek, Acquia Creek, Brent's Mill Run, Chapawamsick Creek, Quantico Creek, Cockspit Point, Powels Creek, Stripling, Neapsco Creek, Gregsby, Occoquon River, Baxter, Accatink Creek, Potrick Creek, Dogne Creek, Washington, Little Hunting Creek, Clifton, Blake, Smith, Hunting Creek, Warehouse, Four Mile Creek, Falls, Sinigar Falls, Mackearty, Rose, James, Broad Run, Lee, Lee's Island,

A Map of the Northern Neck in Virginia

<u>Left Bank Potomack River (Continued)</u>

Goose Creek, Tarp, Awbrey, **nestone Creek, Sinclare, Canoy Island, Mobley, Falls, Shenandoa River, Peterson, Friend, Taylor, Spurgeant, Chaplain, Paulson, Williams, Ipeckon Creek, Ferry, Williams, Brooke, Newkirk, Tolus's Creek, Presland, Back Creek.

Also mentioned on the map are: Cohongdrooto River, Paterson's Creek, Nicholas Old Fields, Wappacomma River, Little Cacapchon River

List of Ships Clearing Upper District James River
from 16th November to 28th December 1699

HARRISON OF LONDON	Square Stern, 200 tons John Harrison, Master John Harrison, Benj. Bradley, Arthur North, Thomas Wych, Roger Jones, Jno. Thompson, Wm. Byrd, Benj. Harrison, Henry Hartwell, Wm. Wilson, Rob't Bolling, Frederick Jones, Owners
PERRY & LANE OF LONDON	Square Stern 330 tons James Morgan, Master Christopher Morgan, Micajah Perry, Tho. Lane, Rich'd Perry, Jno. Perry, Wm. Byrd, Henry Hartwell, Nich'o Lock, Tho. Peacock, __ (Richard)? Russell, Sir Jno. Sweetapple, Joseph Pills, Hopefor Bendall, Wm. Bird, Samuel Rawlinson, Owners

List of Ships Clearing Upper District James River
from 23rd April 1702 to 10th July 1702

PERRY & LANE OF LONDON	Square Stern 330 tons James Morgan, Master Xpher (Christopher) Morgan, Mica (Micajah) Perry, Tho. Lane, Rich'd Perry, Jno. Perry, Wm. Byrd, Henry Hartwell, Nicholas Lock, Tho. Peacock, Rich'd Russell, Sir Jno. Sweetapple, Joseph Piles, Hope Furbendal, Will'm Bond, Sarah H. Robinson.

INDEX

AALVES (Alves,Alvos) George 74
ABBITT, Francis 172
ABBOTT, John 125; Robert 157; Rodger 127; William 134
ABDELL, John 228; Thomas 228; William 228
ABERNATHY, Robert 109,222
ACRE, John 141
ACRES, James 134; William 134
ACKSTED, John 189
ADAM, James 157; William 192
ADAMS, Anne 59,172; Ebenezer 49, 102,37; George 58; James 31, 58,69; John 149; Peter 58,59; Thomas 222; William 282,304
ADAMSON, David 149
ADCOCK, Edward 134; Henry 134
ADDIS (Addiss) John 288,312
ADDISON (Adison) John 77,228, 245; William 269
ADKINS, John 216
ADKINSON, Henry 172,180; John 149; Richard 222; Thomas 172
AKINS, James Sr. 216
ALCOCK, John 157
ALDERSEY, Nicholas 37,49
ALDRED, Anne 143
ALDRIDGE, John 163; William 122,222
ALDY, John 216
ALEX (Alexander) Abraham 163
ALEXANDER (Alex) Abraham 163; David 6,23,141,269; James 126; John 33,192,242; Robert 8,18, 40,252,255; Phillip 18,252
ALFORD, Benjamin 298; John 149, 168
ALIAT, John 161
ALLAMAN, Thomas 144
ALLCOCK, Dorothy 149
ALLEGOOD, William 103
ALLEN (Allin) Arthur 40,56,65, 68,72,79,80,81,82,83,85,86,87, 88,89,90,206,235; Benjamin 121; Charles 186; Daniell 163; Hugh 147; Jacob 307; James 65,68; John 24,28,35,40,47,52,56,87,88, 90,96; Joseph 52; Orphans 220; Reynold 163; Richard 163,172; Robert 163; Samuel 163,292; Thomas 100,112,128,207,261,292; William 178,303,309
ALLERTON, Isaac 260; Willoughby 2, 3,7,19,249,260,283,306
ALLIGOOD, Henry 228; John 228
ALLIN (Allen) Arthur 73,210; Edmund 123; Erasmus 134; Richard 131; Thomas 149,182; Widow 216; William 134
ALLVIS, George 163
ALLY, Henry 222
ALVES (Aalves,Alvos) George 101
ALVEY, Robert 157
ALVOS (Aalves,Alves) George 67
AMBLER, Richard 30,41,42,53
AMBROSE, Leonard 145
AMBURGER, Conrade 119,121
AMES (Amos) Joseph 124; Nicholas 163
AMIS, James 141
AMONET, __ 266, Jacob 106,107
AMOS (Ames) Francis 163; Nicholas 163
ANDERSON, Alexander 59,113; Charles 22,222,242,250,267; David 59,97,163; George 4,29, 119,208,252,269; Henry 34, 108,222; James 120,122; John 34,46,79,163,222; Matthew 222; Richard 4,9,14, 24,149,163; Robert 26,163; Thomas 34,46,99,118,120,222; William 4,5,25,69,157,222
ANDREW, William 59,157
ANDREWS, Andrew 228; Bartho. 210; Benjamin 310; David 210; Ezekiel 311; George 134; John 144; Lewis 263; Robert 129, 210,228; Thomas 76,210,216; Thomas Jr. 98; William 44,71, 113,128,250
ANDROS, Bartholomew 72,90,98; Edmund 242,243; Henry 180; Robert 99
ANGELL, James 228
ANGUISH (Angus) Patrick 189
ANGUS (Anguish) Patrick 9
ANTHONY, George 124; Mark 163; Thomas 282,285,287
APERSON, William 172
APPLEBY, Charles 281,287; Richard 263
APPLETHWAITE (Applewaite,Applewhite) Henry 14; Henry Jr. 14
APPLETON, Joseph 303
APPLEWAITE (Applethwaite,Applewhite) Henry 10,24,35,206
APPLEWHITE (Applethwaite,Applewaite) Henry 4,47; Thomas 35,47
ARBUTHNOT, David 295,301
ARCHER, __ 183; Elizabeth 179; George 89,110,216; John 216; Michael 26,34,111,273; Richard 309; Stephen 202

ARCOUTCH, Mary 216
AREN, John 125
ARGO, James 172
ARISE, Margaret 163
ARLIN, Jeremiah 200
ARMESTONE, Joshua 172
ARMIGER, Jacob 38
ARMISTEAD (Armstead)
Anthony 4,9,12,22,33,53,183, 248,261; Henry 23,33,44,46; John 1,37,46,258; Lewis 46; Peter 241; Robert 22,33,45,53; William 12,22,89,95,133,141, 143,144,146,183,262,285
ARMSBY, John 157
ARMSTEAD (Armistead)
Henry 259; John 240,243
ARMTRADING, Henry 124
ARNALL, Goldsmith 274,278; Thomas 274,278
ARNAUD, Isaac 265
ARNOLD,__ 66, Anthony 157; Benjamin 60,157; Edward 68, 92,111,149,198
ARON, Josiah 163
ARRINGTON, William 95
ARUNDELL, Thomas 282
ARVIN, William 134
ASBROOK, Peter Sr. 216
ASCOUGH, John 59,236; Mary 77
ASCOW, Thomas 186
ASHBEE, William 107
ASHBY, Ellis 277,279; Wm. 190
ASHCROFT, Thomas 163
ASHFEILD, Edmund 261
ASHLEY,__ 320; Allis 275; Charles 163; Dennis 192
ASHTON, Burdit 41,53; Charles 2,7,19,269; Henry 19,41,53,269
ASKEW, John 209,272; Nicholas 209
ASQUE, John 149
ATKINS, James Sr. 220; John 205; Thomas 90,93,210
ATKINSON, Christopher 104; James 95,205; James Jr. 87; John 163; Joshua 263; Richard 210; Stephen 314,315; Thomas 110
ATTERBERRY, Thomas 245
ATTWOOD (Atwood) Edward 91,189; John 107; William 275,282,284
ATWELL, Thomas 204,269
ATWATER, Jonathan 299
ATWOOD (ATTWOOD) Richard 131; William 101,277
AUBORNE (Awborn,Awburn)
Richard 234
AUBREY, Mr. 266
AUGELIERE, Elizabeth 264
AUSTIN,__ 163; Daniel 149; James 163; Johanna 147; Richard 163; Thomas 149
AVENT, Thomas 52,107
AVERETT, John 210
AVERY, John 210,222; Isaac 264
AVIS, Widow 192
AWBORN (Auborne,Awburn) Richard 15
AWBREY, Francis 52
AWBURN (Auborne,Awborn) Richard 2
AYLETT, William 14,25,36,48,53, 109,271
AYLEWORTH, Jon't 125
AYLSBERRY, Phillip 202
AYRES (Eyres) Edmund 123; Francis 124; Henry 124; Ragnall 127; William 134

BABB, John 202; Thomas 118,120, 182; Widow 147
BABINGTON, John 192; Richard 192; Thomas 192
BACHELDON, Joseph 192
BACKING, Richard 108
BACON,__ 233,234,235,236; Elizabeth 237; James 309; John 49,71,144; Nathaniel 54,61; Nathaniel Jr. 235,237; Col. 235
BACOP (Bacon)? Thomas 145
BAD, Samuel 164
BADGER, Reynold 126
BADOUET, Etienne 264
BAGBY, Robert 149; Thomas 172
BAGG***, John 115
BAGGALY, Gervis 124
BAGLEY, Peter 90,93; Richard 298
BAGNALL, Joseph 272
BAGWELL, Alex. 123; Edward 123; Henry 32,44,124; John 126; Thomas 128,308
BAILE, John 210
BAILEN, John 135
BAILEY,BAILY (Bayley,Bayly)
Arthur 272,281; Charles 22,27, 81,84,87,106; Jeffery 282; John 22,104; Richard 4,141,146, 282; Robert 281; Thomas 216; Timothy 285; Walter 92,281,286
BAINE, Hugh 5
BAINES, Thomas 182
BAITES, Isaac 222
BAKER, Christopher 163; Joseph 198; Henry 5,10,14,26,37,49,134,199, 206,210,248; James 47,71,149,183 261,262; John 8,17,62,125,157,

BICKLEY, Joseph 157
BICKNALL, Sam'l 309
BIDW'T, Edward 296
BIGG, Thomas 192
BIGGER, Joseph 261,263
BIGGINS, Arthur 222
BIGGS, Jacob 101; John 190
BIGHTON, Richard 210
BILBAND, James 106
BILL, Robert 149
BILLEBO, __ 266
BILLET, Francois 264
BILLING, Edward 305
BILLINGTON (Bellington) Benjamin 216; Mary 134; Robert 216
BILLOT, Catharine 265; John 228
BILLOTT, William 228
BILLOPS, BILLUPS, George 67, 79,144
BIMMS, Christopher 172
BINAM, BINEHAM (Byneham, Bynum), James 80,83,86,90, 98,210
BINCHAM, John 210
BINE, Edmund 149
BINFORD, James 96
BINGLEY, James 172
BIRCHETT, Edward 222; Robert 222
BIRD (Byrd) Robert 149; Widow 134; William 24,95, 98,111,149,157,289,290,295, 296,323
BIRKET, John 106
BISHOP, John Sr. 222; John Jr. 222; Robert 161; William 192
BISWELL, Thomas 201
BISWICK, Richard 314,315
BIVANS (Bevins,Bevens) Wm. 32
BIZELL, John 111
BLACK, George 172; John 281, 287; Mr. 22,32,44
BLACKBOURNE, BLACKBUN,
BLACKBURN, Capt. 147; Rowland 163; William 210
BLACKISTON, BLACKISTONE, Argail 135; Thomas 186
BLACKLEY, Robert 131; Wm. 172
BLACKMAN, William 216
BLACKNALL, Mr. 35,39,46
BLACKSON, John 228
BLACKSTONE, Peter 314,315; Robert 314
BLACKWELL, James 163; James Jr. 163; Robert 59,70; Samuel 50, 38; William 216
BLADEN, William 246
BLAIR, BLAIRE, Archibald 24,41,53; Arthur 34; Henry 27; John 41,42; James 20,24,30,34,42,47,56,242, 250,251,258,267; Mr. 41,53; Rev. James 20,30,42; Richard 28; Samuel 56; Thomas 44
BLAISS, Mrs. 131
BLAKE, Anne 132; Arthur 192; Elias 124; George 132; John 124; Joseph 286,292; William 149,219; William Jr. 149
BLAKEY, Thomas 132,270
BLALOCK, John 164
BLANCH, William 192
BLANCHARD, Benjamin 199
BLANCHET, John 149
BLAND, Giles 235; Henry 149; Richard 9,11,79,108,222,253,281, 285,289; Sarah 210; Theodorick 1
BLANKITT, Henry 172
BLANKS, BLANKES, Henry 172; Richard Sr. 161; Richard Jr. 161; Thomas 161
BLATHWAIT, William 20
BLECKERN, BLENKERN, John 314,315
BLEDSOE, William 39
BLEIGH, James 285
BLENHAM, John 314
BLESSINGTON, John 204
BLEWFORD, Thomas 131
BLEWIT, Daniel 261
BLICO, Christopher 210
BLIGH, Abraham 300,303; Charles 277, 279,295
BLIGHT, James 300
BLIGHTON, George 9,11; Thomas 64
BLITCHODIN, Thomas 222
BLOCKAM, John 125
BLOUET, __ 266
BLOW, Richard 95,104
BLUDWORK, Joseph 119
BLUMPTON, Henry 202
BLUNDAL, BLUNDALL,BLUNDELL, Brian 294; Bryan 287,297,306
BLUNT, Thomas 64,65,68,69,73,80, 83,85,90,101,102,210
BOARRU, Jean 264
BOBBY, Thomas 234
BOBOE, BOBO, Elizabeth 108,157
BOCUS, Reynold 149
BODY, William 208
BOGNAN, __ 266
BOHANNAH, John 143; Joseph 143
BOHANNON, Dunkin 75,143
BOISSEAU, James 267
BOISSON, Jean 264
BOISTEAU, James 149

BOLLARD, __ 266
BOLLING, Colonel 222; George 28; John 2,3,10,13,23,46,68,71,77, 82,103,108,109,216; John Jr. 34,46; Robert 1,9,11,22,28,32, 39,44,51,68,72,77,79,81,82,84, 85,216,295,323; Robert Sr. 79; Robert Jr. 79,80,81,82,83,85, 86,87,88,89; Stith 28,40
BOLLITHO, John 27
BOLTON, Henry 143, Richard 192, William 192
BON, Louys 264
BONAN, __ 172
BOMARD, Catharine 264
BONAM, Samuel 38
BONAMY, Andrew 293; Peter 293, 314,315
BOND, Abell 305; Francis 188, 306; John 149,203; Richard 202; William 192,323
BONHAM, John 172
BONN, James 35
BONNEY, John 107
BONNY, Richard 191
BONWELL, John 101; Thomas 128
BOOKER, Capt. 147; Edward 34; James 250; Mary 141; Richard 10,13,117,180,183,269, 283; Rolp 250
BOOKEY, Edward 210
BOOTH, Alderman 233; George 104; James 257,288,289; John 126, 191; Joseph 200; Thomas 33,46, 103; Widow 134
BORABY, Peter 315
BORDEN, Benjamin 118
BORER, George 228
BOROUGH (Brough) Coleman 12
BORUM, Edward 144
BOSELL, William 290,307
BOSSE, Francois 264
BOSSARD, __ 266
BOSTOCK, John 163; William 163
BOSWELL, Dorothy 146; Joseph 146, William 22,182,295,296
BOSWICK, Richard 276
BOTMAN, Harman 161
BOTTOM, John 216
BOTTOMEY, Stith 5
BOUCHER, John 94
BOUCHET, Jean 264
BOUGHAM, BOUGHAN (Baughan) Henry 80,86,91; James 2,7,12, 67,68,77,88,95,99,102,269; John 94; Susanna 94
BOUGHER, Phillip 210
BOURGOIAN, Joseph 264
BOYER, Jaques 264
BOULES, Thomas 127
BOULMOR, Thomas 180
BOULT, Roger 178
BOURN, BOURNE, Andrew 120,198; George 149; John 134; Wm. 163
BOUSH (Bush), Alexander 27; George 110; Max. 38,50,51; Samuell 2,3,4,6,8,16,26,37,43, 50,107,288; Samuell Jr. 37.38,50
BOWAN, Griffith 30
BOWDEN, Thomas 149
BOWDOIN, John 306;Peter 50
BOW, BOWE, BOWES, BOWS, Henry 80, 82,85,97,164,203; Nicholas 301
BOWER, William 172
BOWERS, Arthur 134; John 192
BOWGER, John 185
BOWKER, Ralph 24,149
BOWLES, Henry 192; John 164,182; Robert 149
BOWLING, John 244
BOWMAN, Edward 109,216; Henry 208; John 109; John Jr. 216; Len 216; Peter 134; Samuel 314,315
BOYD, BOYT, Edward 111; John 314, 315; Thomas 201; Thomas Jr. 111
BOYES, Samuel 291,292,299
BOYKIN, Edward 65,68,73,80,82,85, 90,95,98,105,205
BOYNE, Epapap 199
BRACKITT, Thomas 192
BRADBURN, Richard 134
BRADBURY, George 163
BRADED, William 314
BRADENHAM, Robert 91
BRADFORD, John 126; Richard 2,4, 9,11,22,161,289; William 128
BRADHURST, John 22
BRADINGHAM, Robert 164
BRADLEY, BRADLY, Benjamin 272;295, 323; Henry 204,284; John 80,83, 86,87; Joseph 101,161; Richard 203; Robert 299; Thomas 87,164
BRADY, Joseph 199
BRAFORD, __ 152
BRAGG, James 209
BRAINES, Benjamin 280; James 280
BRAISSEUR, John 202
BRAKINS, *** 135
BRALEY, Hugh 207; William 186
BRAMBLE, Henry 192
BRANCH, Benjamin 216; Chris. 216; Francis 205; James 111,216; John 205; Matthew 74,216,220; Thomas 216
BRAND, Richard 173,301
BRANSDON, Robert 291
BRANSON, Francis 228; Thomas 118
BRANT, Hugh 5

BROWN, BROWNE, Samuell 72,93, 103,263; Thomas 135,149,228; Widow 192; William 10,28,34, 40,52,65,68,72,73,87,90,100, 102,103,105,134,172,181,192, 205,210,247,270; William Jr. 2,18,40
BROWNING, William 284
BRUCE, Abraham 92,192; John 192
BRUER (Brewer) Shackfield 172
BRUH, Major Samuel 192
BRUIN, William 199
BRUMLEY, William 144
BRUN, George le 288
BRUNSKILL, John 44; Mr. 48
BRUSH, Richard 134
BRUTNALL, Richard 134
BRUTON, James 210
BRUXE, Anne 123
BRYAN, BRYON, Charles 164; James 206; John 172,201,209; Lewis 201; Morgan 118,119, 120,122; Robert 71,109,147; Roger 192; William 201
BUBB, John 282,284
BUCK, John 189,300; Thomas 179
BUCKARD, Stephen 106
BUCKEN, William 192
BUCKLIN, Benjamin 300
BUCKLEY, BUCKLY, John 164; Joseph 281,300
BUCKNALL, Samuel 309
BUCKNER, John 41,55,71,102; Philip 8,255; Richard 6,21, 23,44,93,103,134; Thomas 5, 6,10,13,23,44,134,141; William 9,19,21,140,146,179, 239,248,260,261,270,286,291, 308,313
BUD, Thomas 127
BUGG, Samuel 164
BUICHAM, John 210
BUKLY, John 164
BULKLEY, Benjamin 163
BULL, Henry 192; Thomas 192; Robert Sr. 192
BULLAUGH, John 119
BULLARD, Benjamin 302; John 146; Robert 102
BULLINGTON (Billington) __ 216; Benjamin 216; John 221; Robert 216
BULLOCK, Edward 164; George 190,228; John 149; Mary 210; Richard 163; Thomas 208
BUMPUS, Robert 164
BUNBURY, William 18,252
BUNCH, John 164; Paul 157
BUNDIKE, Richard 127
BUNNELL, Hezickiah 210
BUNTING, William 129
BURBANCK, BURBANK, Timothy 295, 303,308
BURBRIDGE, Richard 296; Robert 37
BURCH, Henry 157; John 149; William 149
BURDEN, Benjamin 121
BURFORD, Edward 278,314,315; John 278,308,314,315; Wm. 149
BURGE, Thomas 101
BURGES, Charles 36,48; Edward 157; George 192; Mrs. 316
BURGESS, Stephen 186; William 149
BURGONY, John 216
BURIDGE, BURRIDGE, John 272,306, 312; Robert 305
BURKETT, Thomas 164
BURLOWE, Philip 222
BURNELL, Edward 163; Francis 10; Mary 163
BURNET, BURNETT, John 135,164; Thomas 251; Thomas Jr. 134,135
BURNHAM, John 236,308; Thomas 180
BUROCKE, John 126
BURREL, Suprian 157
BURRELL (Burwell) Lewis 241,243
BURROSS, BURROUGH, BURROUGHS, BURROWS, BURRUS, Benjamin 189; Benoni 9,17,254; Chris. 51; John 60,69,157; Thomas 157; William 190,216,284,294,295, 297,303,308
BURT, Richard
BURTELL, James 103
BURTON, George 185; Henry 161; Isaac 216; James 145; John 97; Ralph 172; Robert Sr. 68,108, 216; Thomas 127; William 22,32, 38,44,50,129,216
BURWELL, Carter 244; Lewis 34,42, 47,56,61,161,164,172,179,206, 239,240,241,256,292,313; Major 147,157; Mary 163; Mr. 244; Nathaniel 21,23,145
BUSBY, Thomas 68,222
BUSH (Boush) John 102,172; Samuell 67,191,192
BUSHELL, James 250; John 261,262
BUSHILL, Cr. 274
BUSHROD, John 19,269
BUTCHER, John 134
BUTLER, BUTTLER, Caleb 7,19; Elizabeth 204; James 201; John 70,72,134,147,201,222; Lawrence 53; Thomas 59,157; William 6,26,37,49,109,204,222

COLE, COLES, Colonel 185; James 309; John 101,111,199; Michael 286; Richard 172; Robert 127,161; Sillvanus 127; Thomas 305; William 29,40,53, 54,55,56,129,135,235,240,304
COLEMAN, COLMAN, Abraham 272; Daniell 63,99,150; John 75, 141,222,280,283; Joseph 148; Francis Sr. 109,222; Robert 4,12,114,135,201,208,269; Thomas 147,150; William Sr. 109; William Jr. 222
COLLAWNS, William 75
COLLENELL, Owen 126
COLLETT, Jer. 309; Thomas 164
COLLEY, John 192
COLLIER, COLLYER, Bartho. 228; Charles 150,179; Edward 81, 84,87; Elizabeth 81,84,87; Giles 191; John 91,150,211; Joseph 211; Mary 179; Peter 250; Robert 150; Sarah 81,84,87; Thomas 28, 40,108,211
COLLINGS, COLLINS, James 77, 202; James Yard 150; John 125,261,287; William 150,193,201; Zeboth 306
COLLIS, Thomas 145
COLLONE, William 141
COLLSON, Robert 255
COLSTON, Robert 8; William 8
COMAN, William 179
COME, Pierre de 265
COMER, COMERS, Thomas 58,69
COMIGYS, William 245
COMINS, John 190
COMPTON, William 135
COMRIE, William 34,47
CONDELL, __ 150
CONDEN, Thomas 192
CONDUTE, Nathaniel 135
CONIBEARE, Thomas 276
CONLEY, Bartholomew 286; Ignatius 286
CONNELL, Alexander 207
CONNER, CONNOR, CONNERS, John 103; Lewis 75,92,193, 239,281,294,313; Timothy 77,89,91,150
CONNIERS, Henry 40
CONNOLY, Edward 135
CONQUEST, Richard 109
CONSALOMS, William 128
CONSTANTIN, Jean 264
CONWAY, Edwin 25,36,48; Francis 44
CONY, Perog'n 251
COOK, COOKE, Abraham 164; Benjamin 150; Capt. 145; Christopher 27; Elizabeth 210, 211; Giles 23,33,46,145; James 222; John 75,135,150, 280,282,283,286; Mordecai 1, 10,13,75; Mordeccy 23; Reubin 205; Richard 172; Thomas 3,13,23,25,33,36,46,49, 96,141,150,205; Thomas Jr. 150; William 141,186
COOLEY, Charles 182
COOPER, Charles 182; Edward 189; George 1,3,4,16,182,261,270; James 211; John 53,55,192,261, 272; Joseph 69,74,185,199; Philip 145; Richard 135; Samuel 181; Thomas 4,67,135, 172,275,277; Wm. 135,192,282
COPELAND, Christopher 182,261, 262; Francis 199; Henry 199; James 78,101,108,109,202; John 201
COPER, Thomas 128
COPLAND, John 135; Nicholas 135
COPPAGE, John 27
COPPEDGE, John 36
COPPIN, Thomas 288
CORANTE, Pierre 264
CORBAN, George 228
CORBELL, Thomas 203
CORBET, CORBETT, James 293; John 291; Moses 293; Richard 99
CORBIN, Colonel 131; Gawin 10,15, 24,35,48,79,114,115,138,150,239, 270,282,305,313; George 130; John 203; Thomas 79,135,138,268
CORDELL, Richard 148
CORDEY, Thomas 164
CORE, Henry 80,83,86,97,101,201
CORMECK, Michael 228
CORNECK, William 188
CORNEX, John 91; William 2,9
CORNICK, Joel 17; John 5,6,27,38
CORNU, __ 266
CORNWELL, Samuel 95
CORPREW, John 92,101,192; No. 192; Thomas 27,92
COSBY, Charles 172
COSLIN, John 126
COSTEN, Susan 110
COSTIN, Francis 228
COTERILL, COTTERILL, John 314,315
COTTELL, Thomas 192
COTTEN, COTTON, Catherine 150; James 186; John 95,96,105,183, 206; Thomas 211; Walter 211; William 186

DENNIS, DENNISS, DENNISSE, David 257; Richard 6,22, 288; Timothy 190
DENSON, James 70,90,108; John 90,96,107,208
DENT, Thomas 130; Wm. 246
DENTON, Thomas 228,293
DENUS, James 282
DEPREST, Robert 165
DEPTFORD, Hugh 285
DERBY, Daniel Sr. 123; Daniel Jr. 123; Dorman 123
DERICK, Stephen 307
DE SAILLY, Charles 265
DESHAZO, Peter 150
DESNALL, William 193
DEUPUY, Andrew 294
DEVILLARD, Jacob 135
DEWIS, Richard 150
DEWIT, DEWITT, Charles 121; John 121; Martin 121; William 120
DEWS, William 68
DEWY, George 228; Jacob 228
DIAMOND, James 305
DIBBS, John 299
DIBDALE, DIBDALL, John 26,165
DICEY, Jacob 38
DICKASON, Griffeth 110; Thomas 110,157; Wm. 157
DICKS, James 211
DICKENS, Christopher 102; William 129
DIDLACK, John 95
DIDLAKE, James 150
DIGGES, DIGGS, Cole 30,33,40, 42,45,53,97,114,115; Dudley 46,79,179,182,185, 240,241,243; Edward 236; John 144; Mr. 244; Wm. 236
DIGHDON, Isaac 305
DILL, John 308; Joseph 308
DILLAND, Thomas 150
DILLARD, George 150
DILLIARD, Edward 150; Nicholas 150
DILLING, Henry 59
DILLON, Henry 158
DILWORTH, John 307
DIMMOCK, Thomas 150
DINWIDDIE (Dunwiddie)? Mr. 244
DIPFORD, Jonathan 281,287
DISMUKES, William 150
DISON, Nicholas 217
DIX, Isaac 126; John 126
DIXON, Christopher 143; John 48,62,63,193; Michael 229; Nicholas 202,217; Richard 148,180; Thomas 141
DOAGE, James 191
DOBBINS, Daniell 7,12,135
DOBEY, DOBOY, DOBY, Edward 276; John 72,173,223
DOBSON, Edmund 147; Francis 133; John 147; William 147
DOCKER, Edward 71
DOCTON, Thomas 198
DOD, DODD, John 101,165
DODSON, Samuell 276,278; William 217
DODSWORTH, Cuthbert 238
DOE, William 150
DOLE, Erasmus 282
DOLERD, William 165
DOLEY, John 190
DOLLER, Joseph 190
DOLMAN, William 8
DOLSON, Richard 305
DONAPHAN, DONAPHON, DONIPHAN, DONIPHIN, Alexander 4,269; Alex. 8,17,28
DONAS, Arthur 123
DONBARR, Mr. 48
DONBOWE (Denbow) James 277
DORMAR, John 173
DORRELL, Sampson 145,157
DOUGHTY, James 75
DOUGLAS, DOUGLASSE, DOWGLAS, DOWGLASS, DUGLAS, DUGLASS, Charles 217,221; Douglas 59; George 59; James 150; John 180, 223; John Jr. 180; Robert 59, 63,75; Thomas 237; Wm. 102,157
DOSWELL, John 180; John Jr. 180
DOWIE, John 131
DOWING, George 223; John 228
DOWLES, John 205
DOWMAN, John 228
DOWNER, John 89,102,157
DOWNES, DOWNS, Elias 60,97,157; Henry 121
DOWNMAN, John 2; William 17,39,51
DOWS, Jonathan 283,298
DOWTY, Rowland 228
DOYLEY, Cope 186,242
DOYLY, Cope 54,250,251
DRAKE, Henry 306; Richard 90,95, 96; Richard Jr. 108; Thomas 90,95,96
DRANE, John 315
DRASON, Thomas 118
DRAUGHT, Richard 190
DRAWLER, Abraham 205
DRAYTON, Roger 222
DRESDALL, Robert 193
DRESSALL, Timothy 135

DREW, Edward 211; John 96,314, 315; Thomas 10,18,211; William 28
DREWITT, Jonathan 99
DREWRY, DRURY, Charles 2,8,15, 26,37,49,67,202; John 80,83, 86,102,200; Thomas 202; William 204
DREWUTT, John 180
DRUMMOND, Hill 32,134; John 126,173; Richard 22,32, 44,127; Stephen 127; William 9,13,173
DRUMONDS, Joan 60
DRUMONT, John 141
DRYSDALE, Hoh. Hugh 30,259
DUBERRY, Samuell 186
DUCHIMIN (Dachimin) Samuel 83,86,99
DUCK, John 118; Martin 118; William 208
DUCKITT, Abraham 173
DU CLOS, __ 266
DUDDING, Andrew 135
DUDDLESTON, DUDDLESTONE, DUDLESTONE, Sir John 282, 284,298,312
DUDLEY, Ambrose 5,10,13,23; Capt. 143; Christopher 199; James 133,141; Richard 141, 143; Richard Jr. 146; Robert 2,10,15,35,48,132,249; Thomas 132,141,233; William Sr. 233; Wm. Jr. 233
DUETT, Charles 150
DUFFIELD, William 204
DUKE, Henry 1,5,9,13,28,91,165, 173,178,248; Henry Jr. 173, 271; James 24,32; John 74,92, 198; Thomas 135,173,198; Thomas Jr. 92,198
DULLARD, Henry 208
DULLOCK, John 229
DUMARESQ, Elie 288; Elias 293
DUMAS, Jerimiah 165; Jerome 264
DUMFORD, Phillip 91
DUNBAR, Mr. 35; Richard 261
DUNCKLEY, DUNKLEY, John 150; Robert 257,272
DUNCON, David 191
DUNKIN, Thomas 223
DUNLOP, Daniel 314,315
DUNN, DUNNE, Gabriell 262; Henry 182,262; Mrs. 183; William 135,182,261,262
DUNTON, Benjamin 229; John 228; Thomas Sr. 229; Thomas Jr. 229; William 229
DUNWIDDIE (Dinwiddie) Mr. 244
DUPARKS, Thomas 229
DUPEE, Bartholomew 111; Francis 106
DUPRA, Giles 183
DU PYN, Loys 264
DURAND, __ 266
DURDEN (Darden) Jacob 92,209; Stephen 97
DURELL, Thomas 293
DURHAM, Charles 96; James 165; John 102,150
DURRAT, Widow 150
DUSON, Thomas 150
DUTART, __ 266
DUTOUT, __ 266
DU TASTIE, Francois 264
DU TOY, Pierre 264
DUTOY, (Deitoy) Peter 89,97
DUVIVIER, Philippe 264
DUVOLE, John 246
DYATT, Thomas 131
DYER, Benjamin 311; Giles 298; Henry 179; John 126,239,313; Jeffrey 135; Richard 275; William 135,189

EACHOLS, John 151
EALAM, Martin 217; Robert 217
EALES (Eules) John 287
EASE, Peter 126
EASON, John 200; Peter 199; William 199
EAST, Edward 217; Thomas Sr. 217; Thomas 217
EASTER, Grace 145; John 145
EASTES, Abraham 151
EASTHAM, EASTUM, Edward 151; Edward Jr. 151; George 151; Thomas 312
EASTLEY, Robert 76
EATON, John 47,102,178
EBBERY, George 282
EDDING, William 119
EDEY, Henry 305
EDGAR, John 288
EDGCOMB, Robert 278
EDINSON, Benjamin 307
EDLOE, Henry 44; John 32,44
EDMONDS, EDMONS, EDMUND, EDMUNDS, David 229; Elizabeth 173; Howell 28,40,72; Jeremiah 202; John 100,193; Lowell 52; Thomas 181; William 72,90,96,211
EDMONDSON, EDMUNDSON, James 136; Thomas 7,12,136; William 283, 285,313

FLOYD, Berry 229; Charles 27, 229; George 107,161; James 186; John 143; Matthew 229; Morris 71
FOCKES, Thomas 128
FOCKNER, William 141
FOGG, Nathaniel 102
FOLK, Richard 202
FOLLETT, Thomas 70
FOLWER, Richard 161
FONSIGH, Thomas 151
FONVILLE, __ 266
FOOLE, Richard 18
FOORD (Ford) John Jr. 158; William 158
FORBES, Alex. 24
FORCURAN, John 106
FORD (Foord) Elias 211; George 211,282; Peter 61, 66; William 98
FORDET, Isaac 265
FOREMAN, John 274,277
FOREST, FORREST, Anne 75, 144; James 217; John 217 Joseph 261
FORGESON, FORGINSON, FORGISON, FORGUSON, Adam 191; John 102,180; Widow 141; William 165
FORSETT, Charles 151
FORSE, James 38,50
FORSTER, John 296
FORTSON, Charles 151
FOSAKER, FOSSAKER(Fassaker) Richard 2,8,18
FOSSETT, William 136
FOSTER (Fawster) Anne 211; Benjamin 72,223; Christopher 211; John 26, 136,284,294,303,308,309; James 144; Joseph 4,5,10, 16,26,37,165,248; Henry 193; Richard 147; Robert 136,229; Thomas 35,48; William 211
FOTHERGILL, Richard 151; Robert 151
FOULCHER, William 146
FOUASSE, Jean 265
FOULSHAM, Anthony 206
FOUNDAINE, John 223
FOUNTAIN, FOUNTAINE, Francis 41,43,47,53,56; James 36,48; John 110; Peter 32,44
FOURE, Daniel 106; Peter 107
FOUVILLE, John 106
FOVACE, Stephen 56,173,179, 250,251
FOWLER, Elizabeth 305; George 191; Godfrey 110,217; James 198,300, 302; Matthew 71; Robert 305; Samuel 141
FOX, Daniel 1; David 7,15; Henry 9,14,36,48,61,113,158,271; John 56,158; Margarett 151; Robert 261; Samuell 269; Thomas 95; William 7,15,173,271
FOXCRAFT, FOXCROFT, Capt 232; Mr. 236
FRAME, Arthur 123
FRANCIS, John 42,183; Robert 145, 148; Thomas 165
FRANCISCO, Daniel 229
FRANK, John 229; Thomas 136
FRANKLIN, FRANKLYN, James Sr. 217,220; James Jr. 217; Nicholas 136; Philip 284;299; Richard 282,284,285,287,299,304, 314; Symon 190
FRASIER, FRAYSEE, FRAYSER, FRAZIER, John 4,13,24,173,247,251,271
FREED, Richard 262
FREEMAN, Alexander 193; George 173; George Jr. 96; Henry 131; James 285,287; John 70,72,80,83, 86,101,108,193,223; Robert 145; William 165
FRENCH, Nicholas 286; Robert 302
FRETH, William 274
FRIMMER, Samuell 204
FRIPS, John 181
FRISBY, James 245
FRITH, Joseph 178
FRIZELL, George 229
FROKE, William 277
FROST, John 118; Thomas 229; William 119,223
FROSTWATER, George 229; William 229
FRY, Joshua 47,56
FRYER, William 92
FULCHER, FULSHER, John 68,92,193
FULGHAM, Nicholas 79
FULLALOVE, Thomas 158
FULLER, Anthony 62,71,113,158; Edward 178
FULLERTON, James 136; Robert 67
FULTON, Michael 310
FURGISON (Ferguson,Forgison) Thomas 193
FURBENDAL, Hope 323
FURNBUSH, William 173

GLASUCK, George 253
GLEAM, John 165
GLEN, James 108
GLOVER, John 136,272;
William 73,99,158
GLOVERS, Thomas 234
GLYN, Widow 208
GOAR, GOARE, GORE,
Daniell 123; John 293,297,
308,314,315
GOATLY, Sarles 301;
Stephen 301
GOBBEE, Edward 132
GODEON, Andrew 234
GODFREY, GODFRY, John 189,
193; Matthew 4,8,16,26,
50,191,193; Waren 193;
William 101
GODNAT, Catharine 264
GODWIN (Goodwin)
Devereux 38; Devorix 229;
Edmund 96,202,209;
Colonel 209; Joseph 6,24,
35,47,207,308; Thomas 6,
26,37,49,98,100,203,300;
Thomas Jr. 49,200; Wm. 207
GOELIGHTLY, GOLITELY,
Hugh 105;223; John 223
GOFFE, Thomas 93
GOGNI, David 229
GOLDEN, John 185
GOLDMAN, GOULDMAN,
Edward 99,269; Francis 7,
12,23,136,140; Thomas 99
GOLDSBOROUGH, Robert 246
GOLDSBY, Thomas 99
GOLLOY (Gallop) Benj. 306
GONTHIER, __ 266
GONTON, John 165
GOOCH, Jane 59; William 42
GOOD, John 151,217,285;
Richard 136; Samuell 217
GOODALL, John 173
GOODGAME, David 223
GOODGER, John 165
GOODIN, Major 158
GOODLOE, George 131;
Henry 39,52
GOODMAN, Henry 92; John 173;
William 211
GOODRICH, GOODRICHE, GOODRICK,
Benjamin 173; Charles 2,9,
11,28,72,80,83,86,206,248;
Edward 28,93,100; John 131;
Major 223; Robert 34,47,102
GOODRING, Alexander 166
GOODSON, Edward 88,100;
John 146
GOODWIN (Godwin), __ 61;
Benjamin 21,92; Elizabeth 181;
Isaac 185; John 9,19,92,261,
268,272,293,308; Mathew 68;
Nicholas 308; Peter 181;
Robert 173; Thomas 110,223,
281,285,289,300; Ursula 204
GOODWYN (Goodwin) Thomas 288,297
GOOSCOTT, John 54
GORD, Richard 223
GORDEN, GORDON, GORDONE,
John 71,198,250,267;
William 30,31,42,43,181
GORMAN, William 129
GORRY, __ 266
GORY, Claude 106
GOSS, Charles 173
GOSTOGAN, Thomas 229
GOSWILL, Abraham 280; Isaac 280
GOTLING, William 166
GOUFAUT, La 266
GOUGE, Jane 69
GOUGH, Alice 151; Hugh 199;
John 60; Ralph 40,53,114;
Thomas 199; William 9,60
GOULD, James 295,301; Price 140
GOULDING, Edward 136; John 136;
William 136
GOURD, Richard 70
GOWER, James 217
GOWING, Edward 143; Thomas 305
GRACE, Thomas 207
GRADY, Philip 145,148
GRAEME, John 52
GRAHAM, Thomas 165
GRANCHARD, Thomas 165
GRANDBERRY, William 204
GRANDY, Robert 285
GRANES, Thomas 274,314,315
GRANGER, John 76,217
GRANT, Daniell 62; William 75,190
GRATHMEE, Owen 148
GRAVATT, Henry 158
GRAVES, John 151,158; Joseph 173;
Robert 151; Thomas 147,158,278
GRAY (Grey), James 125; John 211;
Joseph 151; Samuel 56,151;
Thomas 261; William 6,28,40,52,
211,270; William Jr. 52,88,100,211
GRAYSON, John 52; John Jr. 52
GREEN, Dorcas 141; Edward 165,211,
290; George 136,207; John 72,112,
158,223; Lewis 39,51,223; Lewis
Jr. 28; Richard 201,212; Robert
121,178; Sarah 143; Samuel 140;
Thomas 173,278; Tobias 296;
Widow 143; William 173,208
GREENAWAY, Christopher 145
GREENBERRY, Charles 245

GREENE, John Sr. 229;
Lawrence 71; Thomas 173
GREENFIELD, Francis 165
GREFON, John 193
GREG, GREGG, Thomas 8,18,29
GREGORY (Grigory)
Anthony 4,10,13,146;
Frances 151; Nicholas 173;
Richard 9,14; Roger 89,92
GREGSON, Ann 81,84,86;
James 311; Thomas 75
GRENDALL, Richard 127
GRENDON, Thomas 233,237
GRESHAM, Edward 151;
George 151; John 151;
Thomas 82,84,88,99,151
GRESTHIAN, James 223
GREWELL, Walter 145
GREY (Gray), Abner 136;
Edward 261; John 125;
Thomas 262
GRICE, Aristotle 173;
Peter 229
GRIFFIN, Andrew 105;
Charles 190; Corbin 15;
David 151; Edward 151;
Henry 111; Humphrey 103,
111; James 198,223;
John 77,126,211,313;
Joseph 111; Samuel 16;
Thomas 28,39,51,136,190
GRIFFITH, Benjamin 229;
Jeremiah 229; Richard 223
GRIG, GRIGG, GRIGGS, __ 217,
Anthony 183; Francis 151;
Robert 71; Thomas 1,3;
William 223
GRIGORY (Gregory) Roger 82,85
GRIGSBY, Thomas 52
GRIGSON, Thomas 136,269
GRILLS, Richard 99; Wm. 98,99
GRIMES, GRYMES, (Crymes)
Capt. 132; Charles 39,42,51;
Hustis 211; John 10,15,25,
30,42,49,91,141,239,313;
Mr. 244
GRIMMALL, William 140
GRINLEY, Susannah 141
GRINTO, William 190
GROMORIN, Gilly 101
GROOM, Edward 246
GROSSE, Edward 161
GROUT, John 141
GROVES, Elianor 237; John 104;
Joseph 303; Samuel 81,84,86,
100,186; William 237
GRUCHIE, John 293
GUDVIN, Etienne 264
GUNDRY, James 278; Nathaniel 312
GUNRY, John 277
GUERRAN, GUERRIN, __ 266
GUEST, George 131
GUICHET, Jean 264
GUILSBY, Thomas 173
GUINGS (GUINNEY)? Michael 104
GULLDING, Charles 229
GULLIAN (Gillum) Peter 284
GULSTONE, Joseph 297
GULLY, Richard 211
GUMMS, Anthony 198
GUNDREY, William 144
GUNN, James 161
GUNTER, Edward 124
GURIDGE, Richard 166
GURROW, William 181
GUTCHINS, Joseph 201
GUTHRIE, John 100
GUTTERY, John 151
GUY, James 193; John 193;
Thomas 272; William 314,315
GWALNEY, William 211
GWIN, GWINN, GWYN, GWYNN, GWYNNE,
Capt. 144; Christopher 199;
David 8,17,138,239,269,313;
Edmond 236; Humphrey 236;
John 2,10,13,173,269;
Rowland 74,203

HACHELL, William 93
HACK, George Nicholas 2,8,11,
124,271; Peter 16,27,38,270,
283,293,295,301,306
HACKLEY, Henry 71,77,199
HACKNEY, Widow 132
HACKSLEY, Edward 113
HACKSTEP (Huckstep) Edward 62
HADLEY, Ambrose 209; Dyonisia 173
HAFFIELD (Harvild,Havield,Havild,
Haveild), Luke 204
HAGARD, HAGGARD, David 129;
Nathaniel 40
HAGES, Walter 129
HAGGAMAN, Isaac 229
HAIL, John 136
HAINES, HAINS, Richard 73;
Thomas 2
HAINIE, HAINY, HAYNIE,
John 166; Richard 3,270
HAISELWOOD, HASELWOOD, HAZELLWOOD,
John 166; Richard 166;
Thomas 166; Widow 131
HAISTWELL, E. 257; Thomas 257
HAKINS, Jane 206; Robert 127
HALEY, James 174

HALL, Anne 77; Christopher 312; Duke 189; Edward 218; Francis 230; Isaac 224, John 148,173; Justance 224; Moses 198; Robert 39,51,141; Thomas 189; William 82,85,102
HALLEMAN, HALLIMAN, HALLOMAN, Richard 64; Thomas 64,81,83, 86,97; William 64
HALLET, George 296
HALLIHAM, Morris 227
HALSTEAD (Holsted) John 6
HAM, Richard 65,69,212
HAMBLETON, James 218; John 203
HAMILTON, George 105
HAMLEN, HAMLIN, HAMLYN, Elizabeth 224,281; John 4, 28,77,161,214,223,285,289; Richard 28,224; Stephen 161; Thomas 161; William 39,51
HAMMELL, HAMMILL, Hans 263,287
HAMMOND, HAMOND, Charles 246; John 245,246
HAMNER, Nicholas 174
HAMPTON, John 71,113,158; William 143
HANBY, Charles 229; Daniell 229; John 229; Richard 229
HANCOCK, HANDCOCK, George 5, 27,107; John 212; Robert 104,174,218; Samuel 218; Symon Sr. 188; Symon Jr. 188; Thomas 61,158,202
HAND, Thomas 151
HANDBACKE, William 72
HANDBERRY, ___ 194
HANDEY, HANDY, Samuell 246; William 166
HANDIFORD, John 132
HANELL, Richard 111
HANES, John 141
HANFIELD, Michael 173
HANFORD, Widow 132
HANIE (Hainie,Hainy,Haynie) Richard 2
HANKIN, HANKINS, Charles 166; Richard 314,315
HANSBURGER, John 120
HANSELL, John 185
HANSER, William 136
HANSFIELD, Luke 72
HANSFORD, ___ 236; Charles 9, 19,237; Elizabeth 179,237; John 178; Thomas 179,187, 233,237; William 114,141, 178,253,271
HARBIN, Henry 282
HARDGROVE, William 152
HARDE, Thomas 212
HARDIMAN, HARDYMAN, Francis 32,44; John 9,11,28, 88,224,281,285,289
HARDIN, Thomas 107
HARDING, George 49; William Sr. 288; William Jr. 288
HARDY, Henry 246; Richard 205
HARDYWAY, Thomas 80,82,85,94
HARE, Anne 203; John 37,81,84, 87,92,100,111,203
HARFORD (Hartford) Charles 284,287,305,312; Charles Jr. 298,304; Edward 280,287,305,312; Widow 132
HARGRAVE, Benjamin 194
HARGROVE, Bryan 212
HARLE, John 274,279,313
HARLOW, Andrew 44; John 35; Mr. 48; Thomas 166
HARMANSON, HARMASON, HARMONSON, George 7,17,27,38,229; Henry 229; John 27,229; Matthew 38; Thomas 229; William 7,17,229
HARMON, Elizabeth 161; Henry 136; William 166
HARNEY, Richard 272
HARNISON, Thomas 96
HARPER, John 79,136,141; Thomas 136
HARRALD, HARROLD, Adam 97; Thomas 199
HARRAR, HARROW, Abraham 52
HARRELL, Adam 109; John 109
HARRELLTON, Paul 166
HARRIOT, Samuell 296
HARRIS, HARRISS, Benjamin 166; Edward 80,83,86,96,100,166, 206,209; James 292; John 2, 16,166,194,199,205,233,278, 279; Joseph 182; Mary 218; Matthew 93; Samuel 261; Robert 166; Thomas 166,209, 218; Timothy 218; Richard 34, 46; William 95,97,109,111, 152,166,174,212,309
HARRISON, Alexander 123; Andrew 75,136; Arnell 123; Benjamin 11,13,19,32,44,56, 64,66,68,72,79,81,83,86,90, 110,161,212,241,243,244,248, 284,285,288,290,295,296,298, 301,323; Benjamin Jr. 61, 174,288,289,301; Capt. 73, 270; Col. 223; Daniell 212; Gabriell 224; Henry 5,28,40, 47,51,52,90,99,110,189;

HARRISON, Henry Jr. 31; James 136,224; John 276, 295,323; Matthew 39,40; Nathaniel 10,18,20,30,64, 68,72,73,87,89,97,98,99, 104,212,258,260,289; Robert 178,179; Selby 127; Samuell 261,280,302; Thomas 40,71,73,90,103, 214,224,252,269; William 28, 39,51,174,178,223
HARROD, Thomas 100
HART, __ 152; Edward 8,18,252; George 296; Henry 212; Robert 212; Thomas 72,90, 102,152
HARTFORD (Harford), Charles 285; Edward 285
HARTHORN, Robert 223
HARTNELL, John 297
HARTWELL, Henry 56,233,295, 323; James 284; Richard 194; William 233,234
HARVEY, George 173; John 8; Richard 194
HARVILD, HAVIELD, HAVILD, HAVEILD, Isabel 98; Luke 2,3, 8,15
HARWAR (?) Samuel 137
HARWAY, Thomas 136
HARWOOD, Daniel 123; Humphry 4, 5,8,18,185,261; Joseph 22,161, John 161,185; Peter 136; Philip 275,303; Robert 161; Samuel 22,32,44,161; Samuel Jr. 32,44,98,100; Thomas 9,185; William 29,40, 53,185,238
HASKINS, Edward 218
HASLYITT, William 183
HASSACAR, Richard 252
HASTUP, George 124
HATCHER, Benjamin Sr. 218; Edward Sr. 218; Henry 218; John 218; William Sr. 77, 218; William Jr. 218
HATFIELD, Richard 174; William 166
HATHORN, Robert 70
HATLEY, Benjamin 257,281; George 257
HATTERSBY, Thomas 188
HATTLE, Shard 161
HATTON, John 8,186; Robert 261; Samuell 185
HAULE, Thomas 127
HAUSLAND, Thomas 26
HAWES, George 265; Haughton 166
HAWKES, Jeffry 224
HAWKINS, Gideon 230; John 23,136, 174,230,245,246,282,283; John Jr. 230; Thomas 182,262;
HAWTHORN, John 96
HAY, John 138; William 203
HAYDEN, HAYDON, Charles 277; John 58,69,158
HAYE, Gilbert 224
HAYES, Adams 189; George 280; Peter 205; Owen 54; Robert 180; Thomas 33,53,143; William 194
HAYFIELD, HAYFEILD, James 62,69; William 158
HAYLE, HAYLES, John 151,152; Joseph 62,151,158
HAYLEY, Daniel 162
HAYMAN, HEYMAN, HYMEN, Peter 260,281
HAYMAND, Thomas 310
HAYNES (Haines,Hains) Nicholas 161; Richard 280,301; Thomas 3,8,18,29,38,40,51,64, 68,73,185; Thomas Jr. 29; William 63,152
HAYS, Ann 75
HAYWARD, HAYWOOD, Francis 41,53; Henry 94,102; Hugh 309,312; John 100; Thomas 145,152
HEABERD, William 108
HEALE, George 4,25,36,48
HEARON, Matthew 276
HEARD, Henry 263; William 269
HEART, Thomas 212
HEATH, HEITH, Adam 77,212,224; Adam Jr. 98; Abraham 108; James 191; Samuel 38,50; Thomas 92; William 111,223
HEDGMAN, Peter 52
HEDGPATH, HIDGPATH, HODGPATH, John 201; John Jr. 82,85,99
HEIT, HIGHT, HYTE, John 166; John Jr. 118; John Wm. 121; Joseph 120; Just. 122
HELME, William 224
HEMINGWAY, Mary 148
HENDERSON, James 59,69; John 152,179,229; Widow 152; William 152
HENDLEY, Charles 189
HENDON, William 152
HENDRICK, Hance 69; Hans 158; Thomas 59; William 93
HENLAND, John 194
HENLEY, John 174; Leonard 174
HENNING, Arthur 152
HENSLEY (Honsley) Richard 182
HENSTONE, Price 313

HOLLICOM, John 294
HOLLIER, Simon 6,22,33,45,183
HOLLIMAN, HOLLOMAN, HOLLYMAN, HOLYMAN, Christopher 205; James 174; Josiah John 106; Mary 212; Richard 71,73,212; Thomas 205,212; William 73
HOLLINGWORTH, HOLLINSWORTH, Abraham 122; Henry 212
HOLLINS, John 158
HOLLIS, William 246
HOLLOWAY, Edward 223,224; John 20,21,22,24,31,41,43, 53,104; William 151
HOLLOWELL, Elener 194; John 194; Joseph 194
HOLLYGOOD, Thomas 194
HOLMAN, Daniel 120; Orphans 187; William 17
HOLMES, Edward 74; John 186; Richard 218; Thomas 218
HOLSTED (Halstead) Henry 194; John 26,194
HOLT, Benjamin 276,278; David 79; Elizabeth 186,212; Jerimah 147; Jerimah Jr. 147; John 28,212; Joseph 104,152; 242; Samuell 296; Thomas 1,2, 3,10,18,212,214,270; Wm. 212
HOLYCROSS, Joseph 224
* HOME, George 52
HOMES, Edward 201; George 151; Walter 119
HOMEWOOD, Thomas 246
HONE, Theoph. 236
HONEY, James 151
HONSLEY (Hensley) Richard 182
HOOD, Abraham 298; John 118, 174; William 199
HOOGLAND, Christopher 289
HOOK, HOOKE, Abraham 293;305; John 275,277,279; Michael 174
HOOKER, Edward 174; Robert 92
HOOKES, John 68
HOOMES, George 151
HOPE, George 125
HOPER, Thomas 40
HOPKINS, John 74,91,174,290; Joseph 268; William 30,166
HORBETT, Thomas 194
HORKEEY, John 166
HORMAN, Robert
HORNE, Matthew 279; Richard 212; William 132,199
HORNING, Robert 200
HORSLEY, Rowland 166
HORSELL, Elias 293
HORSEPOOLE, William 309
HORSTEAD, Henry 94
HORTON, Daniell 199; Thomas 105; William 7
HOSE, Elias 52
HOSKINS, Hugh 190
HOSLEP, John 203
HOUCHINS, Charles 93
HOULD, David 136
HOULGHAN, Nicholas 207
HOULT, Richard 136
HOUSBURROUGH, Morris 152
HOUSE, Job 160; John 183
HOUSS, HOUSSLER, Thomas 111,204
HOW, HOWE, Alex. 141, ** 136
HOWARD, Allen 45; Cornelius 246; Hugh 147; Jacob 310,312; James 96,161,200,203; John 173; Peter 152; Robert 294; Samuell 246; Thomas 101; William 141, 181,233
HOWDEE, John 208
HOWDEN, William 152
HOWELL, James 9,239,281,313; John 93,224,278; Joseph 307; Samuel 141; Thomas 71,206, 224; William 212
HOWERTON, Thomas 136,152
HOWES, HOWSE, Job 10,61,166
HOWLE, John 166; John Jr. 166
HOWLETT, William 144
HOWSEN, HOWSON, John 16,27, 270; Leonard 16,50,270; Robert 21,27
HOYAT, Robert 52
HUBARD, HUBBARD, HUBBERD, HUBERD, HUBBERT, John 166; Ralph 178; Robert 8,18,185,187; Richard 141; William 185
HUBERT, Matthew 174
HUCKSTEP (Hackstep) Edward 71,158
HUDLEY, John 285
HUDNELL, Widow 204
HUDSON, Charles 34,46,80,83,86,97; Christopher 99; George 174; Leonard 174; Richard 72,87,100, 224; Robert 218; Thomas 136; William 129,136,173

* George Home, George Hume. The name is written in both ways; one in the Virginia records, the other in English copies. However, the difference is not due to careless penmanship, as "Hume" is pronounced "Home" in Scotland; both refer to the same man, and the variation is a matter of phonetics.

HUES, HUGHS, HUGH, HUGHES, Edward 68,194,218; Geo. 173; John 166,309; Mr. 46; Rees 166; Rice 102; Robert 166; Thomas 33,309; Wm. 307
HUESTON, Levinus 293,297,308
HUGHLET, HUGHLETT, Thomas 27,38
HUGO, __ 266
HUGON, __ 266
HUIMENT, Robert 105
HULING, John 294
HULL, John 125; Richard 27,141
HULLETT (Hughlett)? John 194
HULSCLAW, Jacob 120
HULYN, Jaques 264
HUMFORT, Hugh 212; William 212
HUMFREY, HUMPHREY, HUMPHRIE, Evan 212; Joe 136; Nicholas 314,315
HUNDLEY, HUNLEY, James 143; John 143; Philip 143; Richard 143; Timothy 143
HUNINGS, Phillip 292
HUNKINS, John 303
HUNT, Anne 233; Christopher 288; Gawton 38; George 22,88,107, 218; Godfrey 202,207,209; Groton 230; John 27,88,94,101, 161,180,230,262; Lawrence 96; Thomas 73,81,83,86,88,97,100, 230; William 4,9,64,65,68,70, 72,73,87,93,152,161,174,212,233
HUNTER, Elizabeth 81,84,86; Nicholas 74,81,84,86,92,203; William 8,15,45,68,99,190, 201,209
HUNTON, Daniel 143
HURSLEY, Richard 261
HURST, John 246; William 145, 289,310
HURT, John 62,63,79,109,158; William 70,71,158; William Jr. 59,158
HUSBANDS, Jane 60; Thomas 60
HUTCHING, HUTCHINGS, HUTCHINS, HUTHINS, Charles 245; Francis 87, 93; Garrott 124; Nicholas 71, 218,307; Richard 208; Robert 277
HUTCHINSON, Robert 8,11,126; William 158
HUTSON, William 262
HUTT, Gerrard 7,19
HUTTINGTON, John 125
HUTTON, George 166; Thomas 136
HYDE, John 268,272; Robert 179; William 161
HYERD, Thomas 212
HYLAM, Thomas 121
HYLAND, Richard 120

ILAND, Richard 110
ILES, Frances 237; John 203,237
IMBER, __ 266
IMBERT, Jean 264
INCH, John 174
INGE, Vincent 158
INGLES, INGLIS, James 35,47; Mongo 5,24,56,94; Mungo 174, 179
INGRAM, John 27,299,303; Roger 205
IRBY, Edmund 70,72; Edward 224; Joshua 224; William 161
IRWIN, Alexander 47,56; Henry 114
ISAACS, John Jr. 230
ISABELL, ISBELL, William 60,158
IVES, John 194; Timothy 194; Timothy Jr.194
IVESON, Abraham Sr. 145
IVEY, IVIE, IVY, Adam 224; George 194; Gilbert 110; John 105; Robert 181; Thomas 88,92
IZARD, Francis 166

JACKMAN, Edward 18; Joseph John 4,88,212
JACKSON, Andrew 250; Charles 20,37; Christopher 49,273; Elizabeth 174; Francis 314, 315; George 147,186; James 224,284; John 44,105,230; Jonah 230; Jonas 129; Joseph 257; Margery 92; Ralph 218,224; Richard 174; Robert 180; Sarah 191; Symon 194; Thomas 77,166, 224,296; William 55,178
JACOB, JACOBS, Abraham 67, 230; Phillip Sr. 230; Richard 230; Thomas 67,310
JACQUELIN, JAQUELIN, JAQUELINE, JAQUILIN, Edward 4,5,6,24,34, 47,174
JAMES, __ 236; Elisha 283,293, 296,305,312,319; Henry 183; Joan 230; John 191,274,277, 296; Jonathan 125,158; Robert 21; Thomas 38
JAMESON, JAMSON, James 6,29; John 218

JORDAN, JORDEN, JORDIN,
Margarett 204; Matthew 205;
River 215; Robert 203,263;
Thomas 4,26,37,49,203,207,
237; Thomas Jr. 37; Wm. 178
JOSEPH, ___ 266
JOSLIN, James 188
JOSSEY, James 198
JOUANY, John 71
JOUIDON, Marie 265; Symon 265
JOURNEY, William 137
JOUX, Benjamin de 250;
Mr. de 266
JOVANY, Jean 265
JOWLES, Henry 245
JOY, JOYE, Henry 224;
Thomas 188
JOYCE, John 91,194
JOYNER, JOYNES, Bridgman 73,
90,101,207; Bridgman Jr. 90,
95; Edmund 230; Edward 185,
230; James 105; John 104;
Major 230; Nehemiah 106;
Theophilus 90,96,111,112,
207; Thomas 104,206
JUDKINS, Samuell 212;
William 212
JUNIPER, Major 236
JURDAN, George 212;
Richard 212
JUSTICE, JUSTIS,
Justinian 161; Ralph 127

KAINE, KAINES, John 121
Richard 194
KABBALL, William 45
KALLANDER, Timothy 152
KANADAY, Francis 21
KAVENAUGH, KAVANAH,
Arthur 104,224
KAY, Robert 233
KEARNY, James 105
KEATE, William 206
KEATON, KEETON, John 204;
William 98
KEBLE, Walter 144
KEELEY, George 202
KEELING, KEELEING, Adam 188;
George 4,10,16,26,167;
John 188; Thomas 27,191
KEENE, KEEN, John 38; Wm. 200
KEETCH, James 245
KEITH, Mr. 46
KELLEBY, James 263
KELLY, KELLEY, John 100,142;
William 91
KEMBROW, KEMBRO (Kimbro)
John 102,167; John Jr. 97,
102,167
KEMP, Colonel 133,144;
George 51,91; James 22,188;
John 188; Matthew 2,3,10,15,
25,36,49,235,249; Peter 2,13,
23,146,160; Richard 4,131;
Thomas 144; William 23,148
KENDALL, John 32,44; Richard
178,218; William 5,27,130,
230; William Jr. 27
KENION, Jonas 287
KENLERISE, Symon 159
KENNEN, KENNON, Elizabeth 218;
Richard 34,46,89; William 23,
46,110
KENNER, KENNOR (Konnor)
Matthew 50; Mr. 52; Richard
305,306; Rodham 1,249,271,
295,305,306
KENNEY, KENNY, William 37,49
KENNIFF, Darby 152
KEOCH, James 245
KERBY, Henry 137
KERLE, William 202
KERNEY, KERNY, Barnaby 37,49,203
KERSEY, Thomas 97
KERTCH, Dorothy 146
KEY, Robert 10,14,137
KEYSER, Timothy 268,272
KIBBEE, William 132
KIDD, Thomas 131
KIGAN, Mary 212
KILLAM, Edward 123; Richard 126;
William 128
KILLINGWORTH, William 212
KILMAN, Thomas 245
KILLY, John 125
KILPIN, KILPING, William 88,102
KIMBRO (Kembro, Kembrow) John 79
KIMPLAND, James 284
KINAMONT, Ambrose 245
KINDER, Thomas 200
KINCHIN, KINHIN, KINLIN,
William 35,47,72,88,98,104
KINDRICK, John 145
KING, Alexander 60; Daniell 87,
91,152; Edward 152; Elizabeth
167; Eusebius 224; Henry 70,
72,200,224; Jane 79; John 2,
16,22,33,45,69,108,152,200,
207,224,282; Julien 200;
Michael 200; Robert 60,158,
209; Samuel 293; Thomas 69,
79; William 200
KINGSON, John 141

KINK, Anne 152
KINKEAD, Lewis 294
KINNERY, James 121; Thomas 121
KINSBROW (Kembrow) John 61
KIPPAX, Peter 28,251,267
KIRBY, Robert 180; Thomas 88, 96,180
KIRKHAM, William 302
KIRKLAND, Richard 224
KIRKMAN, Richard 42
KIRRY, Elias 246
KIRLE, Joseph 280,306
KITTERELL, Jonathan 198
KITTSON, __ 148; Richard 127
KITSON, Richard 22
KNETON, Hugh 255
KNIBB, Samuell 218; Solomon 218
KNIGHT, Edmund 301; Henry 143; Isaac 305,309; James 198; John 230; Simon 109
KNIPE, Rand. 272
KNOTT, Gilbert 276; James 202; William 69,212
KNOWLES, Capt. 143; Dorothy 152; Sands 10,13,233,234
KNOWSTARP, __ 174
KONNOR (Kenner,Kennor) Rodham 7,16,270
KYMBAL, KYMBALL, Charles 31,43

LACEY, LACY, LASY, Mary 212; John 137; Joseph 272; Thomas 167; William 159,167
LA COUGON, Pierre 264
LADD, William 218
LADDON, Joseph 309
LADWELL (Lodwell,Ludwell, Ludwall), Philip 256
LAFEAVOUR, Isaac 107
LAFEIT, Isaac 103
LAFFOON, John 174
LAFORCE, Ren. 45,218
LAGG, William 162
LA GOUFAUT, __ 266
LAILLER, LAILOR, Francis 130; Luke 230
LAINER, Robert 96
LAIS, Henry 184
LAMB, Hannah 180
LAMBESDON, Abraham 123
LAMBKIN, John 204
LAMONT, LAMMOUNT, Edward 27,92
LAMSEY, Henry 310
LANCASTER, Robert 212
LAND, Brewer 185; Edward 189; Francis 38,51; John Loft 125; Lindsey 144; Woodman 186
LANDON, Thomas 10
LANDRUM, James 137; John 120,137
LANDY, James 105
LANE, LANES, Benjamin 147; Daniell 191; John 278; Joseph 87,99,101; Robert 71, 194; Thomas 167,212,268,270, 272,307,323; Thomas Jr. 212; Valentine 147
LANEERE, George 212
LA NEVE (Leneve) William 31
LANG, Mary 212
LANGFORD, John 153
LANGHONRE, John 40,53; Orphans 185
LANGLEY, LANGLY, LAUNGLEY, Thomas 69,194; William 4,8, 16,26,68,194
LANGSTON, John 58,59
LANIER, Robert 88
LANKFORD, Thomas 95
LANSON, Anthony 240
LANTHORN (Linthorne) Thomas 295
LANYON, Thomas 309
LAPITER, John 204; William 204
LARD, John 278
LARKHAM, John 199
LAROUX, John 289
LARRENCE, LARRANCE (Lawrence) John 204
LARY, James 125
LASCELLE, Mary 146
LASHER, Thomas 281
LASHLEY, LASHLY, LASLEY, Patrick 68,85,212; Walter 99
LASISTER (Lassiter) John 68
LASSELLS, Edward 238
LASSITER (Lasister) Robert 198; William 74
LATANE, LATTAME, Lewis 23,33, 114,137,250,267; Mr. 45
LATHAM, William 182
LATIN, John 178
LATON, Reubin 167
LATTIMORE, Edward 183
LAUGHAN, David 255
LAUGHTER, John 212
LAUNDEY, Jeremiah 247
LA TOIX, __ 266
LAURET, Pierre 264
LAURIEN, William 291
LA VIFUE FAURE, __ 265
LAVERCOMBE, William 298
LAVILLIAN, John 106
LAW, James 167; John 137
LAWLEY, Patrick 199
LAWRENCE, LAWRANCE (Larrence) __ 236; George 109,201;

LAWRENCE, LAWRANCE, Henry 92, 200; James 162,201; John 72, 89,101,206,230; Matthew 152; Richard 74,111,174,200; Robert 70,201,203,208; Thomas 111,313
LAWREY, James 200
LAWSON, Anthony 9,54,190,248; George 298; John 167,181; Nicholas 167; Rowland 25; Thomas 17,254,302
LAWTON, Claude 137
LAYCOCK, Richard 274,279
LAYFIELD, George 246
LAYWELL, Thomas 277
LEA, LEE, LEIGH, LIEGH, Charles 2,16,38,50; Edward 167; Francis 205,272; Hancock 16,119,130,260; Henry 41,53; Hugh 104,224; James 257; John 35,48,97, 152,159,201; Mary 77; Mr. 244; Peter 108; Richard 27,38,50,141,235, 239,249,260,269,282,283, 295,313; Robert 237; Samuel 108; Thomas 6,21,25, 30,36,41,42,53,131; William 9,14,56,63,102,152, 178,249,256
LEAD, Amos 99,110; Wm. 97
LEADBETTER, LEADBITER, Francis 224; John 72,107, 224
LEAK, William 167
LEAR, LEARE, John 26,37,105, 236
LEARL, Joseph 276
LEATHERBONY, Charles 123
LEATHERBURY, Perry 126
LE BRUN, George 288
LEENOIR, John 224
LEECH, Joseph 279
LE FEBURE, __ 266
LEFTWICH, Thomas 153
LEGGETT, LEGATT, John 125,190
LEGRAN, James 88
LEHARDY, Charles 288
LEMESURIER, Leonard 293
LEMON, Elizabeth 152; James 189
LEMPREERE, James 293
LENEVE (La Neve) William 47
LENKEN, Heritage 272
LENNON, James 54
LENTON, William 194
LEONARD, LENARD, Daniel 81,83, 86,92
LESNARD, Jean 264
LESPLAH, Peter 167
LESTER, Dareus 218; John 31, 43; William 7,15
LESTRANGE, Thomas 167
LETTEVE, William 34
LETTS, Arthur 152
LEUSQUE, Marie 264
LEUVEAU, Moyse 264
LEVERCONE, __ 138
LEVERMORE, Phillip 167
LEVERITT, Robert 137
LEVETT, Francis 257,308; Richard 257,308
LEVIMA, John 194
LEVINGSTONE (Livingston) John 152,153
LEVRAUX, __ 266
LEWELLAIN, LEWELLING (Llewellen) Daniell 9; Widow 185
LEWGIR, Samuel 281
LEWIS, Abraham 280,284; Charles 37,49; David 120, 122,152; Edward 75,141,152; Henry 262; John 1,10,16,20, 21,46,91,148,152,167,179, 236,244,256,258; Joseph 313; Nicholas 141; Richard 107, 208; Robert 49,127,230; Thomas 53,167,224; William 129,218; Zachary 160
LIDDALL (Lyddall) George 167
LIDE, LIDIE, Robert 98,174
LIECHFIELD, William 129
LIGGATT, William 297
LIGGON, LIGON, Elizabeth 218; Hugh 218; Mary 218; Matthew 82,85; Richard 1,13,79,80, 81,82,83,84,85,86,87,88,89, 218; Richard Jr. 82,85
LIGHTFOOT, Francis 21,24,30, 32,102,258; George 52; Goodrich 39,52,117,121; Henry 24; John 12,13,16,18, 19,140,167,174,248; Mr. 244; Philip 9,13,41,174,235,260, 271,281; Richard 53
LILBURN, Alexander 188
LILLEY, Edward 277
LILLINGTONE, Benjamin 174
LILLY, LILLIR, Samuel 291, 294,306
LIMA, Robert 118
LIME, David 263
LIMPANY, John 261
LINDSEY, LINDSAY, LINSEY, Caleb 143; Jeremiah 82,85, 89,103; Joseph 167; Thomas 311; William 167

MARINEX, Hugh 145; John 145
MARKHAM, Lemuel 19; Lewis 2,7
Thomas 168
MARKS, Mathew 100,225
MARLER, Elizabeth 200
MARLOW, Thomas 67
MARR, George 168; John 159
MARRAW, Dennis 175
MARSHALL, MARSHAL (Marchall)
Daniell 306; George 230;
Humphry 4,5,10,14,207;
John 27,125,230,275,277,300;
Mary 207; Thomas 38,50,232;
William 291
MARSTON, Thomas 175;
William 6,24,34,174
MARTIN, __ 266; Cordelia 153;
Elizabeth 153; Henry 205;
James 168; Jacob 294,301,
306; John 44,104,106,137,
144,153,168,225,277,278;
Martin 167; Michael 263;
Nicholas 48; Thomas 7,15,
167,239,313; William 168,188
MARVELL, Thomas 162
MASH, George 94
MASEY, MASIE (Massey)
Dade 52; Peter 168
MASK, John 168
MASNIBRED, Roger 183
MASON, Edward 202; French 40,521
George 1,2,4,8,16,18,29,40,
195,249,252,255,269; George Jr.
5,6,29; James 10,18,48; John
40,52,104,107; Lemuel 8,16,
188,195,237,248; Rebecca 75;
Thomas 8,168,190,195,202;
Widow 132
MASSAN, __ 266
MASSIE, MASSEE, MASSEY,MASSY,
Charles 49; Dade 29,40,52;
Peter 67; Thomas 37,49
MASSENDAU, Rene 264
MASTERS, Thomas 295
MASTIN, MASTEN, Elizabeth 142;
Thomas 274
MATHEWS, MATTHEW, MATTHEWS,
Baldwin 9,19,179,263;
Benjamin 137; Edmund 212;
Edward 153,218; Hugh 104;
James 107,225; John 230;
Jonathan 268,293,300,302,
308; Mr. 55; Owen 77;
Richard 137; Samuel 4,5,24,
234; William 128
MATHIAS, Matthew 111,190,194
MATTICKS, Thomas 308
MATTLOW (Muttlow) James 168;
John 175
MATTOONE, MATON, MATTON,
__ 266; Anthony 106,107,265
MAULDIN, MAULDING, Richard 108
MAUND, William 79,195
MAUNDER, MAUNDES (Manders)
James 22,44
MAXEN, Benjamin 272
MAY, MAYS, MAYES, Henry 74,89,
111; John 75,82,84,89,94,
100,102,153,225; Thomas 153;
William 72,73,225; Matthew 89
MAYBANK, William 68,93,159
MAYBERRY (Maberry) Francis 95
MAYFIELD, Robert 137
MAYO, MAYHO, John 191;
Joseph 34,46; Valentine 71,131;
William 34,45,90,95,206
MAZEL, __ 266
McCARTY (Marcartee) Daniel 4,5,
21,53; Dennis 52
McCLANAHAN, McCLENAHAN, McCLENAN,
McCLENAHAN; McCLONAHAM,
David 51; M't. 302;
Nathaniel 290,307;
William 38,258
McDONNELL, John 159
McKAY, Robert 121,122
McKENSIE, Alexander 45;
Malcolm 120
McKERRELL, Robert 297
McKING, Alexander 168
M'KINYON, Stephen 314
McKOY, John 168
McQUEEN, Alexander 120
MEACHEN, John Jr. 143
MEACHAM, Edward 70
MEACON (Macon,Macom) Gideon 168
MEADE, MEAD, Andrew 37,49;
William 153
MEANLEY, William 167
MECOY, Dennis Sr. 195;
Dennis Jr. 195; James 188
MEDLOCK, John 168
MEDON, Thomas 137
MEDOR, John 137
MEECH, Daniell 313; Thomas 313
MEEKINGS, Thomas 175
MEEKS, John 98
MELLOCHOP (Mollchop) Mary 129
MELSON, John 125
MELTON, Richard 168
MENAGER, Jean 264
MENDUE, Thomas 206
MENETRUERE, __ 266
MENFIELD, John 168
MERCER, James 95,111,208;
Thomas 194
MERCHANT, Christopher 191;
Richard 144; Thomas 293;

MOODY, MOODIE, John 140; Samuel 93,162,225
MOOKINS, Roger 174
MOON, MOONE, Edward 168; John 168; Robert 287,294, 297,306; Stephen 102,168; Thomas 168
MOORE, MOOR, MOORES, MORE, MORES, Anne 168; Augustine 6, 12,25,36,48,114,183,258,273; Augustus 9; Austines 153; Cason 103,107; Denis 123; David 175; Edward 8,11,124, 200; Eliner 230; Francis 92, 137; George 10,14,35,48,145, 205; Gilbert 230; Henry 107; Jacob 191; James 120,202; John 5,22,67,104,109,183,201, 202,230,274,277,278,302; Joseph 147; Matthew 230; Pelham 167; Richard 201,225; Samuel 153; Sarah 54,145; Thomas 94,188,190; William 105,128,189,191
MOORLAND, Edward 213
MORCE, MORSE, David 24,55; Francis 9,17,38,91,189; John 137
MOREAU, Jean 264
MORECOCK, Thomas 175
MOREING, John 213
MORELAND, Jacob 261
MORELL, __ 266
MOREY, Alexander 130
MORGAN, MORGAIN, Christopher 276,278,323; Edward 168; Jacob 275,277; James 323; John 137; Matthew 168; Morgan 118; Rebeckha 183; Richard 120; William 120, 144,276; William Jr. 144
MORLAND, John 178
MORLEY, John 199
MORRAH, MORRA, MORREIGH, Alexander 188; John 168, 188; Robert 277
MORRIANIE, John 230
MORRIL, Lewis 106
MORRIN, Robert 145
MORRIS, Edward Jr. 175; Henry 153; Jacob 125; James 145,175,180; John 125,137,168,175,178; Joseph 129; Josias 190; Robert 129,167; Thomas 188; William 59,71,108,146,153, 159
MORRISET, __ 266; Peter 106; Pierre 264
MORRISON, MORYSON, Charles 236; Henry 30,42,50; William 285
MOSEBY, Edward 218
MOSELEY, MOSELY, Arthur 103,218; Benjamin 12,137; Edward 3,4,9, 17,27,38,51,137,188,254,269; Edward Jr. 254; Francis 51; Francis Jr. 51; George 101; Hillary 38,51; Howard 51; John 17,24,27,38,51,101,191, 254; Robert 137; Widow 195; William 1,7,191,249
MOSS, Edward 181; James 10,16, 26,168; John 181; Robert 137; Samuel 167; Thomas 167; William 91,213
MOSSELEY, Marvill 131
MOSSUM, Mr. 49
MOTTLEY, John 137
MOUL, Timothy 265
MOULIN, MOULLINS, __ 266; Abraham 264
MOUNTFORD, MOUNTFORT, Jeffry 162; Joseph 178,187; Robert 6; Thomas 2,13,175,186,286
MOUNTJOY, Edward 269; Thomas 285,292
MOXON, William 168
MOYEN, William 310
MOYSER, Nicholas 102
MUCE, Olivier de la 265
MUFREY, Alexander 195
MULLENY, James 198
MULLINS, MULLEN, Matthew 62,69; William 132
MULLONE, Matthew 159
MUMFORD, MUNFORD, Jeffrey 94; Robert 28,39,51,72,75,79, 110,224
MUNDAY, Thomas 137
MUNROE (Monro,Monroe) John 94
MURDAH, MURDAUGH, John 74, 107,198
MURDEN, Widow 195
MURDOCK, Mr. 34
MURFREY, MURPHREE, James 204; Mary 98
MURPHY, William 208
MURRA, MURRER, Robert 275,278
MURRAY, MURRY, Alexander 132; John 205; Thomas 261
MURRELL, Edward 225
MURROW, MURROHO, John 168,204; Robert 204
MUSCHAMP, John 162
MUSCOE, Salvador 33,45,140
MUSGRAVE, Elizabeth 71
MUSGROVE, Edward 142
MUSICK, George 153

MUSTEN, MUSTIN, Edward 190; Thomas 277
MUTTLOW (Mattlow) James 167
MUTRAY, Thomas 168
MYERS, MYRES, Roger 275,277, 279; William Jr. 175
MYHILL, John 179
MYLNE, Francis 23

NACE, Pierre 264
NAGLEER, Sarah 182
NAPIER, Robert 62,159
NASARETH, Colonel 197
NASH, Richard 195; Robert 67; Thomas 195
NASON, Joshua 153
NAWSTEAD, Thomas 111
NAYLOR, NAILER, Joseph 186; Thomas 182; William 175
NEAL, NEALE, Christopher 16, 27,270; George 313; John 122,153; Lewis 122; Richard 27,38,50; Thomas 142
NEAVES, James 168
NEECH, Daniel 17,239
NEEDHAM, Thomas 182,262; Walter 305
NEEDLER, NEDLER, Benjamin 43; Mr. 185
NELSON, Henry 153; John 230; Thomas 41,53,258; Wm. 244
NELTHORPE, NELTHORS, George 257,272
NEPHEW, William 282
NESHAMAH, Mary 177
NETHERLAND, John 34,47; Robert 96
NETTLES, Robert 142
NEVILL, Benjamin 200; John 143,208; Roger 209
NEW, Edmund 162; Edmund Jr. 82,85; Robert 162
NEWBURY, NEWBERRY, Nathaniel 138; William 186
NEWBY, Nathaniel 102,198
NEWMAN, Richard 225; Thomas 205
NEWSOM, NEWSOME, Thomas 100; William 10,18
NEWSON, Robert 213; Wm. 213
NEWTON, Henry 140; John 301; George 26,37,50,54,100, 195,273; Lemuel 6,26,27,79, 81,91,94,98; Nathaniel 37, 50; Nicholas 138; Samuell 83,86,88; Thomas 41,53; Willoughby 51
NIBLITT, Burwell 123
NICHOLLS, NICHELL, NICHILLS, NICHOLL, NICHOLS, NICKELLS, NICKOLLS, Edward 183; Elizabeth 190; George 213; Henry 175; Jane 183; John 28,99,100,101, 111,132; Richard 309; Robert 213; Thomas 58,70
NICHOLAS, George 33; William 313
NICHOLSON, Francis 56,238,239, 246,255,271,279; Henry 195; 255; John 175,195; William 92, 129,195,230
NICOD, __ 266; Abraham 264
NICOLAY, Jacques 264; Soubragon 264
NIEUWENHUYSTEN, William 308
NISBETT, Thomas 272
NIXON, Henry 138; Richard 180
NOBLE, Mark 186
NOBLING, Thomas 183
NOCK, John 125; William Sr. 128; William Jr. 129
NOELL, NOWELL, Dall 140; Daniell 100; Josiah 305; Widow 140
NOEWAY, Barefoot 213
NONIA, NONICE, Richard 168
NORCOTT, Thomas 195
NORE, John 279
NORFLEET, NORFLET, Christopher 81,84,86,92,203; Edward 200; John 200; Thomas 26,199
NORMAN, NORMAND, James 286, 314,315; Joshua 62; Thomas 255; William 142,153
NORMANT, NORMENT, Joseph 159; Samuell 3,80,83,86,159
NORRELL, Hugh 175
NORRINGTON, William 274,278
NORRIS, James 153; Thomas 199; William 168
NORSWORTHY, NOSWORTHY, NORTHWORTHY, George 2,8,15,24,35,73,203, 209,248,290,295,302; James 297; Jos. 288,289; John 26,37; Thomas 207
NORTH, Arthur 295,323; John 132,263; William 138
NORTHERN, John 87,93,180
NORTHEY, David 310; David Jr. 309; John Sr. 309; Samuell Jr. 309
NORTON, Robert 127
NORVELL, NORVILL, Hugh 9,271
NORWENT, Samuel 103
NORWOOD, George 213; Richard 213
NOTTIBOY, Daniell 208

PARISH, Abraham 183; Charles 162; Edward 162; Guy 142; John 162,183; Joseph 162; Mark 183; Thomas 175; William 162
PARKE, PARK, PARKES, PARKS, Col. 159,169; Daniel 56,61, 159,175,179,235,239,281, 286,287,289,295,299,304, 313; Graves 41,273; James 153; John 77,168; Mary 213
PARKER, Alexander 43,45; Andrew 246; Charles 103, 109; Col. 171; Francis 198; Francis Jr. 204; George 8, 11,22,32,44,115,124; Hugh 277,279; James 162; John 80,83,86,102,125,126,138, 199,201; Peter 202; Phillip 109,126; Richard 31,72,88,91,97,100,103,198, 213; Sacker 44; Samuel 100; Thomas 59,74,162,175,198, 202; William 79,129,198, 202,219,292
PARKINS, Nicholas Sr. 219
PARKINSON, John 76
PARMENTIER, Jean 264
PARNELL, John 82,85,101,207
PARRALL, Hugh 118
PARRAM, PARRUM, Edward 72; Thomas 72,80,83,86,93,109
PARRAMOSE, Thomas 231
PARRANSOS, Jean 264
PARRANTES, __ 266
PARRELL, Hugh 120
PARROT, PARROTT, PARRETT, PARRIOTT, Gabriell 246; Henry 270; Lawrence 143; Michael 143; Richard 97; Thomas 302
PARSON, PARSONS, John 47,205; John Jr. 94; William 142
PARTRIDGE, PATRIDGE, Nicholas 105; William 307
PASLEY, Robert 169
PASQUE, Peter 180
PASSENGER, Capt. 315
PASSEUR, __ 266
PASSMORE, PASMORE, George 72, 82,84,88,101,110,111,225
PASSONES, John 183
PATE, John 142,154
PATEET, John 120
PATRIACH, Philip 288,293
PATTERSON, PATISON, PATTISON, PATTISSON, Alexander 15; Catherine 175; David 97; Francis 69; John 28; Joseph 219,225; Robert 195; Thomas 175; William 75,128
PATTRAM, Francis 219
PAULIN, PAULLIN, Elizabeth 154; Thomas 9,14
PAULMER, James 181
PAXTON, Thomas 309
PAYNE, PAYN, Ebenezer 307; George 45; Samuel 311; Thomas 286; Widow 138
PAYNTER, John 292
PEA, Ralph 102
PEABODY, David 301; Francis 302
PEACHEY, PEACHY, Samuel 2,8, 39,51
PEACOCK, Thomas 323
PEAKE, John 252
PEALE, Robert 26,204; William 67,204
PEARCE, PEARSE, PEIRCE, PIERCE, Francis 219; George 70,72, 73,290; John 219; Matthew 41,53,178; Peter 182; Phillip 95,207,209; Samuell 182; Widow 185; William 1,7, 19,120,195,219
PEARMAN, John 175; William 175
PEARSON, Christopher 77, John 110; Michael 120; Simon 122
PEASE, PEICE, John 168,219
PEASLEY, Robert 57; Samuel 51
PEATROSS, Thomas 94
PEE, Thomas 159
PEEK, John 159
PEELE, Ephraim 91; Joseph 91
PEERS, George 293
PEKITHMAN, William 179
PEMBERTON, George 159; Thomas 153
PENDER, Paul 198,203; Mr. 45
PENDEXTER, PENDEXTRE, Charles 293; Thomas 168,175
PENDLETON, Henry 154; Philip 154
PENDRY, Henry 111
PENIX, Edward 168
PENN, William 278
PENNELL, William 276
PENNY, Bryan 183; John 207; Joseph 191; Thomas 191
PEOPLES, David 225; Elizabeth 225; William 225
PEPER, Stephen 175
PEPPERELL, PEPPERILL, William 296,300
PEPUY, Jean 265
PERAULT, Charles 107
PERCE, Francis 68
PERKINS, PERKIN, Charles 175; Isaac 118,122; John 169,273

PERKINS, William 169,195
PERKINSON, John 100,218; Seth 219
PERRAT, Pierre 264
PERRIN, Ann 218
PERRING, Thomas 63
PERROTT, Henry 131; Richard 143
PERRU, __ 266
PERRY, Grace 225; John 126, 200,323; Joseph 225; Micajah 113,225,268,272,280, 307,323; Nicholas 200; Richard 116,268,272,307,323; Robert 277; Samuel 138; Thomas 128; William 278
PERRYMAN, Daniell 274
PERSONS, James 180; John 180, 213
PERVINE, Lewis 189
PETEATE, John 118
PETENAS, Thomas 138
PETERS, Elizabeth 204; James 190,204; John 204; Robert 178; Thomas 143; Widow 195
PETERSON, John 82,84,88,105, 111
PETEVER, PETTIVER, John 113; Thomas 169
PETTIT, PETTITT, PETIT, PETITT, __ 266; Thomas 3,5, 14,24,153
PETIVER, John 71
PETT, Thomas 299
PETTEWAY, Elizabeth 213
PETTERSON, John 225
PETTFORT, John 213; Wm. 213
PETTIS, Thomas 74
PETTROS, PETROSS, Thomas 94
PETTUS, John 140
PETTY, John 169; Robert 49
PETTYPOOLE, William 109
PEW, Arnold 96; Henry 219
PEYTON, PAYTON, __ 154; Robert 143,239,286,291, 313; Robert Jr. 286; Thomas 143
PHELPS, Humphrey 213; Thomas 153
PHIBB, Henry 272
PHILIPS, PHILIP, PHILIPE, PHILIPPE, PHILLIP, PHILLIPS, __ 266; Charles 153; Claude 265; David 119; Edward 175; George 168,279; John 175,213; Nathaniel 96, 225; Nicholas 181; Samuel 279,281,294,298; William 119,120,128,175,213
PHILIPSON, PHILLIPSON, Robert 40,53
PHILPOT, Richard 195
PHINKETT, Elizabeth 153
PICKETT, PICKET, John 120,138
PICKFORD, __ 275
PICKLES, John 95; Thomas 153
PICKLEY, Thomas 169
PICKMAN, Joshua 311
PICKRELL, Gabriell 159
PICOT, __ 266
PIDGEON, PIGEON, Joseph 302; Richard 225
PIGG, Edward 82,84,88,99,108, 153; Henry 81,84,88,108,153; John 74,82,84,89,102,154
PIGOTT, PIGGOTT, PIGOT, Benjamin 175; Ralph 17,50, 175,231
PILES, PILLS, Joseph 323
PILLSON, Thomas 252
PINCHER, Francis 118
PINKARD, PINCKARD, John 7,15; Thomas 4,5,15,25,269
PINKETHMAN, William 5,54,247
PINKITT, John 219; Thomas 219; William 219
PIPKIN, John 199
PIPON, Philip 288
PISBURN, John 189
PISKELL, John 138
PITMAN, PITTMAN, Thomas 144; Thomas Jr. 80,82,85,98, 103,213
PITT, PITTS, Henry 207; John 2,138,206,303,308; Robert 8,11,127; Thomas 1, 24,54,206
PITTETT (Pettit)? John 231; Justian 231; Thomas 231
PITTLADER, Thomas 169; William 169
PLAISTED, Francis 300
PLANTINE, Peter 168
PLATER, George 246
PLATT, Randale 5,28
PLEASANT, PLEASANTS, Dorothy 109; John 68,76, 95,99,103,218,237; Joseph 87,95,104,219
PLEDGE, John 219
PLEY, Widow 138
PLOWMAN, PLOYMAN, John 90,95; Richard 288,290
PLUMER, Isaac 144; Thomas 108, 144; William 143
PLUMSTEE, Robert 290
POE, Samuel 138; William 120
POINTESTRE, Charles 288

POLE, Geofrey 38; Godfrey 31, 43,50
POLLAND, Henry 219; Thomas Sr. 219; Thomas Jr. 219
POLLARD, John 246; Robert 24,153; Thomas 238; William 153,159
POLLOCK, POLLICK, Thomas 283,292
POMEA, Francis 153
POND, Charles 263; Dr. 54; John 180; Stephen 179
POOLE, POLL, George 93,188; Robert 74; Thomas 75,145,183
POPE, Henry 96,104,208; John 94,208; Michael 282; Richard 282; William 105,200
PORLOCK, James 17
PORTENS, John 208,209
PORTER, John 54,169,203,219; John Jr. 311; Samuell 195; William 219
PORTEUS, Madam 142; Robert 4, 20,75,142,268; William 93
PORTLAND, John 298
PORTLOCK, __ 195; Edward 267; Elizabeth 219; John 92
PORTUE, Edward 240
POTTER, POTTORS, Frances 153; John 38,50,180; Joseph 180; Roger 234
POTTS, Thomas 225
POUNCE, George 124
POWELL, Frances 231; Honor 138; Isaac 180; John 4,5,6, 7,17,27,71,97,198,231; Lemuell 195; Mark 182,190; Major 236; Place 138; Richard 195; Robert 153, 219; Seamor 179; Seymon 185; Samuell 231; Thomas 138,145,208; Widow 209; William 91,92,138,195,208
POWERS, Charles 183; David 159; Edward 186; Henry 34,47,273
POYTHRES, POYTHERS, POYTHRESS, POYTHRISS, Francis 65,225; John 28,39,51,70,80,83,86, 105,109; John Jr. 72,225; Thomas 104,225; William 39,51
PRATT, J. 258; John 125; William 119
PREACHARD (Prichard) Roger 89,93
PREEDAY, Daniell 183
PREESON, PRESON, Thomas 75,130, 231,300,303,314,315
PRERIOT, __ 266
PRESCOT, Moses 195
PRESLEY, PRESLY, Peter 5,27, 38,50,270
PRESTON, Henry 143
PRESWOOD, Thomas 98
PRETTEJOHN, Thomas 276,278
PRETTY, Henry 242
PREVOST, Adam 264; Marie 264
PREWITT, William 153
PRICE, Calem 121; Edward 202; Elizabeth 199; John 25,36, 131,138,145,213,225,280,299; Meredith 35; Richard 52,127, 142; Robert 313; Thomas 97; William 94,138
PRICHARD (Preachard) Joseph 107
PRIDDON, Thomas 302,310
PRIDE, William Sr, 219
PRIEST, James 183,187
PRIME, John 35
PRINCE, George 175; Richard 299
PRINCE GEORGE of Denmark 257
PRINGLE, James 263; John 263; William 281
PRITCHETT, David 95,153; John 142; Joseph 225; Roger 138
PROCTER, PROCTOR, PROCKTER, Joshua 213; Joseph 79; Reuben 65,206; Robert 111
PROEMAN, Thomas 279
PROSSER, John 138
PROVERB, Catherine 95; Elianor 95
PRYAN, William 208
PRYNNE, Nicholas 233
PRYOR, Christopher 154; Robert 145
PUGH, Anne 199; Daniel 37, 49,67; Theo. 49
PULLAM, William 168
PULLY, William 213
PULYSTONE, John 213
PURCELL, Arthur 208
PURCHASE, George 3,25,153
PURDY, Nicholas 168
PURLEVANT, Arthur 159
PURLY, John 169
PURNELL, Cornelius 238; Thomas 145
PURVIS, John 275,277,279
PYKE, Henry 231
PYN, Loys due 264
PYNES, Nathaniell 159
PYRAUL, James 168
PYWELL, Charles 123

ROLAND, William 246
ROLLINGS, Gregory 213; Peter 154
RONAN, William 231
RONNO, Stephen 106
ROOKINS, ROOKINGS, William 94,96,99,237
ROOTS, Philip 48
ROPER, John 80,82,85,100,162
ROSCOW, ROSCON (Rascow,Ruscow) William 18,40,53,284
ROSE, __ 321; John 195; Mr. 45; Richard 213; Robert 195; Thomas 128; William 96; William Jr. 104
ROSS, Alexander 118; Andrew 74,99,203; Henry 7; Wm. 169
ROUCH, Rachell 219
ROUNDTREE, John 198; Robert 198; Thomas 199; Wm. 169
ROUSBY, Thomas 64
ROUTEN, ROUTON, Richard 261,262
ROUX, __ 266; Michal 264
ROVELL, John 175
ROWE, ROW, Captain 238; James 147; John 154; William 96,103,180
ROWELL, John 125
ROWEN, ROWIN, Francis 219; Robert 308
ROWLAND, William 234
ROWLES, John 125; William 185
ROWLETT, William 219
ROWLING, John 213
ROWTTON, Richard 183
ROWZEE, ROWZE, Edward 138, 269; Ralph 138
ROY, Daniel 265; Jaques 264; Richard 154
ROYAL, ROYALL, Henry 182, 184,186,261; Joseph 10,13, 46,89,110,162,219,314,315; Joseph Jr. 34
ROYSTON, John 138,142; Thomas 236
RUCKER, Peter 138
RUDD, RUDDS, John 276,278; William 250,267
RUDOLPH, Thomas 23
RUFFICE, Elizabeth 213
RUFFIN, Robert 6,28
RULE, Widow 169
RUSHELL, John 262
RUSCOW (Rascow,Roscow) William 261
RUSHIN, Matthew 88,100
RUSSELL, Alexander 154; Charles 219; Francis 312; John 169,190,219,221; Jos. 186; Nathaniel 147; Peter 121; Richard 272,323; Samuel 70,162,175; William 121
RUST, Jeremiah 53; Mr. 316
RUTHERFORD, Thomas 121
RUTTER, John 203,207; Thomas 203; William 203
RYDER, Mary 70,175
RYLAND, Thomas 143

SABLET (Soblet) Abraham 264
SABOTTE, Peter 106
SADLER, Edward 144; John 80,81,82, 85,87,92,147; Robert 144
SAFFIN, Francois 264
SAILLY, Charles de 265
SALE, SAIL, SALL, SALLE, SALES, Abraham 23,89,92,104,106; Cornelius 138; Mr. 266; Stephen 190; Widow 139
SALMON, James 226; John 139; Thomas 170
SAMMONS, John 189
SAMPSON, James 205; John 246; Widow 162
SAMUEL, __ 266; Anthony 138
SAND, John 54
SANDBORNE, SANDBOURNE, Daniel 207; William 226
SANDERS, Eustick 231; Edward 16,27, 270; Francis 206; Henry 208; James 169; John 27,105,139,169, 175,179,198,202,313; Jonathan 190; Joshua 159; Nathaniel 154; Richard 74,108,203,231; Richard Jr. 200; Robert 108; Thomas 148, 170; William 169,198; William Jr. 198
SANDERSON, John 231; Richard 281, 286,292,293; Richard Jr. 293
SANDERVER, John 181
SANDFORD, SANDEFORD, SANDIFORD, SANFORD, John 68,74; Samuel 127; Sarah 189
SANDIDGE, John 169
SANDLAN, Nicholas 159
SANETIER, Isaac 264
SANTO, Robert 175
SARDIN, Symon 264
SARGENTON, Jean 265
SARRAZIN, SARRZEN, Stephen 219,220
SASSIN, __ 266; Francis 109
SATTERWHITE, Charles 159; John 147
SAUNDERS, Jonathan 242

SHARP, SHARPE, Francis 178; John 176; Robert 219; Thomas 26,107,213,250,267
SHARPLESS, SHARPLES, Cuthbert 274,277; Henry 196
SHAW, Peter 263
SHEA, Luke 202; Patrick 154
SHEARS, Paul 170
SHEENE, Frank 189
SHELDON, William 80,84,87, 92,181
SHEPHERD, SHEAPARD, SHEPERD, SHEPHEARD, SHEPPARD, Isaac 154; Isreall 204; Jeremiah 139; John 183, 231,262; Joseph 154; Morris 32; Thomas 231; Widow 231; William 94,128
SHERLAND, John 188
SHERMAN, Elizabeth 176; Michael 9,13
SHERRER, Thomas 205
SHERRIFF, Henry 170
SHERWOOD, Grace 99; James 190; Will 236; William 239,313
SHETTO, Edward 198; Francis 198; Isaac 198
SHIEFFIELD, Martin 226
SHIELDS, SHIELD, Delight 123; Robert 180
SHILLING, George 93,113,159
SHIP, SHIPPE, Edward 307; Joe 139; William 189
SHIPLEY, John 139; Ralph 144
SHIPMAN, John 263
SHIPWASH, Ambrose 112
SHOEHORN, Cornelius 179
SHOLTWATER, Benjamin 177
SHOOT, Thomas 154
SHORE, Sampson 306
SHORT, John 175; Thomas 100, 139; William 214
SHOWELL, __ 275
SHOWMAKE, Moses 73
SHREWSBURY, SHREWBURY, Francis 214; Joseph 214; Thomas 214
SHURLY, Richard 131
SIBLEY, John 120
SIKES (Seikes) John 101, 195; Walter Sr. 195
SILATOR, Richard 204
SILL, Thomas 298; William 128
SILVERTHORN, Sebastian 127; William 129
SILVESTER, SILLVESTER (Selvester) Benjamin 314,315
SIMCOCKE, John 125
SIMES (Sims) William 176
SIMKINS, Ann 123
SIMMONS, SIMONS, George 263; James 94; John 28,40,52,87,98, 107,214; Mary 183; Thomas 94, 107; Samuel 145
SIMPIO, Charles 154
SIMPSON, SIMSON, John 255; Thomas 128,142
SIMS (Simes) George 213; John 169
SINCLEAR, James 263
SINEH (?) Widow 144
SINGLETON, Henry 144; Robert 144; Samuel 144
SKAIFE, John 24,35; Mr. 48
SKERIN, Widow 219
SKINKER, Samuel 35,47
SKINNER, John 182; Lewis 92
SKIPWORTH, SKIPWITH, Sir William 1,2,10,15,25,49, 133,155
SKELTON, John 154
SLADE, Henry 286; William 175
SLATER (Sclater) James 170,251
SLATLER (Statler) Thomas 261
SLAUGHTER, SLOUGHTER, Francis 8,17,269; George 93, 159; Henry 160; James 180; John 160; Martin 71,159; Phoebe 139; Richard 113,180; Robert 121
SLEDD, SLED, John 313; Joshua 313
SLEDGE, Charles 106; Joseph 310
SLYFOOT, John 263
SMALL, Benjamin 204; John 81,83, 86,97,99,111,198; William 253
SMALLPAGE, Robert 175
SMART, Matthew 226
SMELL, SMELLY, SMELT, Lewis 209; Matthew 182; Robert 70,208; William 182,209
SMETHIE, Robert 72
SMITH, SMYTH, Abraham 231; Alexander 154; Ambrose 63; Arthur 2,10,14,25,35,47,74,207; Augustine 23,39,52,93,114,115; Augustin 77,142; Augustin Jr. 142; Austin 155; Benjamin 122, 183; Brian 234; Bryan 237; Captain 144; Charles 12,83,86, 17,116,139,269; Christopher 108,154,175; Dorothy 94; Edmund 63,160; Francis 139,155; George 58,59,96,188,231;

SMITH, SMYTH, Guy 23,93,147, 250,267; Henry 1,130; Humphry 188,195,219; James 97,125,132,169,226; John 10,13,15,20,23,25,44, 45,55,56,71,91,94,97,119, 132,139,140,142,147,175,179, 195,199,231,235,258,262,263, 270,285,290,297,304; John Cooper 154; John Sawyer 154; Jonas 139; Jonathan 307; Joseph 4,5,6,23,94,231,297; Lancelot Jr. 247; Lawrence 4,41,53,94,115,181,235,241, 256,270; Major 101; Mr. 49; Nathaniel 85,102,169; Nicholas 4,28,35,45,47,79, 106,142,154,278; Obidiah 162,219; Philip 6,23,38,50, 145; Poplar 132; Peter 231; Richard 70,109,155,162,188, 195,213,226,231; Richard (Minor) 231; Robert 105,120, 245,246; Roger 102,169; Samuel 35,48,50,98,199,231, 273,302; Symon 127; Thomas 10,16,79,104,128,139,160, 214,231,232,295,312; Tully 254; William 6,23,25,26,36, 39,52,93,101,113,138,139, 148,169,186,191,207,254, 269,280,285,287,309; Smith in Bristoll 154
SMOUT, Edward 303
SNAILL, Henry 191
SNEAD, SNEED, Charles 32; John 75,169; Robert 22,181, 288; Thomas 169
SNELL, John 154
SNELLING, Elizabeth 146
SNELSON, Charles 34
SNOOKINS (?) William 28
SNOUD, Thomas 139
SNUGGS, Charles 219
SOANE, SOAN, SOAMES, SONES, Henry 6,9,13,32,44,176; Henry Jr. 24; John 1,34,44; Thomas 154; William 71,219
SOBLET (Sablet) __ 266; Abraham 105; Peter Jr. 106
SOBRICHE, __ 266
SOLEAGER, John 106
SOLEMAN, Joseph 294
SOMMERS (Summers) John 282
SORRELL, SORRALL, Martin 103; Mary 176; Thomas 41,177
SOSQUE, Symon 127
SOUDEN (Souter)? John 314,315
SOULLIE, Nicholas 106
SOUTER (Souden) Joseph 284,294, 295,303
SOUTH, Humphrey 272
SOUTHACK, Cyprian 303
SOUTHERLAND, Daniel 154; George 62,113; George Jr. 62 Joseph 62, Philip 62; William 24,35,154
SOUTHERN, SOUTHERNE, John 97,131
SOUTHWORTH, William 131
SPAINE, John 226
SPANN, Mr. 27
SP**N (Spann)? Richard 27
SPARKS, John 155
SPARROW, George 310; John 106; William 196
SPEAR, SPEARES, George 162; Robert 169
SPEARMAN, Job 139
SPEIR, SPEIRS, SPIER, SPIERS, James 70,199; John 4,8,15, 139,198; William 83,85,200
SPENCER, SPENCE, Alexander 1,7, 19; Katherine 155; Nicholas 7, 235,260; Robert 237; Thomas 63, 155,160
SPICER, John 35; Will 261; William 182
SPIGHT, SPEIGHT, SPITE, Francis 201; Francis Jr. 74; William 68,80,83,85,201; William Jr, 74,92
SPINKS, John 91,145
SPIVEY, SPIVY, George 198; James 198; Matthew 2,15,26, 195; Thomas 199
SPOTSWOOD, Alexander 20,273; Colonel 116,117
SPRACKLIN, SPRACLING, Richard 314,315
SPRANGER, Alexander 272
SPRATT, Henry 17,38,91,188,191, 254; Izabell 54; Thomas 190
SPRING, Robert 99,195,237
SPRATTLEY, John 175
SPRATTLIN, Andrew 169
SPRUE, Alexander 269
SPRUCE, Jeremy 159
SPRY, Lewis 277,278
SQUIRES, Richard 267; Waller 113
STACOMB, Robert 127
STAFFORD, Mary 175; William 296
STAGE, STAIGE, STAGG, Mr. 28,39,53
STAGSDALL, Benjamin 179
STAICE, Symon 180
STAINBACK, William 94
STALEY, STALY, Thomas 246
STALLARD, Samuel 139

STALLING, STALLINGS, Elias 198; Elias Jr. 198; John 198; Nicholas 68,198; Richard 198
STAMP, Ralph 170
STANBRIDGE, William 142
STANDARD, STANARD, William 36, 49,77,94,114,160
STANDBACK, William 226
STANDBRO, John 196
STANERS, Thomas 139
STANLEY, STANDLEY, Edward 219; James 101; John 263; Richard 196; Thomas Sr. 101; Thomas Jr. 101; William 169
STANLIN, Richard 127
STANSELL, John 201
STANSFORD, Charles 54
STANTON, James 96; John 125; 139; Thomas 110
STANUP, STANOP, Captain 170; John 10,16,26; Richard 170
STAPELY, Thompson 109
STAPLES, STAPELL, STAPLE, John 261,305; Michael 314, 315; William 202
STAPLETON, Samuel 263; Thomas 74,131,155
STARK, STARKE, John 159; Robert 178,284,306; Thomas 119,155,282; William 41,53
STARKEY, Robert 147,280
STATLER, Thomas 261
STAVALL (?) Bartholomew 103
STEAD, Francis 95
STEAR, Thomas 179
STEERES, Thomas 309
STEPHENS, STEAVENS, STEPHYNS, STEVENS, Edward 89,95,142, 147,272; Charles 147; Henry 147; James 147; John 102,139,279,280, 284,285,287,291,299,301; Michael 310; Roger 263; William 169
STEPHENSON, STEVENSON, Abraham 105; John 205
STEPP, Abraham 138; John 282,289
STEPPING, Thomas 170
STEPTO, John 27
STERLING, Anne 93; Mary 93; Captain 144
STEWARD, Daniel 219; John 213; John Jr. 219,220; Mr. 40,52; William 25
STEWART, John Jr. 77; Samuel 263,309
STHRASHLEY, Thomas 139
STIFF, Thomas 132
STITH, Captain 226; Drury 22,32, 39,44,51,68,74,162; John 5,22, 32,44,162
STOCKLAY, STOCKLEY, STOCKLY, STOKLEY, STOKLY, Charles 123; Christopher 123; John Sr. 231; Joseph 124; Richard 24; Thomas 128
STOGDALE, Philip 119
STOGELL, John 139
STOKES, STOAKES, STOCKES, George 291; Henry 124; John 68,95,147,162; Richard 139; Silvanus 111; Silvanus Jr. 92
STONE, Eusebius 119; John 154; Mary 154
STONER, Daniel 34,45,273; David 178
STORK, William 40
STORY, John 14,155,258,271; Joshua 9,249
STOVOLL, Bartholomew 219
STOWERS, Widow 219
STRANGE, Alexander 169; John 138,274,279,284
STRATON, STRATTON, Anthony 282; Benjamin 231
STREATOR, STREATER, Edmund 26; Edward 37,204
STREET, John 298; William 159
STRINGER, Colonel 236; Henry 4; Hillary 4,27,129,231; Jacob 38,50; Margaret 155; Thomas 127
STRINGFELLOW, Richard 213
STRONGYE, John 277
STROTHER, Benjamin 35; Joseph 35, 47; William 35,47; William Jr. 35,47
STROUD, John 109,226
STRUTTON, Thomas 77,159
STUBBS, STUBS, John 71,74,102, 142; Susannah 147
STUBBLEFIELD, STUBBELFIELD,STUBELFIELD, George 154,155; Simon 145
STUKEY, Charles 186
STURDIVANT, Chichester 105,226; Daniell 226; Mathew 110,226
STURMAN, STURMER, John 4,5,6,7
STUSTER, Galnel 265
STYLES, John 169
SUGG, George 195; Joseph 196; William 195
SUGER, John 213
SULLENGER, Peter 139
SULLIVAN, SULLIVANT, Daniel 15, 203; John 189; Owen 67
SUMERLIN, Jacob 112

TONY, Alexander 170
TOOKE, TOOKER, Henry 10,18,214, 226,248; Joseph 226; Major 226; Robert 226; Thomas 206
TOOMER, John 180
TOPLADIE, Robert 180
TOOPE, Nicholas 234
TOPPING, Joseph 55
TOPSHAM, John 277
TORIN, __ 266
TORRY, John 9
TOTTERDALE, Hans (Henry)? 275,277
TOULES, Henry 124
TOUNSON, TOWNSON, John 124; Thomas 128
TOUSER, Joseph 125
TOUSON, Thomas 128
TOVIS (Tevis) Edmund 170
TOWLAND, William 186
TOWLER, TOWLEY, John 155; Matthew 160
TOWN, Elizabeth 170
TOY, Humphrey 143; Pierre du 264; Thomas 155
TRANTOR, Edward 188
TRAPLEY, John 8
TRAVERS, TRAVERSE, TRAVIS, TRAVRES, Giles 252; John 272; Mr. 55; Rawleigh 8,17,29; Samuel 239,313
TRAYLOR, Edward 220; William 220
TREBUE (Tribue) Anthony 111
TREEMAN, John Jr. 105
TREGIAN, Richard 314,315
TREMEER, TREMERE, TREMIER, John 70,93,180
TRENT, Henry 219; John 294; Leonard 6; William 302
TREVELHAN, TREVETHAN, Sampson 21; Sampson Jr. 27
TREVILLIAN, TREVILIAN, John 187,291
TRIBE, Richard 302
TRIBLE, Peter 139
TRIBUE (Trebue) Anthony 81, 87,106
TRICE, James 155
TRIGONEY, Henry 196
TRIM, TRIMM, Mathew 274,279
TRION, __ 266
TRIPLETT, William 52
TRISTAM, Robert 302
TROTMAN, Anne 162
TROTT, Richard 119
TROTTY, Thomas 220
TRUBYER, Helen 265
TRUETT, Henry 124
TRYFORT, Bartholomew 232
TRYGELL, William 207
TUCKER, TUKER, Charles 182,261; Elizabeth 226; Francis 109; John 109,196,291,304; Richard 196; Robert 110; Thomas 170, 182,183,196; William 196
TUGILL, Henry 132
TULLE, Benjamin 286,292,312
TULLERY, Cornelius 197
TULLETT, John 176
TULLY, John 196; Mark 190; Thomas 191; William 170
TUNISON, Aaron 245
TUNSTALL, Thomas 155
TUPPER, Peter 293
TURBERFIELD, Richard 226
TURBERVILLE, TUBERVILE, TURBARVILLE, TURBERVILL, George 41,53; John 2,3,7,15, 25,36
TUREMAN, Ignatius 155
TURLINGTON, Peter 126
TURLS, William 246
TURMER, John 184
TURNER, Edward 123,162; Elizabeth 148; George 59,60, 139,144,170; George Jr. 170; Henry 170,207,219; James 58, 59,60; James Jr. 58,170; John 184,186,206,237,287,314; Joseph 104; Joshua 92; Richard 155,232; Thomas 35, 47,155; William 59,170
TURPIN, Philip 219; Thomas 219,220
TURTLELOTT, Abraham 294
TURTON, Thomas 189
TUTT, Benjamin 119; Richard 119,120
TWICHARD, Antoine 264
TWITTY, Thomas 170
TWNIE (Twine)? Thomas 176
TYERY, William 176
TYNEY, TYNNEY, Alexander 170; James 170; Thomas 170
TYLER, TYLOR, Edward 311; Francis 20,21,47,94; Henry 2,9,19,41,53,178; John 34
TYNER, Nicholas 208
TYOUS, Thomas 214
TYSON, Matthew 130

UBANKES, Henry 124
UDALL, Mathew 176
UMPLEET, William 182
UNDERHILL, John 54,87
UNDERWOOD, Thomas 209; William 8,17,269

WALLSWORTH, William 189
WALPOLE, WALLPOOLE, Horatia 30, 42; Richard 227
WALSTONE, Henry 189; William 190
WALTER, WALTERS, Elizabeth 232; John 232; Richard 294; William 50,201
WALTHALL, Henry 220; Richard 220; William 220
WALTHAM, Elizabeth 70; John 130; Peter 130; Teagle 130
WALTON, Edward 170,171; Thomas 6,24,35,47
WAPLE, WAPPLE, John 90,214
WARBERTON, Thomas 176
WARD, George 140; John 101,197; Jonathan 121; Richard 220; Robert 176; Samuel 155; Seth 13,220; Thomas 176,214,232, 281,290,292,295,296,301,302, 307; Widow 139; William 80, 84,86,92,101
WARDROPE, Michael 62
WARE, Edward 155; Elizabeth 71; Jacob 250; Nicholas 155; Thomas 62,71; Valentine 155
WARING, Thomas 33,45
WARNER, Augustine 235; Edward 268; John 47; Madam 55; Thomas 275,277,278,282,283, 298
WARRINGTON, WARINGTON, John 126; Stephen 127
WARPOOLE, John 72,73
WARRELL, Francis 263
WARREN, WAREN, WARRIN, WARRING, Allen 214; Argoll 232; James 232; Jacob 274,277; John 162, 232; Joseph 232; Peter 170; Robert 95,199,214,232; Thomas 214; William 190
WARRICK, John 214
WASHBURN, WASHBURNE, John 8,23
WASHING (Washington)? John 52
WASHINGTON, WASHINGTAIN, Arthur 65,73; Augustine 41, 53; John 8,18,29,65,73,239, 252,253,313; Richard 64,68, 73,88,101; Robert 53
WATERFIELD, WATERFEILD, John 146; Peter 146; William 77,232
WATERS, WATER, WATTERS, Charles 144,146; John 140, 148; Richard 130; Samuel 307; Walter 142,208; William 7,17, 21,27,232,249
WATERSON, Richard 232; William 232
WATFORD, Joseph 197
WATKINS, WATTKINS, Benjamin 155; Edward 155,220; Henry Sr. 220; John 103,110, 208,214; Joseph 220; Philip 155; Rebecha 181; Richard 214; Thomas 103,140,196,220; Thomas Jr. 155; William 155, 171,220
WATSON, WATTSON, David 82,84, 89,123; John Sr. 220; Robert 82,84,89,126,196; Samuel 201; Theophilus 171; William 120
WATTS, WATT, Bartholomew 278; Hugh 132; John 2,8,11,22,104, 126,237; Lazarus 288; Matthew 9,77,183,261; Peter 245; Thomas 155,263; William 245
WAUGH, Alexander 252; John 6,29; John Jr. 2,8,18,255; Joseph 109
WAUGHOP, John 50
WAY, Benjamin 272
WAYMAN, John 181
WAMMOUTH, John 276
WEAD, William 140
WEATHERS, Thomas 176
WEAVER, Peter 119; Samuel 170
WEBB, Charles 232; Edward 232; Elizabeth 77; Giles 2,10,13, 220,227; Henry 131,232; Isaac 140; James 140; John 140,220,263; Mary 171,197; Richard 81,84,86,93,203; Robert 110,111,140,214; Thomas 128; William 313
WEBBER, Henry 36,48,114; Phillip 97; Thomas 276
WEBSTER, Godfrey 272; Joseph 171; Thomas 272
WEDDICK, Henry 197
WEEDON, WHEDON, WHEEDEN, Edward 139; George 7,19; John Jr. 196; William 196
WEEKS, WEEKES, Francis 10,15, 131; Widow 131
WELBURN, WELBURNE, Arcado 123; Thomas 1,11
WELCH, WELSH, Edward 203; Henry 214; Rand. 33; Reuben 45,258,273
WELDEY, Dorothy 197; George 176
WELDON, Benjamin 273; Sarah 176
WELLS, Elias 185; Elizabeth 185; Emanuel 185; Habk. 274; John 180; Mills 185; William 185
WERRELL, Josheph 67
WESHART (Wishart,Wishard) John 196

WILL, Roger 214
WILLAROY, WILLEROY, Abraham 77,160
WILLBOURNE, Thomas 155
WILLETT, William 129,232
WILLIAMS, WILLIAM, Anne 206; Charles 80,83,85,93,132, 214; Charles Jr. 109; Clark 171; Daniel 312; David 109; Edward 132; Elizabeth 155; Emanuel 140; George 70,98,142,227; Griffin 113; Griffith 160; Jacob 285; James 71,189, 227; Jane 197; John 44,73, 94,107,109,139,143,155, 160,179,196,206,208,234; Matthew 176,313; Nathaniel 126; Nicholas 97,101; Overton Mack 126; Philip 60,62,74,113,160; Rice 89, 102; Richard 93,96; Robert 220; Roger 214; Rowland 186; Samuel 63, 77,89,101,160; Thomas 171,208,304; William 8, 73,74,105,139,171,182, 207,208,214,242,255,282, 283,289
WILLIAMSON, Bartholomew 188; Francis 65,68,73,206; George 64,65,68,73,206; John 140,176,196; Jones 109; Richard 188; Robert 131; Thomas 140,155,220; Valentine 227; William 129,140
WILLIS, Alexander 191; Francis 33,46,145,171,268, 272,281; Henry 33,53,118, 120,121; James 237; John 125,196; John Jr. 125; Miles 40; Richard 10,281; Stephen 171; Thomas 278; William 160
WILLORY, Abraham 59
WILLOUGHBY, John 246; Thomas 2,8,16,26,37,50, 196
WILLS, Edward 311; John 1103; Miles 2,6,8,18,29, 40,53; Owen 188; Thomas 40,232
WILMORE, John 171
WILNECKE, Phillip 276
WILSON, WILLSON, Benjamin 155; Capt. 290; Capt W. 296; David 139; Ephraim 245; George 302; Henry 109; James 5,8,16,37, 50,100,171,196,197,248,307; James Jr. 5,16,196; Jane 295; John 118,170,176,209, 220,313; John Jr. 220; Lemuel 16,26,196; Solomon 37,50; Thomas 232; Will 295; Willis 9,37,50,239,284,290, 296,313; William 9,12,180, 239,248,256,260,290,300,302, 307,308,313,323
WILTON, Richard 139
WILTSHIER, Joseph 155
WINBOURNE, John 203
WINDER, Thomas 16,270
WINFIELD, WINGFIELD, WINKFIELD, Jarvis 72,105,227; Robert 227; Thomas 170
WINFREE, WINFREA, WINFRY, Charles 106,170; Henry 160; Valentine 113
WINKLEY, WINKLES, Richard 95,227
WINN(Wyn,Wynn,Wynne) Robert 110
WINNINGHAM, Edward 227; John Jr. 227; Thomas 227
WINSLOW, Henry 139; Thomas 139
WINSTON, WINSTONE, Anthony 69, 171; Isaac 34; Theophilus 171; Sarah 171; William 61, 68,97,160
WINTBY, Jacob 170
WINTER, Timothy 176; William 183
WISDOM, Francis 142
WISE, John Sr. 126; John Jr. 126; Richard 156; Robert 268,272; William 128,179
WISHART, WISHARD (Weshart) James 44,101,190; William 190
WITHERINGTON, Nicholas 214
WITHY, Thomas 155
WOLBOURNE, Thomas 8
WOLLOPE, Shimner 127
WOLTHAM, Stephen 127
WOMACK, Abraham 220; John 227; William 103,220
WOOD, Edward 176,188,197; Edward Jr. 74; Gilbert 282; Henry 34,45,171; James 122, 155,160; Joseph 261; Matthew 185; Moses 71,220; Patrick 198; Richard 176; Thomas 131,139,160,176,220; Walter 171
WOODAM, Thomas 162